PERCEPTUAL COMPUTING

Books in the IEEE Press Series on Computational Intelligence

PERCEPTUAL COMPUTING
Aiding People in Making Subjective Judgments

JERRY M. MENDEL
DONGRUI WU

IEEE Computational Intelligence Society, *Sponsor*

IEEE Press Series on Computational Intelligence
David B. Fogel, *Series Editor*

IEEE PRESS

A JOHN WILEY & SONS, INC., PUBLICATION

Library of Congress Cataloging-in-Publication Data:

Mendel, Jerry M., 1938-
  Perceptual computing : aiding people in making subjective judgments / Jerry M. Mendel and
Dongrui Wu.
    p. cm.
  ISBN 978-0-470-47876-9 (cloth)
  1. Human-computer interaction. 2. Computational intelligence. 3. Decision making. 4. Fuzzy sets. I.
Wu, Dongrui. II. Title.
  QA76.9.H85M428 2010
  006.3—dc22   2009041401

Printed in the United States of America.

10 9 8 7 6 5 4 3 2 1

To

Lotfi Zadeh, founder of computing with words and fuzzy logic

Letty Mendel, wife of Jerry M. Mendel

Shunyou Wu, Shenglian Luo, and Ying Li,
parents and wife of Dongrui Wu

Contents

■■■ Preface

Life is full of subjective judgments: those we make that affect others and those that others make that affect us. Such judgments are personal opinions that have been influenced by one's personal views, experience, or background, and can also be interpreted as personal assessments of the levels of variables of interest. They are made using a mixture of qualitative and quantitative information. Emotions, feelings, perceptions, and words are examples of qualitative information that share a common attribute: they cannot be directly measured; for example, eye contact, touching, fear, beauty, cloudiness, technical content, importance, aggressiveness, and wisdom. Data (one- or multidimensional) and possibly numerical summarizations of them (e.g., statistics) are examples of quantitative information that share a common attribute: they can be directly measured or computed from direct measurements; for example, daily temperature and its mean value and standard deviation over a fixed number of days; volume of water in a lake estimated on a weekly basis, as well as the mean value and standard deviation of the estimates over a window of years; stock price or stock-index value on a minute-to-minute basis; and medical data, such as blood pressure, electrocardiograms, electroencephalograms, X-rays, and MRIs.

Regardless of the kind of information—qualitative or quantitative—there is uncertainty about it, and more often than not the amount of uncertainty can range from small to large. Qualitative uncertainty is different from quantitative uncertainty; for example, words mean different things to different people and, therefore, there are linguistic uncertainties associated with them. On the other hand, measurements may be unpredictable—random—because either the quantity being measured is random or it is corrupted by unpredictable measurement uncertainties such as noise (measuring devices are not perfect), or it is simultaneously random and corrupted by measurement noise.

Yet, in the face of uncertain qualitative and quantitative information one is able to make subjective judgments. Unfortunately, the uncertainties about the information propagate so that the subjective judgments are uncertain, and many times this happens in ways that cannot be fathomed, because these judgments are a result of things going on in our brains that are not quantifiable.

It would be wonderful to have an interactive device that could aid people in making subjective judgments, a device that would propagate random and linguistic uncertainties into the subjective judgment, but in a way that could be modeled and observed by the judgment maker. This book is about a methodology, perceptual computing, that leads to such a device: a perceptual computer (Per-C, for short). The Per-C is not a single device for all problems, but is instead a device that must be designed for each specific problem by using the methodology of perceptual computing.

In 1996, Lotfi Zadeh, the father of fuzzy logic, published a paper with the very provocative title "Fuzzy Logic = Computing With Words." Recalling the song, "Is That All There Is?," his article's title might lead one to incorrectly believe that, since fuzzy logic is a very well-developed body of mathematics (with lots of real-world application), it is straightforward to implement his paradigm of computing with words. The senior author and his students have been working on one class of applications for computing with words for more than 10 years, namely, subjective judgments. The result is the perceptual computer, which, as just mentioned, is not a single device for all subjective judgment applications, but is instead very much application dependent. This book explains how to design such a device within the framework of perceptual computing.

We agree with Zadeh, so fuzzy logic is used in this book as the mathematical vehicle for perceptual computing, but not the ordinary fuzzy logic. Instead, interval type-2 fuzzy sets (IT2 FSs) and fuzzy logic are used because such fuzzy sets can model first-order linguistic uncertainties (remember, words mean different things to different people), whereas the usual kind of fuzzy sets (called type-1 fuzzy sets) cannot.

Type-1 fuzzy sets and fuzzy logic have been around now for more than 40 years. Interestingly enough, type-2 fuzzy sets first appeared in 1975 in a paper by Zadeh; however, they have only been actively studied and applied for about the last 10 years. The most widely studied kind of a type-2 fuzzy set is an IT2 FS. Both type-1 and IT2 FSs have found great applicability in function approximation kinds of problems in which the output of a fuzzy system is a number, for example, time-series forecasting, control, and so on. Because the outputs of a perceptual computer are words and possibly numbers, it was not possible for us to just use what had already been developed for IT2 FSs and systems for its designs. Many gaps had to be filled in, and it has taken 10 years to do this. This does not mean that the penultimate perceptual computer has been achieved. It does mean that enough gaps have been filled in so that it is now possible to implement one kind of computing with words class of applications.

Some of the gaps that have been filled in are:

- A method was needed to map word data with its inherent uncertainties into an IT2 FS that captures these uncertainties. The *interval approach* that is described in Chapter 3 is such a method.
- Uncertainty measures were needed to quantify linguistic uncertainties. Some uncertainty measures are described in Chapter 2.

- How to compare IT2 FSs by using similarity was needed. This is described in Chapter 4.
- How to rank IT2 FSs had to be solved. A simple ranking method is also described in Chapter 4.
- How to compute the subsethood of one IT2 FS in another such set had to be determined. This is described in Chapter 4.
- How to aggregate disparate data, ranging from numbers to uniformly weighted intervals to nonuniformly weighted intervals to words, had to be determined. Novel weighted averages are a method for doing this. They include the interval weighted average, fuzzy weighted average and the linguistic weighted average, and are described in Chapter 5.
- How to aggregate multiple-fired if–then rules so that the integrity of word IT2 FS models is preserved had to be determined. Perceptual reasoning, which is described in Chapter 6, does this.

We hope that this book will inspire its readers to not only try its methodology, but to improve upon it.

So that people will start using perceptual computing as soon as possible, we have made free software available online for implementing everything that is in this book. It is MATLAB-based (MATLAB® is a registered trademark of The Mathworks, Inc.) and was developed by the second author, Feilong Liu, and Jhiin Joo, and can be obtained at http://sipi.usc.edu/~mendel/software in folders called "Perceptual Computing Programs (PCP)" and "IJA Demo." In the PCP folder, the reader will find separate folders for Chapters 2–10. Each of these folders is self-contained, so if a program is used in more than one chapter it is included in the folder for each chapter. The IJA Demo is an interactive demonstration for Chapter 7.

We want to take this opportunity to thank the following individuals who either directly contributed to the perceptual computer or indirectly influenced its development: Lotfi A. Zadeh for type-1 and type-2 fuzzy sets and logic and for the inspiration that "fuzzy logic = computing with words," the importance of whose contributions to our work is so large that we have dedicated the book to him; Feilong Liu for codeveloping the interval approach (Chapter 3); Nilesh Karnik for codeveloping the KM algorithms; Bob John for codeveloping the wavy slice representation theorem; Jhiin Joo for developing the interactive software for the investment judgment advisor (Chapter 7); Terry Rickard for getting us interested in subsethood; and Nikhil R. Pal for interacting with us on the journal publication judgment advisor.

The authors gratefully acknowledge material quoted from books or journals published by Elsevier, IEEE, Prentice-Hall, and Springer-Verlag. For a complete listing of quoted books or articles, please see the References. The authors also gratefully acknowledge Lotfi Zadeh and David Tuk for permission to publish some quotes from private e-mail correspondences.

The first author wants to thank his wife Letty, to whom this book is also dedicated, for providing him, for more than 50 years, with a wonderful and supportive environment that has made the writing of this book possible. The second author wants to thank his parents, Shunyou Wu and Shenglian Luo, and his wife, Ying Li, to whom this book is also dedicated, for their continuous encouragement and support.

JERRY M. MENDEL
DONGRUI WU

Los Angeles, California
September 2009

CHAPTER 1

Introduction

1.1 PERCEPTUAL COMPUTING

Lotfi Zadeh (1996, 1999, 2008), the father of fuzzy logic, coined the phrase "computing with words." Different acronyms have been used for computing with words, such as CW and CWW. In this book, the latter is chosen because its three letters coincide with the three words in "computing with words." According to Zadeh (1999):

> CWW is a methodology in which the objects of computation are words and propositions drawn from a natural language. [It is] inspired by the remarkable human capability to perform a wide variety of physical and mental tasks without any measurements and any computations. CWW may have an important bearing on how humans . . . make perception-based rational decisions in an environment of imprecision, uncertainty and partial truth.

In a December 26, 2008, e-mail, Zadeh further stated:

> In 2008, computing with words (CW or CWW) has grown in visibility and recognition. There are two basic rationales for the use of computing with words. First, when we have to use words because we do not know the numbers. And second, when we know the numbers but the use of words is simpler and cheaper, or when we use words to summarize numbers. In large measure, the importance of computing with words derives from the fact that much of human knowledge is described in natural language. In one way or another, the fuzzy-logic-based machinery of computing with words opens the door to a wide-ranging enlargement of the role of natural languages in scientific theories, including scientific theories which relate to economics, medicine, law and decision analysis.

Of course, Zadeh did not mean that computers would actually compute using words—single words or phrases—rather than numbers. He meant that computers would be activated by words, which would be converted into a mathematical representation using fuzzy sets (FSs), and that these FSs would be mapped by a CWW engine into some other FS, after which the latter would be converted back into a word (Fig. 1.1).

Perceptual Computing. By Jerry M. Mendel and Dongrui Wu
Copyright © 2010 the Institute of Electrical and Electronics Engineers, Inc.

Figure 1.1. The CWW paradigm.

Zadeh's definition of CWW is very general and does not refer to a specific field in which CWW would be used. In this book, our focus is on CWW for making subjective judgments, which we call *perceptual computing*.[1]

A subjective judgment is a personal opinion that has been influenced by one's personal views, experience, or background. It can also be interpreted as a personal assessment of the level of a variable of interest and is made using a mixture of qualitative and quantitative information. Examples of subjective judgments are given in Section 1.2.

Zadeh (2001) also states he is interested in developing a computational theory of perceptions—the development of machinery for computing and reasoning with perceptions. Our thesis is that humans make subjective judgments by not only using perceptions but by also using data. Psychologists [e.g., Wallsten and Budescu (1995)] have evidence that although humans prefer to communicate using words, they also want to receive data to support the words. For example, if you are receiving a performance evaluation from your boss, and she tells you that your performance is below average, you will certainly want to know "Why," at which point she will provide quantitative data to you that supports her evaluation. Hence, perceptual computing, as used in this book, is associated with machinery for computing and reasoning with perceptions and data.

Our architecture for perceptual computing is depicted in Fig. 1.2. It is called a *perceptual computer* or Per-C for short [Mendel (2001, 2002, 2007)]. The Per-C consists of three components: encoder, CWW engine, and decoder. Perceptions—words—activate the Per-C and are the Per-C output (along with data); so it is possible for a human to interact with the Per-C using just a vocabulary.

A vocabulary is application (context) dependent, and must be large enough so that it lets the end user interact with the Per-C in a user-friendly manner. The encoder transforms words into FSs and leads to a *codebook*—words with their associated FS models. The outputs of the encoder activate a CWW engine, whose output is one or more other FSs, which are then mapped by the decoder into a recommendation (subjective judgment) with supporting data. The recommendation may be in the form of a word, group of similar words, rank, or class.

This book explains how to design the encoder, CWW engines, and decoders. It provides the reader with methodologies for doing all of this, so that, perhaps for the

---

[1]According to *Merriam Webster's On-Line Dictionary,* the word *perceptual* means "of relating to, or involving perception especially in relation to immediate sensory experience"; *perception* means "a result of perceiving"; and *perceive* means "to attain awareness or understanding of," or "to become aware of through the senses." Hopefully, this explains our choice of the word perceptual in perceptual computing.

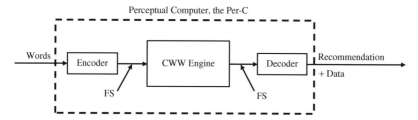

Figure 1.2. Specific architecture for CWW—the perceptual computer.

first time, CWW can be fully implemented, at least for making subjective judgments.

1.2 EXAMPLES

In this section, four examples are provided that illustrate CWW for making subjective judgments: investment decision making, social judgment making, hierarchical decision making, and hierarchical and distributed decision making. These examples are taken up later in this book, in much greater detail, in Chapters 7–10.

1.2.1 Investment Decision Making

Tong and Bonissone (1980) illustrated their approach to linguistic decision making using an investment decision example:

> A private citizen has a moderately large amount of capital that he wishes to invest to his best advantage. He has selected five possible investment areas $\{a_1, a_2, a_3, a_4, a_5\}$ and has four investment criteria $\{c_1, c_2, c_3, c_4\}$ by which to judge them. These are:
> - a_1—the commodity market, a_2—the stock market, a_3—gold,[2] a_4—real estate,[3] and a_5—long-term bonds;
> - c_1—the risk of losing the capital sum, c_2—the vulnerability of the capital sum to modification by inflation, c_3—the amount of interest[4] [profit] received, and c_4—the cash realizeability of the capital sum [liquidity].

The individual's goal is to decide which investments he should partake in. In order to arrive at his decisions, the individual must first rate each of the five alternative

---

[2]Tong and Bonissone called this "gold and/or diamonds." In this book, this is simplified to "gold."
[3]The term *real estate* is somewhat ambiguous because it could mean individual properties, ranging from residential to commercial, or investment vehicles that focus exclusively on real estate, such as a real estate investment trust (REIT) or a real estate mutual fund. In this chapter, real estate is interpreted to mean the latter two.
[4]By *interest* is meant the profit percent from the capital invested; so, in this chapter the term *profit* is used.

investment areas for each of the four criteria. To do this requires that he either knows about the investments or becomes knowledgeable about them. His ratings use words and, therefore, are linguistic ratings. In order to illustrate what the linguistic ratings might look like, the ones used by Tong and Bonissone are provided in the investment alternatives/investment criteria array in Table 1.1. For example, the individual's linguistic ratings about commodities are that there is a high risk of losing his capital sum from investing in commodities, commodities have a more or less high vulnerability to inflation, the amount of profit received from commodities is very high, and commodities are fairly liquid.

What makes the individual's investment choices challenging is that his knowledge about the investments is uncertain; hence, his linguistic ratings are uncertain. Additionally, each individual does not necessarily consider each criterion to be equally important. So, he must also assign a linguistic weight to each of them. The weights chosen by Tong and Bonissone are given in Table 1.2. This individual views the risk of losing his capital as moderately important, the vulnerability to inflation as more or less important, the amount of profit received as very important, and liquidity as more or less unimportant. Although common weights are used for all five investment alternatives, they could be chosen separately for each of the alternatives.

The problem facing the individual investor is how to aggregate the linguistic information in Tables 1.1 and 1.2 so as to arrive at his preferential ranking of the five investments (Fig. 1.3). Clearly, the results will be very subjective because these tables are filled with words and not numbers. The investor may also want to play "what-if" games, meaning that he may want to see what the effects are of changing the words in one or both of the tables on the preferential rankings.

Table 1.1. Investment alternatives/investment criteria array. Example of the linguistic ratings of investment alternatives for investment criteria, provided by an individual[a]

	Investment criteria			
Investment alternatives	c_1 (Risk of losing capital)	c_2 (Vulnerability to inflation)	c_3 (Amount of profit received)	c_4 (Liquidity)
a_1 (commodities)	High	More or less high	Very high	Fair
a_2 (stocks)	Fair	Fair	Fair	More or less good
a_3 (gold)	Low	From fair to more or less low	Fair	Good
a_4 (real estate)	Low	Very low	More or less high	Bad
a_5 (long-term bonds)	Very low	High	More or less low	Very good

[a]An individual fills in this table by answering the following questions: To me, the risk of losing my capital in investment alternative a_j seems to be _____? To me, the vulnerability of investment alternative a_j to inflation seems to be_____? To me, the amount of profit that I would receive from investment alternative a_j seems to be _____? To me, the liquidity of investment alternative a_j seems to be_____?

Table 1.2. Example of the linguistic weights for the investment criteria provided by an individual[a]

c_1 (Risk of losing capital)	c_2 (Vulnerability to inflation)	c_3 (Amount of profit received)	c_4 (Liquidity)
Moderately important	More or less important	Very important	More or less unimportant

[a]An individual fills in this table by answering the following question: The importance that I attach to the investment criterion c_i is _____?

The Per-C that is associated with this application is called an *investment judgment advisor,* and its design is studied in detail in Chapter 7. One of the interesting features of this application is that any person, such as the reader of this book, can fill in Tables 1.1 and 1.2, and immediately find out his/her preferential rankings of the five investments.

1.2.2 Social Judgment Making

According to Mendel et al. (1999):

> In everyday social interaction, each of us is called upon to make judgments about the meaning of another's behavior. Such judgments are far from trivial, since they often affect the nature and direction of the subsequent social interaction and communications. But, how do we make this judgment? By *judgment* we mean the assessment of the *level* of the variable of interest. Although a variety of factors may enter into our decision, behavior is apt to play a critical role is assessing the level of the variable of interest.

Some examples of behavior are kindness, generosity, flirtation, jealousy, harassment, vindictiveness, and morality.

Suppose the behavior of interest is flirtation, and the only indicator of importance is eye contact. The following user-friendly vocabulary could be established for both eye contact and flirtation: none to very little, very little, little, small amount, some, a moderate amount, a considerable amount, a large amount, a very

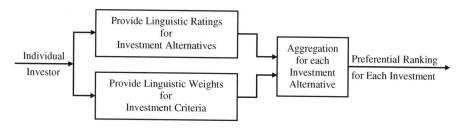

Figure 1.3. Investment judgment advisor.

large amount, and a maximum amount. Surveyed subjects could be asked a question such as, "On a scale of zero to ten, where would you locate the end points of an interval for this word?" These data could then be mapped by means of the encoder into a FS model for each word. The 10 words and their FS models constitute the codebook for the subjective judgment of flirtation and for eye contact.

A small set of five rules could then be established, using a subset of five of the 10 words: none to very little, some, a moderate amount, a large amount, and a maximum amount. One such rule might be:

IF eye contact is a *moderate amount,* THEN the level of flirtation is *some.*

Another survey could be conducted in which subjects choose one of these five flirtation terms for each rule (i.e., for the rule's consequent). Because all respondents do not agree on the choice of the consequent, this introduces uncertainties into this if–then rule-based CWW engine. The resulting rules from the group of subjects are then used as a *consensus flirtation advisor* (Fig. 1.4).

An individual user could interact with this flirtation adviser by inputting any one of the 10 words from the codebook for a specific level of eye contact. Rules within the consensus flirtation advisor would be fired using the mathematics of FSs (as described in Chapter 6), the result being a fired-rule FS for each fired rule. These FSs could then be aggregated into a composite FS that would be compared to the word FSs in the codebook. This comparison would be done using fuzzy set similarity computations, as described in Chapter 4, the result being the word that best describes the consensus flirtation level to the individual.

Such a flirtation adviser could be used to train a person to better understand the relationship between eye contact and flirtation, so that they reach correct conclusions about such a social situation. Their perception of flirtation for each of the 10 words for eye contact leads to their individual flirtation level (Fig. 1.4) for each level of eye contact, and their individual flirtation level is then compared with the corresponding consensus flirtation level. If there is good agreement between the consensus and individual's flirtation levels, then the individual is given positive feedback about this; otherwise, he or she is given advice on how to reinterpret the level of flirtation for the specific level of eye contact. It is not necessary that there be exact agreement between the consensus and individual's flirtation levels for the individual to be given positive feedback, because the consensus and individual's flirtation levels may be similar

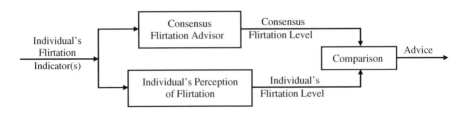

Figure 1.4. Flirtation advisor.

enough. Chapter 4 provides quantitative levels of similarity for words in a codebook, so that it will be possible to quantify what is meant by "similar enough."

Of course, in this very simple example of only one flirtation indicator not much confusion can occur; however, when more indicators are used (e.g., eye contact and touching, or primping and acting witty), then in an actual social situation it is possible to get "mixed signals," that is, a certain level of touching may indicate a large amount of flirtation, whereas a certain level of eye contact may indicate none to very little flirtation. So which is it? In this case, more than one rule will fire and the totality of fired rule FSs is an indicator of what is meant by "mixed signals." By aggregating the fired rule FSs and comparing the resulting FS to the word FSs in the codebook the result will again be the word that best describes the flirtation state to the individual user.

In this way, the flirtation adviser can be used to train a person to reach correct conclusions about social situations when he or she is receiving mixed signals. And, as is well known, the same levels of flirtation indicators can mean different levels of flirtation to women and men; so, a female flirtation advisor could be used to sensitize men to those differences, and vice-versa.

It is easy to extend this social judgment application, which some may feel is light-hearted, to many other social judgments and also to nonsocial judgments. Examples of the latter include global warming, environmental impact, water quality, audio quality, toxicity, and terrorism (terrorist).

The details of a social judgment advisor are described in Chapter 8.

1.2.3 Hierarchical Decision Making

By "hierarchical decision making" (Fig. 1.5) is meant decision making made by a single individual, group, or organization that is based on comparing the performance of competing alternatives, such as an individual's performance in an athletic, dancing, or cooking competition; a group or individual's proposal for solving a problem or building a product; or product selection (e.g., which flat-panel display should I purchase?) Each alternative is first evaluated or scored (this process may itself involve a hierarchical process involving criteria and subcriteria), after which the evaluations or scores are compared at a higher level to arrive at either a single winning competitor or a subset of winners. What can make this challenging is that the evaluations or scores of the subcriteria and criteria can use numbers, uniformly weighted intervals of numbers, nonuniformly weighted intervals of numbers, or even words. How to aggregate such disparate information (the subject of Chapter 5) is very challenging and lends itself very nicely to perceptual computing.

Two examples are:

1. Tzeng and Teng (1993) define a fuzzy multiobjective transportation selection problem as "a given finite set of n potential projects $x_1, x_2, \ldots, x_n$ is evaluated with respect to m objectives $o_1, o_2, \ldots, o_m$, and q resources constraints $c_1, c_2, \ldots, c_q$." The subset of projects that give the highest improvement urgency index (IUI) are the winners. Some of the m objectives are expressed

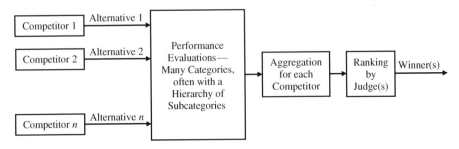

Figure 1.5. Hierarchical decision making.

linguistically, for example, environmental impact is {very good, good, fair, poor, very poor}. Each project's IUI is computed by using a fuzzy weighted average (see Chapter 5) and its resulting FS is then converted into a crisp number, N_{IUI}. Each project's profitability index (PI) is then computed as the ratio N_{IUI}/cost, after which all of the n PIs are ranked. Projects not satisfying the constraints are removed, and the winning projects are selected from the highest PI to the lowest PI, within the limits of an available budget.

2. Mon et al. (1994) consider the following hierarchical multicriteria missile evaluation system. A contractor has to decide which of three companies is going to get the final mass production contract for the missile. The contractor uses five criteria to arrive at his final decision, namely: tactics, technology, maintenance, economy, and advancement. Each of these criteria has some associated technical subcriteria; for example, for tactics the subcriteria are effective range, flight height, flight velocity, reliability, firing accuracy, destruction rate, and kill radius, whereas for economy the subcriteria are system cost, system life, and material limitation.

   The contractor creates a performance evaluation table (Table 1.3) in order to assist in choosing the winning company. Contained within this table are three columns, one for each of the three competing companies. The rows of this table are partitioned into the five criteria, and each of the partitions has additional rows, one for each of its subcriteria. Entries into this table are evaluations of the subcriteria. Additionally, weights are assigned to all of the subcriteria, because they are not of equal importance. These weights are fuzzy numbers such as around seven and around five. The subcriteria evaluations range from numbers to words.

   Somehow, the contractor has to aggregate this disparate information, and this is even more difficult because the five criteria are themselves not of equal importance and have their own fuzzy weights assigned to them.

This application is the subject of Chapter 9, where it is shown how the Per-C can be used to assist the contractor to choose the winning company. Other hierarchical decision making applications are also reviewed in that chapter.

Table 1.3. Performance evaluation table. Criteria and subcriteria with their kinds of weights, and kinds of subcriteria data provided for the three companies

Item	Weighting	Company A	Company B	Company C
Criterion 1: Tactics Effective range (km) Flight height (m) Flight velocity (Mach no.) Reliability (%) Firing accuracy (%) Destruction rate (%) Kill radius (m)	Fuzzy numbers	Numerical evaluations	Numerical evaluations	Numerical evaluations
Criterion 2: Technology Missile scale (cm) (l × d-span) Reaction time (min) Fire rate (round/min) Antijam (%) Combat capability	Fuzzy numbers	Numerical and linguistic evaluations	Numerical and linguistic evaluations	Numerical and linguistic evaluations
Criterion 3: Maintenance Operation condition requirement Safety Defilade Simplicity Assembly	Fuzzy numbers	Linguistic evaluations	Linguistic evaluations	Linguistic evaluations
Criterion 4: Economy System cost (10,000) System life (years) Material limitation	Fuzzy numbers	Numerical and linguistic evaluations	Numerical and linguistic evaluations	Numerical and linguistic evaluations
Criterion 5: Advancement Modularization Mobility Standardization	Fuzzy numbers	Linguistic evaluations	Linguistic evaluations	Linguistic evaluations

1.2.4 Hierarchical and Distributed Decision Making

By "hierarchical and distributed decision making" (Fig. 1.6) is meant decision making that is ultimately made by a single individual, group or organization, but that is based on aggregating independently made recommendations about an object from other individuals, groups, or organizations (i.e., judges). An object could be a person being considered for a job, an article being reviewed for publication in a journal, a military objective, and so on. It is the independent nature of the recommendations that leads to this being called "distributed," and it is the aggregation of the distributed recommendations at a higher level that leads to this being called "hierarchical."

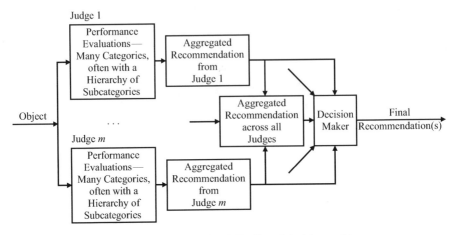

Figure 1.6. Hierarchical and distributed decision making.

There can be multiple levels of hierarchy in this process, because each of the independent recommendations may also involve a hierarchical decision making process, as just described in subsection 1.2.3. Additionally, the individuals, groups, or organizations making their independent recommendations may not be of equal expertise, and so a weight has to be assigned to each of them when they are aggregated. The independent recommendations can involve aggregating numbers, uniformly weighted intervals of numbers, nonuniformly weighted intervals of numbers, and even words. The final recommendation (or decision) is made by a decision maker who not only uses an aggregated recommendation that is made across all of the judges but may also use the aggregated recommendation from each of the judges.

Consider the problem of hiring a new employee.[5] For this process, there often is a selection team with a diversity of views. Typically, the selection team is comprised of the position owner, peers (technical experts), customers, and a manager. Prior to posting a job, selection criteria are created and each candidate is evaluated against those criteria. Each selection team member may be weighted differently, and more weight may be applied to the selection criteria in which they have the greatest expertise. For example, peers might care more about a candidate's technical skills and teamwork ability, so more weight could be applied to a peer's evaluation of the candidate's technical and teamwork capabilities. On the other hand, customers might want to know if the individual has the skills to help them with their business problems, and managers might be looking for candidates who can be used in other roles, so for them more weight could be applied to these selection criteria.

Today, a traditional decision sciences hierarchical matrix is used to assist in making the final hiring decision. For this matrix, everyone on the selection team must rate the candidate on a scale from, say, 1 to 10, and usually this is done in a distributed

[5]This example was provided to us by David Tuk (Chevron Corp.).

manner. Individuals are uncomfortable distinguishing between a 7 and an 8, but they might be willing to say outstanding, strong, fair, and poor. So looking at the difference between how the hiring decision is made deterministically versus what would be discovered if FL were used would be very interesting. The paper by Doctor et al. (2008) is the first attempt to develop a version of the Per-C for this problem.

Chapter 10 explains in detail how the Per-C can be applied to the so-called *journal publication judgment advisor,* in which, for the first time, only words are used at every level of the following hierarchical and distributed decision making process.

n reviewers have to provide a subjective recommendation about a journal article that has been sent to them by the Associate Editor, who then has to aggregate the independent recommendations into a final recommendation that is sent to the Editor-in-Chief of the journal. Because it is very problematic to ask reviewers to provide numerical scores for paper-evaluation subcategories (the two major categories are technical merit and presentation), such as importance, content, depth, style, organization, clarity, references, and so on, each reviewer will only be asked to provide a linguistic score for each of these categories. They will not be asked for an overall recommendation about the paper because in the past it was quite common for reviewers who provided the same numerical scores for such categories to give very different publishing recommendations. By leaving a specific recommendation to the Associate Editor, such inconsistencies can hopefully be eliminated.

Aggregating words to reflect each reviewer's recommendation as well as the expertise of each reviewer about the paper's subject matter is done using a linguistic weighted average (explained in Chapter 5).

Although the journal publication judgment advisor uses reviewers and an associate editor, the word "reviewer" could be replaced by judge, expert, low-level manager, commander, referee, etc, and the term "associate editor" could be replaced by control center, command center, higher-level manager, etc. So, this application has potential wide applicability to many other applications.

1.3 HISTORICAL ORIGINS OF PERCEPTUAL COMPUTING

Although Mendel (2001, 2002) was the first to use the term perceptual computer, it is interesting to go back into the literature of fuzzy sets and systems, earlier than 2001, to trace the origins of anything that resembles it. Although perceptual computing is a subset of CWW, it has a much longer history than CWW, as is demonstrated next.

The earliest article that we found that demonstrates an approach for making subjective judgments using FSs is by Tong and Bonissone (1980). In their words:

> A technique for making linguistic decision is presented. Fuzzy sets are assumed to be an appropriate way of dealing with uncertainty, and it is therefore concluded that decisions taken on the basis of such information must themselves be fuzzy. It is inappropriate then to present the decision in numerical form; a statement in natural language is much better. The basic problem is to choose between a set of alternatives $\{a_i : i = 1,$

..., m}, given some fuzzy information about the "suitability" of each of them. This information is given as a set of fuzzy sets, {$S_i : i = 1, \ldots, M$}, where each of the S_i is defined by a membership function that maps the real line onto a closed interval [0,1]. Suitability is simply interpreted as a measure of the ability of an alternative to meet our decision criteria and is essentially a fuzzification of the idea of a rating. We have to select the preferred alternative on the basis of {$S_i : i = 1, \ldots, M$} and then generate a linguistic statement about our decision.

Their article includes an example of perceptual computing for making a choice about investments when each of five possible investments is evaluated using four criteria. The resulting investment evaluations use words, that is, they are linguistic. This application has been described in more detail in Section 1.2.1.

Next is the monograph by Schmucker (1984). On the one hand, it contains the essence of perceptual computing, but on the other hand, by today's standards its theoretical depth is not high. Although Schmucker does not use the term perceptual computing, he talks about natural language computations and risk analysis. Figure 1.7, which uses some parts of Fig. 5.1 of his book, is an indication that the three elements of the Per-C are in his fuzzy risk analyzer (FRA). In Schmucker's figure, the "PARSE Natural Language to Fuzzy Set" block contains a collection of words, including more or less, very, normally, fairly, and extremely; the CWW Engine is the fuzzy weighted average;[6] and, the Decoder uses best fit, successive approximation, or piecewise decomposition.

Schmucker states:

It is the goal of the system designer of an automated risk analysis facility to (1) have a sufficiently rich set of primary terms and hedges so that the user feels almost unrestricted in his range of expression, and (2) associate with each possible natural language expression that can be generated by rules a technical precise meaning that is consistent with the imprecise nebulous English meaning.

Zadeh (1996) summarizes CWW using a figure like the one in Fig. 1.8 (it is Part b of his Fig. 3). He states [Zadeh (1999)]:

Computing with words (CW) is inspired by the remarkable human capability to perform a wide variety of physical and mental tasks without any measurements and any computations. . . . Underlying this remarkable capability is the brain's crucial ability to manipulate perceptions. . . . Manipulation of perceptions plays a key role in human recognition, decision and execution processes. As a methodology, computing with words provides a foundation for a computational theory of perceptions—a theory which may have an important bearing on how humans make—and machines might make—perception-based rational decisions in an environment of imprecision, uncertainty and partial truth. . . . A basic difference between perceptions and measurements is that, in general measurements are crisp whereas perceptions are fuzzy. . . . The computational theory of perceptions, or CTP for short is based on the methodology of CW. In CTP, words play the role of labels of perceptions and, more generally, perceptions

[6]The fuzzy weighted average is covered in Chapter 5.

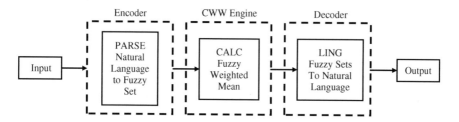

Figure 1.7. Schmucker's (1984) FRA. The dashed blocks and their associated labels which relate his blocks to the Per-C were put in by us.

are expressed as propositions in a natural language. CW-based techniques are employed to translate propositions expressed in a natural language into what is called a Generalized Constraint Language (GCL). In this language, the meaning of a proposition is expressed as a generalized constraint X *isr* R, where X is the constrained variable, R is the constraining relation and *isr* is a variable copula in which r is a variable whose value defines the way in which R constrains X. Among the basic types of constraints are: possibilistic, veristic, probabilistic, random set, Pawlak set, fuzzy graph and usuality. . . . In CW, the initial and terminal data sets, IDS and TDS, are assumed to consist of propositions expressed in a natural language. These propositions are translated, respectively, into antecedent and consequent constraints. Consequent constraints are derived from antecedent constraints through the rules of constraint propagation. The principal constraint propagation rule is the generalized extension principle. The derived constraints are retranslated into a natural language, yielding the terminal data set (TDS).

Some of the blocks in Fig. 1.8 have been enclosed in dashed shapes so that this figure conforms to the Per-C in Fig. 1.2. The two blocks called "propositions in NL" (natural language) and "initial data set (IDS)" comprise our encoder. We have interpreted those blocks to mean: establishing a vocabulary for an application, collecting data about the words in that vocabulary, and modeling the words as fuzzy

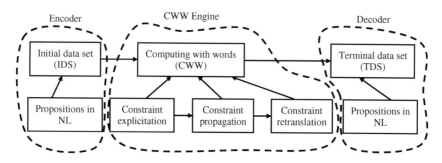

Figure 1.8. Zadeh's (1996) CWW. The dashed shapes and their associated labels which relate the enclosed blocks to the Per-C, were put in by us (Zadeh, 1996; © 1996, IEEE).

sets. The two blocks called "propositions in NL" and "terminal dataset (TDS)" comprise our decoder. We have interpreted those blocks to mean mapping the FS output from the CWW block into a linguistic recommendation. Finally, the four blocks called "constraint explicitation," "constraint propagation," "computing with words (CWW)," and "constraint retranslation" are our CWW engine. We have interpreted these four blocks to mean choosing and implementing a specific CWW engine.

Buckley and Feuring (1999) include Fig. 1.9 that contains within in it a Per-C. In their summary, they state:

> This chapter describes the design of a supervisory fuzzy controller for human operators of a complex plant (nuclear reactor). The human operators are allowed to verbally describe the status of various variables used to control the plant. These verbal descriptions come from a very limited vocabulary recognized by the input translator. The input translator translates these descriptions into fuzzy numbers for input to a fuzzy expert system. The fuzzy expert system processes these fuzzy numbers into fuzzy number outputs describing suggestions to the human operators. The output translator, which is a neural net, takes the fuzzy number output from the fuzzy expert system, and produces verbal suggestions, of what to do, for the human operators. The translation of fuzzy numbers into words is called inverse linguistic approximation.

In Fig. 1.9 verbal evaluations made by a human operator (who is interacting with a complex plant) who has access to a vocabulary of words for the application of supervisory control, are translated into fuzzy numbers by the input translator (hard-

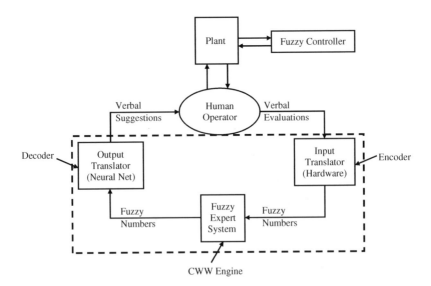

Figure 1.9. Buckley and Feuring's (1999) supervisory fuzzy controller. The dashed block and its associated labels relate the other blocks to the Per-C, and were put in by us (Buckley and Feuring, 1999; © 1999, Springer-Verlag).

ware). This is equivalent to our encoder. The translator's fuzzy numbers are processed by a fuzzy expert system whose outputs are other fuzzy numbers. Clearly, the fuzzy expert system is equivalent to one kind of CWW engine. Its output fuzzy numbers are translated into verbal suggestions by the output translator (neural net). This is equivalent to our Decoder.

Finally, Yager (1999, 2004) has the diagram shown in Fig. 1.10.[7] Clearly, translation, manipulation, and retranslation are synonymous with our Encoder, CWW engine, and decoder. In his 2004 article, the manipulation block is called inference/granular computing, and he states:

> We shall assume that as a result of our inference process we obtain the proposition V is A, where A is a fuzzy subset of the universe X. Our concern is to express this with a natural language statement. The process of retranslation is one of substituting the proposition V is F for V is A, where F is some element from $\mathfrak{I}$ and then expressing the output as V is L, where L is the linguistic term associated with F. The key issue in this process is the substitution of V is F for V is A.

The conclusions to be drawn from this brief historical foray are:

- The elements of the perceptual computer did not originate in Mendel (2001, 2002).
- Tong and Bonissone should be credited with originating the perceptual computer, although they did not call it by that name; but, as William Shakespeare wrote: "What's in a name?"
- Additionally, the essence of perceptual computing has been reinvented a number of times and no doubt will continue to be reinvented.

1.4 HOW TO VALIDATE THE PERCEPTUAL COMPUTER

It is our belief[8] that for the Per-C to be successful it must provide end users with results that are equivalent to those from a human. This agrees in spirit with what the great computer scientist and philosopher Alan Turing (1950) [see, also, Hodges (1997)] proposed as a test, the Turing Test for machine intelligence. This test is as applicable to perceptual computing as it is to machine intelligence, because perceptual computing is a form of artificial intelligence.

Consider an "imitation game" played with three players, a human being, a machine and an interrogator. The interrogator stays in a room apart from the others. The object is for the interrogator to determine which of the others is the human being or the machine. If the machine cannot be distinguished from the human being

---

[7]Yager's interests in CWW can be found as early as 1981 [Yager (1981)]. Although the three elements of a perceptual computer are not in the paper, the methodology of the paper is that of CWW; for example, his main example only uses words.

[8]The material in this section is taken from Mendel (2007c).

Figure 1.10. Yager's (1999) CWW diagram (Yager, 1999; © 1999, Springer-Verlag).

under these conditions, then the machine must be credited with human intelligence [Hodges (1997)]. This is the essence of a Turing Test.

According to Saygin et al. (2000), "The Turing Test is one of the most disputed topics in artificial intelligence and cognitive sciences," because it can be interpreted in many different ways, for example, by philosophers, sociologists, psychologists, religionists, computer scientists, and so on. We are not interested in using a Turing Test to establish whether the Per-C can think so as to demonstrate that it is intelligent. We are interested in using a Turing Test, as explained in Saygin et al. (2000, p. 467), as "a test to assess a machine's ability to pass for a human being."

In order to implement the Per-C, data will be needed. This data must be collected from people who are similar to those who will ultimately be interacting with the Per-C. If such data collection is feasible, then the design of the Per-C can proceed by using some of the data for training[9] and the rest for validation (testing).[10] The validation of the designed Per-C using some of the collected data (the validation set) can be interpreted as a Turing Test.

If, on the other hand, such data collection is not feasible, then the designer of the Per-C must fabricate it or, even worse, design the Per-C using no data at all. After such a design, the Per-C will have to be validated on a group of subjects, and such a validation will again constitute a Turing Test.

Hence, one way or another, validation of a Per-C is accomplished through a Turing Test.

1.5   THE CHOICE OF FUZZY SET MODELS FOR THE PER-C

Because words can mean different things to different people, it is important to use an FS model for a word that lets us capture word uncertainties.[11] At present, there are two possible choices, a type-1 (T1) FS or an interval type-2 (IT2) FS[12] [Mendel (2001b, 2003, 2007b)]. These sets are fully covered in Chapter 2, a high-level syn-

---

[9]When the CWW Engine (Fig. 1.2) is a set of if–then rules (described in Chapter 6), then a training set can be used to optimize the parameters of antecedent and consequent membership functions, to establish the presence or absence of antecedent terms, and to even determine the number of significant rules, after which the optimized rules can be tested using a testing set.

[10]In traditional supervised system design (e.g., using the back-propagation algorithm), the validation dataset is used to determine whether the training should be terminated and the testing dataset is used to evaluate the generalization performance. In this chapter, validation and testing are used interchangeably, and both terms mean to evaluate the performance of the Per-C.

[11]The material in this section is taken from Mendel (2007c).

[12]General type-2 FSs are presently excluded, because they model higher degrees of uncertainty (see Chapter 3, Section 3.2, Premise 2), and how to do this is not generally known.

opsis of which is given at the end of the present chapter, in Section 1.8.1. In order to decide which FS to use as a word model, two different approaches can be taken:

1. Ignore the adage "words can mean different things to different people," use a T1 FS as a word model, design the Per-C, and see if it passes a Turing Test. If it does, then it is okay to use such an FS as a word model.

2. Adhere to the adage "words can mean different things to different people" and try to decide between using a T1 FS and an IT2 FS as a word model before designing the Per-C. Then design the Per-C and see if it passes a Turing Test.

Because we believe in the adage "words can mean different things to different people," the first approach is not taken in this book. Regarding the second approach, in order to choose between using a T1 FS or an IT2 FS as a word model, we shall rely on the great 20th century scientific philosopher, Sir Karl Popper, who proposed *falsificationism* [Popper (1959, 1963) and Thornton (2005)] as a way to establish if a theory is or is not scientific. Falsificationism states:

A theory is scientific only if it is refutable by a conceivable event. Every genuine test of a scientific theory, then, is logically an attempt to refute or to falsify it, and one genuine counterinstance falsifies the whole theory. [Thornton (2005)]

According to Thornton (2005), by falsifiability Popper meant:

If a theory is incompatible with possible empirical observations it is scientific; conversely, a theory which is compatible with all such observations, either because, as in the case of Marxism, it has been modified solely to accommodate such observations, or because, as in the case of psychoanalytic theories, it is consistent with all possible observations, is unscientific.

For a theory to be called scientific it must be testable. This means that it must be possible to make measurements that are related to the theory. A scientific theory can be correct or incorrect. An incorrect scientific theory is still a scientific theory, but is one that must be replaced by another scientific theory that is itself subject to refutation at a later date.

We suggest that using either a T1 FS or an IT2 FS as a word model can be interpreted as a scientific theory.[13] Whether or not each FS word model qualifies as a scientific theory, and then if each is a correct or incorrect scientific theory, must, therefore, be questioned.

Many methods have been reported for making measurements about words and then using those measurements to model a word as either a T1 FS or as an IT2 FS. Hence, as explained next, both kinds of FSs are "scientific" word models.

---

[13]Note that this is very different from T1 FSs and IT2 FSs as mathematics, which are not scientific theories, and about which we should not raise any issues.

Data collection and mapping into the parameters of a T1 membership function (MF) for a word has been reported on by a number of authors [e.g., Klir and Yuan (1995)] and has also been reported on for a T2 MF for a word [Liu and Mendel (2007, 2008), Mendel and Wu (2006, 2007a,b)]. Names for the different T1 methods include: *polling* [Hersch and Caramazza (1976), Lawry (2001)], *direct rating* [Klir and Yuan (1995), Norwich and Turksen (1982, 1984)], *reverse rating* [Norwich and Turksen (1984), Turksen (1986, 1988, 1991), Turksen and Wilson (1994)], *interval estimation* [Cornelissen (2003), Civanlar and Trussel (1986), Dubois and Prade (1986), Zwick (1987)], and *transition interval estimation* [Cornelissen (2003)]. These methods are described in Chapter 3. Names for the different T2 methods are: *person footprint of uncertainty* [Mendel (2007a)], *interval end points* [Mendel and Wu (2006, 2007a,b), Mendel (2007a)], and *interval approach* [Liu and Mendel (2007, 2008)]. These methods are also described in Chapter 3.

The term *fuzzistics* has been coined [Mendel (2003b, 2007a)] for mapping data that are collected from a group of subjects into an FS model, and represents an amalgamation of the words *fuzzy* and *statistics*. It is a term that is used in this book.

Because of the existence of both type-1 and type-2 fuzzistic's works, we conclude that using type-1 or interval type-2 fuzzy sets as models for words is scientific.

That using a T1 FS model for a word is an incorrect scientific theory follows from the following line of reasoning [Mendel (2003b)]:

- A T1 fuzzy set A for a word is well-defined by its MF $\mu_A(x)$ $(x \in X)$ that is totally certain once all of its parameters are specified.
- Words mean different things to different people and so are uncertain.
- Therefore, it is a contradiction to say that something certain can model something that is uncertain.

In the words of Popper, associating the original T1 FS with a word is a "conceivable event" that has provided a "counterinstance" that falsifies this approach to fuzzy sets as models for words.

Chapter 3 explains that an IT2 FS model for a word is only a first-order uncertainty model; hence, an IT2 FS is a scientifically correct first-order uncertainty model for a word and is the one used in this book.[14] As a result, the Fig. 1.2 diagram for the Per-C is modified to the diagram in Fig. 1.11, in which "FS" has been replaced by "IT2 FS."

An objection may be raised that a fixed MF also applies to an IT2 FS model; that is, once the parameters of an IT2 FS model are specified, there no longer is anything uncertain about the IT2 FS. This objection is incorrect because the IT2 FS is a first-order uncertainty model, that is, at each value of the primary variable the MF is an interval of values. For a T1 FS, the MF is a point value, and it is the interval nature of

---

[14]In the future, perhaps the scientifically correct IT2 FS model for a word will be falsified by a more complete T2 FS model. This will only be possible when more kinds of data than are described in Chapter 3 can be collected about words, or if the data that are presently collected are reinterpreted.

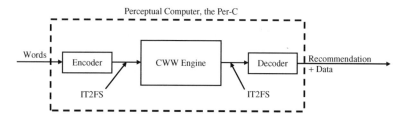

Figure 1.11. The perceptual computer that uses IT2 FS models for words (Mendel, 2007c; © 2007, IEEE).

the MF that provides the uncertainty in the IT2 FS model. This argument is similar to one that can be given for a probability distribution function. Once we agree that such a function does indeed model unpredictable (random) uncertainties, then fixing its parameters does not cause us to conclude that it no longer is a probability model.

One may argue that a T1 FS model for a word is a model for a *prototypical word* [Rosch (1975, 1983)]; however, if one also believes that words mean different things to different people, then this calls into question the concept of a prototypical word.

When random uncertainties are present, most of us have no problem with using probability models and analyses from the very beginning; hence, when linguistic uncertainties are present, we suggest that one must have no problem with using IT2 FS models and analyses from the very beginning. Some may ask the question, "How much linguistic uncertainty must be present before an IT2 FS should be used?" Maybe, in the very early days of probability, a similar question was asked; however, it no longer seems to be asked. When randomness is suspected, probability is used. So, when linguistic uncertainties are suspected, IT2 FSs should be used.

Finally, even a Per-C that is designed using IT2 FSs needs to be validated by a Turing Test. The difference in this second approach is that the design is begun using an FS word model that is scientifically correct. This, in itself, does not mean that the resulting Per-C will pass a Turing Test, because that test is applied to the outputs of the Per-C, and it is (Fig. 1.11) the combination of a scientifically correct FS input word model, the CWW engine, and a good decoder that leads to the output recommendation.

Consequently, in this book IT2 FSs are used to model words.

1.6 KEEPING THE PER-C AS SIMPLE AS POSSIBLE

Many choices have to be made when designing a Per-C.[15] For example, if the CWW engine is a set of if–then rules (see Chapter 6), then choices must be made about:

- Shapes of MFs for each IT2 FS.

---

[15]The material in this section is taken from Mendel (2007c).

- Mathematical operators used to model the antecedent connector words *and* and *or*. Such operators are called t-norms and t-conorms, respectively, and there are many t-norms and t-conorms to choose from [e.g., Klir and Yuan (1995)].
- Implication operators (an if–then rule is mathematically modeled using an implication operator), and there are many such operators [e.g., Klir and Yuan (1995)].
- How to aggregate fired rules, i.e., when more than one rule is fired, rule outputs must be combined (aggregated), and there are many different ways to do this [e.g., Klir and Yuan (1995)]. The result is an aggregated IT2 FS.
- How to go from the aggregated IT2 FS to a word, that is, the decoder-design in which, for example, a similarity measure is used, and there are many kinds of similarity measures [e.g., (Wu and Mendel (2008a)].

On the one hand, it is the multitude of choices that provide fuzzy logic with versatility and flexibility. On the other hand, having so many choices with none to very few guidelines on how to make them is confusing.

How does one make the choices needed to implement a Per-C?

Occam's (or Ockham's) Razor[16] is a principle attributed to the 14th century logician and Franciscan friar, William of Occam. The most useful statement of the principle is, when you have two competing theories that make exactly the same predictions, the one that is simpler is the better. This principle is sometimes misstated as "keep it as simple as possible." One can have two (or more) competing theories that lead to different predictions. Occam's Razor does not apply in that case, because the results that are obtained from the competing theories are different.

All of our fuzzy set and fuzzy logic operators originate from crisp sets and crisp logic. In the crisp domain, although there can be many different operators, they all give the same results; hence, we propose that, for the Per-C, Occam's Razor should be applied to the multitude of t-norm, t-conorms, implication operators, and so on in the *crisp domain*. It should not be applied after the operators have been fuzzified, because then it is too late as they give different results. By this argument, one would choose, for example, minimum or product t-norm and maximum t-conorm, because they are simplest t-norms and t-conorm.

Finally, note, that even a Per-C that is designed using IT2 FSs and the "simplest" operators needs to be validated by a Turing Test. If, for example, a Per-C that uses the simplest operators does not pass a Turing Test, then more complicated operators should be used.

1.7   COVERAGE OF THE BOOK

Many of the chapters in this book are very technical in nature, because to really understand the Per-C so that one can apply it and extend it to new situations, it is our firm belief that one must master the details. Realizing that some readers will be

---

[16]See Wikipedia, the free encyclopedia: http://en.wikipedia.org/wiki/William_of_Ockham, "Occam's Razor" in http://en.wikipedia.org/wiki/Occam%27s_razor, or "What is Occam's Razor" in http://www.weburbia.com/physics/occam.html. Accessed on Jan. 1, 2010.

more interested in the application chapters (Chapters 7–10) rather than in the detail chapters (Chapters 2–6), a summary is given in Section 1.8 for each detail chapter that provides the applications-oriented reader with high-level understandings of the main points of the chapter. After reading these five summaries, it should be possible to read Chapters 7–10.

Chapter 2 is about IT2 FSs since, as has been argued above, they are the ones used by the Per-C. The coverage of these FSs is extensive, but all of the concepts and results of this chapter are used in later chapters of the book, so they must be mastered. Chapter 2 begins with a brief review of T1 FSs. It includes careful defin-itions of many new terms that are associated with IT2 FSs and are needed to com-municate effectively about such sets, including the *footprint of uncertainty* (FOU) and convexity of an IT2 FS. It also includes a representation of IT2 FSs in terms of type-1 FSs that is extremely useful in that it lets all theoretical results about IT2 FSs be developed using T1 FS mathematics; derivations of set theoretic operations of union, intersection and complement for IT2 FSs; the centroid of an IT2 FS, because it provides a measure of uncertainty of such a FS and is a very widely used calcula-tion in later chapters; properties of the centroid; iterative algorithms for computing the centroid; and cardinality and average cardinality of an IT2 FS.

Chapter 3 is about the encoder, that is, about how to model a word using an IT2 FS. It covers two methods for doing this, one called the *person footprint of uncer-tainty method* and the other called the *interval approach method.* The person foot-print of uncertainty method can only be used by persons who are already familiar with interval type-2 fuzzy sets because they must provide a footprint of uncertainty (defined in Chapter 2) for each word; hence, it is limited to so-called *fuzzy experts.* The interval approach (IA) method is based on collecting interval end-point data from a group of subjects and does not require any a priori knowledge about FSs; hence, it can be used by anyone. Because collecting interval data about words using surveys is so important to the IA, this chapter has extensive discussions about it. The IA makes very heavy use of statistics and is a very practical method for map-ping subject's data intervals into an FOU for a word. The resulting FOUs are either interior, left-shoulder, or right-shoulder FOUs, and it is the data that establishes which FOU models a word. The IA is applied to a vocabulary of 32 words and their associated IT2 FS models are obtained. The resulting codebook is frequently used throughout the rest of this book. Hedges are also discussed along with reasons for why we choose not to use them. Finally, methods for eliciting T1 MF information from either a single subject or a group of subjects are described in Appendix 3A.

Chapter 4 is about the decoder, that is, about how to go from IT2 FSs (and asso-ciated data) at the output of the CWW engine to a recommendation and associated data. The recommendation may be a word, similarity of a group of words, a rank, or a class. For example, in social judgment advising, the decoder recommendations are words; in investment judgment advising and procurement award judging, the de-coder recommendations are rankings and similarities; and in journal publication ad-vising, the decoder recommendations are classes (e.g., accept, rewrite, or reject). To map an FOU to a word, a similarity measure is used. Because the output of the CWW engine is often mapped into a codebook word by the decoder, this FOU must resemble such an FOU; therefore, a successful similarity measure for the Per-C is one that simultaneously measures similarity of both FOU shape and proximity of that FOU to a correct word. Hence, in this chapter several similarity measures for IT2 FSs are reviewed, and reasons are provided for why the Jaccard similarity measure is preferred. Additionally, two ranking methods are reviewed for IT2 FSs and a preferred ranking method is obtained, one that ranks the FOUs according to their centers of centroids. Finally, a classification method is presented that is based on the subsethood between two IT2 FSs. Some similarity measures and ranking methods for T1 FSs are described and tabulated in Appendix 4A.

Chapter 5 is about one family of CWW engines called *novel weighted averages* (NWAs) that are a new and very powerful way to aggregate disparate information ranging from numbers to uniformly weighted intervals of numbers to nonuniformly weighted intervals of numbers to words that are modeled using IT2 FSs. The novel weighted averages are grouped into three categories: *interval weighted average* (IWA), in which weights and subcriteria in the weighted average are described by uniformly weighted intervals of real numbers; *fuzzy weighted average* (FWA), in which weights and subcriteria in the weighted average are described by type-1 fuzzy sets; and *linguistic weighted average* (LWA), in which weights and subcriteria in the weighted average are described by interval type-2 fuzzy set models for words. Alpha-cuts and an alpha-cut function decomposition theorem play central roles in computing the FWA and LWA, and so they are reviewed in Chapter 5. Algorithms for computing the IWA, FWA, and LWA are derived. Finally, the *ordered weighted average* (OWA) is described and its relations to NWAs are explained.

Chapter 6 is about one of the most popular CWW engines, called *if–then rules,* and how they are processed so that their outputs can be mapped into a word recommendation by the decoder. We adopt the assumption that the result of combining fired rules must lead to an IT2 FS that resembles the three kinds of FOUs in a CWW codebook, namely, interior and left- and right-shoulder FOUs. This leads to a new way for combining fired rules that is called *perceptual reasoning* (PR), which is a special kind of LWA. The first calculation for PR is a *firing quantity* that may be either a *firing interval* or a *firing level.* The former is computed using the sup–min composition (which should be familiar to people knowledgeable about fuzzy logic systems), whereas the latter is computed using the Jaccard similarity measure (Chapter 4). We prefer a firing level because it leads to FOUs that more closely resemble those in our CWW codebook, whereas using a firing interval does not; hence, later chapters focus exclusively on PR that uses firing levels. Properties are stated and proved for PR that uses firing levels, showing that it leads to IT2 FSs that resemble the three kinds of FOUs in a CWW codebook.

Chapters 7–10 are application chapters. They contain no new theory and illustrate how the Per-C can be used to assist in making investment choices, social judgments, hierarchical decisions, and hierarchical and distributed decisions.

Chapter 7 presents the design of an *investment judgment advisor* (IJA). An investor is given a choice of five investment alternatives—the commodity market, the stock market, gold, real estate, and long-term bonds—and four investment criteria—the risk of losing the capital sum, the vulnerability of the capital sum to modification by inflation, the amount of interest (profit) received, and the cash realizeability of the capital sum (liquidity). The IJA lets an investor provide linguistic ratings for each of the investment alternative's investment criteria, and also linguistic weights for the investment criteria. It then provides the investor with preferential rankings, ranking bands, risk bands, and a similarity array for the investment alternatives so that the investor can establish the components of his/her investment portfolio. The LWA that is explained in Chapter 5 is the basic aggregation tool that is used by the IJA.

Chapter 8 presents the design of a *social judgment advisor* (SJA). The SJA is developed for flirtation judgments, based on if–then rules that are extracted from people. A six-step methodology is presented for designing a SJA. This advisor demonstrates how "I'm getting mixed signals" can be effectively handled within the framework of fuzzy logic, and can be used to sensitize individuals about their (mis-) interpretations of a flirtation situation as compared to the outputs from a consensus flirtation advisor. One of the novel aspects of a SJA is that in an actual flirtation situation, all of the indicators of flirtation will most likely not be observed; hence, a SJA must account for this by means of its architecture, which is an interconnection of subadvisors each for one or two antecedent rules.

Chapter 9 is about how a Per-C can be used to assist in hierarchical decision making. It presents the design of a *procurement judgment advisor* (PJA). A contractor has to decide which of three companies is going to get the final mass production contract for a missile. The contractor uses five criteria to base his/her final decision, namely: tactics, technology, maintenance, economy, and advancement. Each of these criteria has some associated technical subcriteria; for example, for tactics, the subcriteria are effective range, flight height, flight velocity, reliability, firing accuracy, destruction rate, and kill radius, whereas for economy, the subcriteria are system cost, system life, and material limitation. The contractor creates a *performance evaluation table* in order to assist in choosing the winning company. Contained within this table are three columns, one for each of the three competing companies. Entries into this table for the three companies are evaluations of the subcriteria. Additionally, weights are assigned to all of the subcriteria, because they are not of equal importance. These weights are fuzzy numbers such as around seven, around five, and so on. The subcriteria evaluations range from numbers to words. Somehow, the contractor has to aggregate this disparate information, and this is even more difficult because the five criteria are themselves not of equal importance and have their own linguistic weights assigned to them. Chapter 9 demonstrates how novel weighted averages, which are described in Chapter 5, can be used to assist the contractor in making a final decision.

Chapter 10 is about how the Per-C can be used to assist in hierarchical and distributed decision-making. It presents the design of a *journal publication judgment advisor* (JPJA). When an author submits a paper to a journal, the Editor usually assigns its review to an Associate Editor (AE), who then sends it to at least three reviewers. The reviewers send their reviews back to the AE who then makes a publication recommendation to the Editor based on these reviews. The Editor uses this publication recommendation to assist in making a final decision about the paper. In addition to the "comments for the author(s)," each reviewer usually has to complete a review form in which the reviewer has to evaluate the paper based on two major criteria, technical merit and presentation. Technical merit has three subcriteria: importance, content, and depth, and presentation has four subcriteria: style, organization, clarity, and references. Each of the subcriteria has an assessment level that is characterized by some words. A reviewer chooses one assessment level by checking off one of the words. Usually, the reviewer is also asked to give an overall evaluation of the paper and make a recommendation to the AE. The AE then makes a final decision based on the opinions of the three reviewers.

This evaluation process is often difficult and subjective. The JPJA automates the entire process and does not require that the reviewer provide an overall evaluation of the paper. Instead, this is done by the JPJA using LWAs (Chapter 5) followed by classification into one of the classes called accept, rewrite, or reject. This has the potential to relieve much of the burden of the reviewers and the AE, and, moreover, it may be more accurate and less subjective.

Chapter 11 is where we wrap things up. It summarizes the methodology of perceptual computing and provides proposed guidelines for when something should be called computing with words.

1.8 HIGH-LEVEL SYNOPSES OF TECHNICAL DETAILS

In this section, high-level synopses are provide for the most important technical details that are elaborated upon in Chapters 2–6, so that the applications-oriented reader, who may not be interested in those details, can go directly to the application chapters (Chapters 7–10).

1.8.1 Chapter 2: Interval Type-2 Fuzzy Sets

Consider [Mendel (2001b)] the transition from ordinary sets to fuzzy sets. When we cannot determine whether the membership of an element in a set is 0 or 1, we use fuzzy sets of type-1. Similarly, when the circumstances are so fuzzy that we have trouble determining the membership grade even as a crisp number in $[0,1]$, we use fuzzy sets of type-2. A type-1 fuzzy set (T1 FS) has a grade of membership that is crisp, whereas an interval type-2 FS (IT2 FS) has grades of memberships that are fuzzy, so it could be called a "fuzzy fuzzy-set." Symbol A is used for a T1 FS, whereas symbol $\tilde{A}$ is used for an IT2 FS (or, for that matter any T2 FS).

Imagine blurring the type-1 membership function depicted in Fig. 1.12 (a) by shifting the points on the triangle either to the left or to the right and not necessarily by the same amounts, as in Fig. 1.12(b). Then, at a specific value of x, say x', there no longer is a single value for the membership function; instead, the membership function takes on values wherever the vertical line intersects the blur. When all of those values are weighted the same for all x', one obtains an interval type-2 fuzzy set. Such a FS, $\tilde{A}$, is completely described by its footprint of uncertainty (FOU), $FOU(\tilde{A})$, an example of which is depicted in Fig. 1.13. The $FOU(\tilde{A})$, in turn, is completely described by its lower and upper membership functions, $LMF(\tilde{A})$ and

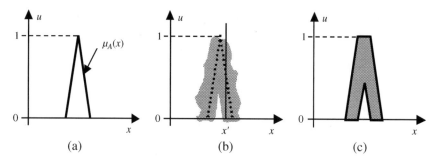

Figure 1.12. (a) Type-1 membership function, (b) blurred type-1 membership function, and (c) FOU for an IT2 FS (Mendel, 2001; © 2001, Prentice-Hall).

$UMF(\tilde{A})$. Although these functions are shown as triangles in Fig. 1.13, they can have many other shapes, for example, trapezoids or Gaussian.

It is very easy to compute the union, intersection, and complement of IT2 FSs just in terms of simple T1 FS operations that are performed only on LMFs or UMFs of IT2 FSs. This makes such FSs very useful for practical applications.

Examining Fig. 1.13, one senses that the uncertainty about an IT2 FS must be related to how much area is enclosed within the FOU, that is, a thinner and narrower FOU has less uncertainty about it than does a fatter and broader FOU. The centroid of $\tilde{A}$, $C_{\tilde{A}}$, provides a measure of the uncertainty about such an FS. It is an interval of numbers that has both a smallest and a largest value, that is, $C_{\tilde{A}} = [c_l(\tilde{A}), c_r(\tilde{A})]$, and $c_r(\tilde{A}) - c_l(\tilde{A})$ is small for thin FOUs and is large for fat FOUs. The trick is to compute $c_l(\tilde{A})$ and $c_r(\tilde{A})$. Unfortunately, there are no closed-form formulas for doing this; however, Karnik and Mendel (2001) have developed iterative algorithms, now known as KM algorithms, for computing $c_l(\tilde{A})$ and $c_r(\tilde{A})$. These algorithms are very heavily used in this book.

Cardinality of a crisp set is a count on the number of elements in that set. The

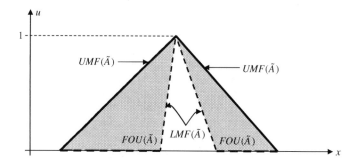

Figure 1.13. FOU for an IT2 FS $\tilde{A}$. The FOU is completely described by its lower and upper membership functions (Mendel, 2007c; © 2007, IEEE).

cardinality of an IT2 FS $\tilde{A}$ is an interval of numbers, the smallest number being the cardinality of $LMF(\tilde{A})$ and the largest number being the cardinality of $UMF(\tilde{A})$. The average cardinality of $\tilde{A}$ is the average of these two numbers.

1.8.2   Chapter 3: Encoding: From a Word to a Model—The Codebook

Words mean different things to different people, so they are uncertain; hence, as we have argued earlier in this chapter, a FS model is needed for a word that has the potential to capture its uncertainties. An IT2 FS is used as a FS model of a word because it is characterized by its FOU and, therefore, has the potential to capture word uncertainties.

In order to obtain an IT2 FS model for a word, the following are required: (1) a continuous scale must be established for each variable of interest, and (2) a vocabulary of words must be created that covers the entire scale. Our methods are described for the continuous scale numbered 0–10.

For perceptual computing, one begins by establishing a vocabulary of application-dependent words, one that is large enough so that a person will feel linguistically comfortable interacting with the Per-C. This vocabulary must include subsets of words that feel, to each subject, like they will collectively cover the scale 0–10. The collection of words, $\tilde{W}_i$, in the vocabulary and their IT2 FS models, $FOU(\tilde{W}_i)$, constitutes a codebook for an application (A), that is, Codebook = $\{(\tilde{W}_i, FOU(\tilde{W}_i)), i = 1, \ldots, N_A\}$.

The term *fuzzistics,* which is a merging of the words *fuzzy* and *statistics,* was coined by Mendel (2003b) to summarize the problem of going from word data collected from a group of subjects, with their inherent random uncertainties that are quantified using statistics, to a word fuzzy set model that captures measures of the word data uncertainties. When the FS model is an IT2 FS, this is called *type-2 fuzzistics.*

After a scale is established and a vocabulary of words is created that is believed to cover the entire scale, interval end-point data are collected from a group of subjects. The method for doing this consists of two steps: (1) randomize the words, and (2) survey a group of subjects to provide end-point data for the words on the scale.

Words need to be randomized so that subjects will not correlate their word-interval end points from one word to the next. The randomized words are used in a survey whose wording might be:

Below are a number of labels that describe an interval or a "range" that falls somewhere between 0 and 10. For each label, please tell us where this range would start and where it would stop. (In other words, please tell us how much of the distance from 0 to 10 this range would cover.) For example, the range "quite a bit" might start at 6 and end at 8. It is important to note that not all ranges be the same and ranges can overlap.

Experiences with carrying out such surveys show that they do not introduce methodological errors and that anyone can answer such questions.

Chapter 3 provides a very practical type-2 fuzzistics method, one that is called the *interval approach* (IA) [Liu and Mendel (2007, 2008)]. The IA consists of two parts, a *data part* and a *fuzzy set* (FS) part. In the data part, data intervals that have been collected from a group of subjects are preprocessed, after which data statistics are computed for the surviving intervals. In the FS part, FS uncertainty measures are established for a prespecified triangle T1 MF [always beginning with the assumption that the FOU is an interior FOU (as in Fig. 1.14), and, if need be, later switching to a shoulder FOU (as in Fig. 1.14)]. Then the parameters of the triangle T1 MF are determined using the data statistics, and the derived T1 MFs are aggregated using union leading to an FOU for a word, and finally to a mathematical model for the FOU.

One of the strong points of the IA is that subject data establish which FOU is used to model a word, that is, the FOU is not chosen ahead of time.

The only FOUs that can be obtained for a word using the IA are the ones depicted in Fig. 1.14, and so these FOUs are referred to herein as *canonical FOUs for a word.*

A word that is modeled by an interior FOU has an UMF that is a trapezoid and a LMF that is a triangle, but, in general, neither the trapezoid nor the triangle are symmetrical. A word that is modeled as a left- or right-shoulder FOU has trapezoidal upper and lower MFs; however, the legs of the respective two trapezoids are not necessarily parallel.

That there are only three canonical FOUs for a word is very different than in function approximation applications of IT2 FSs (e.g., as in fuzzy logic control, or forecasting of time-series) where one is free to choose the shapes of the FOUs ahead of time and many different choices are possible.

1.8.3   Chapter 4: Decoding—From FOUs to a Recommendation

The recommendation from the decoder can have several different forms:

1. *Word.* This is the most typical case. For example, for the social judgment advisor developed in Chapter 8, the FOU at the output of the CWW engine needs to be mapped into a word (or a group of similar words) in the codebook

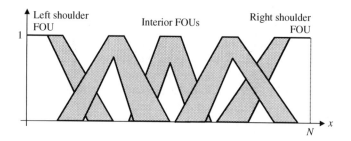

Figure 1.14. Left-shoulder, right-shoulder and interior FOUs, all of whose LMFs and UMFs are piecewise linear (Liu and Mendel, 2008; © 2008, IEEE).

so that it can be understood. Similarity measures that compare the similarity between two FOUs are needed to do this.

2. *Rank.* In some decision-making situations, several strategies/candidates are compared at the same time to find the best one(s). For example, in the investment judgment advisor that is developed in Chapter 7, several investment alternatives are compared to find the one(s) with the best overall match to an investor. In the procurement award judgment advisor developed in Chapter 9, three missile systems are compared to find the one with the best overall performance. Ranking methods are needed to do this.

3. *Class.* In some decision making applications, the output of the CWW engine has to be mapped into a class. For example, in the journal publication judgment advisor that is developed in Chapter 10, the outputs of the CWW engine are IT2 FSs representing the overall quality of a journal article from each reviewer and from the aggregated reviewers, and they need to be mapped into one of three decision categories: accept, revise, and reject. Classifiers are needed to do this.

Obviously, if two FOUs have the same shape and are located very close to each other, they should be linguistically similar; or, if they have different shapes and are located close to each other, they should not be linguistically similar; or, if they have the same or different shapes but are not located close to each other they should also not be linguistically similar.

There are around 50 similarity measures that have been published for T1 FSs, but only six for IT2 FSs. Chapter 4 explains that of these six the Jaccard similarity measure, which utilizes both shape and proximity information about an FOU simultaneously, gives the best results, that is, the Jaccard similarity measure provides a crisp numerical similarity measure that agrees with all three of the previous statements.

Simply stated, the Jaccard similarity measure is the ratio of the average cardinality of the intersection of two IT2 FSs to the average cardinality of the union of the two IT2 FSs. The average cardinality is defined in Chapter 2 and is easy to compute.

There are more than 35 methods for ranking T1 FSs, but only two methods for ranking IT2 FSs. Chapter 4 focuses on one of those methods, one that is very simple and based on the centroid of an IT2 FS. First, the centroid (Chapter 2) is computed for each FOU, and then the center of each centroid is computed, after which the average centroids for all FOUs are sorted in increasing order to obtain the rank of the FOUs.

The classification literature is huge [e.g., Duda et al. (2001)]. Our classifiers are based on subsethood, which defines the degree of containment of one set in another. Subsethood is conceptually more appropriate for a classifier than similarity because $\tilde{A}$ and class-FOUs belong to different domains (e.g., in Chapter 10, the FOU for quality of a journal article is classified into accept, rewrite, or reject). The subsethood between two IT2 FSs, $\tilde{A}$ and $\tilde{B}$, $ss(\tilde{A}, \tilde{B})$, may either be an interval of numbers, $ss(\tilde{A}, \tilde{B}) = [ss_l(\tilde{A}, \tilde{B}), ss_r(\tilde{A}, \tilde{B})]$ or a single number. We prefer to use a single subsethood number for our classifiers.

1.8.4   Chapter 5: Novel Weighted Averages as a CWW Engine

This is the first of two chapters that provide CWW engines. Aggregation of numerical subcriteria (data, features, decisions, recommendations, judgments, scores, etc.) obtained by using a weighted average of those numbers is quite common and widely used. In many situations, however, providing a single number for either the subcriteria or weights is problematic (there could be uncertainties about them), and it is more meaningful to provide intervals, T1 FSs or IT2 FSs, or a mixture of all these, for them. A *novel weighted average* (NWA) is a weighted average in which at least one subcriterion or weight is not a single real number, but is instead an interval, T1 FS, or an IT2 FS. NWAs include the interval weighted average (IWA), fuzzy weighted average (FWA), and linguistic weighted average (LWA).

When at least one subcriterion or weight is modeled as an interval, and all other subcriteria or weights are modeled by no more than such a model, the resulting WA is called an IWA, denoted Y_{IWA}. On the other hand, when at least one subcriterion or weight is modeled as a T1 FS, and all other subcriteria or weights are modeled by no more than such a model, the resulting WA is called a FWA, denoted Y_{FWA}. And, finally, when at least one subcriterion or weight is modeled as an IT2 FS, the resulting WA is called a LWA.

The IWA and FWA are special cases of the LWA; hence, here our focus is only on the latter.[17] The following is a very useful expressive way to summarize the LWA:

$$\tilde{Y}_{LWA} = \frac{\sum_{i=1}^{n} \tilde{X}_i \tilde{W}_i}{\sum_{i=1}^{n} \tilde{W}_i} \tag{1.1}$$

where subcriteria $\tilde{X}_i$ and weights $\tilde{W}_i$ are characterized by their FOUs, and $\tilde{Y}_{LWA}$ is also an IT2 FS. This is called an *expressive* way to summarize the LWA rather than a *computational* way to summarize the LWA, because the LWA is not computed by multiplying, adding, and dividing IT2 FSs. It is more complicated than that. How to actually compute $\tilde{Y}_{LWA}$ is described in Chapter 5, and, somewhat surprisingly, KM algorithms are the bread-and-butter tools for the computations. The exact details of the computations are not needed here. What is needed is the recognition that given FOUs for $\tilde{X}_i$ and $\tilde{W}_i$, it is possible to compute $FOU(\tilde{Y}_{LWA})$.

1.8.5   Chapter 6: If–Then Rules as a CWW Engine

Chapter 6 is the second of two chapters that provide CWW engines. One of the most popular CWW engines uses if–then rules. Chapter 6 is about such rules and how they are processed within a CWW engine so that their outputs can be mapped into a word recommendation by the decoder. This use of if–then rules in a Per-C is quite different from their use in most engineering applications of rule-based sys-

---

[17]In Chapter 5, just the opposite is done, that is, it begins with the IWA, then the FWA, and, finally, the LWA, because the FWA is computed using IWAs, and the LWA is computed using FWAs.

tems—fuzzy logic systems (FLSs)—because in a FLS the output almost always is a number, whereas the output of the Per-C is a recommendation. This distinction has some very interesting ramifications and they are also covered in Chapter 6.

By a *rule* is meant an if–then statement, such as

$$R^l : \text{ IF } x_1 \text{ is } F_1^l \text{ and } \cdots \text{ and } x_p \text{ is } F_p^l, \text{ THEN } y \text{ is } G^l \quad l = 1, \dots, M \quad (1.2)$$

In equation (1.2), x_i are called *antecedents* and y is called a *consequent*. In logic, equation (1.2) is also called an *implication,* and when F_i^l is either a T1 or T2 FS it is called a *fuzzy implication.* There are many mathematical models for a fuzzy implication that have appeared under the subject heading of approximate reasoning, for example, Table 11.1 in Klir and Yuan (1995) lists 14. Each of these models has the property that it reduces to the truth table of material implication when fuzziness disappears, that is, to logical reasoning.

Rational calculation (Chater, et al., 2003) is the view that the mind works by carrying out probabilistic, logical, or decision-theoretic operations (e.g., by the truth table of material implication). *Rational description* is the view that behavior can be approximately described as conforming with the results that would be obtained by some rational calculation. For perceptual computing, logical reasoning will not be implemented as prescribed by the truth table of material implication; instead, rational description is subscribed to.

For CWW, our requirement is that the output of the if–then CWW engine should be an FOU that resembles the three kinds of FOUs in a CWW codebook (as explained in Section 1.8.2). This is so that the decoder can do its job properly (map an FOU into a word in a codebook), and agrees with the adage, "not only do words mean different things to different people," but they must also mean similar things to different people, or else people would not be able to communicate with each other. Because none of the widely used fuzzy reasoning models lead to FOUs that resemble the three kinds of FOUs in a CWW codebook, a new fuzzy reasoning model is proposed, called *perceptual reasoning*[18] (PR) [Mendel and Wu (2008)]. PR not only fits the concept of rational description, but also leads to FOUs that resemble the three kinds of FOUs in a CWW codebook.

PR consists of two steps:

1. A *firing quantity* is computed for each rule by computing the Jaccard similarity measure between each input word and its corresponding antecedent word, and, if a rule has p antecedents, then taking the minumum of the p Jaccard similarity measures.
2. The IT2 FS consequents of the fired rules are combined using a linguistic weighted average in which the "weights" are the firing quantities and the "subcriteria" are the IT2 FS consequents.

---

[18]"Perceptual reasoning" is a term coined in Wu and Mendel (2008) because it is used by the Per-C when the CWW engine consists of if–then rules.

The result is an FOU for PR, and, as proved in Chapter 6, this FOU does indeed resemble the three kinds of FOUs in a CWW codebook.

REFERENCES

J. J. Buckley and T. Feuring, "Computing with words in control," in L. A. Zadeh and J. Kacprzyk (Eds.) *Computing With Words in Information/Intelligent Systems 2: Applications,* Heidelberg: Physica-Verlag, 1999, pp. 289–304.

N. Chater, M. Oaksford, R. Nakisa, and M. Redington, "Fast, frugal and rational: How rational norms explain behavior," *Organizational Behaviour and Human Decision Processes,* vol. 90, no. 1, pp. 63–86, 2003.

S.-M. Chen, "A new method for evaluating weapon systems using fuzzy set theory," *IEEE Trans. on Systems, Man, and Cybernetics—Part A: Systems and Humans,* vol. 26, pp. 493–497, July 1996.

C.-H. Cheng, "Evaluating weapon systems using ranking fuzzy numbers," *Fuzzy Sets and Systems,* vol. 109, pp. 25–35, 1999.

M. R. Civanlar and H. J. Trussel, "Constructing membership functions using statistical data," *Fuzzy Sets and Systems,* vol. 18, pp. 1–14, 1986.

A. M. G. Cornelissen, The Two Faces of Sustainability: Fuzzy Evaluation of Sustainable Development, Ph.D. Thesis, Wageningen Univ., The Netherlands, 2003.

F. Doctor, H. Hagras, D. Roberts, and V. Callaghan, "A Type-2 fuzzy based system for handling the uncertainties in group decisions for ranking job applicants within human resources systems," in *Proceedings of IEEE FUZZ Conference,* Paper # FS0125, Hong Kong, China, June 2008.

D. Dubois and H. Prade, "Fuzzy sets and statistical data," *European J. of Operational Research,* vol. 25, pp. 345–356, 1986.

R. O. Duda, P. E. Hart, and D. G. Stork, *Pattern Classification,* 2nd ed. New York: Wiley, 2001.

F. Herrera and E. Herrera-Viedma, "Aggregation operators for linguistic weighted information," *IEEE Trans. on Systems, Man and Cybernetics, Part-A: Systems and Humans,* vol. 27, pp. 646–656, 1997.

H. M. Hersch and A. Caramazza, "A fuzzy set approach to modifiers and vagueness in natural language," *J. Experimental Psychology,* vol. 105, no. 3, pp. 254–276, 1976.

A. Hodges, *Turing: A Natural Philosopher,* U.K.: Phoenix, 1997.

N. N. Karnik and J. M. Mendel, "Centroid of a type-2 fuzzy set," *Information Sciences,* vol. 132, pp. 195–220, 2001.

G. J. Klir and B. Yuan, *Fuzzy Sets and Fuzzy Logic: Theory and Applications,* Upper Saddle River, NJ: Prentice-Hall, 1995.

J. Lawry, "An alternative to computing with words," *Int. J. of Uncertainty, Fuzziness and Knowledge-Based Systems,* vol. 9, Suppl., pp. 3–16, 2001.

F. Liu and J. M. Mendel, "An interval approach to fuzzistics for interval type-2 fuzzy sets," in *Proceedings of FUZZ-IEEE 2007,* pp. 1030–1035, London, U.K., July 2007.

F. Liu and J. M. Mendel, "Encoding words into interval type-2 fuzzy sets using an *interval approach,*" *IEEE Trans. on Fuzzy Systems,* vol. 16, pp 1503–1521, December 2008.

J. M. Mendel, "The perceptual computer: an architecture for computing with words," in *Proceedings of Modeling With Words Workshop* in the *Proceedings of FUZZ-IEEE 2001*, pp. 35–38, Melbourne, Australia, 2001a.

J. M. Mendel, *Uncertain Rule-Based Fuzzy Logic Systems: Introduction and New Directions*, Upper-Saddle River, NJ: Prentice-Hall, 2001b.

J. M. Mendel, "An architecture for making judgments using computing with words," *Int. J. Appl. Math. Comput. Sci.*, vol. 12, No. 3, pp. 325–335, 2002.

J. M. Mendel, "Type-2 fuzzy sets: some questions and answers," *IEEE Connections*, Newsletter of the IEEE Neural Networks Society, vol. 1, pp. 10–13, 2003a.

J. M. Mendel, "Fuzzy sets for words: a new beginning," in *Proceedings of FUZZ-IEEE 2003*, St. Louis, MO, pp. 37–42, 2003b.

J. M. Mendel, "Computing with words and its relationships with fuzzistics," *Information Sciences*, vol. 177, pp. 998–1006, 2007a.

J. M. Mendel, "Type-2 fuzzy sets and systems: an overview," *IEEE Computational Intelligence Magazine*, vol. 2, pp. 20–29, Feb. 2007b.

J. M. Mendel, "Computing with words: Zadeh, Turing, Popper and Occam," *IEEE Computational Intelligence Magazine*, vol. 2, pp. 10–17, November 2007c.

J. M. Mendel and D. Wu, "Perceptual reasoning for perceptual computing," *IEEE Trans. on Fuzzy Systems*, vol. 16, pp. 1550–1564, December 2008.

J. M. Mendel and H. Wu, "Type-2 fuzzistics for symmetric interval type-2 fuzzy sets: Part 1, forward problems," *IEEE Trans. on Fuzzy Systems*, vol. 14, pp. 781–792, Dec. 2006.

J. M. Mendel and H. Wu, "Type-2 fuzzistics for symmetric interval type-2 fuzzy sets: Part 2, inverse problems," *IEEE Trans. on Fuzzy Systems*, vol. 15, pp. 301–308, April 2007a.

J. M. Mendel and H. Wu, "Type-2 fuzzistics for non-symmetric interval type-2 fuzzy sets: Forward problems," *IEEE Trans. on Fuzzy Systems*, vol. 15, pp. 916–930, October 2007b.

J. M. Mendel, S. Murphy, L. C. Miller, M. Martin, and N. Karnik, "The fuzzy logic advisor for social judgments: A first attempt," in L. A. Zadeh and J. Kacprzyk, (Eds.), *Computing with Words in Information/Intelligent Systems 2, Applications*, pp. 459–483, Heidelberg: Physica-Verlag, 1999.

D.-L. Mon, C.-H. Cheng, and J.-LC. Lin, "Evaluating weapon system using fuzzy analytic hierarchy process based on entropy weight," *Fuzzy Sets and Systems*, vol. 62, pp. 127–134, 1994.

A. M. Norwich and I. B. Türksen, "The construction of membership functions," in *Fuzzy Sets and Possibility Theory: Recent Developments*, (R. R. Yager, Ed.), Oxford: Pergamon Press, pp. 49–60, 1982.

A. M. Norwich and I. B. Türksen, "A model for the measurement of membership and the consequences of its empirical implementation," *Fuzzy Sets and Systems*, vol. 12, pp. 1–25, 1984.

K. Popper, *The Logic of Scientific Discovery* (translation of *Logik der Forschung*), London: Hutchinson, 1959.

K. Popper, *Conjectures and Refutations: The Growth of Scientific Knowledge*, London: Routledge, 1963.

E. Rosch, "Cognitive representations of semantic categories," *J. of Experimental Psychology: General*, vol. 104, pp. 192–233, 1975.

E. Rosch, "Prototype classification and logical classification: the two systems," In Scholnik, E. (Ed.), *New Trends in Cognitive Representation: Challenges to Piaget's Theory,* pp. 73–86, Hillsdale, NJ: Lawrence Erlbaum Associates, 1983.

A. P. Saygin, I. Cicekli, and V. Akman, "Turing test: 50 years later," *Minds and Machines,* vol. 10, pp. 463–518, 2000.

K. S. Schmucker, *Fuzzy Sets, Natural Language Computations, and Risk Analysis,* Rockville, MD: Computer Science Press, 1984.

S. Thornton, "Karl Popper," in *The Stanford Encyclopedia of Philosophy* (Summer 2005 Edition), Edward N. Zalta (ed.), URL = http://plato.stanford.edu/archives/sum2005/entries/popper/.

R. M. Tong and P. P. Bonissone, "A linguistic approach to decision making with fuzzy sets," *IEEE Trans. on Systems, Man, Cybernetics,* vol. 10, pp. 716–723, 1980.

A. M. Turing, "Computing machinery and intelligence," *Mind,* .vol. 59, pp. 433–460, 1950.

I. B. Türksen, "Measurement of membership functions," in W. Karwowski and A. Mital (Eds.), *Applications of Fuzzy Set Theory in Human Factors,* Amsterdam: Elsevier, pp. 55–67, 1986.

I. B. Türksen, "Stochastic fuzzy sets: A survey," in J. Kacprzyk and M. Fedrizzi (Eds.), *Combining Fuzzy Imprecision with Probabilistic Uncertainty in Decision Making,* New York: Springer-Verlag, pp. 168–183, 1988.

I. B. Türksen, "Measurement of membership functions and their acquisition," *Fuzzy Sets and Systems,* vol. 40, pp. 5–38, 1991 (especially Section 5).

I. B. Türksen, "Type-2 representation and reasoning for CWW," *Fuzzy Sets and Systems,* vol. 127, pp. 17–36, 2002

I. B. Türksen and I. A. Wilson, "A fuzzy set preference model for consumer choice," *Fuzzy Sets and Systems,* vol. 68, pp. 253–266, 1994.

G.-H. Tzeng and J.-Y. Teng, "Transportation investment project selection with fuzzy multi-objectives," *Transportation Planning Technology,* vol. 17, pp. 91–112, 1993.

T. S. Wallsten and D. V. Budescu, "A review of human linguistic probability processing: General principles and empirical evidence," *Knowledge Engineering Review,* vol. 10, pp. 43–62, 1995.

D. Wu and J. M. Mendel, "A vector similarity measure for linguistic approximation: Interval type-2 and type-1 fuzzy sets," *Information Sciences,* vol. 178, pp. 381–402, 2008a.

D. Wu and J. M. Mendel, "Perceptual reasoning using interval type-2 fuzzy sets: Properties," in *Proceedings of IEEE FUZZ Conference,* Paper # FS0291, Hong Kong, China, June 2008b.

R. Yager, "A new methodology for ordinal multi-objective decisions based on fuzzy sets," *Decision Sciences,* vol. 12, pp. 589–600, 1981.

R. Yager, "Aproximate reasoning as a basis for computing with words," in L. A. Zadeh and J. Kacprzyk (Eds.), *Computing With Words in Information/ Intelligent Systems 1: Foundations,* Heidelberg: Physica-Verlag, 1999, pp. 50–77.

R. Yager, "On the retranslation process in Zadeh's paradigm of computing with words," *IEEE Trans. on Systems, Man, and Cybernetics—Part B: Cybernetics,* vol. 34, pp. 1184–1195, 2004.

L. A. Zadeh, "Fuzzy logic = computing with words," *IEEE Trans. on Fuzzy Systems,* vol. 4, pp. 103–111, 1996.

L. A. Zadeh, "From computing with numbers to computing with words—from manipulation of measurements to manipulation of perceptions," *IEEE Trans. on Circuits and Systems-1, Fundamental Theory and Applications,* vol. 4, pp. 105–119, 1999.

L. A. Zadeh, "A new direction in AI," *AI Magazine,* pp. 73–84, Spring 2001.

L. A. Zadeh, "Toward human level machine intelligence—Is it achievable? The need for a new paradigm shift," *IEEE Computational Intelligence Magazine,* vol. 3, pp. 11–22, August 2008.

R. Zwick, "A note on random sets and the Thurstonian scaling methods," *Fuzzy Sets and Systems,* vol. 21, pp. 351–356, 1987.

CHAPTER 2

Interval Type-2 Fuzzy Sets

2.1 A BRIEF REVIEW OF TYPE-1 FUZZY SETS

It is said that before you can learn to run you must first learn to walk. Although most readers of this book will already be familiar with type-1 fuzzy sets (T1 FSs), before discussions are given about interval type-2 fuzzy sets (IT2 FSs)—our analog of "running"—a short review of T1 FSs is provided—our analog of "walking." Doing this will also let us establish common notations and definitions for T1 FSs. To begin, a T1 FS is defined.

Definition 2.1. A *fuzzy set* (in this book called a type-1 fuzzy set) A is comprised of a domain D_A of the real numbers (also called the *universe of discourse* of A and frequently denoted X) together with a *membership function* (MF) $\mu_A : D_A \rightarrow [0,1]$. For each $x \in D_A$, the value of $\mu_A(x)$ is the *degree of membership,* or *membership grade,* of x in A. If $\mu_A(x) = 1$ or $\mu_A(x) = 0$ for $\forall x \in D_A$, then the fuzzy set A is said to be a *crisp set.*

Recall that a crisp set A can be described by listing all of its members, or by identifying the elements in A by specifying a condition or conditions that the elements must satisfy, or by using a zero-one MF (also called characteristic function, discrimination function, or indicator function) for A. On the other hand, a T1 FS can only be described by its MF; hence, the T1 FS A and its MF $\mu_A(x)$ are synonyms and are, therefore, used interchangeably, that is, $A \Leftrightarrow \mu_A(x)$. Additionally, the terms degree of membership, membership function (MF), and membership grade are also used interchangeably.

When D_A is continuous (e.g., the real numbers), A is written as

$$A = \int_{D_A} \mu_A(x) / x \tag{2.1}$$

In this equation, the integral sign does not denote integration; it denotes the collection of all points $x \in D_A$ with associated MF $\mu_A(x)$. When D_A is discrete (e.g., the integers), A is written as

$$A = \sum_{D_A} \mu_A(x) / x \tag{2.2}$$

Perceptual Computing. By Jerry M. Mendel and Dongrui Wu

In this equation, the summation sign does not denote arithmetic addition; it denotes the collection of all points $x \in D_A$ with associated MF $\mu_A(x)$; hence, it denotes the set theoretic operation of union. The slash in equations (2.1) and (2.2) associates the elements in D_A with their membership grades, where $\mu_A(x) > 0$.

Sometimes, a T1 FS may depend on more than a single variable, in which case its MF is multivariate; for example, if the T1 FS B depends on two variables, x_1 and x_2, where $x_1 \in D_{X_1}$ and $x_2 \in D_{X_2}$, then, in general, its MF is $\mu_B(x_1, x_2)$ for $\forall(x_1, x_2)$ $\in D_{X_1} \times D_{X_2}$. This MF is three-dimensional and can be quite complicated to establish. For more than two variables, it may be quite hopeless to establish a multivariate MF.

In this book all multivariate MFs are assumed to be separable, that is, $\mu_B(x_1, x_2)$ is expressed directly in terms of the univariate MFs $\mu_B(x_1)$ and $\mu_B(x_2)$ as

$$\mu_B(x_1, x_2) = \min \left\{ \mu_B(x_1),\ \mu_B(x_2) \right\} \tag{2.3}$$

For CWW this is a very plausible assumption because, as explained in Chapter 3, only univariate word MFs are established from data.

Definition 2.2. The *support* of a T1 FS A is the crisp set of all points $x \in D_A$ such that $\mu_A(x) > 0$. A T1 FS whose support is a single point in D_A with $\mu_A(x) = 1$ is called a (type-1) *fuzzy singleton*.

Definition 2.3. A *normal* T1 FS is one for which $\sup_{x \in D_A} \mu_A(x) = 1$.

Definition 2.4. A T1 FS A is *convex* if and only if $\mu_A(\lambda x_1 + (1 - \lambda)x_2) \geq \min[\mu_A(x_1), \mu_A(x_2)]$, where $x_1, x_2 \in D_A$ and $\lambda \in [0, 1]$ [Klir and Yuan (1995)].

This can be interpreted as follows [Lin and Lee (1995)]. Take any two elements x_1 and x_2 in FS A; then the membership grade of all points between x_1 and x_2 must be greater than or equal to the minimum of $\mu_A(x_1)$ and $\mu_A(x_2)$. This will always occur when the MF of A is first monotonically nondecreasing and then monotonically nonincreasing.

The most commonly used shapes for MFs are triangular, trapezoidal, piecewise linear, Gaussian, and bell. Examples of triangle and trapezoidal MFs are depicted in Fig. 2.1. Observe that both of the T1 FSs are normal and convex, the support of T1 FS A is $D_A = [1, 11]$, the support of T1 FS B is $D_B = [7, 20]$, and for $x \in [7, 11]$ x resides simultaneously in both A and B but with different grades of membership.

In general, MFs can either be chosen arbitrarily, based on the experience of an individual (hence, the MFs for two individuals could be quite different depending upon their experiences, perspectives, cultures, etc.), or, they can be designed using optimization procedures [e.g., Horikawa et al. (1992), Jang (1992), Wang and Mendel (1992a, b)]. Much more will be said about how to choose MFs in Chapter 3.

In this book, great use is made of linguistic variables. Wang (1997) provides the following informal definition of a linguistic variable.

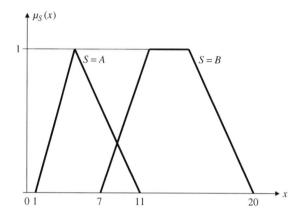

Figure 2.1. Examples of two T1 FSs, A and B.

Definition 2.5. If a variable can take words in natural languages as its values, it is called a *linguistic variable,* where the words are characterized by fuzzy sets defined in the universe of discourse in which the variable is defined.

Let v denote the name of a linguistic variable (e.g., eye contact, force, or economy). Numerical (measured) values of a linguistic variable v are denoted x, where $x \in D_v$. A linguistic variable is usually decomposed into a set of terms, T, which cover its universe of discourse. This decomposition is based on syntactic rules (a grammar) for generating the terms. Examples of terms for eye contact or force are: none to very little, small amount, some, moderate amount, large amount, and extreme amount. Examples of terms for economy are: poor, moderate, good, and excellent. Each of the terms is treated as a FS and is modeled by a MF.

A more formal definition of a linguistic variable, due to Zadeh (1973, 1975), taken from Klir and Yuan (1995), is:

Definition 2.5'. Each *linguistic variable* is fully characterized by a quintuple (v, T, X, g, m) in which v is the name of the variable, T is the set of linguistic terms of v that refer to a base variable whose values range over the universal set X, g is a syntactic rule for generating linguistic terms, and m is a semantic rule that assigns to each linguistic term $t \in T$ its meaning, $m(t)$, which is a fuzzy set[1] on X [i.e., $m : T \rightarrow F(X)$]).

Just as crisp sets can be combined using the union and intersection operations, so can FSs; and, just as a crisp set can be complemented, so can a FS.

Definition 2.6. Let T1 FSs A and B be two subsets of X that are described by their MFs $\mu_A(x)$ and $\mu_B(x)$. The *union* of A and B is described by the MF $\mu_{A \cup B}(x)$, where

---

[1]$F(X)$ denotes the set of all ordinary (i.e., type-1) fuzzy sets of X.

$$\mu_{A\cup B}(x) = \max[\mu_A(x), \mu_B(x)] \quad \forall x \in X \tag{2.4}$$

The *intersection* of A and B is described by the MF $\mu_{A\cap B}(x)$, where

$$\mu_{A\cap B}(x) = \min[\mu_A(x), \mu_B(x)] \quad \forall x \in X \tag{2.5}$$

The *complement* of A is described by the MF $\mu_{A^c}(x)$, where

$$\mu_{A^c}(x) = 1 - \mu_A(x) \quad \forall x \in X \tag{2.6}$$

Although $\mu_{A\cup B}(x)$ and $\mu_{A\cap B}(x)$ can be described using t-conorms and t-norms [e.g., Klir and Yuan (1995)], in this book only the maximum t-conorm and the minimum t-norm are used in equations (2.4) and (2.5), respectively, because our focus is on CWW.

Example 2.1. The union and intersection of the two TI FSs A and B that are depicted in Fig. 2.1, are shown in Figs. 2.2a and b, respectively.

Some other aspects of T1 FSs are reviewed in later chapters of this book, as they are needed.

2.2   INTRODUCTION TO INTERVAL TYPE-2 FUZZY SETS

A T1 FS[2] has grades of membership that are crisp, whereas a type-2 fuzzy set (T2 FS) has grades of membership that are fuzzy, so it could be called a "fuzzy fuzzy-set." Such a set is useful in circumstances where it is difficult to determine the exact MF for an FS, as in modeling a word by an FS. As an example [Mendel (2003)], suppose the variable of interest is eye contact, denoted x, where $x \in [0, 10]$ and this is an intensity range in which 0 denotes no eye contact and 10 denotes maximum amount of eye contact. One of the words (terms) that might characterize the amount of perceived eye contact (e.g., during an airport security check or during flirtation) is "some eye contact."

Suppose that 50 men and women are surveyed, and are asked to locate the ends of an interval for some eye contact on the scale 0–10. Surely, the same results will not be obtained from all of them because words mean different things to different people. One approach for using the 50 sets of two end points is to average the end point data and to then use the average values to construct an interval associated with some eye contact (SEC). A triangular (other shapes could be used) MF, $\mu_{SEC}(x)$, could then be constructed, one whose base end points (on the x-axis) are at the two end-point average values and whose apex is midway between the two end points. This T1 triangular MF can be displayed in two dimensions; see the dashed MF in

---

[2]The material in this section is taken from Mendel (2007a).

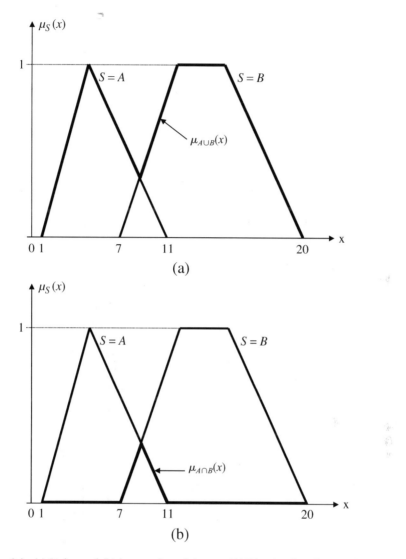

Figure 2.2. (a) Union and (b) intersection of the two T1 FSs A and B, that are depicted in Fig. 2.1.

Fig. 2.3. Unfortunately, it has completely ignored the uncertainties associated with the two end points.

A second approach is to make use of the average end-point values and the standard deviation of each end point to establish an uncertainty interval about each average end-point value. By doing this, one can think of the locations of the two end points along the x-axis as blurred. Triangles can then be located so that their base

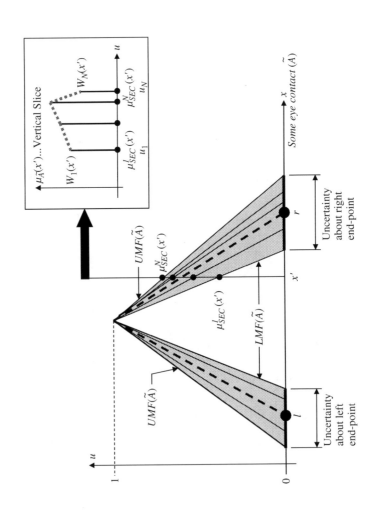

Figure 2.3. Triangular MFs when base end points (l and r) have uncertainty intervals associated with them. The insert depicts the secondary MF (vertical slice) at x' (Mendel, 2007a; © 2007, IEEE).

end points can be anywhere in the intervals along the x-axis associated with the blurred average end points. Doing this leads to a continuum of triangular MFs sitting on the x-axis, as in Fig. 2.3. For purposes of this discussion, suppose there are exactly N such triangles. Then at each value of $x = x'$ there can be up to N MF values $\mu_{SEC}^1(x')$, $\mu_{SEC}^2(x')$, ..., $\mu_{SEC}^N(x')$. Each of the possible membership values has a weight assigned to it, say $W_1(x')$, $W_2(x')$, ..., $W_N(x')$ (see the top insert in Fig. 2.3). These weights can be thought of as the *possibilities* associated with each triangle's grade at this value of x. Consequently, at each x' the collection of grades is a function $\{(\mu_{SEC}^i(x'), W_i(x')), i = 1, ..., N\}$ called the *secondary MF*. The resulting T2 MF is three-dimensional.

If all uncertainty disappears, then a T2 FS reduces to a T1 FS, as can be seen in Fig. 2.3; for example, if the uncertainties about the left and right end points disappear, then only the dashed triangle survives. This is similar to what happens in probability, when randomness degenerates to determinism, in which case the probability density function collapses to a single point. In brief, a T1 FS is embedded in a T2 FS, just as determinism is embedded in randomness.

It is not as easy to sketch three-dimensional figures of a T2 MF as it is to sketch two-dimensional figures of a T1 MF. Another way to visualize a T2 FS is to sketch its *footprint of uncertainty* (FOU) on the two-dimensional domain of the T2 FS, and this is easy to do. The heights of a T2 MF (its *secondary grades*) sit atop its FOU. In Fig. 2.3, if the continuum of triangular MFs is filled in (as implied by the shading), then the FOU is obtained. Other examples of an FOU are shown in Fig. 2.4. They include left- and right-shoulder FOUs and interior FOUs. The uniform shading over the entire FOU means that uniform weighting (possibilities) is assumed. Because of the uniform weighting, this T2 FS is called an *interval type-2 FS* (IT2 FS). IT2 FSs are the only T2 FSs that are used in this book.

With this as a somewhat qualitative introduction to IT2 FSs, more formal definitions are provided next.

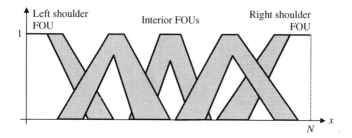

Figure 2.4. Left-shoulder, right-shoulder, and interior FOUs, all of whose LMFs and UMFs are piecewise linear (Liu and Mendel, 2008b; © 2008, IEEE).

2.3 DEFINITIONS

In this section[3] mathematically well-defined terms are provided that let us communicate effectively about IT2 FSs because these terms are used extensively in the rest of the book.

Definition 2.7. An *IT2 FS* $\tilde{A}$ is characterized by the MF $\mu_{\tilde{A}}(x, u)$, where $x \in X$ and $u \in J_x \subseteq [0, 1]$, that is,

$$\tilde{A} = \left\{ ((x, u), \mu_{\tilde{A}}(x, u) = 1) \mid \forall x \in X, \forall u \in J_x \subseteq [0, 1] \right\} \tag{2.7}$$

This can also be expressed as [Mendel (2001), Mendel and John (2002)]

$$\tilde{A} = \int_{x \in X} \int_{u \in J_x \subseteq [0,1]} 1/(x, u) = \int_{x \in X} \left[\int_{u \in J_x \subseteq [0,1]} 1/u \right] / x \tag{2.8}$$

where x, called the *primary variable,* has domain X; $u \in [0, 1]$, called the *secondary variable,* has domain $J_x \subseteq U = [0, 1]$ at each $x \in X$; J_x, is called the *primary membership* (or the codomain) of x, and is defined below in equation (2.14); and, the amplitude of $\mu_{\tilde{A}}(x, u)$, called a *secondary grade* of $\tilde{A}$, equals 1 for $\forall x \in X$ and $\forall u \in J_x \subseteq [0, 1]$. The bracketed term in equation (2.8) is called the *secondary MF,* or vertical slice, of $\tilde{A}$, and is denoted[4] $\mu_{\tilde{A}}(x)$, that is,

$$\mu_{\tilde{A}}(x) = \int_{u \in J_x \subseteq [0,1]} 1/u \tag{2.9}$$

so that $\tilde{A}$ can also be expressed in terms of its vertical slices as

$$\tilde{A} = \int_{x \in X} \mu_{\tilde{A}}(x) / x \tag{2.10}$$

For continuous X and U, equation (2.8) means $\tilde{A} : X \rightarrow \{[a, b]: 0 \le a \le b \le 1\}$. Observe that each $\mu_{\tilde{A}}(x)$ is a T1 FS.

Equation (2.10) is called a *vertical-slice representation* (decomposition) of an IT2 FS.

Definition 2.8. Uncertainty about $\tilde{A}$ is conveyed by the union of all its primary memberships, which is called the *footprint of uncertainty* (FOU) of $\tilde{A}$ (see Fig. 2.5), that is,

---

[3]Some of the material in this section is taken from Mendel, Hagras, and John (2006).
[4]$\mu_{\tilde{A}}(x)$ is actually a function of secondary variable u; hence, a better notation for it is $\mu_{\tilde{A}}(u|x)$. Because the notation $\mu_{\tilde{A}}(x)$ is already widely used by the T2 FS community, it is not changed here.

$$FOU(\tilde{A}) = \bigcup_{\forall x \in X} J_x = \left\{ (x,u) : u \in J_x \subseteq [0,1] \right\} \qquad (2.11)$$

The size of an FOU is directly related to the uncertainty that is conveyed by an IT2 FS. So, an FOU with more area is more uncertain than one with less area. How to quantify the uncertainty about an FOU is discussed in Section 2.6.

According to Zadeh (2008), a "*granule* [is] a clump of attribute values drawn together by indistinguishability, equivalence, proximity, or functionality." According to Bargiela and Pedrycz (2008), "Information granulation is a grouping of elements based on their indistinguishability, similarity, proximity or functionality." An IT2 FS can be interpreted as a granule, and when words are modeled by IT2 FSs (as is done in Chapter 3), those models are granular models.

Definition 2.9. The *upper membership function* (UMF) and *lower membership function* (LMF) of $\tilde{A}$ are two type-1 MFs that bound the FOU (Fig. 2.5). $UMF(\tilde{A})$ is associated with the upper bound of $FOU(\tilde{A})$ and is denoted $\overline{\mu}_{\tilde{A}}(x)$, $\forall x \in X$, and $LMF(\tilde{A})$ is associated with the lower bound of $FOU(\tilde{A})$ and is denoted $\underline{\mu}_{\tilde{A}}(x)$, $\forall x \in X$, that is,

$$UMF(\tilde{A}) \equiv \overline{\mu}_{\tilde{A}}(x) = \overline{FOU(\tilde{A})} \qquad \forall x \in X \qquad (2.12)$$

$$LMF(\tilde{A}) \equiv \underline{\mu}_{\tilde{A}}(x) = \underline{FOU(\tilde{A})} \qquad \forall x \in X \qquad (2.13)$$

Comment: For notational simplicity, in some later chapters we sometimes use $\overline{A}$ ($\underline{A}$) to denote the $UMF(\tilde{A})$ [$LMF(\tilde{A})$], and consequently $\mu_{\overline{A}}(x)$ [$\mu_{\underline{A}}(x)$] for the membership grade on $\overline{A}$ ($\underline{A}$).

Definition 2.10. The *support* of $LMF(\tilde{A})$ [$UMF(\tilde{A})$] is the crisp set of all points $x \in X$ such that $LMF(\tilde{A}) > 0$ [$UMF(\tilde{A}) > 0$]. The *support* of $\tilde{A}$ is the same as the support of $UMF(\tilde{A})$.

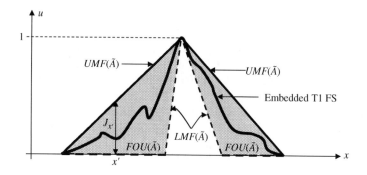

Figure 2.5. Interval T2 FSs and associated quantities (Mendel, 2007a, © 2007, IEEE).

Definition 2.11. IT2 FS $\check{A}$ is *convex* if both $LMF(\check{A})$ and $UMF(\check{A})$, which are T1 FSs, are convex over their respective supports (see Definition 2.4).

In general, the supports of $LMF(\tilde{A})$ and $UMF(\tilde{A})$ are different, and the support of $LMF(\tilde{A})$ is contained within the support of the $UMF(\tilde{A})$. All of our word FOUs (Chapter 3) satisfy this definition of convexity.

Note that the primary membership J_x is[5] an *interval set,* that is,

$$J_x = \left[\underline{\mu}_{\tilde{A}}(x), \bar{\mu}_{\tilde{A}}(x)\right] \tag{2.14}$$

This set is continuous when U is continuous and is discrete when U is discrete, in which case it is denoted $J_x\{\underline{\mu}_{\tilde{A}}(x), \ldots, \bar{\mu}_{\tilde{A}}(x)\}$. Using equation (2.14), the $FOU(\tilde{A})$ in equation (2.11) can also be expressed as

$$FOU(\tilde{A}) = \bigcup_{\forall x \in X} \left[\underline{\mu}_{\tilde{A}}(x), \bar{\mu}_{\tilde{A}}(x)\right] \tag{2.15}$$

A very compact way to describe an IT2 FS is

$$\tilde{A} = 1 / FOU(\tilde{A}) \tag{2.16}$$

where this notation means that the secondary grade equals 1 for all elements of $FOU(\tilde{A})$. Because all of the secondary grades of an IT2 FS equal 1, these secondary grades convey no useful information; hence, an IT2 FS is completely described by its FOU.

Definition 2.12. For continuous universes of discourse X and U, an *embedded T1 FS A_e* is

$$A_e = \int_{x \in X} u/x \qquad u \in J_x \tag{2.17}$$

The set A_e is embedded in $FOU(\tilde{A})$. An example of A_e is given in Fig. 2.5. Other examples are $\bar{\mu}_{\tilde{A}}(x)$ and $\underline{\mu}_{\tilde{A}}(x)$ ($\forall x \in X$).

When the universes of discourse X and U are continuous then there are an uncountable number of embedded T1 FSs in $\tilde{A}$. Because such sets are only used for theoretical purposes and are not used for computational purposes, this poses no problem.

For discrete universes of discourse X and U, an embedded T1 FS A_e has N elements, one each from $J_{x_1}, J_{x_2}, \ldots, J_{x_N}$, namely $u_1, u_2, \ldots, u_N$, that is,

---

[5]The notation J_x is entrenched in the T2 FS literature; however, it fails to designate for which IT2 FS it is applicable, so, a better notation might be $J_{\tilde{A}}(x)$ or $J_x^{\tilde{A}}$. The ambiguous notation J_x is retained in this book so that the reader will be able to easily connect with the T2 FS literature.

$$A_e = \sum_{i=1}^{N} u_i / x_i \quad u_i \in J_{x_i} \tag{2.18}$$

There are a total of $\Pi_{i=1}^{N} M_i$ embedded T1 FSs.

2.4 WAVY-SLICE REPRESENTATION THEOREM

So far, the vertical-slice representation of an IT2 FS, given in equation (2.10), has been emphasized. In this section a different representation is provided for such a fuzzy set, one that is in terms of so-called *wavy slices*. This representation, which makes very heavy use of embedded T1 FSs, was first presented in Mendel and John (2002) for an arbitrary T2 FS, and is the bedrock for the rest of this book.[6] It is stated here for a discrete IT2 FS.

Theorem 2.1 (Wavy-Slice Representation Theorem). Assume that the primary variable x of an IT2 FS is sampled at N values, $x_1, \ldots, x_N$, and at each of these values its primary memberships u_i are sampled at M_i values, $u_{i1}, \ldots, u_{iM_i}$. Then $\tilde{A}$ is represented by equation (2.16) in which

$$FOU(\tilde{A}) = \bigcup_{j=1}^{n_A} A_e^j = \left\{ \underline{\mu}_{\tilde{A}}(x), \ldots, \overline{\mu}_{\tilde{A}}(x) \right\} \equiv [\underline{\mu}_{\tilde{A}}(x), \overline{\mu}_{\tilde{A}}(x)] \tag{2.19}$$

This theorem expresses $FOU(\tilde{A})$ as a union of simple T1 FSs. Equation (2.19) is called a wavy-slice representation of $\tilde{A}$.

Proof: The results in Equation (2.19) are obvious using the following simple geometric argument. Create all of the possible embedded T1 FSs in $FOU(\tilde{A})$ and take their union to reconstruct $FOU(\tilde{A})$. Same points, which occur in different embedded T1 FSs, only appear once in the set-theoretic union.

Note that both the union of the vertical slices and the union of embedded T1 FSs can be interpreted as *covering representations,* because they both cover the entire FOU.

In the sequel it will be seen that one does not need to know the explicit natures of any of the wavy slices in $FOU(\tilde{A})$ other than $\underline{\mu}_{\tilde{A}}(x)$ and $\overline{\mu}_{\tilde{A}}(x)$. In fact, for an IT2 FS, everything can be determined just by knowing its lower and upper MFs.

2.5 SET-THEORETIC OPERATIONS

The goal of this section[7] is to obtain formulas for the union and intersection of two IT2 FSs and also the formula for the complement of an IT2 FS, because these operations are frequently used in a CWW engine that is based on if–then rules (Chapter

---

[6]Although this representation theorem is usually referred to as the Representation Theorem, we now prefer to call it the Wavy-Slice Representation Theorem (RT, for short), in order to distinguish it from the vertical slice representation.

[7]The material in this section follows Mendel, John, and Liu (2006).

6). There are different approaches to deriving such formulas [e.g., extension principle (Zadeh, 1975) and interval arithmetic (Klir and Yuan, 1995)]. The approach that is taken here is based entirely on the Wavy-Slice Representation Theorem 2.1 and the formulas for the union and intersection of two T1 FSs, and the complement of a T1 FS that are given in equations (2.4)–(2.6).

Theorem 2.2. For continuous universes of discourse, (a) The *union* of two IT2 FSs, $\tilde{A}$ and $\tilde{B}, \tilde{A} \cup \tilde{B}$, is another IT2 FS, with $FOU(\tilde{A} \cup \tilde{B})$, that is,

$$\tilde{A} \cup \tilde{B} = 1/FOU(\tilde{A} \cup \tilde{B}) = 1/[\underline{\mu}_{\tilde{A}}(x) \vee \underline{\mu}_{\tilde{B}}(x), \overline{\mu}_{\tilde{A}}(x) \vee \overline{\mu}_{\tilde{B}}(x)] \quad (2.20)$$

where $\vee$ denotes the disjunction operator (e.g., maximum); (b) the *intersection* of two IT2 FSs, $\tilde{A}$ and $\tilde{B}, \tilde{A} \cap \tilde{B}$, is also another IT2 FS, with $FOU(\tilde{A} \cap \tilde{B})$, that is,

$$\tilde{A} \cap \tilde{B} = 1/FOU(\tilde{A} \cap \tilde{B}) = 1/[\underline{\mu}_{\tilde{A}}(x) \wedge \underline{\mu}_{\tilde{B}}(x), \overline{\mu}_{\tilde{A}}(x) \wedge \overline{\mu}_{\tilde{B}}(x)] \quad (2.21)$$

where $\wedge$ denotes the conjunction operator (e.g., minimum); and, (c) the *complement* of IT2 FS $\tilde{A}, \tilde{A}^c$, is an IT2 FS, with $FOU(\tilde{A}^c)$, that is,

$$\tilde{A}^c = 1/FOU(\tilde{A}^c) = 1/[1 - \overline{\mu}_{\tilde{A}}(x), 1 - \underline{\mu}_{\tilde{A}}(x)] \quad (2.22)$$

For discrete universes of discourse, replace the interval sets $[\bullet, \bullet]$ by the sets $\{\bullet, \ldots, \bullet\}$.

The proof of part (a) is given in Appendix A. The proofs of parts (b) and (c) are left to the reader.

It is very important to observe, from equations (2.20)–(2.22) that all of their calculations only involve calculations between T1 FSs.

Example 2.2. Two IT2 FSs, $\tilde{A}$ and $\tilde{B}$, are depicted in Fig. 2.6a. Their union and intersection are depicted in Figs. 2.6b and 2.6c, respectively.

The generalizations of parts (a) and (b) of Theorem 2.2 to more than two IT2 FSs follows directly from equations (2.20) and (2.21) and the associative property of T2 FSs, for example:

$$\mu_{\tilde{A} \cup \tilde{B} \cup \tilde{C}}(x) = 1/[\underline{\mu}_{\tilde{A}}(x) \vee \underline{\mu}_{\tilde{B}}(x) \vee \underline{\mu}_{\tilde{C}}(x), \overline{\mu}_{\tilde{A}}(x) \vee \overline{\mu}_{\tilde{B}}(x) \vee \overline{\mu}_{\tilde{C}}(x)] \quad (2.23)$$

$$\mu_{\tilde{A} \cap \tilde{B} \cap \tilde{C}}(x) = 1/[\underline{\mu}_{\tilde{A}}(x) \wedge \underline{\mu}_{\tilde{B}}(x) \wedge \underline{\mu}_{\tilde{C}}(x), \overline{\mu}_{\tilde{A}}(x) \wedge \overline{\mu}_{\tilde{B}}(x) \wedge \overline{\mu}_{\tilde{C}}(x)] \quad (2.24)$$

2.6   CENTROID OF AN IT2 FS

2.6.1   General Results

The centroid of an IT2 FS, which is the most important computation in this book, provides[8] a measure of the uncertainty of such a FS. This is explained more careful-

---

[8]Most of the material in this section is taken from Mendel and Wu (2007a).

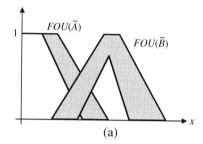

(a)

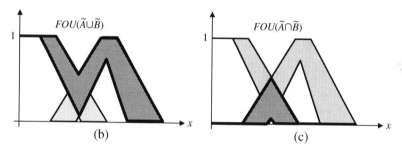

(b)   (c)

Figure 2.6. (a) Two IT2 FSs, $\tilde{A}$ and $\tilde{B}$; (b) $FOU(\tilde{A} \cup \tilde{B})$; and (c) $FOU(\tilde{A} \cap \tilde{B})$.

ly at the end of this subsection. Using equation (2.19), the centroid of IT2 FS $\tilde{A}$, $C_{\tilde{A}}(x)$, is defined as follows.

Definition 2.13. The *centroid* $C_{\tilde{A}}(x)$ of an IT2 FS $\tilde{A}$ is the union of the centroids of all its embedded T1 FSs , $c(A_e)$, that is,

$$C_{\tilde{A}}(x) = \bigcup_{\forall A_e} c(A_e) = \{c_l(\tilde{A}), ..., c_r(\tilde{A})\} \equiv [c_l(\tilde{A}), c_r(\tilde{A})] \tag{2.25}$$

where

$$c_l(\tilde{A}) = \min_{\forall A_e} c_{\tilde{A}}(A_e) = \min_{\forall \theta_i \in [\underline{\mu}_{\tilde{A}}(x_i), \bar{\mu}_{\tilde{A}}(x_i)]} \frac{\sum_{i=1}^{N} x_i \theta_i}{\sum_{i=1}^{N} \theta_i} \tag{2.26}$$

$$c_r(\tilde{A}) = \max_{\forall A_e} c_{\tilde{A}}(A_e) = \max_{\forall \theta_i \in [\underline{\mu}_{\tilde{A}}(x_i), \bar{\mu}_{\tilde{A}}(x_i)]} \frac{\sum_{i=1}^{N} x_i \theta_i}{\sum_{i=1}^{N} \theta_i} \tag{2.27}$$

$C_{\tilde{A}}(x)$ is shown as an explicit function of x because the centroid of each embedded T1 FS falls on the x-axis. Recall that there are n_A embedded T1 FSs that are contained within $FOU(\tilde{A})$; hence, computing their centroids leads to a collection of n_A numbers, $\sum_{i=1}^{N} x_i \theta_i / \sum_{i=1}^{N} \theta_i$, that have both a smallest and largest element, $c_l(\tilde{A}) \equiv c_l$ and $c_r(\tilde{A}) \equiv c_r$, respectively.[9] That such numbers exist is because $\sum_{i=1}^{N} x_i \theta_i / \sum_{i=1}^{N} \theta_i$ is a bounded number. When discretizations of the primary variable and primary membership approach zero, $\{c_l(\tilde{A}), \ldots, c_r(\tilde{A})\} \to [c_l(\tilde{A}), \ldots, c_r(\tilde{A})]$, an interval set. In the literature about the centroid, it is customary write $C_{\tilde{A}}$ as $[c_l(\tilde{A}), c_r(\tilde{A})]$, something that we also do.

Because x_i are sampled values of the primary variable, it is true that in equations (2.26) and (2.27),

$$x_1 < x_2 < \cdots < x_N \tag{2.28}$$

in which x_1 denotes the smallest sampled value of x and x_N denotes the largest sampled value[10] of x.

Examining equations (2.26) and (2.27) it seems that c_l and c_r could be computed by adding and then dividing interval sets. Klir and Yuan (1995) provide the following closed-form formula for the division of two interval sets:

$$[a,b]/[d,e] = [a,b] \times [1/e, 1/d] \tag{2.29}$$
$$= [\min(a/d, a/e, b/d, b/e), \max(a/d, a/e, b/d, b/e)]$$

It would seem that this result could be applied to determine closed-form formulas for c_l and c_r. Unfortunately, this cannot be done because the derivation of this result assumes that a, b, d, and e are independent. Due to the appearance of θ_i in both the numerator and denominator of equations (2.26) and (2.27), the required independence is not present; hence, this interesting closed-form result cannot be used to compute c_l and c_r.

Karnik and Mendel (2001) have developed iterative algorithms—now known as KM Algorithms—for computing c_l and c_r. These algorithms, which are very heavily used in many later chapters of this book, are derived and discussed in Section 2.7. In that section, it is shown that c_l and c_r each has the following structure:

$$c_l = \frac{\sum_{i=1}^{L} x_i \overline{\mu}_{\tilde{A}}(x_i) + \sum_{i=L+1}^{N} x_i \underline{\mu}_{\tilde{A}}(x_i)}{\sum_{i=1}^{L} \overline{\mu}_{\tilde{A}}(x_i) + \sum_{i=L+1}^{N} \underline{\mu}_{\tilde{A}}(x_i)} \tag{2.30}$$

---

[9]When there is no ambiguity about the IT2 FS whose centroid is being computed, it is common to shorten $c_l(\tilde{A})$ and $c_r(\tilde{A})$ to c_l and c_r, respectively, something that is done in this book.

[10]If Gaussian MFs are used, then in theory $x_1 \to -\infty$ and $x_N \to \infty$; but, in practice, when truncations are used x_1 and x_N are again finite numbers.

$$c_r = \frac{\sum_{i=1}^{R} x_i \underline{\mu}_{\tilde{A}}(x_i) + \sum_{i=R+1}^{N} x_i \overline{\mu}_{\tilde{A}}(x_i)}{\sum_{i=1}^{R} \underline{\mu}_{\tilde{A}}(x_i) + \sum_{i=R+1}^{N} \overline{\mu}_{\tilde{A}}(x_i)} \qquad (2.31)$$

In these equations, L and R are called *switch points,* and it is these switch points that are determined by the KM algorithms. Observe that in equation (2.30) when $i = L + 1$, θ_i in equation (2.26) switches from values on the UMF, $\overline{\mu}_{\tilde{A}}(x_i)$, to values on the LMF, $\underline{\mu}_{\tilde{A}}(x_i)$; and, in equation (2.31) when $i = R + 1$, θ_i in equation (2.27) switches from values on the LMF, $\underline{\mu}_{\tilde{A}}(x_i)$, to values on the UMF, $\overline{\mu}_{\tilde{A}}(x_i)$. An example that illustrates the two switch points is given in Fig. 2.7.

It is well known from information theory that entropy provides a measure of the uncertainty of a random variable [Cover and Thomas (1991)]. Recall that a one-dimensional random variable that is uniformly distributed over a region has entropy

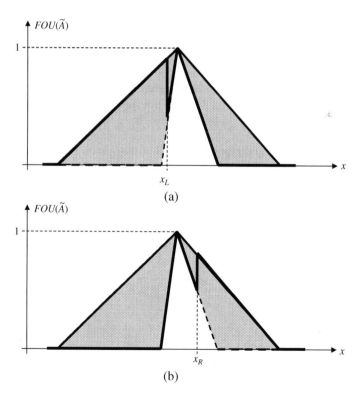

(a)

(b)

Figure 2.7. The embedded T1 FSs that are used to compute switch points L and R are shown by the heavy lines in (a) and (b), respectively (Mendel, 2007a; © 2007, IEEE).

equal to the logarithm of the length of that region. Comparing the MF $\mu_{C_{\tilde{A}}}(x)$ of the interval fuzzy set $C_{\tilde{A}}(x)$, where $\mu_{C_{\tilde{A}}}(x) = 1$ when $x \in [c_l, c_r]$ and $\mu_{C_{\tilde{A}}}(x) = 0$ when $x \notin [c_l, c_r]$, with the probability density function $p_X(x)$ that is uniformly distributed over $[c_l, c_r]$, where $p_X(x) = 1/(c_r - c_l)$ when $x \in [c_l, c_r]$ and $p_X(x) = 0$ when $x \notin [c_l, c_r]$, it is clear that they are almost the same except for their amplitudes. Therefore, it is reasonable to consider the extent of the uncertainty of the fuzzy set $C_{\tilde{A}}(x)$ to be the same as (or proportional to) that of the random variable X. The length of $C_{\tilde{A}}(x)$, $c_r - c_l$, can therefore be used to measure the extent of the uncertainty of an IT2 FS [Wu and Mendel (2002)].

2.6.2 Properties of the Centroid

Since the introduction of the centroid, its properties have been studied by Mendel and Wu (2007a), Liu and Mendel (2008), and Mendel (2005). Here, some of those properties are stated without proof, because they provide insights about the centroid and can also greatly simplify its computation.[11]

Property 1 [Mendel and Wu (2007a)]: Let $\tilde{A}$ be an IT2 FS defined on X, and $\tilde{A}'$ be $\tilde{A}$ shifted by[12] Δm along X, that is, $\underline{\mu}_{\tilde{A}'}(x) = \underline{\mu}_{\tilde{A}}(x - \Delta m)$ and $\overline{\mu}_{\tilde{A}'}(x) = \overline{\mu}_{\tilde{A}}(x - \Delta m)$. Then the centroid of $\tilde{A}'$, $C_{\tilde{A}'}(x) = [c_l(\tilde{A}'), c_r(\tilde{A}')]$, is the same as the centroid of $\tilde{A}$, $C_{\tilde{A}}(x) = [c_l(\tilde{A}), c_r(\tilde{A})]$, shifted by Δm, that is, $c_l(\tilde{A}') = c_l(\tilde{A}) + \Delta m$ and $c_r(\tilde{A}') = c_r(\tilde{A}) + \Delta m$.

This property lets $FOU(\tilde{A})$ be relocated to a more convenient place for the actual computations of c_l and c_r, and demonstrates that it is only the shape of $FOU(\tilde{A})$ that affects $c_r - c_l$ and not where that shape resides on the axis of the primary variable.

Property 2 [Mendel and Wu (2007a)]: If the primary variable x is bounded, that is, $x \in [x_1, x_N]$, then $c_l(\tilde{A}) \geq x_1$ and $c_r(\tilde{A}) \leq x_N$.

Although the centroid cannot be computed in closed form, this property provides bounds for the centroid that are available from knowledge of the domain of the primary variable.

Property 3 [Mendel and Wu (2007a)]: If $LMF(\tilde{A})$ is entirely on the primary-variable (x) axis, and $x \in [x_1, x_N]$, then the centroid does not depend upon the shape of $FOU(\tilde{A})$ and, as long as x_1 and x_N are included in the sampling points, it equals $[x_1, x_N]$.

An example of a FOU for which $LMF(\tilde{A})$ is entirely on the primary-variable (x) axis, and $x \in [x_1, x_N]$, is depicted in Fig. 2.8. It is called a *completely filled-in FOU*. Although the results of this property may seem strange, remember that each of the centroids in equation (2.25) that make up the centroid of $\tilde{A}$ provides a center of

---

[11]The statements of the properties and their accompanying discussions have been taken from Mendel (2007b).
[12]Δm can be positive or negative.

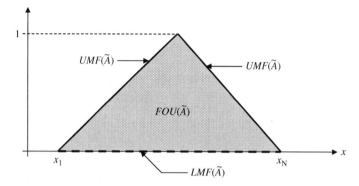

Figure 2.8. Completely filled-in FOU (Mendel and Wu, 2007a; © 2007, Elsevier).

gravity about the vertical (primary membership) axis and, according to Property 2, each of these centroids must be contained within $[x_1, x_N]$. For a completely filled-in FOU, the centroid actually equals $[x_1, x_N]$. This property also demonstrates that for such a FOU its UMF plays no role in determining the centroid. In this book, this is considered to be an undesirable property for a FOU because such a FOU is one of maximum area (for a fixed UMF) and, therefore maximum uncertainty.

Symmetrical FOUs can occur, for example, create an FOU by starting with a Gaussian primary MF and allowing its mean, standard deviation or both to vary over intervals; then the resulting FOU will be symmetrical (Fig. 2.9). For such an FOU, the following properties hold.

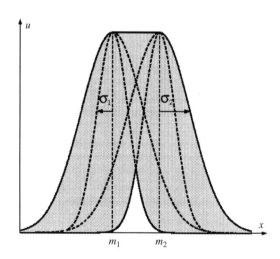

Figure 2.9. FOU that is symmetrical about $m = (m_1 + m_2)/2$, (Wu and Mendel, 2007; © 2007, IEEE).

Property 4 [Mendel (2005)]: If $\tilde{A}$ is symmetrical about primary variable x at $x = m$, then the centroid of such an IT2 FS is symmetrical about $x = m$, and the center of the centroid (i.e., the defuzzified value) equals m.

Note that by using Property 4, one only has to compute $c_l(\tilde{A})$, because $[c_l(\tilde{A}) + c_r(\tilde{A})]/2 = m$, so that $c_r(\tilde{A}) = 2m - c_l(\tilde{A})$. This represents a 50% savings in computation.

Property 5 [Mendel and Wu (2007a)]: If $\tilde{A}$ is symmetrical about $m \in X$, then $c_l(\tilde{A}) \leq m$ and $c_r(\tilde{A}) \geq m$.

This property can be combined with Property 2 to provide lower and upper bounds for $c_l(\tilde{A})$ and $c_r(\tilde{A})$. Other bounds for $c_l(\tilde{A})$ and $c_r(\tilde{A})$, that are explicit functions of the geometry of $FOU(\tilde{A})$, are given in Mendel and Wu (2006, 2007b); but because they are not used in this book they are not presented here.

Next, we turn to the KM algorithms because they are needed to implement many of the results that are described in later chapters.

2.7   KM ALGORITHMS

2.7.1   Derivation of KM Algorithms

Let[13]

$$y(\theta_1,...,\theta_N) \equiv \frac{\displaystyle\sum_{i=1}^{N} x_i\theta_i}{\displaystyle\sum_{i=1}^{N} \theta_i} \tag{2.32}$$

If the usual calculus approach to optimizing $y(\theta_1, ..., \theta_N)$ is taken and it is differentiated with respect to any one of the N θ_i, say θ_k, it follows that

$$\frac{\partial y(\theta_1,...,\theta_N)}{\partial \theta_k} = \frac{\partial}{\partial \theta_k} \left[\frac{\displaystyle\sum_{i=1}^{N} x_i\theta_i}{\displaystyle\sum_{i=1}^{N} \theta_i} \right] = \frac{x_k - y(\theta_1,...,\theta_N)}{\displaystyle\sum_{i=1}^{N} \theta_i} \tag{2.33}$$

Because $\sum_{i=1}^{N} \theta_i > 0$, it is easy to see from equation (2.33) that

$$\frac{\partial y(\theta_1,...,\theta_N)}{\partial \theta_k} \begin{cases} \geq 0 & \text{if } x_k \geq y(\theta_1,...,\theta_N) \\ < 0 & \text{if } x_k < y(\theta_1,...,\theta_N) \end{cases} \tag{2.34}$$

---

[13]Our presentation follows that of Mendel and Wu (2007a).

Unfortunately, equating $\partial y / \partial \theta_k$ to zero does not give us any information about the value of θ_k that optimizes $y(\theta_1, \ldots, \theta_N)$, that is,

$$y(\theta_1,\ldots,\theta_N) = x_k \Rightarrow \frac{\sum\limits_{i=1}^{N} x_i \theta_i}{\sum\limits_{i=1}^{N} \theta_i} = x_k \Rightarrow \frac{\sum\limits_{i \neq k}^{N} x_i \theta_i}{\sum\limits_{i \neq k}^{N} \theta_i} = x_k \qquad (2.35)$$

Observe that θ_k no longer appears in the final expression in equation (2.35), so that the direct calculus approach does not work.

Equation (2.34) does give the direction in which θ_k should be changed in order to increase or decrease $y(\theta_1, \ldots, \theta_N)$:

$$\left. \begin{array}{ll} \text{If } x_k > y(\theta_1,\ldots,\theta_N) & y(\theta_1,\ldots,\theta_N) \text{ increases (decreases) as } \theta_k \text{ increases (decreases)} \\ \text{If } x_k < y(\theta_1,\ldots,\theta_N) & y(\theta_1,\ldots,\theta_N) \text{ increases (decreases) as } \theta_k \text{ decreases (increases)} \end{array} \right\} \tag{2.36}$$

Recall [see equations (2.26) and (2.27)] that the maximum value that θ_k can attain is $\overline{\mu}_{\tilde{A}}(x_k)$ and the minimum value that it can attain is $\underline{\mu}_{\tilde{A}}(x)$. Equation (2.36) therefore implies that $y(\theta_1, \ldots, \theta_N)$ attains its maximum value, c_r, if

$$\theta_k = \begin{cases} \overline{\mu}_{\tilde{A}}(x_k) & \forall k \ni x_k > y(\theta_1,\ldots,\theta_N) \\ \underline{\mu}_{\tilde{A}}(x_k) & \forall k \ni x_k < y(\theta_1,\ldots,\theta_N) \end{cases} \qquad (2.37)$$

Similarly, it can be deduced from equation (2.36) that $y(\theta_1, \ldots, \theta_N)$ attains its minimum value, c_l, if

$$\theta_k = \begin{cases} \overline{\mu}_{\tilde{A}}(x_k) & \forall k \ni x_k < y(\theta_1,\ldots,\theta_N) \\ \underline{\mu}_{\tilde{A}}(x_k) & \forall k \ni x_k > y(\theta_1,\ldots,\theta_N) \end{cases} \qquad (2.38)$$

Because there are only two possible choices for θ_k that are stated above, to compute c_r (c_l) θ_k switches only one time between $\overline{\mu}_{\tilde{A}}(x_k)$ and $\underline{\mu}_{\tilde{A}}(x_k)$. A KM algorithm locates the switch point, and, in general, the switch point for c_r, R, is different from the switch point for c_l, L; hence, there are two KM algorithms, one for L and one for R. The final expression for c_l and c_r is equations (2.30) and (2.31), respectively.

2.7.2 Statements of KM Algorithms

Each of the KM algorithms has five steps.[14] Both algorithms are stated in Table 2.1. Observe that the first two steps of each KM algorithm are identical.

---

[14]This procedure is a special case of computing a fractionally linear function [Kreinovich et al. (1998)]; however, it was developed independently of their work and at about the same time.

Table 2.1. KM algorithms for computing the centroid end points of an IT2 FS, $\tilde{A}$

KM Algorithm for c_l	KM Algorithm for c_r
Step^a $c_l = \min\limits_{\forall \theta_i \in \left[\underline{\mu}_{\tilde{A}}(x_i),\overline{\mu}_{\tilde{A}}(x_i)\right]} \left(\sum\limits_{i=1}^{N} x_i \theta_i \Big/ \sum\limits_{i=1}^{N} \theta_i \right)$	$c_r = \max\limits_{\forall \theta_i \in \left[\underline{\mu}_{\tilde{A}}(x_i),\overline{\mu}_{\tilde{A}}(x_i)\right]} \left(\sum\limits_{i=1}^{N} x_i \theta_i \Big/ \sum\limits_{i=1}^{N} \theta_i \right)$

1   Initialize θ_i by setting $\theta_i = [\underline{\mu}_{\tilde{A}}(x_i) + \overline{\mu}_{\tilde{A}}(x_i)]/2$, $i = 1, \ldots, N$, and then compute

$$c' = c(\theta_1, \ldots, \theta_N) = \sum_{i=1}^{N} x_i \theta_i \Big/ \sum_{i=1}^{N} \theta_i$$

2   Find k ($1 \le k \le N-1$) such that $x_k \le c' \le x_{k+1}$

3   Set $\theta_i = \overline{\mu}_{\tilde{A}}(x_i)$ when $i \le k$, and   Set $\theta_i = \underline{\mu}_{\tilde{A}}(x_i)$ when $i \le k$, and
$\theta_i = \underline{\mu}_{\tilde{A}}(x_i)$ when $i \ge k+1$, and then $\theta_i = \overline{\mu}_{\tilde{A}}(x_i)$ when $i \ge k+1$, and then
compute   compute

$$c_l(k) \equiv \frac{\sum_{i=1}^{k} x_i \overline{\mu}_{\tilde{A}}(x_i) + \sum_{i=k+1}^{N} x_i \underline{\mu}_{\tilde{A}}(x_i)}{\sum_{i=1}^{k} \overline{\mu}_{\tilde{A}}(x_i) + \sum_{i=k+1}^{N} \underline{\mu}_{\tilde{A}}(x_i)} \qquad c_r(k) = \frac{\sum_{i=1}^{k} x_i \underline{\mu}_{\tilde{A}}(x_i) + \sum_{i=k+1}^{N} x_i \overline{\mu}_{\tilde{A}}(x_i)}{\sum_{i=1}^{k} \underline{\mu}_{\tilde{A}}(x_i) + \sum_{i=k+1}^{N} \overline{\mu}_{\tilde{A}}(x_i)}$$

4   Check if $c_l(k) = c'$. If yes, stop and set   Check if $c_r(k) = c'$. If yes, stop and set
$c_l(k) = c_l$ and call k L. If no, go to Step 5. $c_r(k) = c_r$ and call k R. If no, go to Step 5.

5   Set $c' = c_l(k)$ and go to Step 2.   Set $c' = c_r(k)$ and go to Step 2.

^{a}Note that $x_1 \le x_2 \le \ldots \le x_N$.

Example 2.3 [Mendel (2001, p. 264)]. Figure 2.10 depicts an FOU for an IT2 FS, and four of its embedded T1 FSs. The center of gravity for each of these embedded T1 FSs is $c_{(a)} = 4.5603$, $c_{(b)} = 4.5961$, $c_{(c)} = 3.9432$, and $c_{(d)} = 5.2333$. By using the KM algorithms, it is established that $c_l = c_{(c)}$ and $c_r = c_{(d)}$; hence, this example should dispel any mistaken belief that the end points of the centroid of an IT2 FS are associated with the centroids of its lower- and upper-membership functions, $c_{(a)}$ and $c_{(b)}$. They are associated with embedded T1 FSs that involve segments from both the lower- and upper-membership functions.

2.7.3 Properties of KM Algorithms

The two most important properties about the KM algorithms are that [Mendel and Liu (2007)] (1) they are *monotonically convergent,* and, (2) within a quadratic domain of convergence, they are *superexponentially convergent,* which explains why they converge in so few iterations. Simulations in Mendel and Liu (2007) have revealed that, for two significant figures of accuracy, the convergence of the KM algorithms occurs in two to six iterations regardless of n.

Additional properties about the KM algorithms can be found in Liu and Mendel (2008a), and Mendel and Wu (2007a).

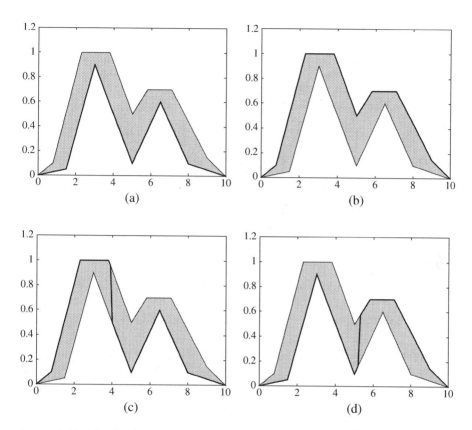

Figure 2.10. FOU and four embedded T1 FSs. (a) and (b) correspond to the lower and upper MFs, respectively; (c) and (d) (which are a result of using the KM algorithms) are associated with c_l and c_r, respectively.

Example 2.4. Figure 2.11 provides a graphical interpretation of the KM algorithm that computes L and c_l. For justifications of both the shape and location of $c_l(k)$ (in relation to the line $y = x_k$) see Liu and Mendel (2008a). The large dots are values of $c_l(k)$ that were obtained by evaluating $c_l(k)$ given in Table 2.1 for $k = 1, \ldots, 9$, and are connected by dotted lines for artistic purposes, that is, no values exist between the dots on those lines. Note that k is associated with the subscript of x_k. The 45° line $y = x_k$ is shown because of the computations in Step 2 of the KM algorithm.

c' is chosen using the equation that is given in Table 2.1, Step 1, and is shown on the vertical axis located between x_7 and x_8. After c' is computed, a horizontal line is drawn until it intersects $y = x_k$, and the intersection point slides down the 45° line until x_7 is reached,[15] at which point $c_l(7)$ is computed. This is the downward-direct-

---

[15]The sliding down is due to the discrete nature of x_i and is in conformance with using $\overline{\mu}_{\tilde{A}}(x_i)$ for $i \leq k$ as required by Step 3 in Table 2.1.

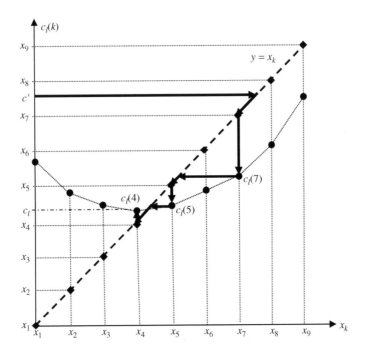

Figure 2.11. Graphical interpretation of the KM algorithm for computing L and c_l. The dashed $45°$ line $y = x_k$ only has values at $x_1, x_2, \ldots, x_9$. The large dots are $c_l(k)$, $k = 1, \ldots, 9$.

ed vertical line at x_7 that intersects a large dot. Because $c_l(4) \neq c'$, the algorithm then goes through three additional iterations before it stops, at which time $c_l(4)$ has been determined to be c_l. For this example, the KM algorithm converges in four iterations. In the fourth iteration the test $c_l(4) = c'$ is passed, and the algorithm stops.

This diagram and its accompanying discussion reveals that the KM algorithm is an alternating projection algorithm, and that it seems to converge very fast. Figure 2.11 shows $c_l(4) = c_l$ for convenience purposes. Convergence of $c_l(k)$ to the true value of c_l only occurs for very small sampling intervals. For larger values of the sampling interval, convergence still occurs but not to the true value of c_l. Instead, convergence occurs according to Step 2 in Table 2.1, as $x_L \leq c_l(L) < x_{L+1}$.

Enhanced KM (EKM) algorithms [Wu and Mendel (2007a, 2008)] that reduce the computational cost of the original ones are described in Appendix B.

2.8   CARDINALITY AND AVERAGE CARDINALITY OF AN IT2 FS

Cardinality[16] of a crisp set is a count of the number of elements in that set. Cardinality of a T1 FS is more complicated because the elements of the FS are not

---

[16]The material in this section is taken from Wu and Mendel (2007b).

equally weighted as they are in a crisp set. Definitions of the cardinality of a T1 FS have been proposed by several authors, including De Luca and Termini (1972), Kaufmann (1977), Gottwald (1980), Zadeh (1981), Blanchard (1982), Klement (1982), Wygralak (1983), and so on. Basically, there have been two kinds of proposals [Dubois and Prade (1985)]: (1) those that assume that the cardinality of a T1 FS can be a crisp number, and (2) those that claim that it should be a fuzzy number.

De Luca and Termini's (1972) definition of the cardinality of a T1 FS is

$$\text{card}(A) = \int_X \mu_A(x)dx \tag{2.39}$$

It is the one that is adopted in this book.

The cardinality of an IT2 FS $\tilde{A}$ [Wu and Mendel (2007b)] is obtained by using the wavy-slice representation Theorem 2.1 as the union of the cardinalities of its embedded T1 FSs, A_e, that is,

$$\text{card}(\tilde{A}) = \bigcup_{\forall A_e} \text{card}(A_e) = \bigcup_{\forall A_e} \int_X \mu_{A_e}(x)dx = \left[\min_{\forall A_e} \int_X \mu_{A_e}(x)dx, \max_{\forall A_e} \int_X \mu_{A_e}(x)dx \right] \tag{2.40}$$

Theorem 2.3 [Wu and Mendel (2007b)]. $\text{card}(\tilde{A})$ in equation (2.40) can be reexpressed as

$$\text{card}(\tilde{A}) = \left[\text{card}(\underline{\mu}_{\tilde{A}}(x)), \text{card}(\bar{\mu}_{\tilde{A}}(x)) \right] \tag{2.41}$$

Proof: It follows from equation (2.40), that

$$\min_{\forall A_e} \int_X \mu_{A_e}(x)dx = \int_X \left[\min_{\forall A_e} \mu_{A_e}(x) \right]dx = \int_X \underline{\mu}_{\tilde{A}}(x)dx = \text{card}(\underline{\mu}_{\tilde{A}}(x)) \tag{2.42}$$

and

$$\max_{\forall A_e} \int_X \mu_{A_e}(x)dx = \int_X \left[\max_{\forall A_e} \mu_{A_e}(x) \right]dx = \int_X \bar{\mu}_{\tilde{A}}(x)dx = \text{card}(\bar{\mu}_{\tilde{A}}(x)) \tag{2.43}$$

Equation (2.41) is obtained by substituting equations (2.42) and (2.43) into equation (2.40).

Definition 2.14. The *average cardinality* of $\tilde{A}$ [Wu and Mendel (2007b)] is the average of its minimum and maximum cardinalities, that is,

$$AC(\tilde{A}) = \frac{\text{card}(\underline{\mu}_{\tilde{A}}(x)) + \text{card}(\bar{\mu}_{\tilde{A}}(x))}{2} \tag{2.44}$$

$AC(\tilde{A})$ is used in Chapter 4 to compute the similarity of two IT2 FSs.

2.9 FINAL REMARK

This completes our coverage of IT2 FSs. Only those aspects of such FSs have been covered that are needed in this book. Readers who are interested to learn more about other aspects of IT2 FSs should see Mendel (2001, 2007a), Mendel et al. (2006), Bustince (2000), and Wu and Mendel (2007b).

APPENDIX 2A. DERIVATION THE UNION OF TWO IT2 FSs

Our derivation of equation (2.20) is for discrete universes of discourse. Consider two IT2 FSs $\tilde{A}$ and $\tilde{B}$. From equation (2.19), it follows that

$$FOU(\tilde{A} \cup \tilde{B}) = \bigcup_{j=1}^{n_A} A_e^j \cup \bigcup_{i=1}^{n_B} B_e^i = \bigcup_{j=1}^{n_A} \bigcup_{i=1}^{n_B} A_e^j \cup B_e^i \tag{2A.1}$$

where n_A and n_B denote the number of embedded IT2 FSs that are associated with $\tilde{A}$ and $\tilde{B}$, respectively; hence,

$$\mu_{\tilde{A} \cup \tilde{B}}(x,u) = 1/FOU(\tilde{A} \cup \tilde{B}) = 1/\bigcup_{j=1}^{n_A} \bigcup_{i=1}^{n_B} A_e^j \cup B_e^i \tag{2A.2}$$

This equation can be expressed as:

$$\begin{aligned}
\mu_{\tilde{A} \cup \tilde{B}}(x,u) &= 1/\bigcup_{j=1}^{n_A} \bigcup_{i=1}^{n_B} \left(\bigcup_{x \in X_d} \mu_{A_e^j \cup B_e^i}(x)/x \right) \\
&= 1/\bigcup_{j=1}^{n_A} \bigcup_{i=1}^{n_B} \left(\bigcup_{x \in X_d} \max\{\mu_{A_e^j}(x), \mu_{B_e^i}(x)\}/x \right) \\
&= 1/\bigcup_{x \in X_d} \left(\bigcup_{j=1}^{n_A} \bigcup_{i=1}^{n_B} \max\{\mu_{A_e^j}(x), \mu_{B_e^i}(x)\} \right)/x
\end{aligned} \tag{2A.3}$$

where the formula for the MF of the union[17] of two T1 FSs that is given in equation (2.4) has been used. Observe that at each value of x, $\bigcup_{j=1}^{n_A} \bigcup_{i=1}^{n_B} \max\{\mu_{A_e^j}(x), \mu_{B_e^i}(x)\}$ is a collection of $n_A \times n_B$ numbers that contains a lower-bounding number [found by computing the minimum over all i and j of $\max\{\mu_{A_e^j}(x), \mu_{B_e^i}(x)\}$] and an upper-bounding number [found by computing the maximum over all i and j of $\max\{\mu_{A_e^j}(x), \mu_{B_e^i}(x)\}$], since both $\mu_{A_e^j}(x)$ and $\mu_{B_e^i}(x)$ are bounded for all values of x. Formulas are now obtained for these bounding numbers.

Recall that the upper and lower MFs for an IT2 FS are also embedded T1 FSs. For $\tilde{A}$, $\overline{\mu}_{\tilde{A}}(x)$ and $\underline{\mu}_{\tilde{A}}(x)$ denote its upper MF and lower MF, whereas for $\tilde{B}$, $\overline{\mu}_{\tilde{B}}(x)$ and $\underline{\mu}_{\tilde{B}}(x)$ denote its comparable quantities. It must therefore be true that

---

[17]Although our derivation is presented for the maximum, it is also applicable for a general t-conorm.

$$\min_{\forall j,i} \max\left\{\mu_{A_e^j}(x), \mu_{B_e^i}(x)\right\} = \max\left(\min_{\forall j,i}\left\{\mu_{A_e^j}(x), \mu_{B_e^i}(x)\right\}\right)$$
$$= \max\left\{\underline{\mu}_{\tilde{A}}(x), \underline{\mu}_{\tilde{B}}(x)\right\} \tag{2A.4}$$
$$= \underline{\mu}_{\tilde{A}}(x) \vee \underline{\mu}_{\tilde{B}}(x)$$

$$\max_{\forall j,i} \max\left\{\mu_{A_e^j}(x), \mu_{B_e^i}(x)\right\} = \max\left(\max_{\forall j,i}\left\{\mu_{A_e^j}(x), \mu_{B_e^i}(x)\right\}\right)$$
$$= \max\left\{\overline{\mu}_{\tilde{A}}(x), \overline{\mu}_{\tilde{B}}(x)\right\} \tag{2A.5}$$
$$= \overline{\mu}_{\tilde{A}}(x) \vee \overline{\mu}_{\tilde{B}}(x)$$

From equations (2A.4) and (2A.5), it follows that

$$\bigcup_{x \in X_d}\left(\bigcup_{j=1}^{n_A}\bigcup_{i=1}^{n_B}\max\left\{\mu_{A_e^j}(x), \mu_{B_e^i}(x)\right\}\right)/x = \bigcup_{x \in X_d}\left\{\underline{\mu}_{\tilde{A}}(x) \vee \underline{\mu}_{\tilde{B}}(x),..., \overline{\mu}_{\tilde{A}}(x) \vee \overline{\mu}_{\tilde{B}}(x)\right\}/x$$

$$\tag{2A.6}$$

so that $\mu_{\tilde{A} \cup \tilde{B}}(x, u)$ in equation (2A.3) can be expressed as

$$\mu_{\tilde{A} \cup \tilde{B}}(x,u) = 1 / \left[\bigcup_{x \in X_d}\left\{\underline{\mu}_{\tilde{A}}(x) \vee \underline{\mu}_{\tilde{B}}(x),..., \overline{\mu}_{\tilde{A}}(x) \vee \overline{\mu}_{\tilde{B}}(x)\right\} / x\right] \tag{2A.7}$$

This can also be expressed in terms of secondary MFs, $\mu_{\tilde{A} \cup \tilde{B}}(x)$, as

$$\mu_{\tilde{A} \cup \tilde{B}}(x,u) = \bigcup_{x \in X_d} \mu_{\tilde{A} \cup \tilde{B}}(x) / x \tag{2A.8}$$

$$\mu_{\tilde{A} \cup \tilde{B}}(x) = 1 / \left\{\underline{\mu}_{\tilde{A}}(x) \vee \underline{\mu}_{\tilde{B}}(x),..., \overline{\mu}_{\tilde{A}}(x) \vee \overline{\mu}_{\tilde{B}}(x)\right\} \tag{2A.9}$$

Equation (2.20) is an equivalent way of expressing equations (2A.8) and (2A.9). Of course, for a continuous universe of discourse, the sequence of numbers $\{\underline{\mu}_{\tilde{A}}(x) \vee \underline{\mu}_{\tilde{B}}(x), \ldots, \overline{\mu}_{\tilde{A}}(x) \vee \overline{\mu}_{\tilde{B}}(x)\}$ becomes the interval $[\underline{\mu}_{\tilde{A}}(x) \vee \underline{\mu}_{\tilde{B}}(x), \overline{\mu}_{\tilde{A}}(x) \vee \overline{\mu}_{\tilde{B}}(x)]$.

APPENDIX 2B. ENHANCED KM (EKM) ALGORITHMS

The EKM algorithms [Wu and Mendel (2007b, 2008)] start with the KM algorithms and modify them in three ways: (1) a better initialization is used to reduce the number of iterations; (2) the termination condition of the iterations is changed to remove an unnecessary iteration; and (3) a subtle computing technique is used to reduce the computational cost of each of the algorithm's iterations. The EKM algorithms are summarized in Table 2.2.

The better initializations are shown in Step 1 of Table 2.2, and both were obtained from extensive simulations. A close examination of Steps 2–5 in Table 2.1 reveals that the termination conditions can be moved one step earlier, something that is done in Table 2.2. The "subtle computing technique" uses the fact that very little changes from one iteration to the next, so instead of recomputing everything on the right-hand sides of $c_l(k)$ and $c_r(k)$, as is done in Table 2.1, only the portions of those right-hand sides that do change are recomputed, as is done in Table 2.2. For detailed explanations of how each of the three modifications are implemented, see Wu and Mendel (2009).

Extensive simulations have shown that on average the EKM algorithms can save about two iterations, which corresponds to a more than 39% reduction in computation time.

Table 2.2. EKM algorithms for computing the centroid end-points of an IT2 FS, $\tilde{A}$

	EKM Algorithm for c_l	EKM Algorithm for c_r
Step[a]	$c_l = \displaystyle\min_{\forall \theta_i \in \left[\underline{\mu}_{\tilde{A}}(x_i), \overline{\mu}_{\tilde{A}}(x_i)\right]} \left(\sum_{i=1}^{N} x_i \theta_i \Big/ \sum_{i=1}^{N} \theta_i\right)$	$c_r = \displaystyle\max_{\forall \theta_i \in \left[\underline{\mu}_{\tilde{A}}(x_i), \overline{\mu}_{\tilde{A}}(x_i)\right]} \left(\sum_{i=1}^{N} x_i \theta_i \Big/ \sum_{i=1}^{N} \theta_i\right)$

| 1 | Set $k = [N/2.4]$ (the nearest integer to $N/2.4$) and compute: | Set $k = [N/1.7]$ (the nearest integer to $N/1.7$) and compute |

$$a = \sum_{i=1}^{k} x_i \overline{\mu}_{\tilde{A}}(x_i) + \sum_{i=k+1}^{N} x_i \underline{\mu}_{\tilde{A}}(x_i) \qquad a = \sum_{i=1}^{k} x_i \underline{\mu}_{\tilde{A}}(x_i) + \sum_{i=k+1}^{N} x_i \overline{\mu}_{\tilde{A}}(x_i)$$

$$b = \sum_{i=1}^{k} \overline{\mu}_{\tilde{A}}(x_i) + \sum_{i=k+1}^{N} \underline{\mu}_{\tilde{A}}(x_i) \qquad b = \sum_{i=1}^{k} \underline{\mu}_{\tilde{A}}(x_i) + \sum_{i=k+1}^{N} \overline{\mu}_{\tilde{A}}(x_i)$$

Compute $c' = a/b$

| 2 | Find $k' \in [1, N-1]$ such that $x_{k'} \le c' \le x_{k'+1}$ |

| 3 | Check if $k' = k$. If yes, stop and set $c' = c_l$, and $k = L$. If no, go to Step 4. | Check if $k' = k$. If yes, stop and set $c' = c_r$, and $k = R$. If no, go to Step 4. |

| 4 | Compute $s = sign(k' - k)$ and: | Compute $s = sign(k' - k)$ and: |

$$a' = a + s \sum_{i=\min(k,k')+1}^{\max(k,k')} x_i \left[\overline{\mu}_{\tilde{A}}(x_i) - \underline{\mu}_{\tilde{A}}(x_i)\right] \qquad a' = a - s \sum_{i=\min(k,k')+1}^{\max(k,k')} x_i \left[\overline{\mu}_{\tilde{A}}(x_i) - \underline{\mu}_{\tilde{A}}(x_i)\right]$$

$$b' = b + s \sum_{i=\min(k,k')+1}^{\max(k,k')} \left[\overline{\mu}_{\tilde{A}}(x_i) - \underline{\mu}_{\tilde{A}}(x_i)\right] \qquad b' = b - s \sum_{i=\min(k,k')+1}^{\max(k,k')} \left[\overline{\mu}_{\tilde{A}}(x_i) - \underline{\mu}_{\tilde{A}}(x_i)\right]$$

Compute $c''(k') = a'/b'$

| 5 | Set $c' = c''(k')$, $a = a'$, $b = b'$ and $k = k'$ and go to Step 2. |

[a]Note that $x_1 \le x_2 \le \ldots \le x_N$.

REFERENCES

A. Bargiela and W. Pedrycz, "Toward a theory of granular computing for human-centered information processing," *IEEE Trans. on Fuzzy Systems,* vol. 16, pp. 320–330, April 2008.

N. Blanchard, "Cardinal and ordinal theories about fuzzy sets," in M. M. Gupta and E. Sanchez (Eds.), *Fuzzy Information and Decision Processes,* 1982, Amsterdam: North Holland, pp. 149–157.

H. Bustince, "Indicator of inclusion grade for interval-valued fuzzy sets: Applications to approximate reasoning based on interval valued fuzzy sets," *Int. J. of Approximate Reasoning,* vol. 23, pp. 137–209, 2000.

T. M. Cover and J. A. Thomas, *Elements of Information Theory,* New York: Wiley, 1991.

A. De Luca and S. Termini, "A definition of non-probabilistic entropy in the setting of fuzzy sets theory," *Information and Computation,* vol. 20, pp. 301–312, 1972.

D. Dubois and H. Prade, "Fuzzy cardinality and the modeling of imprecise quantification," *Fuzzy Sets and Systems,* vol. 16, pp. 199–230, 1985.

S. Gottwald, "A note on fuzzy cardinals," *Kybernetika,* vol. 16, pp. 156–158, 1980.

S. Horikawa, T. Furahashi, and Y. Uchikawa, "On fuzzy modeling using fuzzy neural networks with back-propagation algorithm," *IEEE Trans. on Neural Networks,* vol. 3, pp. 801–806, September 1992.

J.-S. R. Jang, "Self-learning fuzzy controllers based on temporal back-propagation," *IEEE Trans. on Neural Networks,* vol. 3, pp. 714–723, September 1992.

N. Karnik and J. M. Mendel, "Centroid of a type-2 fuzzy set," *Information Sciences,* vol. 132, pp. 195–220, 2001.

A. Kaufmann, "Introduction a la theorie des sous-ensembles flous," in *Complement et Nouvelles Applications,* vol. 4, Paris: Masson, 1977.

E. P. Klement, "On the cardinality of fuzzy sets," in *Proceedings of the Sixth European Meeting on Cybernetics and Systems Research,* Vienna, 1982, pp. 701–704.

G. J. Klir and B. Yuan, *Fuzzy Sets and Fuzzy Logic: Theory and Applications,* Upper Saddle River, NJ: Prentice-Hall, 1995.

V. Kreinovich, A. Lakeyev, J. Rohn, and P. Kahl, *Computational Complexity and Feasibility of Data Processing and Interval Computations,* Chapter 10, The Netherlands: Kluwer Academic Publishers, 1998.

C.-T. Lin and C. S. G. Lee, *Neural Fuzzy Systems,* Upper Saddle River, NJ: Prentice-Hall PTR, 1996.

F. Liu and J. M. Mendel, "Aggregation using the fuzzy weighted average, as computed by the KM Algorithms," *IEEE Trans. on Fuzzy Systems,* vol. 16, pp. 1–12, February 2008a.

F. Liu and J. M. Mendel, "Encoding words into interval type-2 fuzzy sets using an Interval Approach," *IEEE Trans. on Fuzzy Systems,* vol. 16, pp 1503–1521, December 2008b.

J. M. Mendel, *Uncertain Rule-Based Fuzzy Logic Systems: Introduction and New Directions,* Upper-Saddle River, NJ: Prentice-Hall, 2001.

J. M. Mendel, "Type-2 fuzzy sets: some questions and answers," *IEEE Connections,* Newsletter of the IEEE Neural Networks Society, vol. 1, pp. 10–13, Aug. 2003.

J. M. Mendel, "On a 50% savings in the computation of the centroid of a *symmetrical* interval type-2 fuzzy set," *Information Sciences,* vol. 172, pp. 417–430, 2005.

J. M. Mendel, "Type-2 fuzzy sets and systems: An overview," *IEEE Computational Intelligence Magazine,* vol. 2, pp. 20–29, February 2007a.

J. M. Mendel, "Advances in type-2 fuzzy sets and systems," *Information Sciences,* Vol. 177, pp. 84–110, 2007b.

J. M. Mendel and R. I. John, "Type-2 fuzzy sets made simple," *IEEE Trans. on Fuzzy Systems,* vol. 10, pp. 117–127, April 2002.

J. M. Mendel and F. Liu, "Super-exponential convergence of the Karnik-Mendel algorithms for computing the centroid of an interval type-2 fuzzy set," *IEEE Trans. on Fuzzy Systems,* vol. 15, pp. 309–320, April, 2007.

J. M. Mendel and H. Wu, "Type-2 fuzzistics for symmetric interval type-2 fuzzy sets: Part 1, Forward problems," *IEEE Trans. on Fuzzy Systems,* vol. 14, pp. 781–792, December 2006.

J. M. Mendel and H. Wu, "New results about the centroid of an interval type-2 fuzzy set, including the centroid of a fuzzy granule," *Information Sciences,* vol. 177, pp. 360–377, 2007a.

J. M. Mendel and H. Wu, "Type-2 fuzzistics for non-symmetric interval type-2 fuzzy sets: Forward problems," *IEEE Trans. on Fuzzy Systems,* vol. 15, pp. 916–930, October 2007b.

J. M. Mendel, H. Hagras, and R. I. John, "Standard background material about interval type-2 fuzzy logic systems that can be used by all authors," IEEE Computational Intelligence Society standard: can be accessed at http://ieee-cis.org/technical/standards, 2006.

J. M. Mendel, R. I. John, and F. Liu, "Interval type-2 fuzzy logic systems made simple," *IEEE Trans. on Fuzzy Systems,* vol. 14, pp. 808–821, December 2006.

L.-X. Wang, *A Course in Fuzzy Systems and Control,* Upper Saddle River, NJ: Prentice-Hall PTR, 1997.

L.-X. Wang and J. M. Mendel, "Fuzzy basis functions, universal approximation, and orthogonal least-squares learning," *IEEE Trans. on Neural Networks,* vol. 3, pp. 807–813, September 1992a.

L.-X. Wang and J. M. Mendel, "Back-propagation of fuzzy systems as nonlinear dynamic system identifiers," *Proc. FUZZ-IEEE 1992,* San Diego, CA, pp. 1409–1418, 1992b.

D. Wu and J. M. Mendel, "Enhanced Karnik-Mendel algorithms," in *Proceedings of NAFIPS 2007,* San Diego, CA, June 2007a.

D. Wu and J. M. Mendel, "Uncertainty measures for interval type-2 fuzzy sets," *Information Sciences,* vol. 177, pp. 5378–5393, 2007b.

D. Wu and J. M. Mendel, "Enhanced Karnik-Mendel algorithms," *IEEE Trans. on Fuzzy Systems,* vol. 17, no. 4, pp. 923–934, August 2009.

H. Wu and J. M. Mendel, "Uncertainty bounds and their use in the design of interval type-2 fuzzy logic systems," *IEEE Trans. on Fuzzy Systems,* vol. 10, no. 5, pp. 622–639, 2002.

H. Wu and J. M. Mendel, "Classification of battlefield ground vehicles using acoustic features and fuzzy logic rule-based classifiers," *IEEE Trans. on Fuzzy Systems,* vol. 15, no. 1, pp. 56–72, February 2007.

M. Wygralak, "A new approach to the fuzzy cardinality of finite fuzzy sets," *Bulletin for Studies and Exchange of Fuzziness and its Applications,* vol. 15, pp. 72–75, 1983.

L. A. Zadeh, "Outline of a new approach to the analysis of complex systems and decision processes," *IEEE Trans. on Systems, Man, and Cybernetics,* vol. SMC-3, no. 1, pp. 28–44, 1973.

L. A. Zadeh, "The concept of a linguistic variable and its application to approximate reasoning-1," *Information Sciences,* vol. 8, pp. 199–249, 1975.

L. A. Zadeh, "Possibility theory and soft data analysis," in L. Cobb and R. M. Thrall (Eds.), *Mathematical Frontiers of the Social and Policy Sciences,* Boulder, CO: Westview Press, pp. 69–129, 1981.

L. A. Zadeh, "Toward human level machine intelligence—Is it achievable? The need for a paradigm shift," *IEEE Computational Intelligence Magazine,* vol. 3, pp. 11–22, August 2008.

CHAPTER 3

Encoding: From a Word to a Model— The Codebook

3.1 INTRODUCTION

We believe that fuzzy set models for words must be derived from data that are collected from a group of subjects. This is in agreement with Pedrycz (2001), who states:

> It is . . . highly justifiable to expect that all information granules used in system development need to be fully legitimized in terms of experimental (numerical) data. This . . . means that information granules used throughout the process should be both *semantically* meaningful and *experimentally* meaningful. . . . Our conjecture is that the linguistic terms emerge only if there is experimental evidence behind them . . . if there are no pertinent experimental data, there is no point in constructing a linguistic label; its existence cannot be justified in terms of numeric data.

In Chapter 1, it was explained that because words mean different things to different people, and so are uncertain, a fuzzy set model is needed for a word that has the potential to capture its uncertainties, and that an IT2 FS should be used as a FS model of a word, because it is characterized by its FOU and, therefore, has the potential to capture word uncertainties. This chapter explains two methods for obtaining IT2 FS models for words: the first for fuzzy experts (i.e., for people who are knowledgeable about a FS), and the second for anyone.

How to collect data from a group of subjects and how to then map that data into the parameters of a T1 MF has been reported on by a number of authors [e.g., Klir and Yuan (1995)]. Names for the different T1 methods include *polling, direct rating, reverse rating, interval estimation,* and *transition interval estimation.* Unfortunately, none of these methods transfers the uncertainties about collecting word data from a group of subjects into the MF of a T1 FS, because a T1 FS does not have enough degrees of freedom to do this; hence, they are not elaborated upon in the main body of this chapter; however, they are summarized in Appendix 3A, because it is important to learn from the past about how to elicit MF information from a group of subjects so that one may choose the most appropriate method(s) for doing this.

Perceptual Computing. By Jerry M. Mendel and Dongrui Wu
Copyright © 2010 the Institute of Electrical and Electronics Engineers, Inc.

In this chapter, all methods require that:

1. A continuous scale is established for each variable of interest (sometimes a natural scale exists,[1] e.g. as in pressure, temperature, volume, etc.; otherwise, a natural scale does not exist, e.g. as in touching, eye contact, beautiful, etc.).
2. A vocabulary of words is created that covers the entire scale.

Our methods are described for the continuous scale numbered 0–10. Of course, other scales could be used.

An interesting issue is whether or not data collected on a scale for one specific application can be rescaled on the same or a different scale for (i.e., transferred to) another application. The probability elicitation literature[2] [e.g., O'Hagan et al. (2006)] indicates that data collection is sensitive to scale and is application (context) dependent. We subscribe to both conclusions and, therefore, caution the reader that, *although we advocate their using this chapter's methodologies, we do not advocate their using this chapter's example word FOUs for their applications.* These examples are meant only to illustrate the methodologies.

For perceptual computing, one begins by establishing a vocabulary of application dependent words, one that is large enough so that a person will feel linguistically comfortable interacting with the perceptual computer. This vocabulary must include subsets of words that feel, to each subject, like they will collectively cover the scale 0–10. Redundant words and their coverage are not issues in this chapter, although they are important issues when designing a CWW engine [e.g., if–then rules are often only created for the smallest (or a small) subset of words that cover the entire scale—a subvocabulary—thereby keeping the number of rules as small as possible (Chapter 6)].

The collection of words, W_i, in the vocabulary and their IT2 FS models, $FOU(W_i)$, constitutes a *Codebook* for an application (A), that is, Codebook = $\{(W_i, FOU(W_i)), i = 1, \ldots, N_A\}$.

The term *fuzzistics,* which is a merging of the words *fuzzy* and *statistics,* was coined by Mendel (2003) to summarize the problem of going from word data collected from a group of subjects, with their inherent random uncertainties that are quantified using statistics, to a word fuzzy set model that captures measures of the

---

[1]Wallsten and Budescu (1995), focus on a variable called *qualitative probability expression* (whose terms are: almost certain, probable, likely, good chance, possible, tossup, unlikely, improbable, doubtful, and almost impossible) for which a natural scale is [0, 1]. Lichtenstein and Newman (1967) collected range data for 41 verbal phrases (e.g., highly probable, rather likely, barely possible, rare, etc.) for which a natural scale is also [0, 1].

[2]The book by O'Hagan et al. (2006) ". . . concerns the elicitation of expert's knowledge about one or more uncertain quantities in probabilistic form, . . . a (joint) probability distribution for the random variable(s) in question." There are many important lessons for workers in the fuzzy set community to be learned from the long history of such probability elicitations, including: (1) although people like to communicate using words, they also want to receive data; (2) aggregation reduces the effects of uncertainty; (3) imprecision cannot be completely removed from elicitation; and, (4) it is impractical to quantify an expert's opinion as a (probability) distribution without imposing some structure on the distribution.

word data uncertainties. When the FS model is an IT2 FS, this is called *type-2 fuzzistics*. The rest of this chapter describes some approaches to type-2 fuzzistics.

3.2 PERSON FOU APPROACH FOR A GROUP OF SUBJECTS

In the *person FOU approach* for a group of subjects[3] [Mendel (2007)]: (1) FOU data that reflect both the intra- and interlevels of uncertainties about a word are collected from a group of people (subjects), and each FOU is called a *person FOU;* (2) an IT2 FS model for a word is defined as a specific aggregation of all person FOUs; and, (3) the aggregated FOU is mathematically modeled and approximated. This approach is based on six premises.[4]

Premise 1. Uncertainty about a word is of two kinds: (1) *intrauncertainty,* which is the uncertainty a person has about the word; and (2) *interuncertainty,* which is the uncertainty that a group of people have about the word.

Focusing first on the intrauncertainty leads us to Premise 2.

Premise 2. *Intrauncertainty* about a word, W, can be modeled using an *interval type-2 person FS*, $\tilde{W}(p_j)$, where $j = 1, \ldots, n_W$. Such an IT2 FS is completely described by its person FOU and so the terms *IT2 person FS* and *person FOU* are used interchangeably. An IT2 FS characterizes a *first-order kind of uncertainty* about a word within each subject, and is chosen because higher-order kinds of uncertainty (explained below) are themselves subject to additional uncertainties, and are, therefore, excluded from this book.

An example of a person FOU is depicted in Fig. 3.1. We believe that a person will only be able to provide a "broad-brush" FOU for a word, where the width of the FOU is associated with how much uncertainty the person has for a specific word. A thin (thick) FOU, or segment thereof, would conceptually be associated with a word for which a person has a small (large) amount of uncertainty. The amount of uncertainty a person has can vary as a function of the primary variable. In the person FOU shown in Fig. 3.1, there is a small range of values for which the person has no uncertainty about the word. Not all persons need to have such an interval.

In principal, a person FOU could be collected from a group of subjects. In practice, this may be very difficult to do because such a subject must understand the

---

[3]The material in this section is taken from Mendel (2007), where this method is called the "person MF approach." Because our emphasis is entirely on IT2 FS models for words, we now prefer to call this method a "person FOU approach."

[4]Wallsten and Budescu's works, which are very relevant to CWW, seem to have been overlooked by the nonpsychological CWW community; for example, their 1995 paper "reviews the relevant literature to develop a theory of how humans process linguistic information about imprecise continuous quantities in the service of decision making, judgment and communication." They summarize their findings as a collection of two background assumptions and six principles. Some of the latter are similar to some of our premises, although they have been formulated for qualitative probability expressions (footnote 1), whereas our premises are more broadly applicable.

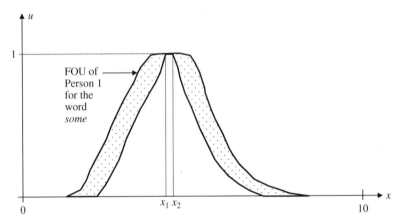

Figure 3.1. FOU of person 1 for the word *some*. The uniform shading indicates that all of the secondary grades equal 1. The flat spot $x \in [x_1, x_2]$ is an interval where Person 1 is absolutely certain about their FOU location. It is not required that there be such a flat spot (Mendel, 2007; © 2007, Elsevier).

concepts of an FS, MF, and an FOU, that is, the subject must be an FS expert. Most subjects (excluding, of course, the readers of this book) have no idea what an FS, MF, or an FOU are. Additionally, no elicitation methodology presently exists to obtain a person FOU from a subject. This is a research opportunity in the new field of type-2 fuzzistics. For the rest of this section, it is assumed [in the spirit of Karl Popper (see Section 1.5)] that, in principal, it is possible to obtain a person FOU.

An IT2 FS captures "first-order uncertainties," whereas a more general T2 FS that has nonuniform secondary grades captures first-and second-order uncertainties. It is the opinion of the authors that to ask subjects to assign anything other than a uniform weighting to their entire FOU is too difficult. It is the senior author's experience from collecting survey information from subjects that they do not like to answer a lot of questions, and they like the questions to be simple. Asking subjects to assign a weighting function to their arbitrarily drawn FOU is much too difficult, even for those of us who are already very familiar with what an FOU is. Asking a subject to provide even a crisp weight (i.e., a number) for a word, about which it has already been argued there is much uncertainty, is contradictory, for how can a subject be absolutely sure about that number? Instead, perhaps a subject might be able to assign linguistic terms (e.g., pretty sure, very sure, etc.) to different regions of their person FOU, indicating their confidence about the FOU in different regions, but such terms are words about which there will be additional uncertainties.

The uncertainty that exists about the person FOU is, therefore, categorized as [Mendel and John (2002)] a *first-order kind of uncertainty,* and the uncertainty that exists about the weight that might be assigned to each element of the person FOU is categorized as a *second-order kind of uncertainty.* When a subject provides their

FOU for a word, the first-order uncertainty is across their entire FOU. Clearly, weight information is itself uncertain, leading to even higher-order (and never-ending) kinds of uncertainty. Although second-order uncertainty may be interesting from a theoretical point of view, in that it lets one use the complete three-dimensional machinery of a T2 FS, it is presently not known how to test the validity of second-order uncertainty by collecting data; hence, in this book, the focus is exclusively on the first-order uncertainty of a person FOU.

A person (p_j) IT2 FS is denoted $\tilde{W}(p_j)$, where symbol W denotes a generic word (term):

$$\tilde{W}(p_j) = \int_{x \in X} \mu_{\tilde{W}}(x \mid p_j)/x \quad j = 1, 2, ..., n_W \tag{3.1}$$

In equation (3.1), there are n_W subjects, and

$$\mu_{\tilde{W}}(x \mid p_j) = \left[a_{\tilde{W}}(x \mid p_j), b_{\tilde{W}}(x \mid p_j) \right] \subseteq [0,1] \quad \forall x \in X \tag{3.2}$$

In equation (3.2), $a_{\tilde{W}}(x|p_j)$ and $b_{\tilde{W}}(x|p_j)$ are the lower and upper bounds, respectively, of the IT2 person FOU. The conditioning notation lets us easily add (or remove) person FOUs to (or from) a database of person FOUs.

Person FOUs are collected from a group of subjects. It is important to collect such FOUs from a representative group; for example, a specific application may only involve teenage girls, beer-drinking men, naturalists, bikers, associate editors, contract managers, airport security personnel, and so on. An example of three person FOUs is depicted in Fig. 3.2 for the word *some*. The FOUs do not have to be smooth, and their upper and lower bounds do not even have to be continuous. The constraints that each person must adhere to when sketching their FOU are that the

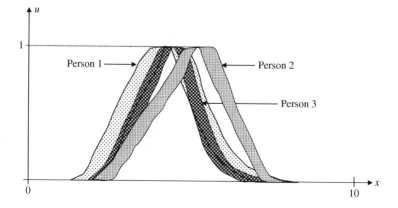

Figure 3.2. FOUs from three people for the word *some*. Again, the uniform shading indicates that all of the secondary grades equal 1 (Mendel, 2007; © 2007, Elsevier).

upper bound cannot exceed 1, the lower bound must not be less than 0, the lower and upper bounds cannot change direction more than one time, and the FOU cannot extend outside of the [0, 10] (or some other established) domain for the primary variable. Each person FOU lets us model the intrauncertainty about a word. The collection of person FOUs lets us model the interuncertainties about a word.

Premise 3: Interuncertainty about a word can be modeled by means of an equally weighted aggregation of each person's word FS, $\tilde{W}(p_j)$ (j = 1, 2, . . . , n_W). This weight can be normalized out of the aggregation, so it can just as well be set equal to 1. Equal weighting also characterizes a first-order kind of uncertainty, but this time across a group of subjects, and is chosen because higher-order kinds of uncertainty (explained below) are themselves subject to additional uncertainties, and are therefore excluded from this book.

Suppose one begins by assuming that interuncertainty about a word can be modeled by means of a weighted aggregation of each person's word FOU, where the weight represents a degree of belief associated with each person. This suggests that a degree of belief is known or can be provided for each person, which may or may not be reasonable. Consider the following three possibilities:

1. All subjects are treated the same, in which case the same weight can be assigned to each person FOU. Although any weight w_W in the range [0, 1] can be assigned to each person (and to all terms), that common weight can always be normalized out of the final description of the fuzzy set; hence, in this case, a unity weight is assigned to each person FOU.
2. Subjects are treated differently, since some subjects may be more knowledgeable about the meaning of a word than others, especially when that word is used in a specific context. In this case, a different weight is assigned to each person, namely $w_W(p_j)$, where that weight is assigned to each person over the entire domain of the word, i.e., over all $x \in X$. The implicit assumptions here are:
   a. Weights $w_W(p_j), j = 1, . . . , n_W$, can be specified as crisp numbers, which is controversial, that is, it is more likely that they can only be assigned linguistically, for example, high confidence or low confidence.
   b. A weight can indeed be assigned to each subject, but who does this—the subject or others?
3. The same as Case 2, except now it is conceivable that a subject's credibility depends on the value of primary variable x, that is, some subjects may be more knowledgeable about a word for certain regions of the variable x than other subjects. Although this may sound far-fetched, this possibility should not be initially excluded when developing a new model. In this case, each weight not only depends upon the specific subject, but also depends upon x, and is, therefore, represented as $w_W(x|p_j)$. The implicit assumptions here are:
   a. Weights $w_W(x|p_j), j = 1, . . . , n_W$, can be specified as crisp functions, which again is controversial; that is, it is more likely that they can only be as-

signed linguistically but now over different regions of primary variable x, for example, high confidence for small values of x, or low confidence for large values of x.

b. A weight function can indeed be assigned to each subject but, again, who does this—the subject or others—and what shape function will be used?

Assuming that each subject can provide their FOU for a word, first-order uncertainty will exist across the entire collection of person MFs, as in Fig. 3.2. Case 1 requires no additional information, whereas Cases 2 and 3 do, and that additional information will itself be uncertain, leading to even higher (and never-ending) kinds of uncertainty; hence, in this book Case 1 is preferred to Cases 2 and 3, and, therefore, it is focused on exclusively.

Premise 4: A natural way to aggregate a group of subject's equally weighted word FOUs is by the mathematical operation of the union.

Two other ways to aggregate are the intersection and addition. The union preserves the commonalities as well as the differences across person FOUs, whereas the intersection preserves only the commonalities[5] across person FOUs. From an information perspective, the intersection discards a lot of information, whereas the union does not. Combining using intersection leads to an FOU that only reveals total agreement across all persons. If a new person came along and their person FOU did not intersect the existing word FOU, then the resulting new word FOU would be vacuous. The union does not have this undesirable property; hence, aggregation of the person FOUs by the union versus the intersection is preferred in this book.

Addition of equally weighted fuzzy sets destroys the underlying requirement that the FOU of the resulting FS must be contained in $[0, 1]^{[0, 1]}$. Of course, an average of the fuzzy sets will preserve this requirement. Because information is lost in averaging, aggregation of the person fuzzy sets by the union is preferred to aggregation by addition.

Finally, the union aggregation preserves the upper and lower bounds that are associated with the set of person FOUs, which to us seems like a desirable property of an aggregator.

Of course, just as data outliers are established and eliminated using statistics, similar things are needed for "outlier person FOUs" (or parts thereof). This can be done on a point-by-point basis (across all n_W person FOUs) for a sampled primary variable. In the rest of this section it is assumed that all outliers have been eliminated.

---

[5]Suppose there are two subsets A and B from the universe of discourse X, where $A = \{a, b, c, d, e, f\}$ and $B = \{a, c, e, f, g, h\}$. Then, the differences (not meant as arithmetic differences) between A and B are the elements g and h in B and the elements b and d in A; hence, $A \cup B = \{a, b, c, d, e, f, g, h\}$ is inclusive in that it does not discard anything. The intersection is exclusive in that it discards g, h, b, and d, that is, $A \cap B = \{a, c, e, f\}$.

From Premise 4, equations (3.1) and (3.2), the following representation for an IT2 FS of a word is obtained:

$$\tilde{W} = \bigcup_{j=1}^{n_W} \tilde{W}(p_j) = \bigcup_{j=1}^{n_W} \int_{x \in X} \mu_{\tilde{W}}(x \mid p_j)/x = \bigcup_{j=1}^{n_W} \int_{x \in X} \left[a_{\tilde{W}}(x \mid p_j), b_{\tilde{W}}(x \mid p_j) \right]/x \quad (3.3)$$

which can also be expressed in terms of vertical slices, as

$$\tilde{W} = \int_{x \in X} \left[\bigcup_{j=1}^{n_W} \mu_{\tilde{W}}(x \mid p_j) \right]/x = \int_{x \in X} \left[\bigcup_{j=1}^{n_W} \left[a_{\tilde{W}}(x \mid p_j), b_{\tilde{W}}(x \mid p_j) \right] \right]/x \quad (3.4)$$

so that the secondary MFs of $\tilde{W}$ can be expressed as:

$$\mu_{\tilde{W}}(x) = \bigcup_{j=1}^{n_W} \mu_{\tilde{W}}(x \mid p_j) = \bigcup_{j=1}^{n_W} \left[a_{\tilde{W}}(x \mid p_j), b_{\tilde{W}}(x \mid p_j) \right] \quad \forall x \in X \quad (3.5)$$

In equations (3.3) and (3.4), $\int$ indicates the union within members of a person fuzzy set, whereas the union sign represents the union across person fuzzy sets; hence, by using both union and $\int$ signs, one is able to distinguish the union of sets versus the union of members within the individual sets. In this representation, duplicate points are not combined, so that the complete identities of the person FOUs are preserved.

This description of a fuzzy set for a word permits us to include both the intra- and interuncertainties that subjects have about the word. It also lets us easily add or remove person fuzzy sets, as desired.

Examining the three person FOUs in Fig. 3.2, it is clear that they are all upper-bounded and lower-bounded. These bounds will be needed shortly, so mathematical equations are developed for them next. Let

$$\underline{\mu}_{\tilde{W}}(x) \equiv \min_{j=1,2,\dots,n_W} a_{\tilde{W}}(x \mid p_j) \quad \forall x \in X \quad (3.6)$$

$$\overline{\mu}_{\tilde{W}}(x) \equiv \max_{j=1,2,\dots,n_W} b_{\tilde{W}}(x \mid p_j) \quad \forall x \in X \quad (3.7)$$

$\underline{\mu}_{\tilde{W}}(x)$ and $\overline{\mu}_{\tilde{W}}(x)$ are the lower (bound) and upper (bound) MF values of $\tilde{W}$ at any $x \in X$, respectively, and

$$\underline{\tilde{W}} \equiv LMF(\tilde{W}) = \int_{x \in X} \underline{\mu}_{\tilde{W}}(x)/x \quad (3.8)$$

$$\overline{\tilde{W}} \equiv UMF(\tilde{W}) = \int_{x \in X} \overline{\mu}_{\tilde{W}}(x)/x \quad (3.9)$$

Note that these lower and upper MFs are T1 (bounding) FSs.

Beginning with the three person FOUs for the word *some* that are depicted in Fig. 3.2, the lower and upper MFs are easily established. They are depicted in Fig. 3.3.

The model in equation (3.4) contains all of the information in the constituent person FOUs. No information has been lost in this model. Although it is possible to develop formulas for performing set-theoretic operations for fuzzy sets modeled by equation (3.4) (which are needed in order to implement a CWW engine), this is not done here, because equation (3.4) is not a parsimonious model. It can result in huge numbers of computations and enormous memory requirements. Instead, parametric models are developed for word fuzzy sets.

In the theory of modeling, for example, system identification [e.g., Ljung (1987) and Soderstrom and Stoica (1989)] a trade-off is always made between preserving all of the data (information) and achieving a useful and parsimonious model. That same fork in the road has now been reached for the fuzzy set of a word, so we shall follow the widely used approach taken in modeling theory, of approximating the data by means of *parametric models.* Recall, for example, that a time series can be approximated using moving average, autoregressive, or autoregressive-moving average models, and many other kinds of time-series models. The point of this example is to illustrate that more than one parametric model is always available. The user (designer) must always make a choice of the model and then fit that model to the data. Parsimony is achieved by choosing a model with the smallest number of parameters that best approximates the data (in some sense). Next, how to obtain a parsimonious model for $\tilde{W}$ is explained.

Figure 3.2 suggests that by including more and more person FOUs, a region will become filled in within which all person FOUs may lay.

Premise 5: When a person FOU has been collected from a sufficient number of subjects, their union will be a filled-in fuzzy set (i.e., an FOU). Let $\tilde{W}_{FI}$ denote the

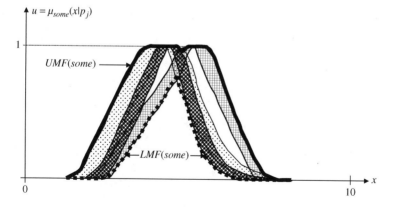

Figure 3.3. Lower and upper MFs for the three person FOUs depicted in Fig. 3.2 (Mendel, 2007; © 2007, Elsevier).

filled-in word fuzzy set. Its associated FOU—the filled-in FOU—is denoted $FOU(\tilde{W}_{FI})$. It is assumed that filling has occurred, or is created, so that the union of person FOUs is itself an IT2 FS (i.e., in order to be a legitimate FOU of an IT2 FS, the FOU of the union of person FOUs must not have gaps).

A filled-in FOU for the example in Fig. 3.2—$FOU(some_{FI})$—is depicted in Fig. 3.4. Observe that the filled-in FOU is bounded from above by $UMF(some)$ and from below by $LMF(some)$, as in Fig. 3.3. Regardless of how many subjects are surveyed, the union of their person FOUs will have lower and upper bounds, so it is not necessary to quantify the phrase "sufficient number of subjects" in order to obtain, or create, a filled-in fuzzy set. Of course, as more subjects are added to the pool, the shapes of these bounds may change.

Let $J_x(\tilde{W}_{FI})$ denote the primary membership of x for filled-in word fuzzy set $\tilde{W}_{FI}$. Because of fill-in, $J_x(\tilde{W}_{FI})$ is now a continuous interval, that is,

$$J_x(\tilde{W}_{FI}) = \left[\underline{\mu}_{\tilde{W}}(x), \overline{\mu}_{\tilde{W}}(x)\right] \tag{3.10}$$

Using equation (3.10), the following representation for the FOU of a filled-in word fuzzy set is postulated:

$$FOU(\tilde{W}_{FI}) = \int_{x \in X} J_x(\tilde{W}_{FI})/x = \int_{x \in X} \left[\underline{\mu}_{\tilde{W}}(x), \overline{\mu}_{\tilde{W}}(x)\right]/x \tag{3.11}$$

It is important to understand that the upper and lower MF values used in equation (3.11) are obtained directly from the person FOUs through a bounding procedure, which occurs automatically though the union aggregation. As explained earlier, often the notations $FOU(\tilde{W}_{FI})$ and $\tilde{W}_{FI}$ are used interchangeably.

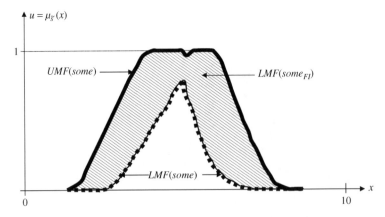

Figure 3.4. Filled-in FOU for *some* based on the three-person upper and lower MFs depicted in Fig. 3.2. Note that *s* stands for *some* (Mendel, 2007; © 2007, Elsevier).

It should be clear by comparing equation (3.11) with equations (3.8) and (3.9), that

$$LMF(\tilde{W}_{FI}) = LMF(\tilde{W}) \tag{3.12}$$

$$UMF(\tilde{W}_{FI}) = UMF(\tilde{W}) \tag{3.13}$$

To partially summarize, what has been done so far is to go from $\tilde{W}$, the union of person FOUs, to $\tilde{W}_{FI}$, the filled-in word fuzzy set, whose FOU is the fill-in of all points between the lower and upper MFs of the FOU of $\tilde{W}$. No parametric approximation has occurred yet.

Premise 6: A filled-in parametric model, $\hat{W}$ ($\hat{W}$ for short), for $\tilde{W}_{FI}$ in equation (3.11) is one that is described by two functions, $\underline{\mu}_{\hat{W}}(x)$ and $\overline{\mu}_{\hat{W}}(x)$. These functions have shapes that are chosen ahead of time (e.g., triangular, piecewise-linear, or trapezoidal) and each shape is characterized by a small number of parameters that are fixed during some sort of design procedure.

$\underline{\mu}_{\hat{W}}(x)$ is an approximation to $LMF(\tilde{W}_{FI})$, and $\overline{\mu}_{\hat{W}}(x)$ is an approximation to $UMF(\tilde{W}_{FI})$. If no parameters are shared by $\underline{\mu}_{\hat{W}}(x)$ and $\overline{\mu}_{\hat{W}}(x)$, then, for example, two independent least-squares approximation problems can easily be established for determining the parameters of $\underline{\mu}_{\hat{W}}(x)$ and $\overline{\mu}_{\hat{W}}(x)$. The approximation problem for $\underline{\mu}_{\hat{W}}(x)$ only uses the data in $LMF(\tilde{W}_{FI})$ and is unconstrained, whereas the approximation problem for $\overline{\mu}_{\hat{W}}(x)$ only uses the data in $UMF(\tilde{W}_{FI})$ but is constrained so that at least at one value of x $\overline{\mu}_{\hat{W}}(x) = 1$. In this way, the resulting T1 upper-bound FS will be a normal FS. Note that the constraint on $\overline{\mu}_{\hat{W}}(x)$ can automatically be satisfied by an appropriate choice for the shape of $\overline{\mu}_{\hat{W}}(x)$ and so one does not have to solve a constrained optimization problem.

Figure 3.5 depicts a trapezoidal function approximation to the UMF of the Fig. 3.4 $FOU(some_{FI})$, and a triangular function approximation to the LMF of the Fig. 3.4 $FOU(some_{FI})$. The trapezoidal function, which is not necessarily symmetrical, is characterized by the four parameters, a, b, c, and d. Because of its built-in flat top between b and c, $\overline{\mu}_{\hat{W}}(x)$ is a normal FS, and the parameters of this UMF approximation can be obtained by solving an unconstrained optimization problem. The triangular function, which is also not necessarily symmetrical, is characterized by the three parameters, e, f, and g, and they can also be obtained by solving an unconstrained optimization problem. Even though it may look like $f = (b + c)/2$, it would be unwise to impose this constraint ahead of time. Instead, the data should establish the seven parameters.

A simpler approach to least-squares approximation is to use a trapezoid to bound the UMF and a triangle to bound the LMF. This approach is consistent with the results that are described in Section 3.5.2.

Just as the filled-in word fuzzy set $\tilde{W}_{FI}$ has an FOU associated with it, namely $FOU(\tilde{W}_{FI})$ [see equation (3.11)], $\hat{W}$ also has a FOU associated with it, namely $FOU(\hat{W})$:

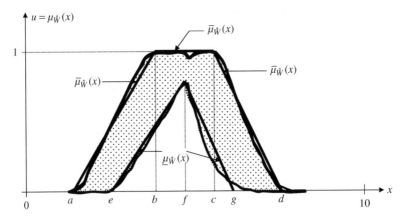

Figure 3.5. Trapezoidal approximation to the filled-in data upper MF, and triangular approximation to the filled-in data lower MF for *some*. Note that $W = some$ (Mendel, 2007; © 2007, Elsevier).

$$FOU(\hat{W}) = \int_{x \in X}\left[\underline{\mu}_{\hat{W}}(x), \overline{\mu}_{\hat{W}}(x)\right]\big/x \qquad (3.14)$$

The closer that $\underline{\mu}_{\hat{W}}(x)$ and $\overline{\mu}_{\hat{W}}(x)$ respectively approximate $\underline{\mu}_{\tilde{W}}(x)$ and $\overline{\mu}_{\tilde{W}}(x)$ over $\forall x \in X$, the closer $FOU(\hat{W})$ approximates $FOU(\tilde{W}_{FI})$.

Adding or removing person FOUs (i.e., increasing or decreasing n_W) will very likely cause $\underline{\mu}_{\hat{W}}(x)$ and $\overline{\mu}_{\hat{W}}(x)$ to change, so if this is done $FOU(\hat{W})$ would have to be recomputed. This is easy to do.

In summary, what has been done in this section is to go from $\tilde{W}$, the union of person FOUs, to $\tilde{W}_{FI}$, the filled-in word fuzzy set, whose FOU is the fill-in of all points between the lower and upper bounds of the FOU of $\tilde{W}$, and finally to $\hat{W}$, a parsimonious approximation to the word fuzzy set. This approximation uses data that are obtained from subjects. This modeling process is encapsulated symbolically as:

$$\tilde{W} \rightarrow \tilde{W}_{FI} \rightarrow \hat{W} \qquad (3.15)$$

Strong points of this approach are:

1. The union of the person FOUs (the data) establishes the shape of the FOU directly.
2. No statistics about the data are used, that is, all of the data (the person FOUs) are used so that no information is lost.
3. If all uncertainty disappears [i.e., all subjects provide the same person MF (not an FOU, but a T1 FS)], then the IT2 FS word model reduces to a T1 FS word model.

The weak point of this approach is it requires subjects to be knowledgeable about fuzzy sets. Unfortunately, this weakness may be so large that (in the opinion of the authors) that it may obliterate the advantages of the approach; hence, to date the person FOU approach is very limited in applicability.

We close this section by reminding the readers that person FOUs can only be collected from FS experts and, therefore, other techniques must be established for collecting word data from the vast majority of subjects. Note that[6] if the method that is used to collect word data from a group of subjects introduces uncertainties because the subjects do not understand something about the method (e.g., they do not understand what an FOU is), then the method's uncertainties become comingled with the subject's uncertainties about the word, and this is not good.

3.3 COLLECTING INTERVAL END-POINT DATA

In the *interval end-points approach* (described in Section 3.4) and *interval approach* (described in Section 3.5) for a group of subjects: (1) interval end-point data about a word are collected; (2) statistics (mean and standard deviation) are established for the data, and (3) those statistics are mapped into a prespecified parametric FS model. These approaches are analogous to statistical modeling in which one first chooses the underlying probability distribution (i.e., data-generating model) and then fits the parameters of that model using data and a meaningful design method, for example the method of maximum likelihood. To begin, a methodology for collecting interval end-point data from a group of subjects is reviewed.

3.3.1 Methodology[7]

After a scale is established and a vocabulary of words is created that is believed to cover the entire scale, the methodology for collecting interval end-point data from a group of subjects consists of two steps: (1) randomize the words, and (2) survey a group of subjects to provide end-point data for the words on the scale.

Words need to be randomized so that subjects will not correlate their word-interval end points from one word to the next. The randomized words are used in a survey, whose wording might be:

> Below are a number of labels that describe an interval or a "range" that falls somewhere between 0 and 10. For each label, please tell us where this range would start and where it would end. (In other words, please tell us how much of the distance from 0 to 10 this range would cover.) For example, the range "quite a bit" might start at 6 and end at 8. It is important to note that *not all ranges are the same,* and *ranges can overlap.*

[6]See also the discussions in Appendix 3A.
[7]The material in this subsection is taken from Mendel (2007) and Mendel (2001, Chapter 2).

Our experiences with carrying out such surveys show that anyone can answer such questions and people understand what an interval is, and, therefore, this method does not introduce methodological errors.

Example 3.1 [Mendel (2001, Chapter 2)]. An example of a 16-word vocabulary is: *None, Very Little, A Small Amount, A Little Bit, A Bit, Some, A Moderate Amount, A Fair Amount, A Good Amount, A Considerable Amount, A Sizeable Amount, A Large Amount, A Substantial Amount, A Lot, An Extreme Amount,* and *A Maximum Amount.* End-point datasets were collected from 87 students; 17 datasets had bad data (e.g., some students filled in 0–10 as the range for of all of the words). Of the remaining 70 datasets, 40 were from men, 11 from women, and 19 were from students who chose not to identify their sex. In the following results, the sex of the respondent is not distinguished, although, clearly, one could do so if it were felt to be important.[8] Survey results are summarized in Table 3.1.

Because a range was requested for each label, and each range is defined by the two numbers *start* and *end,* the survey led to sample statistics for these two numbers, namely, their mean and standard deviation. The two end-point standard deviations represent the uncertainties associated with each label. Observe that standard deviations are not the same for the *start* and *end* values for each label.

The Table 3.1 data are also summarized in Fig. 3.6. For each label, there are two circles with a heavy solid line between them. The circles are located at the mean start and end points for each label. The dashed lines to the left of the left-hand circles and to the right of the right-hand circles each terminate in a vertical bar equal to one standard deviation, listed in Table 3.1 for the mean start and end points, respectively.

Observe, from Fig. 3.6 that:

1. The dashed portions of the intervals for each label represent the label's uncertainty. For illustrative purposes only, minus one standard deviation has been shown for the left end of an interval, whereas plus one standard deviation has been shown for the right end of an interval. Exactly how many standard deviations should be used is discussed below in Section 3.3.2.

2. Except for a small number of words that appear to have equal uncertainties for both end points (a moderate amount, a fair amount, a good amount, and a considerable amount), most words have unequal uncertainties for their end points, and there always is more uncertainty for the end point that is closer to the midpoint of the 0–10 scale, that is, toward the number 5.

3. There is a gap between the mean-value right end point of *none* and left end point of *very little,* implying that either another word should be inserted between them or they should be combined. For illustrative purposes, in our following discussions, the latter is done and the word is called *none to very little.*

---

[8]Perhaps gender differences have to be considered when designing a perceptual computer, for example, touching usually implies a much higher subjective judgment level of flirtation for a man than it does for a woman.

Table 3.1. Processed survey results for16 words

No.	Range label	Mean		Standard deviation	
		Start	End	Start	End
1	None	0.0143	0.2286	0.1195	0.9036
2	Very little	0.8714	2.2571	0.9313	1.3693
3	A small amount	1.3000	3.6429	0.8739	1.1800
4	A little bit	1.3143	3.0714	0.8434	1.6180
5	A bit	1.7000	3.7571	1.4876	1.8371
6	Some	1.8286	4.2857	1.2391	1.6694
7	A moderate amount	4.1429	6.1714	1.1457	1.1668
8	A fair amount	4.2571	6.2286	1.2931	1.3424
9	A good amount	4.9429	7.4429	1.4928	1.3688
10	A considerable amount	5.3571	7.9857	1.5700	1.5834
11	A sizeable amount	5.6571	8.2571	1.9700	1.5575
12	A large amount	6.0857	8.9000	1.6572	1.0377
13	A substantial amount	6.2571	8.6429	1.8703	1.2399
14	A lot	6.7429	9.3857	1.9611	0.7669
15	An extreme amount	7.8857	9.6000	2.1027	0.7690
16	A maximum amount	8.8857	9.7571	2.4349	1.1221

Source: Mendel, 2001; © 2001, Prentice-Hall.

4. People seem to agree that *none* starts at zero, and there is very little uncertainty about this (see the standard deviation in Table 3.1); that is, to people, the word *none* seems to have a very strong connotation with the number zero.

5. The same cannot be said for the label *a maximum amount.* The right-hand mean value for its range is 9.7571 and not 10. One explanation for this is that people may be adverse to assigning the largest possible number to any label, because of an expectation that there could be another label that should have the largest number associated with it.[9] Because the labels were randomized, the students may have expected a phrase even stronger than *a maximum amount,* and they did not check the complete list of 16 words to see if such a stronger phrase actually occurred.

6. The 16 words do not quite cover the 0–10 interval, but this only occurs at the right-most extreme values.

7. There seems to be a linguistic gap between the solid lines for the labels *some* and *a moderate amount* as evidenced by the small degree of overlap between these lines. Perhaps this gap could be filled in by adding the word *somewhat moderate.*

8. In Fig. 3.7, the sets *none* and *very little* have been combined and five labels are shown whose intervals between their mean start and end points cover

[9]Why, for example, if the top grade on an examination is *excellent* and the range for *excellent* is 8–10, are some people assigned an 8, and probably no one is assigned a 10? Perhaps, it is the expectation that someone else will do better, or that no one is perfect.

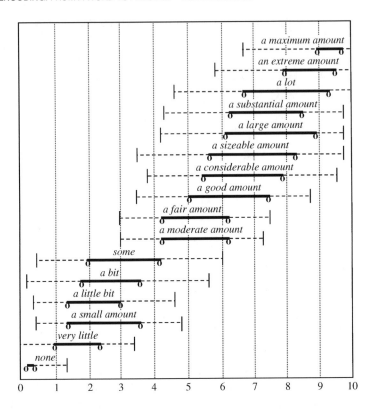

Figure 3.6. All 16 labels with their intervals and uncertainties (Mendel, 2001; © 2001, Prentice-Hall).

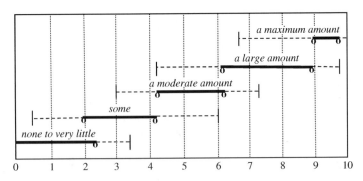

Figure 3.7. Although the five labels cover 0–10, there is not much overlap between some of them. It is when the standard deviation information is used that sufficient overlap is achieved, (Mendel, 2001; © 2001, Prentice-Hall).

the 0–10 range (except for the right-end anomaly). These are not the only five labels that could have been chosen. For example, instead of using *a moderate amount, a fair amount* could have been used, or instead of using *a large amount, a substantial amount* could have been used. This suggests that there is a strong linguistic similarity between certain words, something that is explored in more detail in Chapter 4.

9. The intervals between the mean start and end points in Fig. 3.7 are not of equal size and there is more (or less) overlap between some than between others.

10. It is possible to cover the 0–10 range with five labels, as indicated in Fig. 3.7; however, as just mentioned, there is not much overlap between the solid lines for some of the labels; but, when the standard deviation information is used, then sufficient overlap is achieved.

11. It is also possible to cover the 0–10 interval with four or three labels (see Fig. 3.8). The smallest number of labels from the 16 labels used in our survey that cover the interval is three and this is only possible because of linguistic uncertainties; that is, overlap occurs for the three labels only because of uncertainty.

Linguistic uncertainty appears to be useful in that it lets the 0–10 range be covered with a much smaller number of labels than without it. It also seems pretty clear from the survey results that words do indeed mean different things to different people.

3.3.2 Establishing End-Point Statistics for the Data

The interval end-point data that are collected from a group of subjects are treated as random. Consequently, for each word interval the following four statistics can be computed: sample mean and standard deviation of left end point, x_{avg}^l and s^l, and sample mean and standard deviation of right end-point, x_{avg}^r and s^r. Examples of such statistics are depicted in Figs. 3.6–3.8. Note that when end-point data have

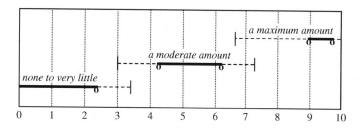

Figure 3.8. The smallest number of labels that cover the interval 0–10 is three, and this is only possible because of uncertainties, (Mendel 2001; © 2001, Prentice-Hall).

been collected from more than 30 subjects who are chosen independently, then these statistics will be approximately normal (via the Central Limit Theorem) [Walpole et al. (2007)].

While it is easy to use the sample means, it is less clear how to use the sample standard deviations; that is, what multiple of them should be used? Fortunately, statistics provides a solution to this difficulty.

For a normal distribution [Walpole et al. (2007)] of measurements with unknown mean and standard deviation, tolerance limits are given by $x_{avg}^l \pm ks^l$ (or $x_{avg}^r \pm ks^r$), where tolerance factor k is determined so that one can assert with $100(1 - \gamma)\%$ confidence that the given limits contain at least the proportion $1 - \alpha$ of the measurements. Table 3.2 gives k for eight values of n (the number of sampled subjects), two values of $1 - \gamma$, and two values of $1 - \alpha$. Knowing n and choosing values for $1 - \gamma$ and $1 - \alpha$, one can obtain k. For example, when data have been collected from 30 subjects, using $k = 2.549$ means one can be 95% confident that 95% of the 30 data fall in the intervals $x_{avg}^l \pm 2.549s^l$ and $x_{avg}^r \pm 2.549s^r$.

3.4 INTERVAL END-POINTS APPROACH

In the interval end-points approach, each subject provides the end points of an interval associated with a word on a prescribed scale, as just described. The mean and standard deviation are computed for the two end points using the data collected from all of the subjects.[10] These end-point statistics are then mapped into an IT2 FS model for the word by using end-point bounds of the centroid of a prespecified FOU [Mendel and Wu (2007a)]. Even though there are no closed-form formulas for the centroid of an IT2 FS (Chapter 2), Mendel and Wu (2006, 2007b) have been able to compute closed-form formulas for the lower and upper bounds of the centroid end points for word W, $c_l(W)$ and $c_r(W)$, namely $\underline{c}_l(W)$, $\overline{c}_l(W)$, $\underline{c}_r(W)$, and $\overline{c}_r(W)$. These bounds are in terms of the geometric properties of $FOU(\tilde{W})$, namely: area under $FOU(\tilde{W})$, area under $LMF(\tilde{W})$, area under $UMF(\tilde{W})$, and centroid of $FOU(\tilde{W})$. Their papers provide many examples for both symmetric and nonsymmetric interior and shoulder FOUs, in which the four bounds are expressed as explicit nonlinear functions of the FOU parameters.

Mendel and Wu (2007b) establish two design equations that let them map interval end-point data statistics into closed-form formulas for the parameters of a[11] two-parameter symmetrical interior FOU. Although a strong point for their method is that it is not limited to people who are knowledgeable about fuzzy sets, because most words do not have symmetrical intervals of uncertainty for both their left and

---

[10]Lichtenstein and Newman (1967) collected range data—interval end points—for 41 verbal phrases that are associated with numerical probabilities on the scale [0, 1]; however, they only provide the mean (as well as the range) for 180 intervals collected for each phrase. They do not provide the standard deviations for the two end points of an interval.

[11]In order to obtain a unique solution for parameters of an FOU, the FOU must be characterized by exactly as many parameters as there are design equations.

Table 3.2. Tolerance factor k for a number of collected data (n), a proportion of the data $(1 - \alpha)$, and a confidence level

n	$1 - \gamma = 0.95$ $1 - \alpha$		$1 - \gamma = 0.99$ $1 - \alpha$	
	0.90	0.95	0.90	0.95
10	2.839	3.379	3.582	4.265
15	2.480	2.954	2.945	3.507
20	2.310	2.752	2.659	3.168
30	2.140	2.549	2.358	2.841
50	1.996	2.379	2.162	2.576
100	1.874	2.233	1.977	2.355
1000	1.709	2.036	1.736	2.718
∞	1.645	1.960	1.645	1.960

Source: Walpole et al. (2007).

right end points (e.g., see Figs. 3.5–3.7), their results are very limited, and comparable results have yet to be obtained for nonsymmetrical interior FOUs and left- and right-shoulder FOUs. Additional difficulties with their approach are the shape of the FOU must be chosen ahead of time, and if all uncertainty disappears (i.e., all subjects provide the same intervals) then their IT2 FS word model does not reduce to a T1 FS word model. The latter is a very serious shortcoming of their interval end-points approach, because adherence to the Karnik–Mendel design requirement [Karnik and Mendel (1998), Mendel (2001)], something that we advocate, requires that, when all sources of uncertainty disappear, a T2 design must reduce to a T1 design. Consequently, no details for the interval end-point approach are provided in this book.

3.5 INTERVAL APPROACH

In this section,[12] the *interval approach* (IA) to T2 fuzzistics is presented. The IA captures the strong points of both the person-MF and interval end points approaches, that is, it (1) collects interval end-point data from a group of subjects, (2) does not require subjects to be knowledgeable about fuzzy sets, (3) has a straightforward mapping from data to an FOU, (4) does not require an a priori assumption about whether or not an FOU is symmetric or nonsymmetric, and, (5) leads to an IT2 FS word model that reduces to a T1 FS word model automatically if all subjects provide the same intervals.

The basic idea of the IA is to map each subject's data interval into a prespecified T1 person MF, and to interpret the latter as an embedded T1 FS of an IT2 FS (this is motivated by the Wavy Slice Representation Theorem for an IT2 FS that is explained in Section 2.4). The IA consists of two parts, the *data part* (Fig. 3.9) and the

[12]The material in this section is taken from Liu and Mendel (2008).

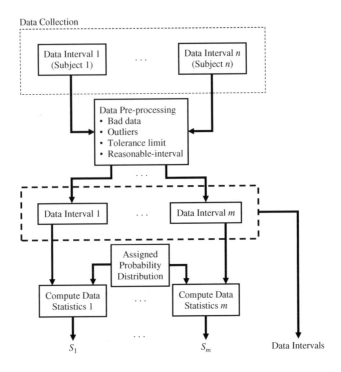

Figure 3.9. Data part of the IA approach. Note that the output statistics $S_1 \ldots, S_m$ feed into the fuzzy part of IA in Fig. 3.10 (Liu and Mendel, 2008; © 2008, IEEE).

Fuzzy Set (FS) Part (Fig. 3.10). In the data part, data that have been collected from a group of subjects are preprocessed, after which data statistics are computed for the surviving intervals. In the FS part, FS uncertainty measures are established for a prespecified T1 MF [always beginning with the assumption that the FOU is an interior FOU (see Fig. 2.4), and, if need be, later switching to a shoulder FOU (see Fig. 2.4)]. Then the parameters of the T1 MF are determined using the data statistics, and the derived T1 MFs are aggregated using union leading to an FOU for a word, and, finally, to a mathematical model for the FOU.

Sections 3.5.1 and 3.5.2 explain each of the blocks in Figs. 3.9 and 3.10.

3.5.1   Data Part

Once data intervals $[a^{(i)}, b^{(i)}]$ have been collected from a group of n subjects ($i = 1, \ldots, n$) for a word, the data part of the IA consists of two major steps: (1) preprocessing the n data intervals, and (2) computing statistics for the data intervals that survive the preprocessing step. The details of these steps are described in this section. They are applied to the data intervals for each codebook word one word at a time.

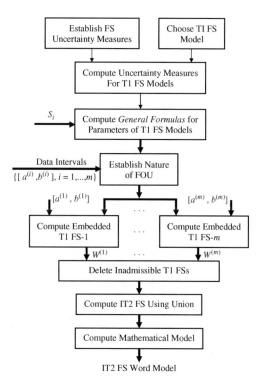

Figure 3.10. FS part of the IA approach (Liu and Mendel, 2008; © 2008, IEEE).

3.5.1.1 *Data Preprocessing.* Preprocessing the n interval end-point data $[a^{(i)},$ $b^{(i)}]$ $(i = 1, \ldots, n)$ consists of four stages: (1) bad data processing, (2) outlier processing, (3) tolerance-limit processing, and (4) reasonable-interval processing. As a result of data preprocessing, some of the n interval data are discarded and the remaining m intervals are renumbered, $1, 2, \ldots, m$. In the rest of this section, details are provided for each of these four stages.

Stage 1—Bad Data Processing. Such processing removes nonsensical results (some subjects do not take a survey seriously and so provide useless results). If interval end points satisfy

$$\left. \begin{array}{l} 0 \le a^{(i)} \le 10 \\ 0 \le b^{(i)} \le 10 \\ b^{(i)} \ge a^{(i)} \end{array} \right\} \; i = 1,...,n \qquad (3.16)$$

then an interval is accepted; otherwise, it is rejected. These conditions are obvious and do not need further explanations. After bad data processing, there will be $n' \le n$ remaining data intervals.

Stage 2—Outlier Processing. Such processing uses a Box and Whisker test [Walpole, et al. (2007)] to eliminate outliers. Recall that outliers are points that are unusually large or small.

A Box and Whisker test is usually stated in terms of first and third quartiles and an interquartile range. The first and third quartiles, $Q(0.25)$ and $Q(0.75)$, contain 25% and 75% of the data, respectively. The interquartile range, IQR, is the difference between the third and first quartiles; hence, IQR contains 50% of the data between the first and third quartiles.

Any point that is more than $1.5IQR$ above the third quartile or more than $1.5IQR$ below the first quartile is considered an outlier [Walpole, et al. (2007)]. Consequently, if the subject interval end-points $a^{(i)}$ and $b^{(i)}$, and the interval's length $L^{(i)}$ satisfy

$$\left.\begin{array}{l} a^{(i)} \in [Q_a(0.25)-1.5IQR_a, Q_a(0.75)+1.5IQR_a] \\ b^{(i)} \in [Q_b(0.25)-1.5IQR_b, Q_b(0.75)+1.5IQR_b] \\ L^{(i)} \in [Q_L(0.25)-1.5IQR_L, Q_L(0.75)+1.5IQR_L] \end{array}\right\} \ i = 1,...,n' \qquad (3.17)$$

a data interval is accepted; otherwise, it is rejected. In these equations, Q_a (Q_b, Q_L) and IQR_a (IQR_b, IQR_L) are the quartile and interquartile ranges for the left (right) end-point and interval length.

After outlier processing, there will be $m' \le n'$ remaining data intervals for which the following data statistics are then computed: m_l, s_l (sample mean and standard deviation of the m' left end-points), m_r, s_r (sample mean and standard deviation of the m' right end-points), and m_L, s_L (sample mean and standard deviation of the lengths of the m' intervals).

Stage 3—Tolerance Limit Processing. If a data interval $[a^{(i)}, b^{(i)}]$ and its length $L^{(i)}$ satisfy [Walpole, et al. (2007)]

$$\left.\begin{array}{l} a^{(i)} \in [m_l - ks_l, m_l + ks_l] \\ b^{(i)} \in [m_r - ks_r, m_r + ks_r] \\ L^{(i)} \in [m_L - ks_L, m_L + ks_L] \end{array}\right\} \ i = 1,...,m' \qquad (3.18)$$

it is accepted, otherwise it is rejected. In equation (3.18), tolerance factor k is determined as explained in Section 3.3.2: if $k = 2.549$ then one can assert with 95% confidence that the given limits contain at least 95% of the subject data intervals.

Assumption: Data interval end points are approximately normal, so that the tolerance limits that are given in Table 3.2 can be used.

After tolerance limit processing, there will be $m'' \le m'$ remaining data intervals ($1 \le m'' \le n$), and the following data statistics are then recomputed: m_l, s_l (sample mean and standard deviation of the m'' left end-points), and m_r, s_r (sample mean and standard deviation of the m'' right end-points).

Stage 4—Reasonable-Interval Processing. In addition to focusing on the maxim, "words mean different things to different people" (which was our rationale for using IT2 FS models for words), one also needs to focus on the maxim, "words mean similar things to different people." In fact, if there is understanding about a word across a group of subjects, it is the latter that causes it. This second maxim led us[13] to require only overlapping intervals be kept. Such intervals are called *reasonable,* as defined below.

Definition 3.1. A data interval is said to be *reasonable* if it overlaps with another data interval in the sense of Fig. 3.11.

In the last step of data preprocessing, only reasonable data intervals are kept. Appendix 3B provides a derivation of the following.

Reasonable-Interval Test: IF

$$\left.\begin{array}{l} a^{(i)} < \xi* \\ b^{(i)} > \xi* \end{array}\right\} \quad \forall i = 1, ..., m'' \tag{3.19}$$

where $\xi*$ is one of the values

$$\xi* = \frac{(m_r \sigma_l^2 - m_l \sigma_r^2) \pm \sigma_l \sigma_r \left[(m_l - m_r)^2 + 2(\sigma_l^2 - \sigma_r^2) \ln(\sigma_l / \sigma_r)\right]^{1/2}}{\sigma_l^2 - \sigma_r^2} \tag{3.20}$$

such that

$$m_l \leq \xi* \leq m_r \tag{3.21}$$

THEN the data interval is kept; OTHERWISE, it is deleted.

As a result of reasonable-interval processing, some of the m'' data intervals may be discarded and there will finally be m remaining data intervals ($1 \leq m \leq n$) that are renumbered, $1, 2, ..., m$.

In summary, data preprocessing starts with all n data intervals and ends with m data intervals:

$$\begin{array}{ccccccc} & \text{Bad Data} & \text{Outliers} & \text{Tolerance Limits} & & \text{Reasonable Interval} & \\ n & \rightarrow & n' & \rightarrow & m' & \rightarrow & m'' & \rightarrow & m \end{array}$$

3.5.1.2 *Compute Data Statistics for Each Interval.* A probability distribution is assigned to each of the m surviving data intervals after which statistics are

---

[13]In a first attempt at the IA [Liu and Mendel (2007)], only the first three stages of data preprocessing were used. FOUs were obtained that did not look so good and many were filled in or almost filled in, that is, $LMF(\tilde{W}) \approx 0$. Because the centroid of a filled-in FOU is completely independent of $UMF(\tilde{W})$, such a FOU is not considered to be a good one [Mendel and Wu (2007c); see, also, Property 3 in Section 2.6.2]. As a result, something else had to be done.

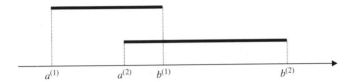

Figure 3.11. An example of two overlapping intervals for the same word. The intervals are raised off of the horizontal axis just for the purpose of clarity (Liu and Mendel, 2008; © 2008, IEEE).

computed for each interval using the assumed probability model and the interval end-points. These statistics are used as described in Section 3.5.2.4.

Although many choices are possible for an assumed probability distribution for a subject's data interval, unless a subject provides more information about that interval (e.g., a greater belief in the center of the interval) then a *uniform distribution* is most sensible, and is the one chosen herein.[14] According to Dubois et al. (2004), "... a uniform probability distribution on a bounded interval ... is the most natural probabilistic representation of incomplete knowledge when only the support is known. It is non-committal in the sense of maximal entropy ... and it applies Laplace's indifference principle stating that what is equipossible is equiprobable."

In order to keep things as simple as possible, only two statistics are used for a uniform distribution: its mean and standard deviation. Recall that if a random variable Y is uniformly distributed in $[a, b]$ [Walpole, et al. (2007)] then

$$m_Y = \frac{a+b}{2} \tag{3.22}$$

$$\sigma_Y = \frac{b-a}{\sqrt{12}} \tag{3.23}$$

In the second stage of the data part, data statistics $S_1, \ldots, S_m$ are computed for each interval, $[a^{(i)}, b^{(i)}]$, where

$$S_i = (m_Y^{(i)}, \sigma_Y^{(i)}) \quad i = 1, \ldots, m \tag{3.24}$$

---

[14]Dubois et al. (2004) explain how to map a collection of confidence intervals into a symmetrical-triangle T1 MF in which the confidence intervals are associated with data that are collected from a group of subjects about a single point. More specifically, in their problem n measurements, $y_1, y_2, \ldots, y_n$, are collected, after which the sample mean, $\overline{m}_y$, is computed, as $\overline{m}_y = \sum_{i=1}^{n} y_i / n$. The α confidence intervals of $\overline{m}_y$, denoted $[\underline{CI}(\alpha), \overline{CI}(\alpha)]$, are then computed for a fixed value of α. When each confidence interval is assumed to be uniformly distributed, their method maps the confidence intervals into a symmetric triangular fuzzy number.

Note, however, their problem is different from ours, because in our problem the starting point is a collection of n intervals rather than a collection of n numbers, so their results have not been used by us.

and these data statistics are then used in the FS part of the IA, where they are mapped into the parameters of a T1 MF, as explained in Section 3.5.2.4.

This completes the data part of the IA.

3.5.2 Fuzzy Set Part

The FS Part of the IA (Fig. 3.10) consists of nine steps, each of which is described in this section.

3.5.2.1 Choose a T1 FS Model. In the present IA, because the mapping from an interval of data to a T1 MF only uses the mean and variance of the (just) assumed uniform probability distribution, only T1 MFs with two degrees of freedom can be used. In this chapter, only a symmetrical triangle interior T1 MF, or a left-shoulder T1 MF, or a right-shoulder T1 MF are used.

3.5.2.2 Establish FS Uncertainty Measures. Although many choices are possible for uncertainty measures of a T1 FS (Klir , 2006) our approach is to focus on simplicity; therefore, we use the mean and standard deviation of a T1 FS.

Definition 3.2. The mean and standard deviation of a T1 FS A are:

$$m_A = \frac{\int_{a_{MF}}^{b_{MF}} x\mu_A(x)dx}{\int_{a_{MF}}^{b_{MF}} \mu_A(x)dx} \tag{3.25}$$

$$\sigma_A = \left[\frac{\int_{a_{MF}}^{b_{MF}} (x - m_A)^2 \mu_A(x)dx}{\int_{a_{MF}}^{b_{MF}} \mu_A(x)dx}\right]^{1/2} \tag{3.26}$$

where a_{MF} and b_{MF} are the parameters of the MFs that are depicted in the figures of Table 3.3.

Obviously, if $\mu_A(x)/\int_{a_{MF}}^{b_{MF}}\mu_A(x)dx$ is the probability distribution of x, where $x \in [a_{MF}, b_{MF}]$, then equations (3.25) and (3.26) are the same as the mean and standard deviation used in probability.

Usually, a_{MF} and b_{MF} denote the left end and right end of the support of a T1 MF; however, shoulder T1 MFs pose a problem because for a left-shoulder T1 MF there is no uncertainty for $x \in [0, a_{MF}]$, whereas for a right-shoulder T1 MF there is no uncertainty for $x \in [b_{MF}, M]$; hence, for shoulder MFs a_{MF} and b_{MF} do not cover the entire span of the MF, and are as shown in the second and third row figures of Table 3.3.

3.5.2.3 Compute Uncertainty Measures for T1 FS Models. The mean and standard deviations for symmetric triangle (interior), left-shoulder and right-shoulder T1 MFs are easy to compute, and they are also summarized in Table 3.3. Observe

Table 3.3. Mean and standard deviation for interior and shoulder T1 MFs

Name	MF	Mean (m_{MF}) and standard deviation (σ_{MF})
Symmetric triangle (interior MF)		$m_{MF} = (a_{MF} + b_{MF})/2$ $\sigma_{MF} = (b_{MF} - a_{MF})/2\sqrt{6}$
Left-shoulder		$m_{MF} = (2a_{MF} + b_{MF})/3$ $\sigma_{MF} = \left[\frac{1}{6}\left[(a_{MF} + b_{MF})^2 + 2a_{MF}^2\right] - m_{MF}^2 \right]^{1/2}$
Right-shoulder		$m_{MF} = (2a_{MF} + b_{MF})/3$ $\sigma_{MF} = \left[\frac{1}{6}\left[(a'_{MF} + b'_{MF})^2 + 2a'^2_{MF}\right] - m'^2_{MF} \right]^{1/2}$ $a'_{MF} = M - b_{MF}$ $b'_{MF} = M - a_{MF}$ $m'_{MF} = M - m_{MF}$

Source: Liu and Mendel, 2008; © 2008, IEEE.

that by using the primed parameters for the right-shoulder T1 MF, the equation for its σ_{MF} looks just like the comparable formula for the left-shoulder T1 MF.

3.5.2.4 *Compute General Formulas for Parameters of T1 FS Models.*
The parameters of a T1 FS (triangle, left- or right-shoulder) are computed by equating the mean and standard deviation of a T1 FS to the mean and standard deviation, respectively, of a data interval, that is, $m_{MF}^{(i)} = m_Y^{(i)}$ and $\sigma_{MF}^{(i)} = \sigma_Y^{(i)}$, where $m_{MF}^{(i)}$ and $\sigma_{MF}^{(i)}$ are in Table 3.3, and $m_Y^{(i)}$ and $\sigma_Y^{(i)}$ are computed using equations (3.22) and (3.23). This is done for each of the m remaining data intervals. The resulting T1 MF parameters, $a_{MF}^{(i)}$ and $b_{MF}^{(i)}$, are summarized in Table 3.4. Although these parameters could have been expressed in terms of $m_Y^{(i)}$ and $\sigma_Y^{(i)}$, our choice has been to express them directly in terms of $a^{(i)}$ and $b^{(i)}$ by using equations (3.22) and (3.23).[15]

3.5.2.5 *Establish Nature of the FOU.*
Given a set of m data intervals, they must be mapped into an interior FOU, left-shoulder FOU, or a right-shoulder FOU.

---

[15]For example, for an interior MF, $a_{MF}^{(i)} = m_Y^{(i)} - \sqrt{6}\sigma_Y^{(i)}$ and $b_{MF}^{(i)} = m_Y^{(i)} + \sqrt{6}\sigma_Y^{(i)}$.

Table 3.4. Transformations of the uniformly distributed data interval $[a^{(i)}, b^{(i)}]$ into the parameters $a_{MF}^{(i)}$ and $b_{MF}^{(i)}$ of a T1 FS

MF	Transformations
Symmetric triangle (interior MF)	$a_{MF}^{(i)} = \frac{1}{2}[(a^{(i)} + b^{(i)}) - \sqrt{2}(b^{(i)} - a^{(i)})]$
	$b_{MF}^{(i)} = \frac{1}{2}[(a^{(i)} + b^{(i)}) + \sqrt{2}(b^{(i)} - a^{(i)})]$
Left-shoulder	$a_{MF}^{(i)} = \dfrac{(a^{(i)} + b^{(i)})}{2} - \dfrac{(b^{(i)} - a^{(i)})}{\sqrt{6}}$
	$b_{MF}^{(i)} = \dfrac{(a^{(i)} + b^{(i)})}{2} + \dfrac{\sqrt{6}(b^{(i)} - a^{(i)})}{3}$
Right-shoulder	$a_{MF}^{(i)} = M - \dfrac{(a'^{(i)} + b'^{(i)})}{2} - \dfrac{\sqrt{6}(b'^{(i)} - a'^{(i)})}{3}$
	$b_{MF}^{(i)} = M - \dfrac{(a'^{(i)} + b'^{(i)})}{2} + \dfrac{(b'^{(i)} - a'^{(i)})}{\sqrt{6}}$
	$a'^{(i)} = M - b^{(i)}$
	$b'^{(i)} = M - a^{(i)}$

Source: Liu and Mendel, 2008; © 2008, IEEE.

This is a classification problem. In this subsection, a rationale for deciding which of these FOUs is chosen, and an FOU classification procedure are explained.

3.5.2.5.1 FOU Rationale. To begin, it is always assumed that the m data intervals can be mapped into an interior FOU, and if this cannot be done that the data can be mapped into a left-shoulder FOU, and if this cannot be done that the data can be mapped into a right-shoulder FOU. This rationale is the basis for the classification procedure that is given next.

3.5.2.5.2 FOU Classification Procedure. To begin, the following *admissibility requirement* for an interior FOU is defined.

Definition 3.3. For the scale [0, 10], an interior FOU is said to be admissible if and only if

$$\left. \begin{array}{l} a_{MF}^{(i)} \geq 0 \\ b_{MF}^{(i)} \leq 10 \end{array} \right\} \; \forall i = 1, ..., m \quad (3.27)$$

By using the formulas for $a_{MF}^{(i)}$ and $b_{MF}^{(i)}$ that are given in the first row of Table 3.4, it is straightforward to show that equation (3.27) is equivalent to

$$\left. \begin{array}{l} 1.207a^{(i)} - 0.207b^{(i)} \geq 0 \\ 1.207b^{(i)} - 0.207a^{(i)} \leq 10 \end{array} \right\} \; \forall i = 1, ..., m , \quad (3.28)$$

or, equivalently,

$$\left.\begin{array}{l} b^{(i)} \leq 5.831 a^{(i)} \\ b^{(i)} \leq 0.171 a^{(i)} + 8.29 \end{array}\right\} \forall i = 1,...,m \qquad (3.29)$$

Additionally, there is the obvious constraint that

$$b^{(i)} \geq a^{(i)} \ \forall i = 1,...,m \qquad (3.30)$$

Figure 3.12 depicts the three inequalities in equations (3.29) and (3.30) and shows the admissible region for an interior FOU. Unfortunately, requiring equations (3.29) and (3.30) to be satisfied for all m data intervals is too stringent. For example, consider two situations: in the first situation only one of the m data pairs (barely) falls outside of the admissible region and in the second situation more than half of the data pairs fall outside of that region. Using equations (3.29) and (3.30), an interior FOU would be rejected for both situations, which does not seem so reasonable; hence, requiring all $\{a^{(i)}, b^{(i)}\}_{i=1}^{m}$ to fall in the admissible region seems too stringent.

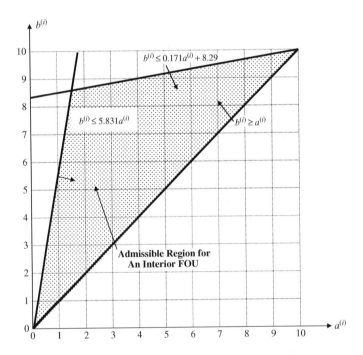

Figure 3.12. Admissible region for an interior FOU that is based on equations (3.29) and (3.30) (Liu and Mendel, 2008; © 2008, IEEE).

To that end, instead of using equations (3.29) and (3.30), their expected values are used:

$$\left.\begin{array}{l} m_b \le 5.831 m_a \\ m_b \le 0.171 m_a + 8.29 \end{array}\right\} \tag{3.31}$$

$$m_b \ge m_a \tag{3.32}$$

A figure that is analogous to Fig. 3.12 could be drawn. It would look just like the one in Fig. 3.12, except that the lines would be for equations (3.31) and (3.32) instead of for equations (3.29) and (3.30). Note that even though equation (3.30) has been re-expressed in equation (3.32) in terms of expected values, it will always be satisfied by all m intervals by virtue of the third line of equation (3.16). Our attention is, therefore, directed at the two inequalities in equation (3.31).

In practice, the population means, m_a and m_b, are not available, so equation (3.31) cannot be used as is. As explained next, our approach to implementing equation (3.31) is to develop two hypothesis tests.

Let

$$c \equiv b - 5.831a \tag{3.33}$$

$$d \equiv b - 0.17a - 8.29 \tag{3.34}$$

From equations (3.31), (3.33), and (3.34), it follows that to determine if equation (3.31) is satisfied is equivalent to determining if the following are satisfied:

$$\left.\begin{array}{l} m_c \le 0 \\ m_d \le 0 \end{array}\right\} \tag{3.35}$$

According to statistics [Walpole, et al. (2007), Chapter 10], to verify equation (3.35) one needs to test the population means m_c and m_d using the following *one-tailed tests* (H_0 denotes the null hypothesis and H_1 denotes the alternative hypothesis):

For m_c :
$$H_0 : m_c = 0 \tag{3.36}$$
$$H_1 : m_c < 0$$

For m_d :
$$H_0 : m_d = 0 \tag{3.37}$$
$$H_1 : m_d < 0$$

It is well known that, for the one-sided hypotheses in equations (3.36) and (3.37), for which the population variances are unknown but sample variances are available, rejection of H_0 occurs when a computed t-statistic is smaller than $-t_{\alpha, m-1}$, where $m - 1$ is the degrees of freedom for the t-distribution, and m is the number of intervals that have survived the preprocessing stages.

For m_c, $t \equiv T_c$, and [Walpole, et al. (2007), Section 10.7]

$$T_c = \frac{\bar{c} - 0}{s_c / \sqrt{m}} < -t_{\alpha, m-1} \tag{3.38}$$

in which $\bar{c}$ is the sample mean of c and s_c is the sample standard deviation of c. From equation (3.33) $\bar{c}$ can be expressed as

$$\bar{c} = \bar{b} - 5.831\bar{a} = m_r - 5.831m_l \tag{3.39}$$

where m_l and m_r are the sample means of the surviving m intervals which are available from the data part of the IA. Substituting equation (3.39) into equation (3.38), it is straightforward to obtain the following decision inequality for m_c:

$$m_r < 5.831m_l - t_{\alpha, m-1} \frac{s_c}{\sqrt{m}} \tag{3.40}$$

For m_d, $t \equiv T_d$, and

$$T_d = \frac{\bar{d} - 0}{s_d / \sqrt{m}} < -t_{\alpha, m-1} \tag{3.41}$$

in which $\bar{d}$ is the sample mean of d and s_d is the sample standard deviation of d. Proceeding as was done for T_c, but beginning with equation (3.34), it is straightforward to obtain the following decision inequality for m_d:

$$m_r < 0.171m_l + 8.29 - t_{\alpha, m-1} \frac{s_d}{\sqrt{m}} \tag{3.42}$$

By these analyses, equation (3.31) is replaced by equations (3.40) and (3.42), and, in addition equation (3.32) is replaced by

$$m_r \geq m_l \tag{3.43}$$

Equations (3.40), (3.42), and (3.43) are plotted in the *classification diagram* depicted in Fig. 3.13, in which the decision regions for interior, left-shoulder, and right-shoulder FOUs are shown shaded. Observe that there is a small region for which no FOU is assigned. It is called the *unreasonable region* because to assign a shoulder FOU for values in it leads to FOUs that extend unreasonably far to the left (for a right-shoulder FOU) or right (for a left-shoulder FOU). No interval data that has been collected to date have led to (m_l, m_r) that fall in the unreasonable region.

Based on these discussions, our FOU Classification Procedure is: compute m_l and m_r, and:

$$\text{IF } m_r \le 5.831 m_l - t_{\alpha,m-1} \frac{s_c}{\sqrt{m}}, \quad m_r \le 0.171 m_l + 8.29 - t_{\alpha,m-1} \frac{s_d}{\sqrt{m}}, \text{ and } m_r \ge m_l$$

THEN FOU is an INTERIOR FOU

$$\text{OTHERWISE, IF } m_r > 5.831 m_l - t_{\alpha,m-1} \frac{s_c}{\sqrt{m}}, \text{ and } m_r < 0.171 m_l + 8.29 - t_{\alpha,m-1} \frac{s_d}{\sqrt{m}}$$

THEN FOU is a LEFT-SHOULDER FOU

$$\text{OTHERWISE, IF } m_r < 5.831 m_l - t_{\alpha,m-1} \frac{s_c}{\sqrt{m}}, \text{ and } m_r > 0.171 m_l + 8.29 - t_{\alpha,m-1} \frac{s_d}{\sqrt{m}} \qquad (3.44)$$

THEN FOU is a RIGHT-SHOULDER FOU

$$\text{OTHERWISE, IF } m_r > 5.831 m_l - t_{\alpha,m-1} \frac{s_c}{\sqrt{m}} \text{ and } m_r > 0.171 m_l + 8.29 - t_{\alpha,m-1} \frac{s_d}{\sqrt{m}}$$

THEN NO FOU

Comments:

1. In order to classify a word's surviving m data intervals, first m_l, m_r, s_c, and s_d must be computed. m_l and m_r are the sample averages of $\{a^{(i)}\}_{i=1}^m$ and $\{b^{(i)}\}_{i=1}^m$, respectively, and s_c and s_d are the sample standard deviations of $\{b^{(i)} - 5.83a^{(i)}\}_{i=1}^m$ and $\{b^{(i)} - 0.171a^{(i)} - 8.29\}_{i=1}^m$, respectively. Although these calcula-

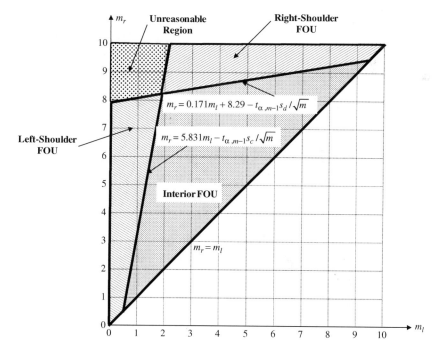

Figure 3.13. Classification diagram with FOU decision regions (Liu and Mendel, 2008; © 2008, IEEE).

tions could have been put into the data part of the IA, we have chosen to put them into the fuzzy set part because s_c and s_d first appear in the fuzzy set part of the IA.

2. Observe from equation (3.44) [or (3.40) and (3.42)] that the nondiagonal decision boundaries depend upon m in two ways: (1) $t_{\alpha,m-1}$ depends upon m (as well as α), and (2) $1/\sqrt{m}$. This means that when m is different for different words (as frequently occurs) the decision diagrams for different words will be different. It also means that when m is large, so that $t_{\alpha,m-1}s_c/\sqrt{m} \to 0$ and $t_{\alpha,m-1}s_d/\sqrt{m} \to 0$, then Fig. 3.13 reduces to the *asymptotic classification diagram* that is depicted in Fig. 3.14.

3. The decision boundaries depend on α. For example, when $m = 20$ and $\alpha = 0.10$, then [Walpole, et al. (2007), Table A.4] $t_{0.10,19} = 1.328$, whereas if $\alpha = 0.05$, then $t_{0.05,19} = 1.729$. From equation (3.40) and these two (representative) examples, observe that as α decreases, the left-shoulder decision line moves to the right; and, from equation (3.42) and these two (representative) examples, observe that as α decreases, the right-shoulder decision line moves downward. Hence, smaller values of α lead to larger left- and right- shoulder decision regions. As in any decision making situation, the specific choice of α is left to the user, although $\alpha = 0.05$ is a very popular choice, since it also corresponds to a 95% confidence interval.

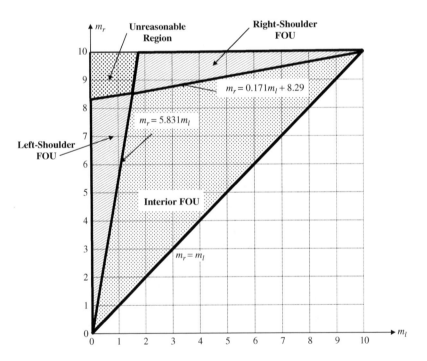

Figure 3.14. Asymptotic classification diagram with FOU decision regions (Liu and Mendel, 2008; © 2008, IEEE).

3.5.2.6 Compute Embedded T1 FSs. Once a decision has been made as to the kind of FOU for a specific word, each of the word's remaining m data intervals are mapped into their respective T1 FSs using the equations that are given in Table 3.4:

$$(a^{(i)}, b^{(i)}) \rightarrow (a_{MF}^{(i)}, b_{MF}^{(i)}), \quad i = 1,...,m \qquad (3.45)$$

These T1 FSs, denoted $W^{(i)}$, are called *embedded T1 FSs,* because they are used to obtain the FOU of the word, as described below in Section 3.5.2.8.

3.5.2.7 Delete Inadmissible T1 FSs. It is possible that some of the m embedded T1 FSs are inadmissible, that is, they violate equation (3.27), because our FOU classification procedure has been based on statistics and not on each realization. Those T1 FSs are deleted, so that there will be m^* remaining embedded T1 FSs, where $m^* \leq m$.

3.5.2.8 Compute an IT2 FS Using the Union. Using the Wavy Slice Representation Theorem for an IT2 FS (Section 2.4) a word's IT2 FS $\tilde{W}$ is computed as

$$\tilde{W} = \bigcup_{i=1}^{m^*} W^{(i)} \qquad (3.46)$$

where $W^{(i)}$ is the just-computed ith embedded T1 FS.

3.5.2.9 Compute the Mathematical Model for FOU($\tilde{W}$). In order to compute a mathematical model for $FOU(\tilde{W})$, both $UMF(\tilde{W})$ and $LMF(\tilde{W})$ must be approximated. There are many ways in which this can be done. Our approach is very simple and guarantees that all m^* embedded T1 FSs are contained within $FOU(\tilde{W})$. Regardless of the type of FOU, the following four numbers must first be computed:

$$\left. \begin{array}{l} \underline{a}_{MF} \equiv \min_{i=1,...,m^*} \{a_{MF}^{(i)}\} \\ \overline{a}_{MF} \equiv \max_{i=1,...,m^*} \{a_{MF}^{(i)}\} \end{array} \right\} \qquad (3.47)$$

$$\left. \begin{array}{l} \underline{b}_{MF} \equiv \min_{i=1,...,m^*} \{b_{MF}^{(i)}\} \\ \overline{b}_{MF} \equiv \max_{i=1,...,m^*} \{b_{MF}^{(i)}\} \end{array} \right\} \qquad (3.48)$$

3.5.2.9.1 Mathematical Model for an Interior FOU. Fig. 3.15 depicts this situation. The steps to approximate $UMF(\tilde{W})$ are:

a. Compute

$$C_{MF}^{(i)} = \frac{a_{MF}^{(i)} + b_{MF}^{(i)}}{2} \qquad (3.49)$$

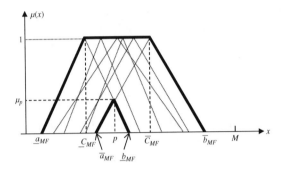

Figure 3.15. An example of the union of T1 triangle MFs. The heavy lines are the lower and upper MFs (Liu and Mendel, 2008; © 2008, IEEE).

b. Compute

$$\underline{C}_{MF} = \min\{C^{(i)}_{MF}\} \tag{3.50}$$

$$\overline{C}_{MF} = \max\{C^{(i)}_{MF}\} \tag{3.51}$$

c. Connect the following points with straight lines: $(\underline{a}_{MF}, 0)$, $(\underline{C}_{MF}, 1)$, $(\overline{C}_{MF}, 1)$, and $(\overline{b}_{MF}, 0)$.

The result is a trapezoidal UMF.
The steps to approximate $LMF(\tilde{W})$ are:

a. Compute the intersection point (p, μ_p) of the right leg and the left leg of the left- and right-most extreme triangles (see Fig. 3.15) using:

$$p = \frac{\underline{b}_{MF}(\overline{C}_{MF} - \overline{a}_{MF}) + \overline{a}_{MF}(\underline{b}_{MF} - \underline{C}_{MF})}{(\overline{C}_{MF} - \overline{a}_{MF}) + (\underline{b}_{MF} - \underline{C}_{MF})} \tag{3.52}$$

$$\mu_p = \frac{\underline{b}_{MF} - p}{\underline{b}_{MF} - \underline{C}_{MF}} \tag{3.53}$$

b. Connect the following points with straight lines: $(\underline{a}_{MF}, 0)$, $(\overline{a}_{MF}, 0)$, (p, μ_p), $(\underline{b}_{MF}, 0)$, and $(\overline{b}_{MF}, 0)$.

The result is a triangle LMF.

3.5.2.9.2 Mathematical Model for a Left-Shoulder FOU. Fig. 3.16 depicts this situation. To approximate $UMF(\tilde{W})$, connect the following points with straight lines: $(0, 1)$, $(\overline{a}_{MF}, 1)$, and $(\overline{b}_{MF}, 0)$. The result is a left-shoulder UMF. To approximate $LMF(\tilde{W})$, connect the following points with straight lines: $(0, 1)$, $(\underline{a}_{MF}, 1)$, $(\underline{b}_{MF}, 0)$, and $(\overline{b}_{MF}, 0)$. The result is a left-shoulder LMF.

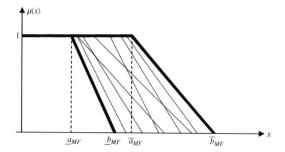

Figure 3.16. An example of the union of T1 left-shoulder MFs. The heavy lines are the lower and upper MFs (Liu and Mendel, 2008; © 2008, IEEE).

3.5.2.9.3 Mathematical Model for a Right-Shoulder FOU. Figure 3.17 depicts this situation. To approximate $UMF(\tilde{W})$, connect the following points with straight lines: $(\underline{a}_{MF}, 0)$, $(\underline{b}_{MF}, 1)$, and $(M, 1)$. The result is a right-shoulder UMF. To approximate $LMF(\tilde{W})$, connect the following points with straight lines: $(\underline{a}_{MF}, 0)$, $(\overline{a}_{MF}, 0)$, $(\overline{b}_{MF}, 1)$, and $(M, 1)$. The result is a right-shoulder LMF.

3.5.3 Observations

3.5.3.1 Canonical FOUs for Words. Figures 3.15–3.17 illustrate the only FOUs that can be obtained for a word using the IA, and so these FOUs are referred to herein as *canonical FOUs for a word.*

A word that is modeled by an interior FOU has an UMF that is a trapezoid and a LMF that is a triangle, but, in general, neither the trapezoid nor the triangle are symmetrical. A word that is modeled as a left- or right-shoulder FOU has trapezoidal upper and lower MFs; however, the legs of the respective two trapezoids are not necessarily parallel.

That there are only three canonical FOUs for a word is very different than in function approximation applications of IT2 FSs (e.g., as in fuzzy logic control, or

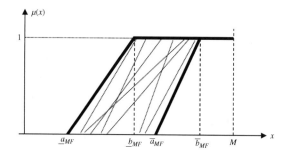

Figure 3.17. An example of the union of T1 right-shoulder MFs. The heavy lines are the lower and upper MFs (Liu and Mendel, 2008; © 2008, IEEE).

forecasting of time series), where one is free to choose the shapes of the FOUs ahead of time, and many different choices are possible. The full implications of knowing the general shapes of the three canonical word FOUs ahead of time will become much clearer in Chapters 5 and 6.

3.5.3.2 No completely Filled-in FOUs. In Mendel and Wu (2007c) (see, also Property 3 in Section 2.6.2), it is explained that when $LMF(\tilde{W}) = 0$, then $FOU(\tilde{W})$ is completely filled in. This is not considered to be a good FOU, because the centroid of such an FOU equals the span[16] of $LMF(\tilde{W})$ and is, therefore, completely independent of $UMF(\tilde{W})$. The following property shows that the IA does not lead to completely filled-in FOUs.

Property of IA: Using the IA, none of the obtained FOUs will be completely filled in, that is, (a) for an interior FOU, $\underline{b}_{MF} > \overline{a}_{MF}$ (see Fig. 3.15); (b) for a left-shoulder FOU, $\underline{b}_{MF} > \underline{a}_{MF} > 0$ (see Fig. 3.16); and, (c) for a right-shoulder FOU, $\overline{a}_{MF} < \overline{b}_{MF} <$ M (see Fig. 3.17).

A proof of this theorem is given in Liu and Mendel (2007b).

3.5.3.3 Whose FOU? In the field of probability elicitation, O'Hagan and Oakley (2004) question how various individual expert probability distributions should be combined into a single distribution, and, regardless of the method used for combining, whose distribution does this represent? The latter question reflects the fact that regardless of how the distributions are combined, the final distribution has lost the uncertainties of the individual subjects, and, in fact, it may correspond to none of the subjects.

One can raise a similar question for the FOU of a word that is obtained from the IA, that is, whose FOU does it represent? Unlike the probability elicitation field, where each expert is assumed to have a probability distribution, no assumption is ever made in our work that a subject has a personal FOU for a word. An FOU is a mathematical model that captures the uncertainties about a word, and is only used in later processing or analyses.

Note, however, that the union method for combining each subject's T1 FS preserves all of their uncertainties because each of their T1 FSs is contained within the FOU.

One can even provide a Bayesian-like interpretation to the construction of a FOU. Allow the analyst to be one of the subjects, so that her T1 FS is the first T1 FS of the remaining m^* T1 FSs. Then the resulting FOU not only uses her a priori FOU, which is a T1 FS, but modifies it by folding in the T1 FSs of the remaining $m^* - 1$ data intervals.

3.5.3.4 Additional Data. If at a later time more subject data become available, then one must repeat the entire IA procedure because such data can affect the data and interval statistics in the data part of the IA, and those statistics are used in the

---

[16]See Definition 2.9.

FS part of the IA. So, it is very important not to discard the subject data intervals. How (or if it is possible) to turn the IA into a data-adaptive procedure remains to be explored.

3.5.4 Codebook Example

A dataset was collected from 28 subjects at the Jet Propulsion Laboratory (JPL)[17] for a vocabulary of 32 words. These words were randomized and for all words each subject was asked the question, "On a scale of 0 to 10, what are the end points of an interval that you associate with the word *W*?" All of the data were processed as described in Sections 3.5.1 and 3.5.2.

Table 3.5 (in which the 32 words have been ordered using a ranking method that is explained later in this section) summarizes how many data intervals survived each of the four preprocessing stages, and how many intervals, m^*, survived the deletion of inadmissible T1 FSs step in the FS part of the IA. Observe that m^* is quite variable. Table 3.5 also gives the final left and right end-point statistics that were used to establish the nature of each word's FOU. These statistics are based on the m remaining data intervals after stage 4 of preprocessing.[18]

Table 3.6 is the codebook for the 32 words. It provides the coordinates (code) for the LMF and UMF of each FOU.[19]

Figure 3.18 depicts the FOUs for all 32 words. Observe that the words have been ordered so that there seems to be a very natural flow from left-shoulder FOUs to interior FOUs to right-shoulder FOUs. This flow was achieved by first computing the centroid of each FOU (Chapter 2) and then the mean of each centroid. The results of these computations are given in the last two columns of Table 3.6. The words were then rank-ordered using the mean of the centroid. Ranking the words by this method seems to give visually acceptable results (see also Section 4.3)

Observe from Fig. 3.18 and Table 3.6, that some words (e.g., *a smidgen* and *tiny; some* and *some to moderate; very sizeable, substantial amount* and *a lot,* and *very high amount* and *extreme amount*) have almost identical FOUs. Similarity of all of the words to one another is examined in great detail in Chapter 4.

One may feel that the words *very small* and *very little* should have been modeled as left-shoulder FOUs, and the words *very large* and *very sizeable* should have been modeled as right-shoulder FOUs. That they were not may be due to the relatively small number of data intervals that were collected from subjects.

Note that the ordering of the words in Fig. 3.18 is due to our ad hoc method for ranking the FOUs. If the reader does not like the positions of the FOUs, he/she can change them without affecting the codebook.

---

[17]This was done in 2002 when J. M. Mendel gave an in-house short course on fuzzy sets and systems at JPL.

[18]The results in Table 3.5 are somewhat different from those given in Table IV of Liu and Mendel (2008). In that article, the term $\sigma_l^2 - \sigma_r^2$, in the numerator of equation (3.20), was coded incorrectly as $\sigma_r^2 - \sigma_l^2$. This was brought to the attention of the authors by Mr. Hussam Hamrawi and Dr. Simon Coupland.

[19]The results in Table 3.6 are somewhat different from those given in Table V of Liu and Mendel (2008). See footnote 18.

Table 3.5. Remaining data intervals and their end-point statistics for m data intervals

| Word | Preprocessing | | | | FS part | Left-end statistic | | Right-end statistic | |
| | Stage 1 | Stage 2 | Stage 3 | Stage 4 | | | | | |
	n'	m'	m''	m	m^*	m_l	s_l	m_r	s_r
None to very little	28	21	20	20	20	0	0	1.09	0.25
Teeny-weeny	28	24	23	8	8	0.09	0.17	1.04	0.20
A smidgen	26	22	20	9	9	0.28	0.26	1.44	0.39
Tiny	28	24	24	9	9	0.22	0.23	1.34	0.47
Very small	28	21	21	16	15	0.79	0.28	1.83	0.28
Very little	28	23	21	10	9	0.67	0.33	2.15	0.53
A bit	28	25	23	12	12	1.00	0	2.63	0.48
Low amount	28	26	24	18	15	0.86	0.50	2.64	0.64
Small	28	26	25	22	20	1.25	0.55	3.23	0.48
Somewhat small	28	27	25	15	15	1.84	0.56	3.45	0.46
Little	28	27	26	19	18	1.33	0.50	3.30	0.63
Some	28	25	24	17	17	3.24	0.59	5.68	0.83
Some to moderate	28	23	23	23	23	3.18	0.67	6.09	0.58
Moderate amount	28	23	20	20	20	3.92	0.29	5.97	0.55
Fair amount	28	24	21	21	21	4.07	0.62	6.24	0.44
Medium	28	24	23	20	20	4.35	0.40	5.84	0.32
Modest amount	28	21	20	19	19	4.32	0.45	6.03	0.31
Good amount	28	25	23	15	15	5.53	0.74	7.57	0.62
Quite a bit	28	23	23	12	12	6.06	0.54	8.13	0.31
Sizeable	28	22	21	18	14	6.62	0.67	8.75	0.80
Considerable amount	28	24	24	16	14	6.59	0.69	8.53	0.72
Very sizeable	28	26	24	13	10	7.42	0.64	9.23	0.48
Substantial amount	28	25	24	17	12	7.50	0.66	9.29	0.53
A lot	28	26	26	16	12	7.26	0.55	9.27	0.49
High amount	28	26	24	20	13	7.53	0.72	9.40	0.48
Large	28	26	26	23	16	7.44	0.54	9.28	0.45
Very large	27	26	25	15	11	7.97	0.58	9.37	0.43
Humongous amount	28	25	23	22	22	9.00	0.58	10.00	0
Huge amount	28	25	21	21	21	8.62	0.45	9.85	0.22
Very high amount	28	27	23	21	21	8.77	0.54	9.97	0.07
Extreme amount	28	28	27	22	22	8.98	0.36	10	0.02
Maximum amount	27	25	23	15	15	9.21	0.27	10	0

Source: Adopted from Liu and Mendel, 2008; © 2008, IEEE.

Herrera, Herrera-Viedma, and Martinez (2000) discuss multigranular linguistic term sets and how in ". . . decision making problems with multiple sources of information, linguistic performance values that are given to the different sources can be represented as linguistic term sets with different granularity and/or semantics." Our interpretation of "linguistic term sets with different granularity" is as a *subvocabu-*

Table 3.6. FOU data for all words (based on m^* data intervals)—the codebook. Each UMF and LMF is represented as a trapezoid (see Fig. 4.5). The fifth parameter for the LMF is its height

Word	UMF	LMF	Centroid	Center of centroid
None to very little	[0, 0, 0.14, 1.97]	[0, 0, 0.05, 0.66, 1]	[0.22,0.73]	0.48
Teeny-weeny	[0, 0, 0.55, 1.97]	[0, 0, 0.09, 1.02, 1]	[0.34,0.74]	0.54
A smidgen	[0, 0, 0.59, 2.63]	[0, 0, 0.09, 1.16, 1]	[0.39,0.99]	0.69
Tiny	[0, 0, 0.63, 2.63]	[0, 0, 0.09, 1.16, 1]	[0.39,0.99]	0.69
Very small	[0.19, 1, 1.50, 2.31]	[0.79, 1.25, 1.25, 1.71, 0.65]	[0.95,1.55]	1.25
Very little	[0.19, 1, 2.00, 3.41]	[0.79, 1.37, 1.37, 1.71, 0.48]	[0.92,2.21]	1.57
A bit	[0.59, 1.50, 2.00, 3.41]	[0.79, 1.68, 1.68, 2.21, 0.74]	[1.42,2.08]	1.75
Low amount	[0.09, 1.25, 2.50, 4.62]	[1.67, 1.92, 1.92, 2.21, 0.30]	[0.92,3.46]	2.19
Small	[0.09, 1.50, 3.00, 4.62]	[1.79, 2.28, 2.28, 2.81, 0.40]	[1.29,3.34]	2.32
Somewhat small	[0.59, 2.00, 3.25, 4.41]	[2.29, 2.70, 2.70, 3.21, 0.42]	[1.76,3.43]	2.59
Little	[0.38, 1.58, 3.50, 5.62]	[1.79, 2.20, 2.20, 2.40, 0.24]	[1.18,4.35]	2.76
Some	[1.28, 3.50, 5.50, 7.83]	[3.79, 4.41, 4.41, 4.91, 0.36]	[2.87,6.13]	4.50
Some to moderate	[1.17, 3.50, 5.50, 7.83]	[4.09, 4.65, 4.65, 5.41, 0.40]	[3.01,6.11]	4.56
Moderate amount	[2.59, 4.00, 5.50, 7.62]	[4.29, 4.75, 4.75, 5.21, 0.38]	[3.74,6.16]	4.95
Fair amount	[2.17, 4.25, 6.00, 7.83]	[4.79, 5.29, 5.29, 6.02, 0.41]	[3.85,6.41]	5.13
Medium	[3.59, 4.75, 5.50, 6.91]	[4.86, 5.03, 5.03, 5.14, 0.27]	[4.19,6.19]	5.19
Modest amount	[3.59, 4.75, 6.00, 7.41]	[4.79, 5.30, 5.30, 5.71, 0.42]	[4.57,6.24]	5.41
Good amount	[3.38, 5.50, 7.50, 9.62]	[5.79, 6.50, 6.50, 7.21, 0.41]	[5.11,7.89]	6.50
Quite a bit	[4.38, 6.50, 8.00, 9.41]	[6.79, 7.38, 7.38, 8.21, 0.49]	[6.17,8.15]	7.16
Sizeable	[4.38, 6.50, 8.00, 9.41]	[7.29, 7.56, 7.56, 8.21, 0.38]	[5.95,8.39]	7.17
Considerable amount	[4.38, 6.50, 8.25, 9.62]	[7.19, 7.58, 7.58, 8.21, 0.37]	[5.97,8.52]	7.25
Very sizeable	[5.38, 7.50, 8.75, 9.81]	[7.79, 8.20, 8.20, 8.71, 0.42]	[6.88,8.88]	7.88
Substantial amount	[5.38, 7.50, 8.75, 9.81]	[7.79, 8.22, 8.22, 8.81, 0.45]	[6.95,8.86]	7.90
A lot	[5.38, 7.50, 8.75, 9.83]	[7.69, 8.19, 8.19, 8.81, 0.47]	[6.99,8.82]	7.91
High amount	[5.38, 7.50, 8.75, 9.81]	[7.79, 8.30, 8.30, 9.21, 0.53]	[7.19,8.82]	8.01
Large	[5.98, 7.75, 8.60, 9.52]	[8.03, 8.36, 8.36, 9.17, 0.57]	[7.50,8.75]	8.12
Very large	[6.59, 8.00, 9.25, 9.89]	[8.61, 8.82, 8.82, 9.21, 0.32]	[7.60,9.34]	8.47
Humongous amount	[7.37, 9.82, 10, 10]	[9.74, 9.98, 10, 10, 1]	[8.68,9.91]	9.30
Huge amount	[7.37, 9.36, 10, 10]	[8.95, 9.93, 10, 10, 1]	[8.99,9.65]	9.32
Very high amount	[7.37, 9.73, 10, 10]	[9.34, 9.95, 10, 10, 1]	[8.95,9.77]	9.36
Extreme amount	[7.37, 9.82, 10, 10]	[9.37, 9.95, 10, 10, 1]	[8.95,9.78]	9.37
Maximum amount	[8.68, 9.91, 10, 10]	[9.61, 9.97, 10, 10, 1]	[9.50,9.87]	9.68

Source: Adopted from Liu and Mendel, 2008; © 2008, IEEE.

lary from the codebook. Figure 3.19 depicts three subvocabularies, where the FOUs in each subvocabulary cover the entire domain [0, 10]. Each subvocabulary was obtained from the results given in Table 3.6 and Fig. 3.18. When a codebook is established, it contains within it many subvocabularies. One important use for a subvocabulary is in designing if–then rules as a CWW engine, in which case it is

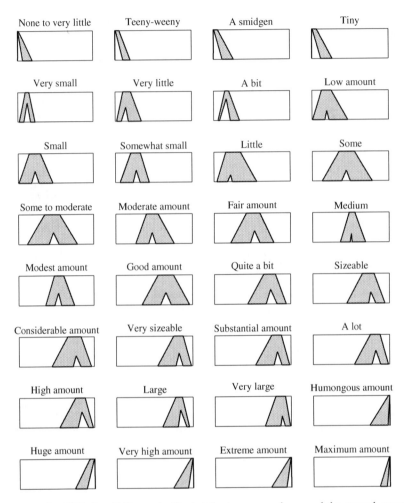

Figure 3.18. FOUs for all 32 words. Start at the top row and proceed downward, scanning from left to right (adopted from Liu and Mendel, 2008; © 2008, IEEE).

expedient to use a small (the smallest) subvocabulary that covers the entire domain in order to avoid rule explosion. This is explored in Chapter 6.

Chapter 7 has results from using the IA for three vocabularies that are associated with the investment judgment advisor.

3.5.5 Software

Software that implements the IA is available at: http://sipi.usc.edu/~mendel/software.

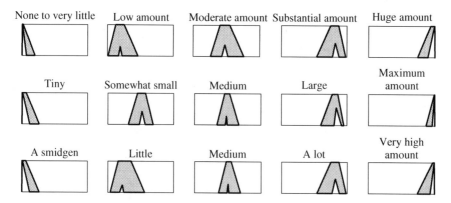

Figure 3.19. FOUs for three subvocabularies (adopted from Liu and Mendel, 2008; © 2008, IEEE).

3.5.6 Concluding Remarks

In May 2009, during the final stages of the writing of this book, the first author was doing some joint research at DeMontfort University with Prof. Robert John, Dr. Simon Coupland, and Mr. Hussam Hamrawi, and together they found some improvements to the IA. These improvements have to do with: (1) removing [0, 10] intervals; (2) removing intervals that are very small, including when $a^{(i)} = b^{(i)}$; and (3) removing intervals that overlap but are too large. Because this work has not yet been published, its details are not included in this book.

A weak point of the IA is that the interval end-point data have to be collected from a group of subjects. Sometimes this is not possible, due, for example, to budget limitations, time constraints, or unavailability of a subject pool. Joo and Mendel (2009) have proposed a method for obtaining an FOU from a single subject by an IA that is called an *individual IA* (IIA). It collects interval end-point and uncertainty-band data from a single subject, maps them into an IT2 FS, and makes very heavy use of the FOU diagram in Fig. 3.14. The IIA is not meant to replace the IA when a group of subjects is available; it is used only when a group of subjects is not available.

3.6 HEDGES

A *linguistic hedge* or modifier, introduced first by Zadeh (1972), is an operation that modifies the meaning of a term or, more generally, of a fuzzy set. For example, if weak pressure is a fuzzy set, then very weak pressure, more-or-less weak pressure, extremely weak pressure, and not-so weak pressure are examples of hedges that are applied to this fuzzy set. There are a multitude of hedges, many additional examples of which can be found in references such as Schmucker (1984) and Cox (1994).

There are two ways to handle hedges:

1. They can be viewed as operators that act on a fuzzy set's membership function to modify it.
2. They can be treated as a new word in the codebook.

Our viewpoint is that every word that is used by a perceptual computer must be in the codebook; hence, the second viewpoint is adopted in this book.

Comments

1. By the first approach, one establishes a set of primary terms and their MFs. The hedge operators then operate on some[20] or all of the primary terms, leading to a larger set of terms and their MFs. This can be interpreted as starting with a codebook of primary words and then obtaining an expanded codebook comprised of primary and hedged words.

2. Two hedge operators introduced by Zadeh (1972) are the concentration operator, $\mu_{con(F)}(x)$, where

$$\mu_{con(F)}(x) \equiv \left[\mu_F(x)\right]^2 \tag{3.54}$$

and the dilation operator, $\mu_{dil(F)}(x)$, where

$$\mu_{dil(F)}(x) \equiv \left[\mu_F(x)\right]^{1/2} \tag{3.55}$$

Note that $\mu_{con(F)}(x)$ leads to a MF that lies within the MF of the original T1 FS [e.g., *weak pressure* has MF $\mu_{WP(F)}(p)$, so that *very weak pressure* is a FS with MF $[\mu_{WP}(p)]^2$], whereas $\mu_{dil(F)}(x)$ leads to a MF that lies outside of the MF of the original T1 FS [e.g., *more or less weak pressure* is a FS with MF $[\mu_{WP}(p)]^{1/2}$]. To the best of our knowledge, hedge operators for IT2 FSs do not yet exist.

3. Using the squaring operator for concentration and the square root operator for dilation are quite arbitrary, as already noticed by Zadeh (1972), who stated:

   It should be emphasized, however, that these representations are intended mainly to illustrate the approach rather than to provide accurate definitions of the hedges in question. Furthermore it must be understood that our analysis and its conclusions are tentative in nature and may require modification in later work.

   Because of the uncertainty about the numerical values of the exponents, hedges (even for a T1 FS) might be more appropriately modeled within the framework of T2 FSs.

---

[20]Hedges should only operate on primary terms for which the hedged term makes linguistic sense. For example, the hedge *much* makes no linguistic sense when it is applied to the primary term *low pressure*.

4. Schmucker (1984) states:

> Representing hedges as operators acting upon the representation of the primary terms has both positive and negative implications. On the positive side, it seems very natural and also allows for an easy implementation of the connection of several hedges. . . . The negative side of representing hedges as operators is that some hedges don't seem to be easily modeled by such an approach. By this we mean that the way people normally use these hedges entails an implementation considerably different and more complex than that of an operator that acts uniformly upon the fuzzy restrictions that represent the various primary terms.

5. Macvicar-Whelen (1978) provide experimental results that indicate the hedge *very* causes a shift in the MF rather than a steepening of the MF as is obtained by the concentration operator; hence, their paper calls into question the use of operators to model hedges.

6. Finally, an IT2 FS model for a word, as obtained in this chapter, includes the uncertainty about that word, through data intervals that are collected from a group of subjects. There is no evidence (yet) to support the transformation of primary word uncertainties by using hedge operators. (In probability theory, if a random variable is squared, then its probability distribution is not the square of the original distribution; probability theory leads to a much more complicated transformation.) Using the IA, the shape of the FOU may change from an interior FOU to a shoulder FOU when the adjective *very* appears before the word. For example, see Fig. 3.18 and the words *high amount* and *very high amount.*

APPENDIX 3A. METHODS FOR ELICITING T1 MF INFORMATION FROM SUBJECTS

3A.1   Introduction

A large literature exists on how to elicit T1 MF information from either a single subject or a group of subjects. The most popular methods are called[21] polling, direct rating, reverse rating, and interval estimation (of which there are two kinds, so they will be called interval estimation-1 and interval estimation-2).

3A.2   Description of the Methods

In *polling* [Cornelissen (2003), Hersch and Caramazza (1976), Lawry (2001), Türksen (1991)] for each $x_i \in X$, a subject s_j ($j = 1, \ldots, n$) indicates whether x_i does ($x_i =$

---

[21]Pedrycz (2001) also formulates a procedure for going from data to T1 MFs. His data are not about words; they are application-related data, e.g. histograms of real-estate prices. This data leads to a data probability distribution function, which is then used to map into a constrained set of MFs. The MF shapes are fixed (triangles), they must form a fuzzy partition, and an equalization condition must be satisfied. The equalization condition leads to an integral equation that is used to design the MF parameters.

$1 \equiv$ yes) or does not ($x_i = 0 \equiv$ no) have a property (is or is not in the FS A), that is, $\mu_A(x_i|s_j) = 1$ or 0. The MF is then constructed as the following average:

$$\mu_A(x_i) = \frac{1}{n}\sum_{j=1}^{n}\mu_A(x_i \mid s_j) \quad \forall x_i \in X \tag{3A.1}$$

Example 3A.1. In polling, subjects are asked questions like: (1) Do you agree that $x = x_i$ is A? (2) Does x_i belong to A? (3) Do you agree that 40 kgs (x_i) is a *thin woman* (A)? (4) This specific value of pressure (x_i) is or is not *high pressure* (A)?

The *group-voting method* [Lawry (2001)] is another kind of polling method in which the (hypothetical) question would be "Do you agree that x is A_1 or A_2 or . . . or A_n?" or "Does x belong to A_1 or A_2 or . . . or A_n?" In this method, x can be simultaneously put into more than one fuzzy set. This is different from the polling method in which x can only be put into, or not put into, one set at a time. Of course, if the polling method used a series of questions such as (1) "Does x belong to A_1?" (2) "Does x belong to A_2?" . . . (n) "Does x belong to A_n?" then such a polling method would be equivalent to the group-voting method.

In *direct rating* [Budescu et al. (2003), Chameau and Santamarina (1987), Civanlar and Trussel (1986), Norwich and Türksen (1982a,b,c; 1984), Türksen (1991)], for each $x_i \in X$, a subject s_j directly provides a numerical value for the MF, $\mu_A(x_i|s_j)$, where that value can be between 0 and 1. Data are collected either M times from a single subject, in which case the MF is then constructed as the following average:

$$\mu_A(x_i) = \frac{1}{M}\sum_{i=1}^{M}\mu_A(x_i \mid s_j) \quad \forall x_i \in X \tag{3A.2}$$

or once from multiple subjects ($j = 1, \ldots, n$), in which case, $\mu_A(x_i)$ is given by equation (3A.1).

Example 3A.2. In direct rating, subjects are asked questions like: (1) How A is x_i? (2) 40 kgs (x_i) corresponds to what degree of *thinness of a woman* (A)? (3) 200 psi (x_i) corresponds to what degree of *high pressure* (A)?

In *reverse rating* [Norwich and Türksen (1982a,b,c; 1984), Türksen (1986, 1988, 1991), Türksen and Wilson (1994)], for each MF value, y, a subject provides a numerical value for the primary variable, x_i, where $x_i \in X$. For a single subject, the same question for the same MF is repeated over a period of time, or it can be used for a group of subjects. This method seems to be limited to monotonically increasing (decreasing) MFs, because it is only for such MFs that there will be a single numerical value of x_i for each y.

Example 3A.3. In reverse rating, subjects are asked questions like: (1) identify x_i that possesses the yth grade of membership in the FS A, (2) identify x_i that is A to the degree $\mu_A(x_i)$, (3) identify a *woman's weight* (x_i) that is thin (A) to the degree 0.7 (y), and (4) identify the *pressure* (x_i) that is *high* (A) to the degree 0.6 (y).

Reverse rating can be performed in different ways. In one approach [Norwich and Türksen (1984)], a collection of female figures (dolls) was built of different heights. The subject had access to all of the figures and was given, for example, the MF value y for *tall female*. The subject then had to choose one of the figures that most represented y for *tall female*. In another approach [Türksen and Wilson (1994)], a small number (e.g., 13) of questions was asked about seven fuzzy sets labeled very poor, poor, somewhat poor, neutral, somewhat good, good, and very good. One such question was "Where (on a scale of 0–100) does good become very good?

In *interval estimation-1* [Civanlar and Trussel (1986), Dubois and Prade (1989), Zwick (1987)], for each MF value (level), y, the subject provides a crisp interval $[x_L(s_j), x_R(s_j)]$ for which a base variable x is, or is not, in the FS A at that level. This is done repeatedly for different values of the MF level, and is an α-cut method.[22] The MF is reconstructed using an α-cut decomposition theorem.

Note that for reverse rating, a single value for the domain variable is requested, whereas for this version of interval estimation an interval is requested for the domain variable. Note also that interval estimation-1 is also known as *set-valued statistics* [Dubois and Prade (1989)].

Example 3A.4. In interval estimation-1, subjects are asked questions like: (1) give an interval that describes the A-ness of x, (2) identify a range of *women's weights* $([x_L(s_j), x_R(s_j)])$ that are thin (A) to the degree 0.7, and (3) identify a range of pressures $([x_L(s_j), x_R(s_j)])$ that are *high* (A) to degree 0.6.

In *interval estimation-2* [Cornelissen (2003), Mendel (1999, 2001)], the subject provides a crisp interval $[x_L(s_j), x_R(s_j)]$ that is associated with an entire term A. In [Cornelissen (2003)], the MF associated with subject s_j for A is assigned the value 1 for all $x \in [x_L(s_j), x_R(s_j)]$ and the value 0 for all $x \notin [x_L(s_j), x_R(s_j)]$. Equation (3A.1) is again used to establish the overall MF for A across a group of n subjects. In [Liu and Mendel (2007a,b)], statistics about the crisp intervals are used to compute prescribed T1 FSs.[23]

Example 3A.5. In interval estimation-2, subjects are asked questions like: (1) identify a range of weights $([x_L(s_j), x_R(s_j)])$ that characterize thin women (A), (2) identify a range of pressures $([x_L(s_j), x_R(s_j)])$ that are high (A), and (3) On a scale of 0–10, where would you locate the end points of an interval that are associated with *high pressure* (A)?

---

[22]α-cuts and an α-cut Decomposition Theorem for T1 FSs are discussed in Chapter 5.
[23]Cornelissen (2003) also introduces the *transition interval estimation method*, in which different nonzero MF assignments are made for all $x \in [x_L(s_j), x_R(s_j)]$ and for all $x \notin [x_L(s_j), x_R(s_j)]$.

3A.3 Discussion

In this section, the five elicitation methods are critiqued based on three criteria:

1. *MF knowledge.* Requiring a subject to understand the concept of a MF limits the elicitation method to subjects who either are already knowledgeable about fuzzy sets or are instructed about a MF just prior to the elicitation. Lack of knowledge about the concept of a MF can introduce methodological (elicitation) uncertainties into the elicitation method, in which case observed word uncertainties are a mixture of methodological uncertainties and actual word uncertainties. The latter cannot be unscrambled from the former because no measure of the methodological uncertainties is available. Consequently, if an elicitation method does not (does) require that a subject know anything about the concept of a MF, this is considered a plus (minus) for that method.

2. *Number of questions.* Our experience from eliciting MF information from groups of subjects [Mendel (1999, 2001)] is that they do not like to answer a lot of questions.[24] Consequently, if an elicitation method does not (does) require that a subject answer many questions, this is considered a plus (minus) for that method. The most favorable situation occurs when a subject only has to answer one question per word.

3. *Difficulty in answering each elicitation method's question.* Although this criterion is more subjective than the other two criteria, difficulty in answering a question may also affect the accuracy of the resulting MFs, since it can introduce yet another methodological uncertainty into the elicitation process.

Everyone will not agree with these three criteria, but when one is faced with five competing elicitation methodologies, a decision about which one(s) to choose has to be based on some rationale. These criteria seem quite reasonable and practical.

Note that there can be different components to *elicitation uncertainty*. Two common components are (the already mentioned) MF knowledge and *scale*. Anytime subjects are asked to provide values or intervals on a given scale, then if they are asked to provide it on a different scale, the answers for the two scales will not be perfectly correlated. All five methods are subject to scale uncertainties, however polling and interval estimation-2 are subject only to scale uncertainty, whereas the other three methods are subject to both MF knowledge and scale uncertainty.

A comparison of the five elicitation methods is summarized in Table 3.7. There is only one method that does not require MF knowledge and uses only one question per word, Interval Estimation-2. It is this method that we therefore prefer to use

---

[24]Türksen and Wilson (1994) also state that people are not willing to spend a lot of time answering survey questions. Note that "a lot of questions" and "many questions" are open to the queries, "How many questions constitute a lot of questions or many questions"? These are very subjective and their answers are something we avoid, because our method of choice for a group of subjects only requires one question per word—the smallest possible number of questions—whereas all other methods require more than one question per word.

Table 3.7. Comparisons of five T1 elicitation methods

Name of method	MF knowledge	Number of questions	Question-difficulty ranking[a]
Polling	Not required	Large	1
Direct Rating	Required	Large	3
Reverse Rating	Required	Large	4
Interval Estimation-1	Required	Large	5
Interval Estimation-2	Not required	One per word	2

[a]Least-difficult is ranked 1 and most difficult is ranked 5. This ranking is ours and is subjective, that is, if a subject is asked a question using polling or interval estimation-2, our feeling is that it can be answered in a very short time and the subject will be quite sure about their answer. On the other hand, if a subject is asked a question using direct rating, reverse rating, or interval estimation-1, our feeling is that it will take a longer time and the subject will not be so sure about their answer; for example, the phrases "to the degree 0.7" or "degree of" sound quite uncertain.

when data are elicited from a group of subjects about words, and it is the method used in this book.

APPENDIX 3B. DERIVATION OF REASONABLE INTERVAL TEST

In this appendix, derivations of equations (3.19)–(3.21) are obtained. They are taken from Liu and Mendel (2008, Appendix A). Examining Fig. 3.11, and using the requirement that reasonable data intervals must overlap, it must be true that

$$\min_{\forall i=1,\dots,m''} b^{(i)} > \max_{\forall i=1,\dots,m''} a^{(i)} \tag{3B.1}$$

A simple way to satisfy equation (3B.1) is to require that

$$\left.\begin{array}{l} a^{(i)} < \xi \\ b^{(i)} > \xi \end{array}\right\}, \ \forall i = 1,\dots,m'' \tag{3B.2}$$

where threshold ξ has to be chosen, and there can be different ways to do this. In the IA, an optimal value of ξ, ξ^*, is chosen so that

$$\xi^* = \arg\min_{\xi}[\,P(a^{(i)} > \xi) + P(b^{(i)} < \xi)\,] \tag{3B.3}$$

By choosing ξ^* in this way, data intervals that do not satisfy equation (3B.2) will occur with the smallest probability.

In order to compute ξ^*, it is assumed that each $a^{(i)}$ ($i = 1, \dots, m''$) is Gaussian with mean m_a and standard deviation σ_a, and each $b^{(i)}$ ($i = 1, \dots, m''$) is also Gaussian, but with mean m_b and standard deviation σ_b. It follows that

$$P(a^{(i)} > \xi) + P(b^{(i)} < \xi) = \frac{1}{\sqrt{2\pi}\sigma_a} \int_\xi^\infty e^{-\frac{1}{2}\left[\frac{a^{(i)}-m_a}{\sigma_a}\right]^2} da^{(i)} + \frac{1}{\sqrt{2\pi}\sigma_b} \int_{-\infty}^\xi e^{-\frac{1}{2}\left[\frac{b^{(i)}-m_b}{\sigma_b}\right]^2} db^{(i)}$$

(3B.4)

Setting the derivative of this function with respect to ξ equal to zero, ξ^* is found to be the solution of

$$\frac{1}{\sqrt{2\pi}\sigma_a} e^{-\frac{1}{2}\left[\frac{\xi^*-m_a}{\sigma_a}\right]^2} = \frac{1}{\sqrt{2\pi}\sigma_b} e^{-\frac{1}{2}\left[\frac{\xi^*-m_b}{\sigma_b}\right]^2}$$

(3B.5)

Observe that ξ^* occurs at the intersection of the two Gaussian distributions $p(a^{(i)})$ and $p(b^{(i)})$. Taking the natural logarithm of both sides of equation (3B.5), one is led to the following quadratic equation:

$$(\sigma_a^2 - \sigma_b^2)\xi^{*2} + 2(m_a\sigma_b^2 - m_b\sigma_a^2)\xi^* + [m_b^2\sigma_a^2 - m_a^2\sigma_b^2 - 2\sigma_a^2\sigma_b^2 \ln(\sigma_a/\sigma_b)] = 0$$

(3B.6)

The two solutions of this equation are

$$\xi^* = \frac{(m_b\sigma_a^2 - m_a\sigma_b^2) \pm \sigma_a\sigma_b\left[(m_a-m_b)^2 + 2(\sigma_a^2 - \sigma_b^2)\ln(\sigma_a/\sigma_b)\right]^{1/2}}{(\sigma_a^2 - \sigma_b^2)}$$

(3B.7)

The final solution is chosen as the one for which

$$\xi^* \in [m_a, m_b]$$

(3B.8)

   That this solution minimizes $P(a^{(i)} > \xi) + P(b^{(i)} < \xi)$, rather than maximizes it follows from showing that the derivative of equation (3B.5) with respect to ξ, after which ξ is set equal to ξ^*, is positive. Because this is a very tedious calculation, an alternative is presented next.

Fact: $P(a^{(i)} > \xi) + P(b^{(i)} < \xi)$ is a concave function and its minimum value, ξ^*, occurs in the interval $[m_a, m_b]$.

   A proof of this fact follows from (a) and (b) of Fig. 3.20. From Fig. 3.20 (a), observe that at $\xi = \xi^*$,

$$P(a^{(i)} > \xi^*) + P(b^{(i)} < \xi^*) = A_1 + (A_2 + A_3)$$

(3B.9)

and at $\xi = \xi'$ ($\xi' < \xi^*$),

$$P(a^{(i)} > \xi') + P(b^{(i)} < \xi') = (A_1 + A_2 + A_4) + A_3$$

(3B.10)

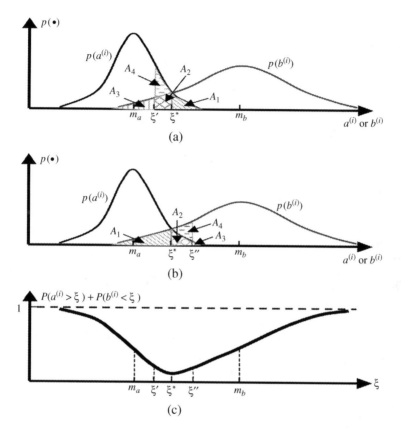

Figure 3.20. $p(a^{(i)})$, $p(b^{(i)})$, and the four areas $A_i = (i = 1, \ldots, 4)$ that can be used to compute $P(a^{(i)} > \xi^*) + P(b^{(i)} < \xi^*)$, and (a) $P(a^{(i)} > \xi') + P(b^{(i)} < \xi')$, $\xi' < \xi^*$; or (b) $P(a^{(i)} > \xi'') + P(b^{(i)} < \xi'')$, $\xi'' > \xi^*$; and, (c) the concave shape of $P(a^{(i)} > \xi) + P(b^{(i)} < \xi)$ (Liu and Mendel, 2008; © 2008, IEEE).

Comparing equations (3B.10) and (3B.9), it follows that

$$P(a^{(i)} > \xi') + P(b^{(i)} < \xi') > P(a^{(i)} > \xi^*) + P(b^{(i)} < \xi^*) \qquad (3B.11)$$

Proceeding in a similar manner for Fig. 3.20 (b), it follows that ($\xi'' > \xi^*$)

$$P(a^{(i)} > \xi'') + P(b^{(i)} < \xi'') > P(a^{(i)} > \xi^*) + P(b^{(i)} < \xi^*) \qquad (3B.12)$$

Equations (3B.11) and (3B.12) together prove that $P(a^{(i)} > \xi) + P(b^{(i)} < \xi)$ is a concave function about $\xi = \xi^*$. The concave shape of $P(a^{(i)} > \xi) + P(b^{(i)} < \xi)$ is depicted in Fig. 3.20 (c).

Above, it has been proven that ξ^* occurs at the intersection of $p(a^{(i)})$ and $p(b^{(i)})$; but, it is clear from Fig. 3.20 (a) or (b) that $\xi^* \in [m_a, m_b]$. Q. E. D.

Because access to the population means and standard deviations is unavailable, they must be estimated in order to compute ξ^* and to perform the test in equation (3B.8). Our approach is to estimate those quantities as

$$\hat{m}_a = m_l, \; \hat{m}_b = m_r, \; \hat{\sigma}_a = \sigma_l, \; \hat{\sigma}_b = \sigma_r \tag{3B.13}$$

Doing this, one obtains equations (3.19)–(3.21). Note that numerical values for m_l, m_r, σ_l, and σ_r are available at the end of tolerance limit processing, so that ξ^* can indeed be computed.

REFERENCES

D. V. Budescu, T. M. Karelitz, and T. Wallsten, "Predicting the directionality of probability words from their membership functions," *J. of Behav. Dec. Making,* vol. 16, 2003, pp. 259–180.

J.-L. Chameau and J. C. Santamarina, "Membership functions I: Comparing methods of measurement," *Int. J. of Approximate Reasoning,* vol. 1, pp. 287–301, 1987.

M. R. Civanlar and H. J. Trussel, "Constructing membership functions using statistical data," *Fuzzy Sets and Systems,* vol. 18, pp. 1–14, 1986.

A. M. G. Cornelissen, *The Two Faces of Sustainability: Fuzzy Evaluation of Sustainable Development,* Ph.D. Thesis, Wageningen Univ., The Netherlands, 2003.

D. Dubois and H. Prade, "Fuzzy sets and statistical data," *European J. of Operational Research,* vol. 25, pp. 345–356, 1986.

D. Dubois and H. Prade, "Fuzzy sets, probability and measurement," *European J. Operation Res.,* vol. 40, pp. 1350–1354, 1989.

D. Dubois, L. Foulloy, G. Mauris, and H. Prade, "Probability-possibility transformations, triangular fuzzy sets, and probabilistic inequalities," *Reliable Computing,* vol. 10, pp. 273–297, 2004.

F. Herrera, E. Herrera-Viedma, and L. Martinez, "A fusion approach for managing multigranularity linguistic term sets in decision making," *Fuzzy Sets and Systems,* vol. 114, pp. 43–58, 2000.

H. M. Hersch and A. Caramazza, "A fuzzy set approach to modifiers and vagueness in natural language," *J. of Experimental Psychology,* vol. 105, pp. 254–276, 1976.

J. Joo and J. M. Mendel, "Obtaining an FOU for a word from a single subject by an Individual Interval Approach," in *Proceedings of IEEE International Conference on Systems, Man, and Cybernetics,* San Antonio, TX, Oct. 2009.

N. N. Karnik and J. M. Mendel, "Introduction to type-2 fuzzy logic systems," in *Proceedings of 1998 IEEE FUZZ Conf.,* Anchorage, AK, May 1998, pp. 915–920.

G. J. Klir, *Uncertainty and Information: Foundations of Generalized Information Theory,* New York: Wiley, 2006.

G. J. Klir and B. Yuan, *Fuzzy Sets and Fuzzy Logic: Theory and Applications,* Upper Saddle River, NJ: Prentice-Hall, 1995.

J. Lawry, "An alternative to computing with words," *Int. J. of Uncertainty, Fuzziness and Knowledge-Based Systems,* vol. 9, Supplement, pp. 3–16, 2001.

S. Lichtenstein and J. R. Newman, "Empirical scaling of common verbal phrases associated with numerical probabilities," *Psychonomic Science,* vol. 9, pp. 563–564, 1967.

F. Liu and J. M. Mendel, "An *Interval Approach* to fuzzistics for interval type-2 fuzzy sets," in *Proceedings FUZZ-IEEE,* London, UK, pp. 1030–1035, July 2007.

F. Liu and J. M. Mendel, "Encoding words into interval type-2 fuzzy sets using an *Interval Approach,*" *IEEE Trans. on Fuzzy Systems,* vol. 16, pp 1503–1521, December 2008.

L. Ljung, *System Identification: Theory for the User,* Englewood Cliffs, NJ: Prentice-Hall, 1987.

P. J. Macvicar-Whelen, "Fuzzy sets, the concept of height, and the hedge 'very'," *IEEE Trans. on Systems, Man, and Cybernetics,* vol. SMC-8, pp. 507–511, June 1978.

J. M. Mendel, "Computing with words, when words mean different things to different people," in *Proceedings of Third International ICSC Symposium on Fuzzy Logic and Applications,* Rochester Univ., Rochester, NY, June 1999.

J. M. Mendel, *Uncertain Rule-Based Fuzzy Logic Systems: Introduction and New Directions,* Upper-Saddle River, NJ: Prentice-Hall, 2001.

J. M. Mendel, "Fuzzy sets for words: a new beginning," in *Proceedings of FUZZ-IEEE,* St. Louis, MO, pp. 37–42, 2003.

J. M. Mendel, "Computing with words and its relationship with fuzzistics," *Information Sciences,* vol. 177, pp. 988–1006, 2007.

J. M. Mendel and R. I. John, "Footprint of uncertainty and its importance to type-2 fuzzy sets," in *Proceedings of 6th IASTED Int'l. Conf. on Artificial Intelligence and Soft Computing,* Banff, Canada, July 2002, pp. 587–592.

J. M. Mendel and H. Wu, "Type-2 fuzzistics for symmetric interval type-2 fuzzy sets: Part 1, Forward problems," *IEEE Trans. on Fuzzy Systems,* vol. 14, pp. 781–792, December 2006.

J. M. Mendel and H. Wu, "Type-2 fuzzistics for symmetric interval type-2 fuzzy sets: Part 2, Inverse problems," *IEEE Trans. on Fuzzy Systems,* vol. 15, pp. 301–308, April 2007a.

J. M. Mendel and H. Wu, "Type-2 fuzzistics for non-symmetric interval type-2 fuzzy sets: Forward problems," *IEEE Trans. on Fuzzy Systems,* vol. 15, pp. 916–930, October, 2007b.

J. M. Mendel and H. Wu, "New results about the centroid of an interval type-2 fuzzy set, including the centroid of a fuzzy granule," *Information Sciences,* vol. 177, pp. 360–377, 2007c.

A. M. Norwich and I. B. Türksen, "The fundamental measurement of fuzziness," in *Fuzzy Sets and Possibility Theory: Recent Developments,* (R. R. Yager, Ed.), Oxford: Pergamon Press, pp. 61–67, 1982a.

A. M. Norwich and I. B. Türksen, "The construction of membership functions," in *Fuzzy Sets and Possibility Theory: Recent Developments,* (R. R. Yager, Ed.), Oxford: Pergamon Press, pp. 49–60, 1982b.

A. M. Norwich and I. B. Türksen, "Stochastic fuzziness," in *Fuzzy Information and Decision Processes,* (M. M. Gupta and E. Sanchez, Eds.), Amsterdam: North-Holland, pp. 13–22, 1982c.

A. M. Norwich and I. B. Türksen, "A model for the measurement of membership and the consequences of its empirical implementation," *Fuzzy Sets and Systems,* vol. 12, pp. 1–25, 1984.

A. O'Hagan and J. E. Oakley, "Probability is perfect, but we can't elicit it perfectly," *Reliability Engineering and System Safety,* vol. 85, pp. 239–248, 2004.

A. O'Hagan, C. E. Buck, A. Daneshkhah, J. R. Eiser, P. H. Garthwaite, D. J. Jenkinson, J. E. Oakley, and T. Rakow, *Uncertain Judgements: Eliciting Expert's Probabilities,* Chichester, UK: John Wiley, West Sussex, England, 2006.

W. Pedrycz, "Fuzzy equalization in the construction of fuzzy Sets," *Fuzzy Sets and Systems,* Vol. 119, pp. 329–335, 2001.

K. S. Schmucker, *Fuzzy Sets, Natural Language Computations, and Risk Analysis,* Rockville, MD: Computer Science Press, 1984.

T. Soderstrom and P. Stoica, *System Identification,* New York: Prentice-Hall International, 1989.

I. B. Türksen, "Measurement of membership functions," in *Applications of Fuzzy Set Theory in Human Factors* (W. Karwowski and A. Mital, Eds.), Amsterdam: Elsevier Science Publishers, pp. 55–67, 1986.

I. B. Türksen, "Stochastic fuzzy sets: a survey," in *Combining Fuzzy Imprecision with Probabilistic Uncertainty in Decision Making,* (J. Kacprzyk and M. Fedrizzi, Eds.), New York: Springer-Verlag, pp. 168–183, 1988.

I. B. Türksen, "Measurement of membership functions and their acquisition," *Fuzzy Sets and Systems,* vol. 40, pp. 5–38, 1991.

I. B. Türksen and I. A. Wilson, "A fuzzy set preference model for consumer choice," *Fuzzy Sets and Systems,* vol. 68, pp. 253–266, 1994.

R. W. Walpole, R. H. Myers, A. L. Myers, and K. Ye, *Probability and Statistics for Engineers and Scientists,"* 8th Ed., Upper Saddlebroock River, NJ: Prentice-Hall, 2007.

T. S. Wallsten and D. V. Budescu "A review of human linguistic probability processing: general principles and empirical evidence," *The Knowledge Engineering Review,* vol. 10, no. 1, pp. 43–62, 1995.

L. A. Zadeh, "A fuzzy-set-theoretic interpretation of linguistic hedges," *J. of Cybernetics,* vol. 2, pp. 4–34, 1972.

R. Zwick, "A note on random sets and the Thurstonian scaling methods," *Fuzzy Sets and Systems,* vol. 21, pp. 351–356, 1987.

CHAPTER 4

Decoding: From FOUs to A Recommendation

4.1 INTRODUCTION

Recall that a Per-C (Fig. 1.7) consists of three components: an encoder, which maps words into IT2 FS models; a CWW engine, which operates on the input words and whose outputs are FOU(s); and a decoder, which maps these FOU(s) into a recommendation. The decoder is discussed in this chapter.

The recommendation from the decoder can have several different forms:

1. *Word:* This is the most typical case. For example, for the social judgment advisor (SJA) developed in Chapter 8, perceptual reasoning (Chapter 6) is used to compute an output FOU from a set of rules that are activated by words. This FOU is then mapped into a codebook word so that it can be understood. The mapping that does this imposes two requirements, one each on the CWW engine and the decoder.

   First, the output of the CWW Engine must resemble the word FOU in the codebook. Recall that in Chapter 3 it was shown that there are only three kinds of FOUs in the codebook—left-shoulder, right-shoulder, and interior FOUs—all of which are *normal*. Consequently, the output of the CWW engine must also be a normal IT2 FS having one of these three shapes. Perceptual reasoning lets us satisfy this requirement.

   Second, the Decoder must compare the similarity between two IT2 FSs so that the output of the CWW engine can be mapped into its most similar word in the codebook. Several similarity measures [Bustine (2000), Gorzalczany (1987), Mitchell (2005), Wu and Mendel (2008, 2009), Zeng and Li (2006b)] for IT2 FSs are discussed in Section 4.2.

2. *Rank:* In some decision-making situations, several alternatives are compared so that the best one(s) can be chosen. In the investment judgment advisor (IJA) developed in Chapter 7, several investment alternatives are compared to find the ones with the best overall matches to an investor. In the procurement judgment advisor (PJA) developed in Chapter 9, three missile systems are compared to find the one with the best overall performance. In these ap-

plications, the outputs of the CWW engines are always IT2 FSs; hence, the decoder must rank them to find the best alternative(s). Ranking methods [Mitchell (2006), Wu and Mendel (2009)] for IT2 FSs are discussed in Section 4.3.

3. *Class:* In some decision-making applications, the output of the CWW engine must be mapped into a class. In the journal publication judgment advisor (JPJA) developed in Chapter 10, the outputs of the CWW Engine are IT2 FSs representing the overall quality of a journal article obtained from reviewers. These IT2 FSs must be mapped into one of three decision classes: accept, rewrite, or reject. How to do this is discussed in Section 4.4.

It is important to propagate linguistic uncertainties all the way through the Per-C, from its encoder, through its CWW engine, and also through its decoder; hence, our guideline for developing decoders is to preserve and propagate the uncertainties through the decoder as far as possible. More will be said about this later in this chapter.

4.2 SIMILARITY MEASURE USED AS A DECODER

In this section, six similarity measures for IT2 FSs are briefly introduced and their performances as decoders are compared. The best of these measures is suggested for use as a decoder in CWW, and is the one used by us in later chapters.

4.2.1 Definitions

Similarity, proximity, and compatibility have all been used in the literature to assess agreement between FSs [Cross and Sudkamp (2002)]. There are many different definitions for the meanings of them [Cross and Sudkamp (2002), Fan and Xie (1999), Kaufmann (1975), Mencar et al. (2007), Setnes et al. (1998), Yager (2004), Zadeh (1971)].

According to Yager (2004), a *proximity relationship* between two T1 FSs A and B on a domain X is a mapping $p: X \times X \rightarrow T$ (often T is the unit interval) having the properties

1. *Reflexivity:* $p(A, A) = 1$
2. *Symmetry:* $p(A, B) = p(B, A)$

According to Zadeh (1971) and Yager (2004), a *similarity relationship* between two FSs A and B on a domain X is a mapping $sm: X \times X \rightarrow T$ having the properties

1. *Reflexivity:* $sm(A, A) = 1$
2. *Symmetry:* $sm(A, B) = sm(B, A)$
3. *Transitivity:* $sm(A, B) \geq sm(A, C) \wedge sm(C, B)$, where C is an arbitrary FS on domain X

Observe that a similarity relationship adds the additional requirement of transitivity to proximity, though whether or not the above definition of transitivity is correct is still under debate [Cock and Kerre (2003), Klawonn (2003)].

There are other definitions of transitivity used in the literature [Bustince (2000), García-Lapresta and Meneses (2003), Switalski (2003)], for example, the one used by Bustince (2000) is:

Transitivity': If $A \leq B \leq C$, that is, $\mu_A(x) \leq \mu_B(x) \leq \mu_C(x)$ $\forall x \in X$ (see Fig. 4.1), then $sm(A, B) \geq sm(A, C)$.

Bustince's transitivity is used by us in this book because it seems more reasonable than the transitivity introduced by Zadeh and Yager.

Compatibility is a broader concept. According to Cross and Sudkamp (2002), "the term compatibility is used to encompass various types of comparisons frequently made between objects or concepts. These relationships include similarity, inclusion, proximity, and the degree of matching."

In summary, similarity is included in proximity, and both similarity and proximity are included in compatibility. T1 FS compatibility measures are briefly discussed in Appendix 4A.1. The rest of this section focuses on similarity measures for IT2 FSs.

4.2.2 Desirable Properties for an IT2 FS Similarity Measure Used as a Decoder

Let $sm(\tilde{A}, \tilde{B})$ be the similarity measure between two IT2 FSs $\tilde{A}$ and $\tilde{B}$, and $c(\tilde{A})$ be the center of the centroid, or average centroid, of $\tilde{A}$ [Section 2.5.A; see also Wu and Mendel (2007)], that is,

$$c(\tilde{A}) = \frac{c_l(\tilde{A}) + c_r(\tilde{A})}{2} \tag{4.1}$$

Definition 4.1. $\tilde{A}$ and $\tilde{B}$ have the same shape if $\overline{\mu}_{\tilde{A}}(x) = \overline{\mu}_{\tilde{B}}(x + \lambda)$ and $\underline{\mu}_{\tilde{A}}(x) = \underline{\mu}_{\tilde{B}}(x + \lambda)$ for $\forall x \in X$, where λ is a constant.

Definition 4.2. $\tilde{A} \leq \tilde{B}$ if $\overline{\mu}_{\tilde{A}}(x) \leq \overline{\mu}_{\tilde{B}}(x)$ and $\underline{\mu}_{\tilde{A}}(x) \leq \underline{\mu}_{\tilde{B}}(x)$ for $\forall x \in X$.

An illustration of $\tilde{A} \leq \tilde{B}$ is shown in Fig. 4.2.

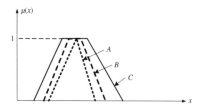

Figure 4.1. An illustration of $A \leq B \leq C$.

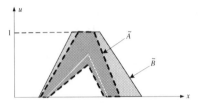

Figure 4.2. An illustration of $\tilde{A} \leq \tilde{B}$ (Wu and Mendel, 2009, © 2009, Elsevier).

Definition 4.3. $\tilde{A}$ and $\tilde{B}$ overlap, i.e., $\tilde{A} \cap \tilde{B} \neq \emptyset$, if $\exists x$ such that $\min(\overline{\mu}_{\tilde{A}}(x), \overline{\mu}_{\tilde{B}}(x)) > 0$. $\tilde{A}$ and $\tilde{B}$ do not overlap, that is, $\tilde{A} \cap \tilde{B} = \emptyset$, if $\min(\overline{\mu}_{\tilde{A}}(x), \overline{\mu}_{\tilde{B}}(x)) = \min(\underline{\mu}_{\tilde{A}}(x), \underline{\mu}_{\tilde{B}}(x)) = 0$ for $\forall x$.

An illustration of overlapping $\tilde{A}$ and $\tilde{B}$ is shown in Fig. 4.2. Nonoverlapping $\tilde{A}$ and $\tilde{B}$ have no parts of their FOUs that overlap.

The following four properties [Wu and Mendel (2008)] are considered desirable for an IT2 FS similarity measure:

1. *Reflexivity:* $sm(\tilde{A}, \tilde{B}) = 1 \Leftrightarrow \tilde{A} = \tilde{B}$.
2. *Symmetry:* $sm(\tilde{A}, \tilde{B}) = sm(\tilde{B}, \tilde{A})$.
3. *Transitivity:* If $\tilde{C} \leq \tilde{A} \leq \tilde{B}$, then $sm(\tilde{C}, \tilde{A}) \geq sm(\tilde{C}, \tilde{B})$.
4. *Overlapping:* If $\tilde{A} \cap \tilde{B} \neq \emptyset$, then $sm(\tilde{A}, \tilde{B}) > 0$; otherwise, $sm(\tilde{A}, \tilde{B}) = 0$.

Observe that the first three properties are the IT2 FS counterparts of those used in Zadeh and Yager's definition of T1 FS similarity measures, except that Bustince's definition of transitivity is used. The fourth property of overlapping is intuitive and is used in many T1 FS similarity measures [Cross and Sudkamp (2002)], so, it is included here as a desirable property for IT2 FS similarity measures.

4.2.3 Problems with Existing IT2 FS Similarity Measures

Though "there are approximately 50 expressions for determining how similar two (T1) fuzzy sets are" [Bustince et al. (2007)], to the best knowledge of the authors, there are only six similarity (compatibility) measures for IT2 FSs [Bustince (2002), Gorzalczany (1987), Mitchell (2005), Wu and Mendel (2008, 2009a), Zeng and Li (2006b)]. The drawbacks of five of them are pointed out in this subsection [an example that demonstrates each of the drawbacks can be found in Wu and Mendel (2008)], and the sixth similarity measure (Jaccard similarity measure, [Wu and Mendel (2009)]) is introduced in the next subsection.

1. Gorzalczany (1987) defined an interval compatibility measure for IT2 FSs; however, it is not a good similarity measure for our purpose because [Wu and Mendel (2008)] as long as $\max_{x \in X} \mu_{\tilde{A}}(x) = \max_{x \in X} \mu_{\tilde{B}}(x)$ and $\max_{x \in X} \overline{\mu}_{\tilde{A}}(x) = \max_{x \in X} \overline{\mu}_{\tilde{B}}(x)$ (both of which can be easily satisfied by $\tilde{A}$ and $\tilde{B}$, even when $\tilde{A} \neq \tilde{B}$), no matter how different the shapes of $\tilde{A}$ and $\tilde{B}$ are, it always gives $sm_G(\tilde{A}, \tilde{B}) = sm_G(\tilde{B}, \tilde{A}) = [1, 1]$, that is, it does not satisfy reflexivity.
2. Bustince (2002) defined an interval similarity measure for IT2 FSs $\tilde{A}$ and $\tilde{B}$

based on the inclusion of $\tilde{A}$ in $\tilde{B}$. A problem with this approach is that [Wu and Mendel (2008)] when $\tilde{A}$ and $\tilde{B}$ are disjoint, no matter how far away they are from each other, $sm_B(\tilde{A}, \tilde{B})$ will always be a nonzero constant, that is, it does not satisfy overlapping.

3. Mitchell (2005) defined the similarity between two IT2 FSs as the average of the similarities between their embedded T1 FSs, when the embedded T1 FSs are generated randomly. Consequently, this similarity measure does not satisfy reflexivity, that is, $sm_M(\tilde{A}, \tilde{B}) \neq 1$ when $\tilde{A} = \tilde{B}$ because the randomly generated embedded T1 FSs from $\tilde{A}$ and $\tilde{B}$ vary from experiment to experiment [Wu and Mendel (2008)].

4. Zeng and Li (2006b) defined the similarity between $\tilde{A}$ and $\tilde{B}$ based on the difference between them. A problem with this approach is that when $\tilde{A}$ and $\tilde{B}$ are disjoint, the similarity is a nonzero constant, or increases as the distance increases, that is, it does not satisfy overlapping.

5. Wu and Mendel (2008) proposed a vector similarity measure, which considers the similarity between the shape and proximity of two IT2 FSs separately. It does not satisfy overlapping [Wu and Mendel (2009)].

4.2.4   Jaccard Similarity Measure for IT2 FSs

The Jaccard similarity measure for T1 FSs ([Jaccard (1908)]; see, also, Table 4A.1) is defined as

$$sm_J(A, B) = \frac{f(A \cap B)}{f(A \cup B)} \tag{4.2}$$

where f is a function satisfying $f(A \cup B) = f(A) + f(B)$ for disjoint A and B. Usually the function f is chosen as the cardinality [see (2.39)], that is, when $\cap \equiv \min$ and $\cup \equiv \max$,

$$sm_J(A, B) \equiv \frac{p(A \cap B)}{p(A \cup B)} = \frac{\int_X \min(\mu_A(x), \mu_B(x))dx}{\int_X \max(\mu_A(x), \mu_B(x))dx} \tag{4.3}$$

whose discrete version is

$$sm_J(A, B) = \frac{\sum_{i=1}^N \min(\mu_A(x_i), \mu_B(x_i))}{\sum_{i=1}^N \max(\mu_A(x_i), \mu_B(x_i))} \tag{4.4}$$

where x_i $(i = 1, \ldots, N)$ are equally spaced in the support of $A \cup B$.

A new similarity measure for IT2 FSs, which is an extension of equation (4.3), is proposed in [Wu and Mendel (2009)]. It uses average cardinality, AC, as defined in equation (2.44), applied to both $\tilde{A} \cap \tilde{B}$ and $\tilde{A} \cup \tilde{B}$, where $\tilde{A} \cap \tilde{B}$ and $\tilde{A} \cup \tilde{B}$ are computed by equations (2.21) and (2.20), respectively:

$$sm_J(\tilde{A}, \tilde{B}) \equiv \frac{AC(\tilde{A} \cap \tilde{B})}{AC(\tilde{A} \cup \tilde{B})} = \frac{\int_X \min(\overline{\mu}_{\tilde{A}}(x), \overline{\mu}_{\tilde{B}}(x))dx + \int_X \min(\underline{\mu}_{\tilde{A}}(x), \underline{\mu}_{\tilde{B}}(x))dx}{\int_X \max(\overline{\mu}_{\tilde{A}}(x), \overline{\mu}_{\tilde{B}}(x))dx + \int_X \max(\underline{\mu}_{\tilde{A}}(x), \underline{\mu}_{\tilde{B}}(x))dx} \tag{4.5}$$

Note that each integral in equation (4.5) is an area, for example, $\int_X \min(\overline{\mu}_{\tilde{A}}(x),$ $\overline{\mu}_{\tilde{B}}(x))dx$ is the area under the minimum of $\overline{\mu}_{\tilde{A}}(x)$ and $\overline{\mu}_{\tilde{B}}(x)$. Closed-form solutions cannot always be found for these integrals, so, the following discrete version of equation (4.5) is used in calculations:

$$sm_j(\tilde{A}, \tilde{B}) = \frac{\sum_{i=1}^{N} \min(\overline{\mu}_{\tilde{A}}(x_i), \overline{\mu}_{\tilde{B}}(x_i)) + \sum_{i=1}^{N} \min(\underline{\mu}_{\tilde{A}}(x_i), \underline{\mu}_{\tilde{B}}(x_i))}{\sum_{i=1}^{N} \max(\overline{\mu}_{\tilde{A}}(x_i), \overline{\mu}_{\tilde{B}}(x_i)) + \sum_{i=1}^{N} \max(\underline{\mu}_{\tilde{A}}(x_i), \underline{\mu}_{\tilde{B}}(x_i))} \quad (4.6)$$

Theorem 4.1. The Jaccard similarity measure, $sm_j(\tilde{A}, \tilde{B})$, satisfies reflexivity, symmetry, transitivity, and overlapping.

The proof is given in Appendix 4B.1.

4.2.5 Simulation Results

The 32 word FOUs shown in Fig. 3.18 are used in this section, and for the convenience of the readers, they are repeated in Fig. 4.3. The similarities among all 32 words, computed using the Jaccard similarity measure in equation (4.5), are summarized in Table 4.1. The numbers across the top of this table refer to the numbered words that are in the first column of the table. Observe that the Jaccard similarity measure gives very reasonable results; generally, the similarity decreases monotonically as two words get further away from each other.[1] The Jaccard similarity measure was also compared with five other similarity measures in Wu and Mendel (2008), and the results showed that to date it is the best one to use in CWW, because it is the only IT2 FS similarity measure that satisfies the four desirable properties of a similarity measure.

Note, also, that once similarities have been computed this never has to be done again; the results in Table 4.1 can be stored in memory for later use (as in perceptual reasoning; see Chapter 6).

Example 4.1. It is interesting to know which words are similar to a particular word with similarity values larger than a prespecified threshold. When the Jaccard similarity measure is used, the groups of similar words for different thresholds are shown in Table 4.2; for example, Row 1 shows that the word *teeny-weeny* is similar to the word *none to very little* to degree ≥ 0.7, and that this word as well as the words *a smidgen* and *tiny* are similar to *none to very little* to degree ≥ 0.6. Observe that except for the word *maximum amount*, every word in the 32-word vocabulary has at least one word similar to it with similarity larger than or equal to 0.6. Observe, also, that there are four words [*very sizeable* (22), *substantial amount* (23), *a lot* (24), and *high amount* (25)] with the most number (8 in this example) of neighbors with similarity larger than or equal to 0.5, and all of them have interior FOUs (see Fig. 4.3).

---

[1]There are some cases in which the similarity does not decrease monotonically, for example, words 8 and 9 in the first row. This is because the distances among the words are determined by a ranking method (see Section 4.3) that considers only the centroids but not the shapes of the IT2 FSs.

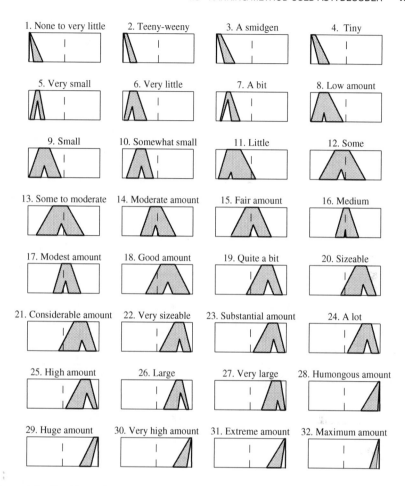

Figure 4.3. The 32 word FOUs ranked by their centers of centroid. To read this figure, scan from left to right, starting at the top of the page. The dashed line is at $x = 5$, which will be useful in Example 4.2 (adapted from Liu and Mendel, 2008; © 2008, IEEE).

The fact that so many of the 32 words are similar to many other words suggests that it is possible to create many subvocabularies that cover the interval [0, 10]. Some examples of five word subvocabularies have already been given in Fig. 3.19.

4.3 RANKING METHOD USED AS A DECODER

Though there are more than 35 reported different methods for ranking type-1 fuzzy numbers ([Wang and Kerre (2001a,b)]; see also Appendix 4A.2), to the best knowledge of the authors, only two methods have been published [Mitchell (2006), Wu

Table 4.1. Similarity matrix when the Jaccard similarity measure is used

	1	2	3	4	5	6	7	8	9	10	11	12	13	14	15	16	17	18	19	20	21	22	23	24	25	26	27	28	29	30	31	32
1. None to very little	1	.78	.63	.62	.25	.19	.11	.16	.13	.08	.09	.01	.01	.01	0	0	0	0	0	0	0	0	0	0	0	0	0	0	0	0	0	0
2. Teeny-weeny	.78	1	.81	.80	.27	.21	.12	.17	.14	.08	.10	.01	.01	0	0	0	0	0	0	0	0	0	0	0	0	0	0	0	0	0	0	0
3. A smidgen	.63	.81	1	.99	.37	.31	.20	.24	.21	.14	.15	.03	.04	0	0	0	0	0	0	0	0	0	0	0	0	0	0	0	0	0	0	0
4. Tiny	.62	.80	.99	1	.38	.31	.20	.24	.21	.14	.16	.03	.04	0	0	0	0	0	0	0	0	0	0	0	0	0	0	0	0	0	0	0
5. Very small	.25	.27	.37	.38	1	.64	.40	.36	.30	.18	.21	.03	.03	0	0	0	0	0	0	0	0	0	0	0	0	0	0	0	0	0	0	0
6. Very little	.19	.21	.31	.31	.64	1	.71	.62	.52	.39	.41	.10	.11	.04	.02	0	0	0	0	0	0	0	0	0	0	0	0	0	0	0	0	0
7. A bit	.11	.12	.20	.20	.40	.71	1	.51	.46	.40	.41	.10	.10	.04	.04	0	0	0	0	0	0	0	0	0	0	0	0	0	0	0	0	0
8. Low amount	.16	.17	.24	.24	.36	.62	.51	1	.83	.65	.65	.21	.21	.10	.12	.03	.03	.03	0	0	0	0	0	0	0	0	0	0	0	0	0	0
9. Small	.13	.14	.21	.21	.30	.52	.46	.83	1	.74	.73	.23	.24	.11	.13	.03	.03	.03	0	0	0	0	0	0	0	0	0	0	0	0	0	0
10. Somewhat small	.08	.08	.14	.14	.18	.39	.40	.65	.74	1	.66	.25	.26	.12	.12	.03	.03	.02	0	0	0	0	0	0	0	0	0	0	0	0	0	0
11. Little	.09	.10	.15	.16	.21	.41	.41	.65	.73	.66	1	.36	.37	.22	.23	.12	.11	.08	.03	0	0	0	0	0	0	0	0	0	0	0	0	0
12. Some	.01	.01	.03	.03	.03	.10	.10	.21	.23	.25	.36	1	.94	.73	.69	.45	.50	.33	.20	.20	.19	.10	.10	.10	0	.06	.03	0	0	0	0	0
13. Some to moderate	.01	.01	.04	.04	.03	.11	.10	.21	.24	.26	.37	.94	1	.75	.70	.45	.51	.33	.19	.19	.19	.10	.10	.10	0	.06	.03	0	0	0	0	0
14. Moderate amount	.01	0	0	0	0	.04	.04	.10	.11	.12	.22	.73	.75	1	.79	.60	.63	.37	.21	.22	.21	.12	.12	.12	.08	.06	.04	0	0	0	0	0
15. Fair amount	0	0	0	0	0	.02	.04	.12	.13	.12	.23	.69	.70	.79	1	.52	.69	.37	.25	.26	.25	.12	.12	.12	.07	.08	.04	0	0	0	0	0
16. Medium	0	0	0	0	0	0	0	.03	.03	.03	.12	.45	.45	.60	.52	1	.76	.46	.26	.27	.25	.11	.11	.11	.07	.03	0	0	0	0	0	0
17. Modest amount	0	0	0	0	0	0	0	.03	.03	.03	.11	.50	.51	.63	.69	.76	1	.46	.26	.27	.25	.11	.11	.11	.07	.02	0	0	0	0	0	0
18. Good amount	0	0	0	0	0	0	0	.03	.03	.02	.08	.33	.33	.37	.37	.46	.46	1	.64	.65	.63	.40	.40	.39	.38	.32	.24	.10	.10	.10	.10	.03
19. Quite a bit	0	0	0	0	0	0	0	0	0	0	.03	.20	.19	.21	.25	.26	.26	.64	1	.95	.90	.53	.52	.52	.51	.43	.31	.12	.12	.11	.11	.02
20. Sizeable	0	0	0	0	0	0	0	0	0	0	.03	.20	.19	.22	.26	.27	.27	.65	.95	1	.93	.55	.55	.55	.53	.45	.32	.12	.12	.12	.12	.02
21. Considerable amount	0	0	0	0	0	0	0	0	0	0	.03	.19	.19	.21	.25	.25	.25	.63	.90	.93	1	.60	.60	.60	.58	.50	.37	.15	.15	.14	.14	.04
22. Very sizeable	0	0	0	0	0	0	0	0	0	0	0	.10	.10	.12	.12	.11	.11	.40	.53	.55	.60	1	.99	.97	.94	.72	.58	.23	.23	.22	.22	.08
23. Substantial amount	0	0	0	0	0	0	0	0	0	0	0	.10	.10	.12	.12	.11	.11	.40	.52	.55	.60	.99	1	.99	.95	.73	.58	.23	.23	.22	.22	.08
24. A lot	0	0	0	0	0	0	0	0	0	0	0	.10	.10	.12	.12	.11	.11	.39	.52	.55	.60	.97	.99	1	.94	.72	.58	.23	.23	.22	.22	.08
25. High amount	0	0	0	0	0	0	0	0	0	0	0	0	0	.08	.07	.07	.07	.38	.51	.53	.58	.94	.95	.94	1	.77	.58	.22	.21	.21	.21	.07
26. Large	0	0	0	0	0	0	0	0	0	0	0	.06	.06	.06	.08	.03	.02	.32	.43	.45	.50	.72	.73	.72	.77	1	.60	.20	.20	.19	.19	.05
27. Very large	0	0	0	0	0	0	0	0	0	0	0	.03	.03	.04	.04	0	.02	.24	.31	.32	.37	.58	.58	.58	.58	.60	1	.36	.37	.34	.33	.14
28. Humongous amount	0	0	0	0	0	0	0	0	0	0	0	0	0	0	0	0	0	.10	.12	.12	.15	.23	.23	.23	.22	.20	.36	1	.70	.85	.88	.52
29. Huge amount	0	0	0	0	0	0	0	0	0	0	0	0	0	0	0	0	0	.10	.12	.12	.15	.23	.23	.23	.21	.20	.37	.70	1	.82	.79	.41
30. Very high amount	0	0	0	0	0	0	0	0	0	0	0	0	0	0	0	0	0	.10	.11	.12	.14	.22	.22	.22	.21	.20	.34	.85	.82	1	.97	.50
31. Extreme amount	0	0	0	0	0	0	0	0	0	0	0	0	0	0	0	0	0	.10	.11	.12	.14	.22	.22	.22	.21	.19	.33	.88	.79	.97	1	.52
32. Maximum amount	0	0	0	0	0	0	0	0	0	0	0	0	0	0	0	0	0	.03	.02	.02	.04	.08	.08	.08	.07	.05	.14	.52	.41	.50	.52	1

Table 4.2. Groups of similar words when the Jaccard similarity measure is used

Word	$sm_J \geq 0.9$	$sm_J \geq 0.8$	$sm_J \geq 0.7$	$sm_J \geq 0.6$	$sm_J \geq 0.5$
1. None to very little			Teeny-weeny	A smidgen Tiny	
2. Teeny-weeny	Tiny A smidgen	A smidgen Tiny	None to very little	None to very little	
3. A smidgen		Teeny-weeny		None to very little	
4. Tiny		Teeny-weeny		None to very little	
5. Very small				Very little	
6. Very little			A bit	Very small Low amount	Small
7. A bit			Very little		Low amount
8. Low amount		Small	Very little	Little Somewhat small Very little	A bit
9. Small		Low amount	Somewhat small Little		Very little
10. Somewhat	small		Small	Little Low amount	
11. Little			Small	Somewhat small Low amount	
12. Some	Some to moderate		Moderate amount	Fair amount	Modest amount
13. Some to moderate	Some		Moderate amount	Fair amount	Modest amount
14. Moderate amount			Fair amount Some to moderate Some	Modest amount	Medium
15. Fair amount			Moderate amount	Some to moderate Some Modest amount	Medium

(continued)

Table 4.2. *Continued*

Word	$sm_J \geq 0.9$	$sm_J \geq 0.8$	$sm_J \geq 0.7$	$sm_J \geq 0.6$	$sm_J \geq 0.5$
16. Medium			Modest amount		Moderate amount Fair amount
17. Modest amount			Medium	Fair amount Moderate amount	Some to moderate Some
18. Good amount				Sizeable Quite a bit Considerable amount	
19. Quite a bit	Sizeable	Considerable amount		Good amount	Very sizeable A lot Substantial amount High amount
20. Sizeable	Quite a bit Considerable amount			Good amount	Very sizeable A lot Substantial amount High amount
21. Considerable amount	Sizeable	Quite a bit		Good amount Very sizeable	Substantial amount A lot High amount
22. Very sizeable	Substantial amount A lot High amount		Large	Considerable amount	Very large Sizeable Quite a bit
23. Substantial amount	Very sizeable A lot High amount		Large		Considerable amount Very large Sizeable Quite a bit

24. A lot	Substantial amount Very sizeable High amount	Large		Considerable amount Very large Sizeable Quite a bit
25. High amount	Substantial amount Very sizeable A lot	Large		Very large Considerable amount Sizeable Quite a bit
26. Large		Very large	High amount Substantial amount Very sizeable A lot	
27. Very large		Large		
28. Humongous amount	Extreme amount Very high amount Very high amount	Huge amount		High amount Very sizeable Substantial amount A lot Maximum amount
29. Huge amount			Extreme amount Humongous amount	
30. Very high amount	Humongous amount Huge amount		Humongous amount	Maximum amount
31. Extreme amount	Very high amount		Huge amount	Maximum amount Extreme amount Humongous amount Very high amount
32. Maximum amount	Humongous amount			

Source: Wu and Mendel, 2009a; © 2009, Elsevier.

and Mendel (2009a)] for ranking IT2 FSs, and they are discussed in this section. Before that, some reasonable ordering properties for IT2 FSs are introduced.

4.3.1 Reasonable Ordering Properties for IT2 FSs

Wang and Kerre (2001a,b) performed a comprehensive study of T1 FSs ranking methods based on seven reasonable ordering properties for T1 FSs. When extended to IT2 FSs, these properties are:[2]

P1. If $\tilde{X}_1 \geq \tilde{X}_2$, and $\tilde{X}_2 \geq \tilde{X}_1$, then $\tilde{X}_1 \sim \tilde{X}_2$.
P2. If $\tilde{X}_1 \geq \tilde{X}_2$, and $\tilde{X}_2 \geq \tilde{X}_3$, then $\tilde{X}_1 \geq \tilde{X}_3$.
P3. If $\tilde{X}_1 \cap \tilde{X}_2 = \emptyset$ and $c(\tilde{X}_1) > c(\tilde{X}_2)$, then $\tilde{X}_1 \geq \tilde{X}_2$.
P4. The order of $\tilde{X}_1$ and $\tilde{X}_2$ is not affected by the other IT2 FSs under comparison.
P5. If $\tilde{X}_1 \geq \tilde{X}_2$, then[3] $\tilde{X}_1 + \tilde{X}_3 \geq \tilde{X}_2 + \tilde{X}_3$.
P6. If $\tilde{X}_1 \geq \tilde{X}_2$, then[4] $\tilde{X}_1\tilde{X}_3 \geq \tilde{X}_2\tilde{X}_3$.

Here, $\geq$ means "larger than or equal to in the sense of ranking" and $\sim$ means "the same rank."

All six properties are intuitive. P4 may look trivial, but it is worth emphasizing because some ranking methods [Wang and Kerre (2001a,b)] first set up a reference set (or sets) and then all FSs are compared with the reference set(s). The reference set(s) may depend on the FSs under consideration, so it is possible (but not desirable) that $\tilde{X}_1 \geq \tilde{X}_2$ when $\{\tilde{X}_1, \tilde{X}_2, \tilde{X}_3\}$ are ranked, whereas $\tilde{X}_1 < \tilde{X}_2$ when $\{\tilde{X}_1, \tilde{X}_2, \tilde{X}_4\}$ are ranked.

4.3.2 Mitchell's Method for Ranking IT2 FSs

Similar to his IT2 FS similarity measure, Mitchell (2006) computes the ranking of IT2 FSs from the rankings of their randomly selected embedded T1 FSs. As a result, the ranking is random and changes from experiment to experiment.

Let N be the number of randomly selected embedded T1 FSs for each IT2 FS and M be the number of IT2 FSs to be ranked. Then, a total of N^M T1 FS rankings must be evaluated by the Mitchell method before the IT2 FS ranks can be computed. For example, to rank the 32 IT2 FSs shown in Fig. 4.3, even if N is chosen as a very small number, say 2, a total of $2^{32} \approx 4.295 \times 10^9$ T1 FS rankings have to be evaluated. Clearly, this is highly impractical. Additionally, because of the random nature of Mitchell's ranking method, it only satisfies Property P3 of the six reasonable properties proposed in Section 4.3.1.

---

[2]There is another property saying that "for any IT2 FS $\tilde{X}_1$, $\tilde{X}_1 \geq \tilde{X}_1$." However, it is not included here since it can be viewed as a special case of P2, and the centroid-based ranking method introduced in Section 4.3.3 satisfies it.
[3]$\tilde{X}_1 + \tilde{X}_3$ is computed using α-cuts and the extension principle, that is, let $\tilde{X}_1^\alpha$, $\tilde{X}_3^\alpha$, and $(\tilde{X}_1 + \tilde{X}_3)^\alpha$ be α-cuts on $\tilde{X}_1$, $\tilde{X}_3$ and $\tilde{X}_1 + \tilde{X}_3$, respectively; then $(\tilde{X}_1 + \tilde{X}_3)^\alpha = \tilde{X}_1^\alpha + \tilde{X}_3^\alpha$ for $\forall \alpha \in [0, 1]$.
[4]$\tilde{X}_1\tilde{X}_3$ is computed using a-cuts and the extension principle, that is, let $\tilde{X}_1^\alpha$, $\tilde{X}_3^\alpha$ and $(\tilde{X}_1\tilde{X}_3)^\alpha$ be α-cuts on $\tilde{X}_1$, $\tilde{X}_3$ and $\tilde{X}_1\tilde{X}_3$, respectively; then $(\tilde{X}_1\tilde{X}_3)^\alpha = \tilde{X}_1^\alpha\tilde{X}_3^\alpha$ for $\forall \alpha \in [0, 1]$.

4.3.3   A New Centroid-Based Ranking Method

A simple ranking method based on the centroids of IT2 FSs is proposed in [Wu and Mendel (2009)].

Centroid-Based Ranking Method. First compute the average centroid for each IT2 FS using equation (4.1) and then sort $c(\tilde{X}_i)$ to obtain the rank of $\tilde{X}_i$.

This ranking method can be viewed as a generalization of Yager's first ranking method for T1 FSs (see Table 4A.2), which first computes the centroid of T1 FSs X_i and then ranks them. Since the average centroid is computed from an IT2 FS and then is used to rank the corresponding IT2 FSs, it can be referred to as an *order-inducing variable,* as called by Yager and Filev (1999).

Theorem 4.2 [Wu and Mendel (2009)]. The centroid-based ranking method satisfies the first four reasonable ordering properties, P1–P4.

The proof is given in Appendix 4B.2.

The centroid-based ranking method does not always satisfy P5 and P6. Counterexamples are given in Wu and Mendel (2009); however, these counterexamples happen only when $c(\tilde{X}_1)$ and $c(\tilde{X}_2)$ are very close to each other. For most cases, P5 and P6 are still satisfied. In summary, the centroid-based ranking method satisfies the reasonable ordering properties P1–P4, whereas Mitchell's method only satisfies P3.

Finally, note that the centroid-based ranking method violates the guideline proposed at the end of Section 4.1, that is, it first converts each FOU to a crisp number and then ranks them. The following concept of ranking band is useful in incorporating more uncertainties and in evaluating the confidence of the ranking.

Definition 4.4. The *ranking band* of an IT2 FS is an interval equal to its centroid.

Clearly, if the ranking bands do not overlap (much) then we are more confident about the rankings than if they overlap a lot.

4.3.4   Simulation Results

The 32 word FOUs shown in Fig. 4.3 have been sorted using the centroid-based ranking method. Observe that:

1. The four smallest terms are left shoulders, the five largest terms are right shoulders, and the terms in between have interior FOUs.
2. Visual examination shows that the ranking is reasonable; it also coincides with the meanings of the words.

In summary, the centroid-based ranking method for IT2 FSs seems to be a good choice for the CWW decoder; hence, it is used in this book.

4.4   CLASSIFIER USED AS A DECODER

In this section, five subsethood measures for IT2 FSs are briefly introduced and their performances as a classifier are compared. The best of these measures is suggested for use as a decoder in CWW, and is the one used by us in later chapters.

4.4.1   Desirable Properties for Subsethood Measure as a Decoder

Subsethood of FSs was first introduced by Zadeh (1965) and then extended by Kosko (1990), who defined the subsethood of a T1 FS A in another T1 FS B as

$$ss_K (A, B) = \frac{\int_X \min(\mu_A (x), \mu_B (x)) dx}{\int_X \mu_A (x) dx} \tag{4.7}$$

whose discrete version is

$$ss_K (A, B) = \frac{\sum_{i=1}^{N} \min(\mu_A (x_i), \mu_B (x_i))}{\sum_{i=1}^{N} \mu_A (x_i)} \tag{4.8}$$

Subsethood measures for FSs have since then been studied extensively [Cornelis and Kerre (2004), Dong et al. (2005), Fan et al. (1999), Nguyen and Kreinovich (2008), Rickard (2009), Sinha and Dougherty (1993), Vlachos and Sergiadis (2007), Wu and Mendel (2010), Yang and Lin (2009), Young (1996)], and many different desirable properties or axioms have been proposed for them. In this section, we are interested in subsethood measures for IT2 FSs, particularly, their role as decoders in the Per-C.

Because the Jaccard similarity measure for T1 FSs [see equation (4.2)] and Kosko's subsethood measure for T1 FSs bare a strong resemblance, and the former is the basis for the Jaccard similarity measure for IT2 FSs and the latter is the basis for almost all subsethood measures for IT2 FSs [Cornelis and Kerre (2004), Dong et al. (2005), Nguyen and Kreinovich (2008), Rickard (2009), Vlachos and Sergiadis (2007), Yang and Lin (2009)], in analogy to the desirable properties for IT2 FS similarity measures proposed in Section 4.2.2, and also considering the properties of FS subsethood measures proposed in the literature [Cornelis and Kerre (2004), Dong et al. (2005), Fan et al. (1999), Liu and Xiong (2002), Sinha and Dougherty (1993), Vlachos and Sergiadis (2007), Young (1996), Zadeh (1965), Zeng and Li (2006a)], the following three[5] properties are considered desirable for an IT2 FS subsethood measure when it is used as a classifier in the Per-C[6] [Wu and Mendel (2010)]:

---

[5]For IT2 FS similarity measures, there is another desirable property called symmetry, for example, $sm_J(\tilde{A}, \tilde{B}) = sm_J(\tilde{B}, \tilde{A})$. However, IT2 FS subsethood measures are generally asymmetrical, that is, $ss(\tilde{A}, \tilde{B}) \neq ss(\tilde{B}, \tilde{A})$. There are special conditions under which $ss(\tilde{A}, \tilde{B}) = ss(\tilde{B}, \tilde{A})$; however, usually these conditions are different for different subsethood measures, and it may be impossible to find an intuitive condition under which $ss(\tilde{A}, \tilde{B}) = ss(\tilde{B}, \tilde{A})$ should hold. So, symmetry is not considered for IT2 FS subsethood measures.
[6]Some authors [Cornelis and Kerre (2004), Nguyen and Kreinovich (2008), Rickard et al. 2008)] define IT2 FS subsethood measures as intervals. For such cases, reflexivity becomes $ss(\tilde{A}, \tilde{B}) = [1, 1] \Leftrightarrow \tilde{A} \leq \tilde{B}$, and overlapping becomes: If $\tilde{A} \cap \tilde{B} \neq \emptyset$, then $ss(\tilde{A}, \tilde{B}) > [0, 0]$; otherwise, $ss(\tilde{A}, \tilde{B}) = [0, 0]$.

1. *Reflexivity:* $ss(\tilde{A}, \tilde{B}) = 1 \Leftrightarrow \tilde{A} \leq \tilde{B}$.
2. *Transitivity:* If $\tilde{C} \leq \tilde{A} \leq \tilde{B}$, then $ss(\tilde{A}, \tilde{C}) \geq ss(\tilde{B}, \tilde{C})$; if $\tilde{A} \leq \tilde{B}$, then $ss(\tilde{C}, \tilde{A}) \leq ss(\tilde{C}, \tilde{B})$ for any $\tilde{C}$.
3. *Overlapping:* If $\tilde{A} \cap \tilde{B} \neq \emptyset$, then $ss(\tilde{A}, \tilde{B}) > 0$; otherwise, $ss(\tilde{A}, \tilde{B}) = 0$.

4.4.2   Problems with Four Existing IT2 FS Subsethood Measures

To the best knowledge of the authors, five T2 FS subsethood measures have been proposed in the literature. Four of them are not used in this book because of their problems pointed out in this subsection. The fifth one, which will be used in this book, is described in more detail in the next subsection.

1. Liu and Xiong (2002) proposed a subsethood measure for intuitionistic FSs [Atanassov (1986)], which can also be applied to IT2 FSs; however, it satisfies only transitivity, not reflexivity and overlapping [Wu and Mendel (2010)].
2. Cornelis and Kerre (2004) introduced an interval inclusion (subsethood) measure for intuitionistic FSs, which can also be used for IT2 FSs; however, it satisfies reflexivity and transitivity, but not overlapping [Wu and Mendel (2010)].
3. Rickard et al. (2008, 2009) and Nguyen and Kreinovich (2008) independently extended Kosko's subsethood measure to IT2 FSs, and they obtained the same result. Their IT2 FS subsethood measure satisfies transitivity and overlapping but not reflexivity [Wu and Mendel (2010)].
4. Yang and Lin (2009) defined an inclusion (subsethood) measure for general T2 FSs, which can also be used for IT2 FSs; however, it satisfies neither of reflexivity, transitivity, nor overlapping [Wu and Mendel (2010)].

4.4.3   Vlachos and Sergiadis's IT2 FS Subsethood Measure

Vlachos and Sergiadis (2007) proposed a subsethood measure for interval-valued FSs, which are the same as IT2 FSs. It is

$$ss_{VS}(\tilde{A}, \tilde{B}) = 1 - \frac{\sum_{i=1}^{N} \max(0, \underline{\mu}_{\tilde{A}}(x_i) - \underline{\mu}_{\tilde{B}}(x_i)) + \sum_{i=1}^{N} \max(0, \overline{\mu}_{\tilde{A}}(x_i) - \overline{\mu}_{\tilde{B}}(x_i))}{\underline{\mu}_{\tilde{A}}(x_i) + \overline{\mu}_{\tilde{A}}(x_i)}$$

$$(4.9)$$

When $\underline{\mu}_{\tilde{A}}(x_i) \geq \underline{\mu}_{\tilde{B}}(x_i)$, it follows that

$$\underline{\mu}_{\tilde{A}}(x_i) - \max(0, \underline{\mu}_{\tilde{A}}(x_i) - \underline{\mu}_{\tilde{B}}(x_i)) = \underline{\mu}_{\tilde{A}}(x_i) - \underline{\mu}_{\tilde{A}}(x_i) + \underline{\mu}_{\tilde{B}}(x_i)$$
$$= \underline{\mu}_{\tilde{B}}(x_i) = \min(\underline{\mu}_{\tilde{A}}(x_i), \underline{\mu}_{\tilde{B}}(x_i))$$

$$(4.10)$$

and when $\underline{\mu}_{\tilde{A}}(x_i) < \underline{\mu}_{\tilde{B}}(x_i)$, it follows that

$$\underline{\mu}_{\tilde{A}}(x_i) - \max(0, \underline{\mu}_{\tilde{A}}(x_i) - \underline{\mu}_{\tilde{B}}(x_i)) = \underline{\mu}_{\tilde{A}}(x_i) = \min(\underline{\mu}_{\tilde{A}}(x_i), \underline{\mu}_{\tilde{B}}(x_i)) \quad (4.11)$$

Hence,

$$\underline{\mu}_{\tilde{A}}(x_i) - \max(0, \underline{\mu}_{\tilde{A}}(x_i) - \underline{\mu}_{\tilde{B}}(x_i)) = \min(\underline{\mu}_{\tilde{A}}(x_i), \underline{\mu}_{\tilde{B}}(x_i)) \quad (4.12)$$

Similarly,

$$\overline{\mu}_{\tilde{A}}(x_i) - \max(0, \overline{\mu}_{\tilde{A}}(x_i) - \overline{\mu}_{\tilde{B}}(x_i)) = \min(\overline{\mu}_{\tilde{A}}(x_i), \overline{\mu}_{\tilde{B}}(x_i)) \quad (4.13)$$

Consequently, equation (4.9) can be rewritten as

$$
\begin{aligned}
ss_{VS}(\tilde{A}, \tilde{B}) &= \frac{\sum_{i=1}^{N} [\underline{\mu}_{\tilde{A}}(x_i) - \max(0, \underline{\mu}_{\tilde{A}}(x_i) - \underline{\mu}_{\tilde{B}}(x_i))]}{\sum_{i=1}^{N} \underline{\mu}_{\tilde{A}}(x_i) + \sum_{i=1}^{N} \overline{\mu}_{\tilde{A}}(x_i)} \\
&\quad + \frac{\sum_{i=1}^{N} [\overline{\mu}_{\tilde{A}}(x_i) - \max(0, \overline{\mu}_{\tilde{A}}(x_i) - \overline{\mu}_{\tilde{B}}(x_i))]}{\sum_{i=1}^{N} \underline{\mu}_{\tilde{A}}(x_i) + \sum_{i=1}^{N} \overline{\mu}_{\tilde{A}}(x_i)} \\
&= \frac{\sum_{i=1}^{N} \min(\underline{\mu}_{\tilde{A}}(x_i), \underline{\mu}_{\tilde{B}}(x_i)) + \sum_{i=1}^{N} \min(\overline{\mu}_{\tilde{A}}(x_i), \overline{\mu}_{\tilde{B}}(x_i))}{\sum_{i=1}^{N} \underline{\mu}_{\tilde{A}}(x_i) + \sum_{i=1}^{N} \overline{\mu}_{\tilde{A}}(x_i)}
\end{aligned}
\quad (4.14)
$$

Observe the analogy of equation (4.14) to the Jaccard similarity measure in equation (4.6). Since equation (4.14) is easier to understand and to compute than equation (4.9), it is used in the rest of this book instead of equation (4.9).

The continuous version of Vlachos and Sergiadis's IT2 FS subsethood measure can be expressed as

$$ss_{VS}(\tilde{A}, \tilde{B}) = \frac{\int_X \min(\underline{\mu}_{\tilde{A}}(x), \underline{\mu}_{\tilde{B}}(x))dx + \int_X \min(\overline{\mu}_{\tilde{A}}(x), \overline{\mu}_{\tilde{B}}(x))dx}{\int \underline{\mu}_{\tilde{A}}(x)dx + \int \overline{\mu}_{\tilde{A}}(x)dx} \quad (4.15)$$

Theorem 4.3. $ss_{VS}(\tilde{A}, \tilde{B})$ satisfies transitivity, reflexivity and overlapping.

The proof is given in Appendix 4B.3.

4.4.4 Simulation Results

In this subsection, an example is used to illustrate Vlachos and Sergiadis's IT2 FS subsethood measure, and to also explain why the Jaccard similarity measure should not be used as a classifier in decoding.

Example 4.2. This example classifies the 32 word FOUs shown in Fig. 4.3 into two classes in the [0, 10] interval (see Fig. 4.4):

$$\tilde{B} = \text{Smaller than or equal to 5} \quad (4.16)$$

$$\tilde{C} = \text{Larger than 5} \quad (4.17)$$

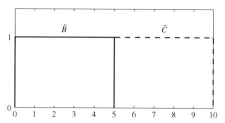

Figure 4.4. $\tilde{B}$ = smaller than or equal to 5 (solid curve) and $\tilde{C}$ = larger than 5 (dashed curve).

Observe that $\tilde{B}$ and $\tilde{C}$ are actually crisp sets; however, they can be viewed as special IT2 FSs; for example, $\tilde{B}$ has a normal trapezoidal UMF [0, 0, 5, 5] and a normal trapezoidal LMF [0, 0, 5, 5]. By viewing the FOUs in Fig. 4.3 in relation to the dashed line drawn at $x = 5$, it is clear that words 1–10 are definitely in $\tilde{B}$ and words 22–32 are definitely in $\tilde{C}$. The subsethood measures of these 32 words in $\tilde{B}$ and $\tilde{C}$, as well as their Jaccard similarities with $\tilde{B}$ and $\tilde{C}$, are summarized in Table 4.3.

Observe from Fig. 4.3 and Table 4.3 that:

1. According to reflexivity, words 1–10 should have $ss(\tilde{A}, \tilde{B}) = 1$ since each of them is completely under or on $\tilde{B}$, and words 11–32 should have $ss(\tilde{A}, \tilde{B}) < 1$ since none of them is completely under or on $\tilde{B}$. ss_{VS} satisfies this requirement. Similarly, words 1–21 should have $ss(\tilde{A}, \tilde{C}) < 1$ and words 22–32 should have $ss(\tilde{A}, \tilde{C}) = 1$. Again, ss_{VS} satisfies this requirement.

2. According to overlapping, words 1–21 should have $ss(\tilde{A}, \tilde{B}) > 0$ since they overlap with $\tilde{B}$, and words 22–32 should have $ss(\tilde{A}, \tilde{B}) = 0$ as they do not overlap with $\tilde{B}$. ss_{VS} satisfies this requirement. Similarly, words 1–10 should have $ss(\tilde{A}, \tilde{C}) = 0$ and words 11–32 should have $ss(\tilde{A}, \tilde{C}) > 0$. Again, ss_{VS} satisfies this requirement.

3. As the word $\tilde{A}$ gets larger sounding, generally $ss_{VS}(\tilde{A}, \tilde{B})$ decreases, whereas $ss_{VS}(\tilde{A}, \tilde{C})$ increases, both of which are reasonable.

4. As shown in Table 4.3, for all words[7] $\tilde{A}$,

$$ss_{VS}(\tilde{A}, \tilde{B}) + ss_{VS}(\tilde{A}, \tilde{C}) = 1 \qquad (4.18)$$

This relationship is always true for complementary crisp sets, for example, $\tilde{B}$ and $\tilde{C}$ in Fig. 4.4, because

$$ss_{VS}(\tilde{A}, \tilde{B}) + ss_{VS}(\tilde{A}, \tilde{C})$$
$$= \frac{\sum_{x_i \leq 5} \min(\overline{\mu}_{\tilde{A}}(x_i), \overline{\mu}_{\tilde{B}}(x_i)) + \sum_{x_i \leq 5} \min(\underline{\mu}_{\tilde{A}}(x_i), \underline{\mu}_{\tilde{B}}(x_i))}{\sum_{i=1}^{N} \overline{\mu}_{\tilde{A}}(x_i) + \sum_{i=1}^{N} \underline{\mu}_{\tilde{A}}(x_i)}$$
$$+ \frac{\sum_{x_i > 5} \min(\overline{\mu}_{\tilde{A}}(x_i), \overline{\mu}_{\tilde{C}}(x_i)) + \sum_{x_i > 5} \min(\underline{\mu}_{\tilde{A}}(x_i), \underline{\mu}_{\tilde{C}}(x_i))}{\sum_{i=1}^{N} \overline{\mu}_{\tilde{A}}(x_i) + \sum_{i=1}^{N} \underline{\mu}_{\tilde{A}}(x_i)}$$

---

[7] In Table 4.3, sometimes equation (4.18) does not hold exactly because of discretization and roundoff errors.

Table 4.3. Comparison of the Vlachos and Sergiadis IT2 FS subsethood measure and the Jaccard similarity measure for the 32 FOUs in Fig. 4.3

$\tilde{A}$	$\tilde{B}$ = smaller than or equal to 5		$\tilde{C}$ = larger than 5	
	ss_{VS}	ss_J	ss_{VS}	ss_J
1. None to very little	1	0.14	0	0
2. Teeny-weeny	1	0.18	0	0
3. A smidgen	1	0.22	0	0
4. Tiny	1	0.22	0	0
5. Very small	1	0.16	0	0
6. Very little	1	0.23	0	0
7. Abit	1	0.22	0	0
8. Low amount	1	0.30	0	0
9. Small	1	0.32	0	0
10. Somewhat small	1	0.27	0	0
11. Little	0.98	0.35	0.03	0.01
12. Some	0.63	0.24	0.38	0.13
13. Some to moderate	0.63	0.25	0.37	0.13
14. Moderate amount	0.54	0.16	0.46	0.13
15. Fair amount	0.46	0.15	0.55	0.18
16. Medium	0.40	0.07	0.60	0.11
17. Modest amount	0.31	0.07	0.69	0.17
18. Good amount	0.14	0.05	0.86	0.36
19. Quite a bit	0.02	0.01	0.98	0.35
20. Sizeable	0.03	0.01	0.97	0.33
21. Considerable amount	0.02	0.01	0.98	0.36
22. Very sizeable	0	0	1	0.30
23. Substantial amount	0	0	1	0.31
24. A lot	0	0	1	0.31
25. High amount	0	0	1	0.32
26. Large	0	0	1	0.25
27. Very large	0	0	1	0.24
28. Humongous amount	0	0	1	0.15
29. Huge amount	0	0	1	0.22
30. Very high amount	0	0	1	0.18
31. Extreme amount	0	0	1	0.17
32. Maximum amount	0	0	1	0.09

$$= \frac{\sum_{x_i \leq 5} \min(\overline{\mu}_{\tilde{A}}(x_i), 1) + \sum_{x_i \leq 5} \min(\underline{\mu}_{\tilde{A}}(x_i), 1)}{\sum_{i=1}^{N} \overline{\mu}_{\tilde{A}}(x_i) + \sum_{i=1}^{N} \underline{\mu}_{\tilde{A}}(x_i)}$$

$$+ \frac{\sum_{x_i > 5} \min(\overline{\mu}_{\tilde{A}}(x_i), 1) + \sum_{x_i > 5} \min(\underline{\mu}_{\tilde{A}}(x_i), 1)}{\sum_{i=1}^{N} \overline{\mu}_{\tilde{A}}(x_i) + \sum_{i=1}^{N} \underline{\mu}_{\tilde{A}}(x_i)}$$

$$= \frac{\sum_{x_i \leq 5} \overline{\mu}_{\tilde{A}}(x_i) + \sum_{x_i \leq 5} \underline{\mu}_{\tilde{A}}(x_i)}{\sum_{i=1}^{N} \overline{\mu}_{\tilde{A}}(x_i) + \sum_{i=1}^{N} \underline{\mu}_{\tilde{A}}(x_i)} + \frac{\sum_{x_i > 5} \overline{\mu}_{\tilde{A}}(x_i) + \sum_{x_i > 5} \underline{\mu}_{\tilde{A}}(x_i)}{\sum_{i=1}^{N} \overline{\mu}_{\tilde{A}}(x_i) + \sum_{i=1}^{N} \underline{\mu}_{\tilde{A}}(x_i)}$$

$$= \frac{\sum_{i=1}^{N} \overline{\mu}_{\tilde{A}}(x_i) + \sum_{i=1}^{N} \underline{\mu}_{\tilde{A}}(x_i)}{\sum_{i=1}^{N} \overline{\mu}_{\tilde{A}}(x_i) + \sum_{i=1}^{N} \underline{\mu}_{\tilde{A}}(x_i)} = 1 . \tag{4.19}$$

5. The Jaccard similarity measure cannot be used as a classifier because it gives counterintuitive results; for example, *none to very little* should belong to the class *smaller than or equal to 5* completely, but its Jaccard similarity is only 0.14. Furthermore, as mentioned in Section 4.1, a classifier is needed when the output of the CWW engine, $\tilde{A}$, is mapped into a decision category $\tilde{B}$. Subsethood is conceptually more appropriate for a classifier because it defines the degree to which $\tilde{A}$ is contained in $\tilde{B}$. On the other hand, it is not reasonable to compare the similarity between $\tilde{A}$ and $\tilde{B}$ because they belong to different domains (vocabularies); for example, in the JPJA (Chapter 10) $\tilde{A}$ represents the overall quality of a paper, whereas $\tilde{B}$ is a publication decision.

In summary, Vlachos and Sergiadis's IT2 FS subsethood measure satisfies all three desirable properties and it is preferred over Jaccard's similarity measure as a classifier in decoding, so it is used in the rest of the book.

APPENDIX 4A

This appendix briefly introduces some compatibility measures and ranking methods for T1 FSs.

4A.1 Compatibility Measures For T1 FSs

The literature on compatibility measures for T1 FSs is quite extensive [Bustince et al. (2007)]. According to Cross and Sudkamp (2002), these measures can be classified into four classes:

1. *Set-theoretic compatibility measures,* in which set-theoretic operations are used to define compatibility measures.
2. *Proximity-based compatibility measures,* which are [Cross and Sudkamp (2002)] "generalizations of geometric and interval models of distance."
3. *Logic-based compatibility measures,* which are [Cross and Sudkamp (2002)] "generalizations of fuzzy logic that construct equality indices using fuzzy logic connectives on fuzzy set membership functions."
4. *Fuzzy-valued compatibility measures,* in which the compatibility measures are themselves FSs.

Some commonly used compatibility measures for T1 FSs are summarized in Table 4A.1. For more details on T1 compatibility, proximity, and similarity measures, see Cross and Sudkamp (2002) and its references.

Table 4A.1. Summary of compatibility measures for T1 FSs. Note that those measures involving α-cuts require the FSs to be convex

Compatibility measure	Equation
Set-Theoretic	
Tversky's (1977) Method	$sm_T(A, B) = f(A \cap B)/[f(A \cap B) + af(A - B) + bf(B - A)]$, where f satisfies $f(A \cup B) = f(A) + f(B)$ for disjoint A and B.
Jaccard's (1908) Method	$sm_J(A, B) = f(A \cap B)/f(A \cup B)$, where f is defined above.
Dubois and Prade's (1982) Method	$sm_D(A, B) = g\left(\overline{(A \cup B)} \cap (A \cup B)\right)$ or $sm_D(A, B) = g\left((A \cup B) \cap \overline{(A \cup B)}\right)$, where g satisfies: (1) $g(\emptyset) = 0$, (2) $g(X) = 1$, and (3) $g(A) \leq g(B)$ if $A \subseteq B$.
Proximity-Based	
Minkowski's r-metric-Based [Zwick et al. (1987)]	$d_r(A, B) \equiv \left(\sum_{i=1}^{n} |\mu_A(x_i) - \mu_B(x_i)|^r\right)^{1/r}$, $r \geq 1$. $d_r(A, B)$ is a distance measure.
Normalization Approach [Cross and Sudkamp (2002)]	$sm_N(A, B) = 1 - d_r(A, B)/n$
Conversion Function Approach [Pal and Majumder (1977)]	$sm_C(A, B) = [1 + (d_r(A, B)/s)^t]^{-1}$, where s and t are positive constants.
Angular Coefficient Based	
Bhattacharya's (1946) Distance	$sm_B(A, B) = \dfrac{\sum_{i=1}^{n} \mu_A(x_i)\mu_B(x_i)}{\left(\sum_{i=1}^{n} \mu_A(x_i)^2\right)^{1/2}\left(\sum_{i=1}^{n} \mu_B(x_i)^2\right)^{1/2}}$
Interval-Based	$A_\alpha \equiv [a_1(\alpha), a_2(\alpha)]$ and $B_\alpha \equiv [b_1(\alpha), b_2(\alpha)]$ are α-cuts on A and B $q(A_\alpha, B_\alpha) \equiv \max(|a_1(\alpha) - b_1(\alpha)|, |a_2(\alpha) - b_2(\alpha)|)$,
Hausdorff Distance-Based [Ralescu (1984), Zwick et al. (1987)]	$sm_H(A, B) = [1 + (q_*(A, B)/s)^t]^{-1}$, where $q_*(A, B)$ can be $q(A_1, B_1)$, $\int_0^1 q(A_\alpha, B_\alpha)d\alpha$, or $\sup_{\alpha \geq 0} q(A_\alpha, B_\alpha)$.
Dissemblance Index Based [Cross and Sudkamp (2002)]	$d(A_\alpha, B_\alpha) \equiv [|a_1(\alpha) - b_1(\alpha)| + |a_2(\alpha) - b_2(\alpha)|]/(2|X|)$, where $|X|$ is the length of the domain of $A \cup B$ $sm_D(A, B) = d(A_1, B_1)$, or $\int_0^1 d(A_\alpha, B_\alpha)d\alpha$, or $\sup_{\alpha \geq 0} d(A_\alpha, B_\alpha)$.
Linguistic Approximation-Based	
Bonissone's (1980) Method	$sm_B(A, B) = \left[1 - \int_X \left(\dfrac{\mu_A(x)\mu_B(x)}{card(A) \cdot card(B)}\right)^{1/2} dx\right]^{1/2}$, where $card(A)$ [$card(B)$] is the cardinality of A (B).
Logic-Based	
Hirota and Pedrycz's (1989, 1991) Method	$[\mu_A(x_i) \Leftrightarrow \mu_B(x_i)] \equiv [\mu_A(x_i) \rightarrow \mu_B(x_i)] \wedge [\mu_B(x_i) \rightarrow \mu_A(x_i)]$ $[\mu_A(x_i) = \mu_B(x_i)] \equiv \{[\mu_A(x_i) \rightarrow \mu_B(x_i)] \wedge [\mu_B(x_i) \rightarrow \mu_A(x_i)]$ $+ [\mu_{\bar{A}}(x_i) \rightarrow \mu_{\bar{B}}(x_i)] \wedge [\mu_{\bar{B}}(x_i) \rightarrow \mu_{\bar{A}}(x_i)]\}/2$, $sm_{L1}(A, B) = \sum_{i=1}^{n} [\mu_A(x_i) = \mu_B(x_i)]/n$, $sm_{L2}(A, B) = \sum_{i=1}^{n} [\mu_A(x_i) \Leftrightarrow \mu_B(x_i)]/n$.

Table 4A.1. *Continued*

Fuzzy-Valued Dubois and Prade's (1982) Method	The similarity is a FS, whose α-cuts are $$sm_F^{\alpha}(A,\ B) = \frac{\text{card}((A_{\alpha} \cap B_{\alpha}) \cap \text{supp}(A \cap B))}{\text{card}((A_{\alpha} \cup B_{\alpha}) \cap \text{supp}(A \cup B))}$$ where $\text{supp}(A \cap B)$ is the support of $A \cap B$.

Source: Wu and Mendel, 2008; © 2008, Elsevier.

4A.2 Ranking Methods for T1 FSs

Wang (1997) and Wang and Kerre (1996, 2001a,b) performed a very comprehensive study on ranking methods for T1 FSs. They partitioned over 35 ranking methods for T1 FSs into three classes:

1. *Class 1.* Reference set(s) is (are) set up, and each T1 FS is mapped into a crisp number based on the reference(s). The T1 FSs are then ranked according to the corresponding crisp numbers.
2. *Class 2.* A function $f(A_i)$ is used to map a T1 FS A_i to a crisp number, which can then be ranked. No reference set(s) is (are) used in the mapping.
3. *Class 3.* T1 FSs A_i ($i = 1, \ldots, M$) are ranked through pairwise comparisons.

They then proposed seven reasonable properties that a ranking method should satisfy ([Wang and Kerre (2001a)]; see also Section 4.3.1). Some simple ranking methods, which are also the most reasonable ones according to the seven properties [Wang and Kerre (2001a,b)], are summarized in Table 4A.2.

APPENDIX 4B

This appendix provides the proofs for Theorems 4.1–4.3.

4B.1 Proof of Theorem 4.1

Our proof of Theorem 4.1 is for the discrete case in equation (4.6). The proof for the continuous case in equation (4.5) is very similar, and is left to the reader.

1. *Reflexivity.* Consider first the necessity, that is, $sm_J(\tilde{A}, \tilde{B}) = 1 \Rightarrow \tilde{A} = \tilde{B}$. When the areas of the FOUs are not zero, $\min(\underline{\mu}_{\tilde{A}}(x_i),\ \underline{\mu}_{\tilde{B}}(x_i)) < \max(\overline{\mu}_{\tilde{A}}(x_i),\ \overline{\mu}_{\tilde{B}}(x_i))$; hence, the only way that $sm_J(\tilde{A}, \tilde{B}) = 1$ [see equation (4.6)] is when $\min(\overline{\mu}_{\tilde{A}}(x_i),\ \overline{\mu}_{\tilde{B}}(x_i)) = \max(\overline{\mu}_{\tilde{A}}(x_i),\ \overline{\mu}_{\tilde{B}}(x_i))$ and $\min(\underline{\mu}_{\tilde{A}}(x_i),\ \underline{\mu}_{\tilde{B}}(x_i)) = \max(\underline{\mu}_{\tilde{A}}(x_i),\ \underline{\mu}_{\tilde{B}}(x_i))$, in which case $\overline{\mu}_{\tilde{A}}(x_i) = \overline{\mu}_{\tilde{B}}(x_i)$ and $\underline{\mu}_{\tilde{A}}(x_i) = \underline{\mu}_{\tilde{B}}(x_i)$, i.e., $\tilde{A} = \tilde{B}$.

   Consider next the sufficiency, that is, $\tilde{A} = \tilde{B} \Rightarrow sm_J(\tilde{A}, \tilde{B}) = 1$. When $\tilde{A} = \tilde{B}$, that is, $\overline{\mu}_{\tilde{A}}(x_i) = \overline{\mu}_{\tilde{B}}(x_i)$ and $\underline{\mu}_{\tilde{A}}(x_i) = \underline{\mu}_{\tilde{B}}(x_i)$, it follows that $\min(\overline{\mu}_{\tilde{A}}(x_i),\ \overline{\mu}_{\tilde{B}}(x_i))$

Table 4A.2. Summary of ranking methods for T1 FSs

Ranking method[a]	Equation used for ranking

Class 1

Jain's (1976, 1977) Method

$$f_J(A_i) = \sup_x \min(\mu_{A_{\max,J}}(x), \mu_{A_i}(x)), \text{ where } \mu_{A_{\max,J}}(x) = \left(\frac{x}{x_{\max}}\right)^k,$$

in which $k > 0$ and $x_{\max}$ is the right end of the x domain.

Chen's (1985) Method

$$f_C(A_i) = [R(A_i) + 1 - L(A_i)]/2,$$

where $R(A_i) = \sup_x \min(\mu_{A_{\max,C}}(x), \mu_{A_i}(x)),$

$$L(A_i) = \sup_x \min(\mu_{A_{\min,C}}(x), \mu_{A_i}(x)),$$

$$\mu_{A_{\max,C}}(x) = \left(\frac{x - x_{\min}}{x_{\max} - x_{\min}}\right)^k, \quad \mu_{A_{\min,C}}(x) = \left(\frac{x_{\max} - x}{x_{\max} - x_{\min}}\right)^k,$$

$k > 0$, and $x_{\min}$ is the left end of the x domain.

Kim and Park's (1995) Method

$$f_{KP}(A_i) = kh_{A_i \cap A_{\max,KP}} + (1 - k)(1 - h_{A_i \cap A_{\min,KP}}),$$

where $k \in [0, 1]$, $h_{A_i \cap A_{\max,KP}}$ is the height of $A_i \cap A_{\max,KP}$,

$$\mu_{A_{\max,KP}}(x) = \frac{x - x_{\min}}{x_{\max} - x_{\min}}, \text{ and } \mu_{A_{\min,KP}}(x) = \frac{x_{\max} - x}{x_{\max} - x_{\min}}.$$

Class 2

Let $A_{i\alpha}$ be an α-cut of a T1 FS A_i.

Adamo's (1980) Method

$$f_A(A_i) = r(A_{i\alpha}), \text{ where } r(A_{i\alpha}) \text{ is the right end of } A_{i\alpha},$$

and α can be any user-chosen number in $(0, 1]$.

Yager's (1978) First Method

$$f_Y(A_i) = \frac{\int_0^1 x\mu_{A_i}(x)\,dx}{\int_0^1 \mu_{A_i}(x)\,dx},$$

where the domain of x is constrained in $[0, 1]$.

Yager's (1980, 1981) Second Method

$$f_Y(A_i) = \int_0^{h_{A_i}} m(A_{i\alpha})\,d\alpha, \text{ where } h_{A_i} \text{ is the height of } A_i,$$

and $m(A_{i\alpha})$ is the center of $A_{i\alpha}$.

Fortemps and Rouben's (1996) Method

$$f_{FR}(A_i) = \frac{1}{h_{A_i}} \int_0^{h_{A_i}} [r(A_{i\alpha}) - l(A_{i\alpha})]\,d\alpha,$$

where $l(A_{i\alpha})$ is the left end of $A_{i\alpha}$.

Class 3

$$d_H(A_i, A_j) \equiv \int_X [\mu_{A_i}(x) - \mu_{A_j}(x)]\,dx,$$

A^l and A^u are T1 FSs defined as

$$\mu_{A^l}(x) \equiv \sup_{y \leq x} \mu_{A_i}(y), \mu_{A^u}(x) \equiv \sup_{y \geq x} \mu_{A_i}(y)$$

$\widetilde{\max}(A, B)$ and $\widetilde{\min}(A, B)$ are T1 FSs defined as

$$\mu_{\widetilde{\max}(A,B)}(x) = \sup_{x = u \vee v} [\mu_A(u) \vee \mu_B(v)]$$

$$\mu_{\widetilde{\min}(A,B)}(x) = \sup_{x = u \wedge v} [\mu_A(u) \wedge \mu_B(v)]$$

Nakamura's (1986) Method

$$r(A_i, A_j) = \frac{kd_H(A_i^l, \widetilde{\min}(A_i^l, A_j^l)) + (1 - k)d_H(A_i^u, \widetilde{\min}(A_i^u, A_j^u))}{kd_H(A_i^l, A_j^l) + (1 - k)d_H(A_i^u, A_j^u)}.$$

Kolodziejczyk's (1986) Method

$$r(A_i, A_j) = \frac{d_H(A_i^l, \widetilde{\min}(A_i^l, A_j^l)) + d_H(A_i^u, \widetilde{\min}(A_i^u, A_j^u)) + d_H(A_i \cap A_j, \emptyset)}{d_H(A_i^l, A_j^l) + d_H(A_i^u, A_j^u) + 2d_H(A_i \cap A_j, \emptyset)}$$

Saade and Schwarzlander's (1992) Method

$$r(A_i, A_j) = d_H(A_i^l, \widetilde{\max}(A_i^l, A_j^l)) + d_H(A_i^u, \widetilde{\max}(A_i^u, A_j^u)).$$

[a]Note that for Classes 1 and 2, each T1 FS is first mapped into a crisp number, and then these numbers are sorted to obtain the ranks of the corresponding T1 FSs. For Class 3, the pairwise ranks are computed directly.

$= \max(\overline{\mu}_{\tilde{A}}(x_i), \overline{\mu}_{\tilde{B}}(x_i))$ and $\min(\underline{\mu}_{\tilde{A}}(x_i), \underline{\mu}_{\tilde{B}}(x_i)) = \max(\underline{\mu}_{\tilde{A}}(x_i), \underline{\mu}_{\tilde{B}}(x_i))$. Consequently, it follows from equation (4.6) that $sm_J(\tilde{A}, \tilde{B}) = 1$.

2. *Symmetry.* Observe from equation (4.6) that $sm_J(\tilde{A}, \tilde{B})$ does not depend on the order of $\tilde{A}$ and $\tilde{B}$; so, $sm_J(\tilde{A}, \tilde{B}) = sm_J(\tilde{B}, \tilde{A})$.

3. *Transitivity.* If $\tilde{C} \leq \tilde{A} \leq \tilde{B}$ (see Definition 4.2), then

$$sm_J(\tilde{C}, \tilde{A}) = \frac{\sum_{i=1}^{N} \min(\overline{\mu}_{\tilde{C}}(x_i), \overline{\mu}_{\tilde{A}}(x_i)) + \sum_{i=1}^{N} \min(\underline{\mu}_{\tilde{C}}(x_i), \underline{\mu}_{\tilde{A}}(x_i))}{\sum_{i=1}^{N} \max(\overline{\mu}_{\tilde{C}}(x_i), \overline{\mu}_{\tilde{A}}(x_i)) + \sum_{i=1}^{N} \max(\underline{\mu}_{\tilde{C}}(x_i), \underline{\mu}_{\tilde{A}}(x_i))}$$

$$= \frac{\sum_{i=1}^{N} \overline{\mu}_{\tilde{C}}(x_i) + \sum_{i=1}^{N} \underline{\mu}_{\tilde{C}}(x_i)}{\sum_{i=1}^{N} \overline{\mu}_{\tilde{A}}(x_i) + \sum_{i=1}^{N} \underline{\mu}_{\tilde{A}}(x_i)} \tag{4B.1}$$

$$sm_J(\tilde{C}, \tilde{B}) = \frac{\sum_{i=1}^{N} \min(\overline{\mu}_{\tilde{C}}(x_i), \overline{\mu}_{\tilde{B}}(x_i)) + \sum_{i=1}^{N} \min(\underline{\mu}_{\tilde{C}}(x_i), \underline{\mu}_{\tilde{B}}(x_i))}{\sum_{i=1}^{N} \max(\overline{\mu}_{\tilde{C}}(x_i), \overline{\mu}_{\tilde{B}}(x_i)) + \sum_{i=1}^{N} \max(\underline{\mu}_{\tilde{C}}(x_i), \underline{\mu}_{\tilde{B}}(x_i))}$$

$$= \frac{\sum_{i=1}^{N} \overline{\mu}_{\tilde{C}}(x_i) + \sum_{i=1}^{N} \underline{\mu}_{\tilde{C}}(x_i)}{\sum_{i=1}^{N} \overline{\mu}_{\tilde{B}}(x_i) + \sum_{i=1}^{N} \underline{\mu}_{\tilde{B}}(x_i)} \tag{4B.2}$$

Because $\tilde{A} \leq \tilde{B}$, it follows that $\sum_{i=1}^{N}\overline{\mu}_{\tilde{A}}(x_i) + \sum_{i=1}^{N}\underline{\mu}_{\tilde{A}}(x_i) = \sum_{i=1}^{N}\overline{\mu}_{\tilde{B}}(x_i) + \sum_{i=1}^{N}\underline{\mu}_{\tilde{B}}(x_i)$ and, hence, $sm_J(\tilde{C}, \tilde{A}) = sm_J(\tilde{C}, \tilde{B})$.

4. *Overlapping.* If $\tilde{A} \cap \tilde{B} = \emptyset$ (see Definition 4.3), $\exists x$ such that $\min(\overline{\mu}_{\tilde{A}}(x_i), \overline{\mu}_{\tilde{B}}(x_i)) > 0$, then, in the numerator of equation (4.6),

$$\sum_{i=1}^{N} \min(\overline{\mu}_{\tilde{A}}(x_i), \overline{\mu}_{\tilde{B}}(x_i)) + \sum_{i=1}^{N} \min(\underline{\mu}_{\tilde{A}}(x_i), \underline{\mu}_{\tilde{B}}(x_i)) > 0 \tag{4B.3}$$

In the denominator of equation (4.6),

$$\sum_{i=1}^{N} \max(\overline{\mu}_{\tilde{A}}(x_i), \overline{\mu}_{\tilde{B}}(x_i)) + \sum_{i=1}^{N} \max(\underline{\mu}_{\tilde{A}}(x_i), \underline{\mu}_{\tilde{B}}(x_i))$$
$$\geq \sum_{i=1}^{N} \min(\overline{\mu}_{\tilde{A}}(x_i), \overline{\mu}_{\tilde{B}}(x_i)) + \sum_{i=1}^{N} \min(\underline{\mu}_{\tilde{A}}(x_i), \underline{\mu}_{\tilde{B}}(x_i)) > 0 \tag{4B.4}$$

Consequently, $sm_J(\tilde{A}, \tilde{B}) > 0$. On the other hand, when $\tilde{A} \cap \tilde{B} = \emptyset$, i.e., $\min(\overline{\mu}_{\tilde{A}}(x_i), \overline{\mu}_{\tilde{B}}(x_i)) = \min(\underline{\mu}_{\tilde{A}}(x_i), \underline{\mu}_{\tilde{B}}(x_i)) = 0$ for $\forall x$, then, in the numerator of equation (4.6),

$$\sum_{i=1}^{N} \min(\overline{\mu}_{\tilde{A}}(x_i), \overline{\mu}_{\tilde{B}}(x_i)) + \sum_{i=1}^{N} \min(\underline{\mu}_{\tilde{A}}(x_i), \underline{\mu}_{\tilde{B}}(x_i)) = 0 \tag{4B.5}$$

Consequently, $sm_J(\tilde{A}, \tilde{B}) = 0$.

4B.2   Proof of Theorem 4.2

P1–P4 in Section 4.3.1 are proved in order.

P1. $\tilde{X}_1 \geq \tilde{X}_2$ means $c(\tilde{X}_1) \geq c(\tilde{X}_2)$ and $\tilde{X}_2 \geq \tilde{X}_1$ means $c(\tilde{X}_2) \geq c(\tilde{X}_1)$, and, hence, $c(\tilde{X}_1) = c(\tilde{X}_2)$, that is, $\tilde{X}_1 \sim \tilde{X}_2$.

P2. For the centroid-based ranking method, $\tilde{X}_1 \geq \tilde{X}_2$ means $c(\tilde{X}_1) \geq c(\tilde{X}_2)$ and $\tilde{X}_2 \geq \tilde{X}_3$ means $c(\tilde{X}_2) \geq c(\tilde{X}_3)$, and hence $c(\tilde{X}_1) \geq c(\tilde{X}_3)$, that is, $\tilde{X}_1 \geq \tilde{X}_3$.

P3. $\tilde{X}_1 \geq \tilde{X}_2$ is obvious because $c(\tilde{X}_1) > c(\tilde{X}_2)$.

P4. Because the order of $\tilde{X}_1$ and $\tilde{X}_2$ is completely determined by $c(\tilde{X}_1)$ and $c(\tilde{X}_2)$, which have nothing to do with the other IT2 FSs under comparison, the order of $\tilde{X}_1$ and $\tilde{X}_2$ is not affected by the other IT2 FSs.

4B.3   Proof of Theorem 4.3

Our proof of Theorem 4.3 is for the discrete case of equation (4.14). The proof for the continuous case of equation (4.15) is very similar, and is left to the reader.

1. *Reflexivity.* When $ss_{VS}(\tilde{A}, \tilde{B}) = 1$, it follows from (4.14) that

$$\min(\underline{\mu}_{\tilde{A}}(x_i), \underline{\mu}_{\tilde{B}}(x_i)) = \underline{\mu}_{\tilde{A}}(x_i), \quad \forall x_i \tag{4B.6}$$

$$\min(\overline{\mu}_{\tilde{A}}(x_i), \overline{\mu}_{\tilde{B}}(x_i)) = \overline{\mu}_{\tilde{A}}(x_i), \quad \forall x_i \tag{4B.7}$$

that is, $\overline{\mu}_{\tilde{B}}(x_i) \geq \overline{\mu}_{\tilde{A}}(x_i)$ and $\underline{\mu}_{\tilde{B}}(x_i) \geq \underline{\mu}_{\tilde{A}}(x_i)$; hence, $\tilde{A} \leq \tilde{B}$ according to Definition 4.2. The sufficiency is hence proved. The necessity can be shown by reversing the above reasoning, and is left to the reader as an exercise.

2. *Transitivity.* It follows from equation (4.14) that

$$ss_{VS}(\tilde{A}, \tilde{C}) = \frac{\sum_{i=1}^{N} \min(\overline{\mu}_{\tilde{A}}(x_i), \overline{\mu}_{\tilde{C}}(x_i)) + \sum_{i=1}^{N} \min(\underline{\mu}_{\tilde{A}}(x_i), \underline{\mu}_{\tilde{C}}(x_i))}{\sum_{i=1}^{N} \overline{\mu}_{\tilde{A}}(x_i) + \sum_{i=1}^{N} \underline{\mu}_{\tilde{A}}(x_i)} \tag{4B.8}$$

$$ss_{VS}(\tilde{B}, \tilde{C}) = \frac{\sum_{i=1}^{N} \min(\overline{\mu}_{\tilde{B}}(x_i), \overline{\mu}_{\tilde{C}}(x_i)) + \sum_{i=1}^{N} \min(\underline{\mu}_{\tilde{B}}(x_i), \underline{\mu}_{\tilde{C}}(x_i))}{\sum_{i=1}^{N} \overline{\mu}_{\tilde{B}}(x_i) + \sum_{i=1}^{N} \underline{\mu}_{\tilde{B}}(x_i)} \tag{4B.9}$$

When $\tilde{C} \leq \tilde{A} \leq \tilde{B}$, it follows from Definition 4.2 that $\underline{\mu}_{\tilde{C}}(x_i) \leq \underline{\mu}_{\tilde{A}}(x_i) \leq \underline{\mu}_{\tilde{B}}(x_i)$ and $\overline{\mu}_{\tilde{C}}(x_i) \leq \overline{\mu}_{\tilde{A}}(x_i) \leq \overline{\mu}_{\tilde{B}}(x_i)$ for $\forall x_i$; hence,

$$\sum_{i=1}^{N} \min(\overline{\mu}_{\tilde{A}}(x_i), \overline{\mu}_{\tilde{C}}(x_i)) + \sum_{i=1}^{N} \min(\underline{\mu}_{\tilde{A}}(x_i), \underline{\mu}_{\tilde{C}}(x_i)) = \sum_{i=1}^{N} \overline{\mu}_{\tilde{C}}(x_i) + \sum_{i=1}^{N} \underline{\mu}_{\tilde{C}}(x_i) \tag{4B.10}$$

$$\sum_{i=1}^{N} \min(\overline{\mu}_{\tilde{B}}(x_i), \overline{\mu}_{\tilde{C}}(x_i)) + \sum_{i=1}^{N} \min(\underline{\mu}_{\tilde{B}}(x_i), \underline{\mu}_{\tilde{C}}(x_i)) = \sum_{i=1}^{N} \overline{\mu}_{\tilde{C}}(x_i) + \sum_{i=1}^{N} \underline{\mu}_{\tilde{C}}(x_i) \tag{4B.11}$$

$$\sum_{i=1}^{N}\overline{\mu}_{\tilde{A}}(x_i) + \sum_{i=1}^{N}\underline{\mu}_{\tilde{A}}(x_i) \le \sum_{i=1}^{N}\overline{\mu}_{\tilde{B}}(x_i) + \sum_{i=1}^{N}\underline{\mu}_{\tilde{B}}(x_i) \qquad (4B.12)$$

Consequently, $ss_{VS}(\tilde{A}, \tilde{C}) \ge ss_{VS}(\tilde{B}, \tilde{C})$ for any $\tilde{C}$. Similarly, it follows from (4.14) that

$$ss_{VS}(\tilde{C}, \tilde{A}) = \frac{\sum_{i=1}^{N}\min(\overline{\mu}_{\tilde{C}}(x_i), \overline{\mu}_{\tilde{A}}(x_i)) + \sum_{i=1}^{N}\min(\underline{\mu}_{\tilde{C}}(x_i), \underline{\mu}_{\tilde{A}}(x_i))}{\sum_{i=1}^{N}\overline{\mu}_{\tilde{C}}(x_i) + \sum_{i=1}^{N}\underline{\mu}_{\tilde{C}}(x_i)}$$

$$(4B.13)$$

$$ss_{VS}(\tilde{C}, \tilde{B}) = \frac{\sum_{i=1}^{N}\min(\overline{\mu}_{\tilde{C}}(x_i), \overline{\mu}_{\tilde{B}}(x_i)) + \sum_{i=1}^{N}\min(\underline{\mu}_{\tilde{C}}(x_i), \underline{\mu}_{\tilde{B}}(x_i))}{\sum_{i=1}^{N}\overline{\mu}_{\tilde{C}}(x_i) + \sum_{i=1}^{N}\underline{\mu}_{\tilde{C}}(x_i)}$$

$$(4B.14)$$

When $\tilde{A} \le \tilde{B}$, it follows from Definition 4.2 that $\underline{\mu}_{\tilde{A}}(x_i) \le \underline{\mu}_{\tilde{B}}(x_i)$ and $\overline{\mu}_{\tilde{A}}(x_i) \le \overline{\mu}_{\tilde{B}}(x_i)$ for $\forall x_i$; hence,

$$\min(\overline{\mu}_{\tilde{C}}(x_i), \overline{\mu}_{\tilde{A}}(x_i)) \le \min(\overline{\mu}_{\tilde{C}}(x_i), \overline{\mu}_{\tilde{B}}(x_i))$$
$$\min(\underline{\mu}_{\tilde{C}}(x_i), \underline{\mu}_{\tilde{A}}(x_i)) \le \min(\underline{\mu}_{\tilde{C}}(x_i), \underline{\mu}_{\tilde{B}}(x_i))$$

$$(4B.15)$$

so that

$$\sum_{i=1}^{N}\min(\overline{\mu}_{\tilde{C}}(x_i), \overline{\mu}_{\tilde{A}}(x_i)) + \sum_{i=1}^{N}\min(\underline{\mu}_{\tilde{C}}(x_i), \underline{\mu}_{\tilde{A}}(x_i))$$
$$\le \sum_{i=1}^{N}\min(\overline{\mu}_{\tilde{C}}(x_i), \overline{\mu}_{\tilde{B}}(x_i)) + \sum_{i=1}^{N}\min(\underline{\mu}_{\tilde{C}}(x_i), \underline{\mu}_{\tilde{B}}(x_i))$$

$$(4B.16)$$

Consequently, $ss_{VS}(\tilde{C}, \tilde{A}) \le ss_{VS}(\tilde{C}, \tilde{B})$ for any $\tilde{C}$.

3. *Overlapping.* According to Definition 4.3, $\tilde{A}$ and $\tilde{B}$ overlap if $\min(\overline{\mu}_{\tilde{A}}(x_i), \overline{\mu}_{\tilde{B}}(x_i)) > 0$ for at least one x_i; hence, if $\tilde{A} \cap \tilde{B} \ne \emptyset$, then

$$ss_{VS}(\tilde{A}, \tilde{B}) = \frac{\sum_{i=1}^{N}\min(\overline{\mu}_{\tilde{A}}(x_i), \overline{\mu}_{\tilde{B}}(x_i)) + \sum_{i=1}^{N}\min(\underline{\mu}_{\tilde{A}}(x_i), \underline{\mu}_{\tilde{B}}(x_i))}{\sum_{i=1}^{N}\overline{\mu}_{\tilde{A}}(x_i) + \sum_{i=1}^{N}\underline{\mu}_{\tilde{A}}(x_i)}$$

$$\ge \frac{\sum_{i=1}^{N}\min(\overline{\mu}_{\tilde{A}}(x_i), \overline{\mu}_{\tilde{B}}(x_i))}{\sum_{i=1}^{N}\overline{\mu}_{\tilde{A}}(x_i) + \sum_{i=1}^{N}\underline{\mu}_{\tilde{A}}(x_i)} \ge 0$$

$$(4B.17)$$

On the other hand, according to Definition 4.3, when $\tilde{A} \cap \tilde{B} = \emptyset$, $\sum_{i=1}^{N}\min(\overline{\mu}_{\tilde{A}}(x_i), \overline{\mu}_{\tilde{B}}(x_i)) = 0$ and $\sum_{i=1}^{N}\min(\underline{\mu}_{\tilde{A}}(x_i), \underline{\mu}_{\tilde{B}}(x_i)) = 0$; consequently, $ss_{VS}(\tilde{A}, \tilde{B}) = 0$.

REFERENCES

J. Adamo, "Fuzzy decision trees," *Fuzzy Sets and Systems,* vol. 4, pp. 207–219, 1980.

K. Atanassov, "Intuitionistic fuzzy sets," *Fuzzy Sets and Systems,* vol. 20, pp. 87–97, 1986.

A. Bhattacharya, "On a measure of divergence of two multinomial populations," *Sankhya,* vol. 7, pp. 401–406, 1946.

P. P. Bonissone, "A fuzzy sets based linguistic approach: Theory and applications," in *Proceedings of 12th Winter Simulation Conference,* Orlando, FL, 1980, pp. 99–111.

H. Bustince, "Indicator of inclusion grade for interval-valued fuzzy sets. Application to approximate reasoning based on interval-valued fuzzy sets," *International Journal of Approximate Reasoning,* vol. 23, no. 3, pp. 137–209, 2000.

H. Bustince, M. Pagola, and E. Barrenechea, "Construction of fuzzy indices from fuzzy DI-subsethood measures: Application to the global comparison of images," *Information Sciences,* vol. 177, pp. 906–929, 2007.

S. Chen, "Ranking fuzzy numbers with maximizing set and minimizing set," *Fuzzy Sets and Systems,* vol. 17, pp. 113–129, 1985.

M. D. Cock and E. Kerre, "On (un)suitable fuzzy relations to model approximate equality," *Fuzzy Sets and Systems,* vol. 133, no. 2, pp. 137–153, 2003.

C. Cornelis and E. Kerre, "Inclusion measures in intuitionistic fuzzy set theory," *Lecture Notes in Computer Science,* vol. 2711, pp. 345–356, 2004.

V. V. Cross and T. A. Sudkamp, *Similarity and Compatibility in Fuzzy Set Theory: Assessment and Applications.* Heidelberg: Physica-Verlag, 2002.

X. D. Liu, S. H. Zheng, and F. L. Xiong, "Entropy and subsethood for general interval-valued intuitionistic fuzzy sets," *Lecture Notes in Computer Science,* vol. 3613, pp. 42–52, 2005.

D. Dubois and H. Prade, "A unifying view of comparison indices in a fuzzy set-theoretic framework," in R. R. Yager (Ed.), *Fuzzy Set and Possibility Theory Recent Developments,* New York: Pergamon Press, 1982, pp. 3–13.

J. Fan and W. Xie, "Some notes on similarity measure and proximity measure," *Fuzzy Sets and Systems,* vol. 101, pp. 403–412, 1999.

J. Fan, W. Xie, and J. Pei, "Subsethood measure: New definitions," *Fuzzy sets and systems,* vol. 106, pp. 201–209, 1999.

P. Fortemps and M. Roubens, "Ranking and defuzzification methods based on area compensation," *Fuzzy Sets and Systems,* vol. 82, pp. 319–330, 1996.

J. L. García-Lapresta and L. C. Meneses, "An empirical analysis of transitivity with four scaled preferential judgment modalities," *Review of Economic Design,* vol. 8, pp. 335–346, 2003.

M. B. Gorzalczany, "A method of inference in approximate reasoning based on interval-valued fuzzy sets," *Fuzzy Sets and Systems,* vol. 21, pp. 1–17, 1987.

K. Hirota and W. Pedrycz, "Handling fuzziness and randomness in process of matching fuzzy data," in *Proceedings 3rd IFSA Congress,* 1989, pp. 97–100.

K. Hirota and W. Pedrycz, "Matching fuzzy quantities," *IEEE Trans. on Systems, Man, and Cybernetics,* vol. 21, no. 6, pp. 908–914, 1991.

P. Jaccard, "Nouvelles recherches sur la distribution florale," *Bulletin de la Societe de Vaud des Sciences Naturelles,* vol. 44, p. 223, 1908.

R. Jain, "Decision making in the presence of fuzzy variables," *IEEE Trans. on Systems, Man, and Cybernetics,* vol. 6, pp. 698–703, 1976.

R. Jain, "A procedure for multiple-aspect decision making using fuzzy set," *International Journal of Systems Sciences,* vol. 8, pp. 1–7, 1977.

A. Kaufmann, *Introduction to the Theory of Fuzzy Subsets: Fundamental Theoretical Elements.* New York: Academic Press, 1975.

J. Kim, Y. Moon, and B. P. Zeigler, "Designing fuzzy net controllers using genetic algorithms," *IEEE Control Systems Magazine,* vol. 15, no. 3, pp. 66–72, 1995.

F. Klawonn, "Should fuzzy equality and similarity satisfy transitivity? Comments on the paper by M. De Cock and E. Kerre," *Fuzzy Sets and Systems,* vol. 133, pp. 175–180, 2003.

W. Kolodziejczyk, "Orlovsky's concept of decision-making with fuzzy preference relation— further results," *Fuzzy Sets and Systems,* vol. 19, no. 1, pp. 11–20, 1986.

B. Kosko, "Fuzziness vs. probability," *International Journal of General Systems,* vol. 17, pp. 211-240, 1990.

F. Liu and J. M. Mendel, "Encoding words into interval type-2 fuzzy sets using an interval approach," *IEEE Trans. on Fuzzy Systems,* vol. 16, no. 6, pp. 1503–1521, 2008.

Y.-H. Liu and F.-L. Xiong, "Subsethood on intuitionistic fuzzy sets," in *Proceedings of 1st International Conference on Machine Learning and Cybernetics,* vol. 3, Beijing, China, 2002, pp. 1336–1339.

C. Mencar, G. Castellano, and A. M. Fanelli, "Distinguishability quantification of fuzzy sets," *Information Sciences,* vol. 177, pp. 130–149, 2007.

H. B. Mitchell, "Pattern recognition using type-II fuzzy sets," *Information Sciences,* vol. 170, no. 2–4, pp. 409–418, 2005.

H. B. Mitchell, "Ranking type-2 fuzzy numbers," *IEEE Trans. on Fuzzy Systems,* vol. 14, no. 2, pp. 287–294, 2006.

K. Nakamura, "Preference relations on a set of fuzzy utilities as a basis for decision making," *Fuzzy Sets and Systems,* vol. 20, no. 2, pp. 147–162, 1986.

H. T. Nguyen and V. Kreinovich, "Computing degrees of subsethood and similarity for interval-valued fuzzy sets: Fast algorithms," in *Proceedings of 9th International Conference on Intelligent Technologies,* Samui, Thailand, October 2008, pp. 47–55.

S. K. Pal and M. M. Majumder, "Fuzzy sets and decision-making approaches in vowel and speaker recognition," *IEEE Trans. on Systems, Man, and Cybernetics,* vol. 7, pp. 625–629, 1977.

A. L. Ralescu and D. A. Ralescu, "Probability and fuzziness," *Information Sciences,* vol. 34, pp. 85–92, 1984.

J. T. Rickard, J. Aisbett, G. Gibbon, and D. Morgenthaler, "Fuzzy subsethood for type-n fuzzy sets," in *Proceedings NAFIPS,* New York, May 2008.

J. T. Rickard, J. Aisbett, and G. Gibbon, "Fuzzy subsethood for fuzzy sets of type-2 and generalized type-n," *IEEE Trans. on Fuzzy Systems,* vol. 17, no. 1, pp. 50–60, 2009.

J. Saade and H. Schwarzlander, "Ordering fuzzy sets over the real line: An approach based on decision making under uncertainty," *Fuzzy Sets and Systems,* vol. 50, no. 3, pp. 237–246, 1992.

M. Setnes, R. Babuska, U. Kaymak, H. R. Van, and N. Lemke, "Similarity measures in fuzzy rule base simplification," *IEEE Trans. on Systems, Man, and Cybernetics-B,* vol. 28, no. 3, pp. 376–386, 1998.

D. Sinha and E. R. Dougherty, "Fuzzification of set inclusion: Theory and applications," *Fuzzy sets and Systems,* vol. 55, pp. 15–42, 1993.

Z. Switalski, "General transitivity conditions for fuzzy reciprocal preference matrices," *Fuzzy Sets and Systems,* vol. 137, pp. 85–100, 2003.

A. Tversky, "Features of similarity," *Psychology Review,* vol. 84, pp. 327–352, 1977.

I. Vlachos and G. Sergiadis, "Subsethood, entropy, and cardinality for interval-valued fuzzy sets—an algebraic derivation," *Fuzzy Sets and Systems,* vol. 158, pp. 1384–1396, 2007.

X. Wang, *A Comparative Study of the Ranking Methods for Fuzzy Quantities,* Ph.D. dissertation, University of Gent, 1997.

X. Wang and E. E. Kerre, "Reasonable properties for the ordering of fuzzy quantities (I)," *Fuzzy Sets and Systems,* vol. 118, pp. 375–387, 2001a.

X. Wang and E. E. Kerre, "Reasonable properties for the ordering of fuzzy quantities (II)," *Fuzzy Sets and Systems,* vol. 118, pp. 387–405, 2001b.

X. Wang and E. E. Kerre, "On the classification and the dependencies of the ordering methods," in *Fuzzy Logic Foundations and Industrial Applications,* D. Ruan (Ed.), Dordrech: Kluwer Academic Publishers, 1996, pp. 73–88.

D. Wu and J. M. Mendel, "Uncertainty measures for interval type-2 fuzzy sets," *Information Sciences,* vol. 177, no. 23, pp. 5378–5393, 2007.

D. Wu and J. M. Mendel, "A vector similarity measure for linguistic approximation: Interval type-2 and type-1 fuzzy sets," *Information Sciences,* vol. 178, no. 2, pp. 381–402, 2008.

D. Wu and J. M. Mendel, "A comparative study of ranking methods, similarity measures and uncertainty measures for interval type-2 fuzzy sets," *Information Sciences,* vol. 179, no. 8, pp. 1169–1192, 2009a.

D. Wu and J. M. Mendel, "Interval type-2 fuzzy set subsethood measures as a decoder for perceptual reasoning," USC-SIPI Report 389, Signal and Image Processing Institute, University of Southern California, 2010.

R. Yager, "Ranking fuzzy subsets over the unit interval," in *Proceedings IEEE Conference on Decision and Control,* vol. 17, 1978, pp. 1435–1437.

R. Yager, "On choosing between fuzzy subsets," *Kybernetes,* vol. 9, pp. 151–154, 1980.

R. Yager, "A procedure for ordering fuzzy sets of the unit interval," *Information Sciences,* vol. 24, pp. 143–161, 1981.

R. Yager, "A framework for multi-source data fusion," *Information Sciences,* vol. 163, pp. 175–200, 2004.

R. R. Yager and D. P. Filev, "Induced ordered weighted averaging operators," *IEEE Trans. on Systems, Man, and Cybernetics-B,* vol. 29, no. 2, pp. 141–150, 1999.

M.-S. Yang and D.-C. Lin, "On similarity and inclusion measures between type-2 fuzzy sets with an application to clustering," *Computers and Mathematics with Applications,* vol. 57, pp. 896–907, 2009.

V. R. Young, "Fuzzy subsethood," *Fuzzy Sets and Systems,* vol. 77, pp. 371–384, 1996.

L. A. Zadeh, "Fuzzy sets," *Information and Control,* vol. 8, pp. 338–353, 1965.

L. A. Zadeh, "Similarity relations and fuzzy orderings," *Information Sciences,* vol. 3, pp. 177–200, 1971.

W. Zeng and H. Li, "Inclusion measures, similarity measures, and the fuzziness of fuzzy sets and their relations," *International Journal of Intelligent Systems,* vol. 21, pp. 639–653, 2006a.

W. Zeng and H. Li, "Relationship between similarity measure and entropy of interval valued fuzzy sets," *Fuzzy Sets and Systems,* vol. 157, pp. 1477–1484, 2006b.

R. Zwick, E. Carlstein, and D. Budescu, "Measures of similarity among fuzzy concepts: A comparative analysis," *International Journal of Approximate Reasoning,* vol. 1, pp. 221–242, 1987.

CHAPTER 5

Novel Weighted Averages as a CWW Engine

5.1 INTRODUCTION

The weighted average (WA) is arguably the earliest and still most widely used form of aggregation or fusion. We remind the reader of the well-known formula for the WA, that is,

$$y = \frac{\sum_{i=1}^{n} x_i w_i}{\sum_{i=1}^{n} w_i} \qquad (5.1)$$

in which w_i are the weights (real numbers) that act upon the subcriteria x_i (real numbers). In this book, the term subcriteria can mean data, features, decisions, recommendations, judgments, scores, and so on. In equation (5.1), normalization is achieved by dividing the weighted numerator sum by the sum of all of the weights. While it is always true that the sum of the normalized weights that act upon each x_i add to one, that is,

$$\sum_{j=1}^{n} \frac{w_j}{\sum_{i=1}^{n} w_i} = 1 \qquad (5.2)$$

it is not a requirement that the sum of the unnormalized weights must add to one. In many situations (described below) requiring $\sum_{i=1}^{n} w_i$ is too restrictive; so, such a requirement is not imposed in this book.

The arithmetic WA (AWA) is the one we are all familiar with and is the one in which all subcriteria and weights in equation (5.1) are real numbers. In many situations, however, providing crisp numbers for either the subcriteria or the weights is problematic (there could be uncertainties about them), and it is more meaningful to provide intervals, T1 or IT2 FSs (or a mixture of all of these), for the subcriteria and weights.

Recall the Per-C introduced in Chapter 1, which consists of three components: encoder, decoder, and CWW engine. The encoder transforms words into IT2 FSs that activate a CWW engine, as has been discussed in Chapter 3. The decoder maps the output of the CWW engine into a word and some accompanying data, as has

Perceptual Computing. By Jerry M. Mendel and Dongrui Wu

been discussed in Chapter 4. The CWW engine maps IT2 FSs into IT2 FSs. There can be several kinds of CWW engines, for example, novel weighted averages (NWAs) and if–then rules. The NWAs are the topic of this chapter. Some extensions of the ordered weighted averages are also introduced.

5.2 NOVEL WEIGHTED AVERAGES

Definition 5.1. An NWA is a WA in which at least one subcriterion or weight is not a single real number but is instead an interval, T1 FS or an IT2 FS, in which case such subcriteria, weights, and the WA are called *novel models.*

How to compute equation (5.1) for these novel models is the main subject of this chapter. What makes the computations challenging is the appearance of novel weights in both the numerator and denominator of equation (5.1). So, returning to the issue about normalized versus unnormalized weights, although everyone knows how to normalize a set of n numerical weights (just divide each weight by the sum of all of the weights) it is not known how to normalize a set of n novel weights.

Because there can be four possible models for subcriteria or weights, there can be 16 different WAs, as summarized in Fig. 5.1.

Definition 5.2. When at least one subcriterion or weight is modeled as an interval, and all other subcriteria or weights are modeled by no more than such a model, the resulting WA is called an *interval WA* (IWA).

Definition 5.3. When at least one subcriterion or weight is modeled as a T1 FS, and all other subcriteria or weights are modeled by no more than such a model, the resulting WA is called a *fuzzy WA* (FWA).

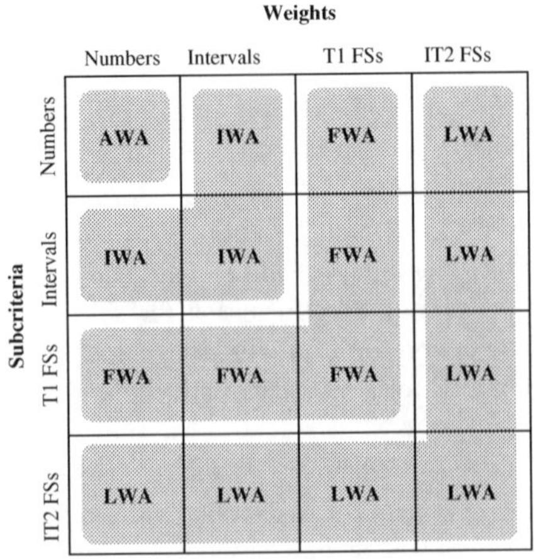

		Weights		
	Numbers	Intervals	T1 FSs	IT2 FSs
Numbers	AWA	IWA	FWA	LWA
Intervals	IWA	IWA	FWA	LWA
T1 FSs	FWA	FWA	FWA	LWA
IT2 FSs	LWA	LWA	LWA	LWA

Figure 5.1. Matrix of possibilities for a WA.

Definition 5.4. When at least one subcriterion or weight is modeled as an IT2 FS, the resulting WA is called a *linguistic WA* (LWA).

Definition 5.1. (continued). By a NWA is meant an IWA, FWA, or LWA.

From Fig. 5.1 it should be obvious that contained within the LWA are all of the other NWAs, suggesting that one should focus on the LWA and then view the other NWAs as special cases of it (a top-down approach). Although this is possible, our approach will be to study NWAs from the bottom up, that is, from the IWA to the FWA to the LWA, because (this is proved in Sections 5.4 and 5.5) the computation of a FWA uses a collection of IWAs, and the computation of a LWA uses two FWAs.

In order to reduce the number of possible derivations from 15 (the AWA is excluded) to three, it is assumed that for the IWA *all* subcriteria and weights are modeled as intervals, for the FWA *all* subcriteria and weights are modeled as T1 FSs, and for the LWA *all* subcriteria and weights are modeled as IT2 FSs.

5.3   INTERVAL WEIGHTED AVERAGE

In equation (5.1) let

$$x_i \in [a_i, b_i] \qquad i = 1, ..., n \tag{5.3}$$

$$w_i \in [c_i, d_i] \qquad i = 1, ..., n \tag{5.4}$$

We associate interval sets X_i and W_i with equations (5.3) and (5.4), respectively, and refer to them as *intervals*.

The WA in equation (5.1) is now evaluated over the Cartesian product space:

$$D_{X_1} \times D_{X_2} \times \cdots \times D_{X_n} \times D_{W_1} \times D_{W_2} \times \cdots \times D_{W_n}$$

Regardless of the fact that this requires an uncountable number of evaluations,[1] the resulting IWA, Y_{IWA}, will be a closed interval of nonnegative real numbers, and is completely defined by its two end points, y_L and y_R:

$$Y_{IWA} = [y_L, y_R] \tag{5.5}$$

Because x_i $(i = 1, \ldots, n)$ appear only in the numerator of equation (5.1), the smallest (largest) value of each x_i is used to find y_L (y_R):

$$y_L = \min_{\forall w_i \in [c_i, d_i]} \frac{\sum_{i=1}^{n} a_i w_i}{\sum_{i=1}^{n} w_i} \tag{5.6}$$

[1]Unless all of the D_{X_i} and D_{W_i} are first discretized, in which case there could still be an astronomically large but countable number of evaluations of equation (5.1), depending upon the number of terms in equation (5.1) (i.e., n) and the discretization size.

$$y_R = \max_{\forall w_i \in [c_i, d_i]} \frac{\sum_{i=1}^{n} b_i w_i}{\sum_{i=1}^{n} w_i} \tag{5.7}$$

where the notations under min and max in equations (5.6) and (5.7) mean that i ranges from 1 to n, and each w_i ranges from c_i to d_i.

Comparing equations (5.6) to (2.26), in which x_i is replaced by a_i, and equations (5.7) to (2.27), in which x_i are replaced by b_i, it then follows by using equations (2.30) and (2.31) that y_L and y_R can be represented as

$$y_L = \frac{\sum_{i=1}^{L^*} a_i d_i + \sum_{i=L^*+1}^{n} a_i c_i}{\sum_{i=1}^{L^*} d_i + \sum_{i=L^*+1}^{n} c_i} \tag{5.8}$$

$$y_R = \frac{\sum_{i=1}^{R^*} b_i c_i + \sum_{i=R^*+1}^{n} b_i d_i}{\sum_{i=1}^{R^*} c_i + \sum_{i=R^*+1}^{n} d_i} \tag{5.9}$$

in which L^* and R^* are *switch points* that are found by using either KM or EKM algorithms (Tables 2.1 and 2.2). In order to use these algorithms, $\{a_1, \ldots, a_n\}$ and $\{b_1, \ldots, b_n\}$ must be sorted in increasing order, respectively; hence, in the sequel, it is always assumed that

$$a_1 \leq a_2 \leq \cdots \leq a_n \tag{5.10}$$

$$b_1 \leq b_2 \leq \cdots \leq b_n \tag{5.11}$$

Example 5.1. Suppose for $n = 5$, $\{x_i\}|_{i=1,\ldots,5} = \{9, 7, 5, 4, 1\}$ and $\{w_i\}|_{i=1,\ldots,5} = \{2, 1, 8, 4, 6\}$, so that the arithmetic WA $y_{AWA} = 4.14$. Let λ denote any of these crisp numbers. In this example, for the IWA, $\lambda \to [\lambda - \delta, \lambda + \delta]$, where δ may be different for different λ:

$$\{x_i\}|_{i=1,\ldots,5} \to \{[8.2, 9.8], [5.8, 8.2], [2.0, 8.0], [3.0, 5.0], [0.5, 1.5]\}$$

$$\{w_i\}|_{i=1,\ldots,5} \to \{[1.0, 3.0], [0.6, 1.4], [7.1, 8.9], [2.4, 5.6], [5.0, 7.0]\}$$

It follows that $Y_{IWA} = [2.02, 6.36]$. Note that the average of Y_{IWA} is 4.19, which is very close to the value of y_{AWA}. The important difference between y_{AWA} and Y_{IWA} is that the uncertainties about the subcriteria and weights have led to an uncertainty band for the IWA, and such a band may play a useful role in subsequent decision making.

Finally, the following is a useful *expressive* way to summarize the IWA:

$$Y_{IWA} \equiv \frac{\sum_{i=1}^{n} X_i W_i}{\sum_{i=1}^{n} W_i} \tag{5.12}$$

where X_i and W_i are intervals whose elements are defined in equations (5.3) and (5.4), respectively, and Y_{IWA} is also an interval. Of course, in order to explain the right-hand side of this expressive equation, one needs equations (5.5)–(5.7) and their accompanying discussions.

5.4   FUZZY WEIGHTED AVERAGE

In the IWA, subcriteria and weights are modeled as intervals. In some situations, it may be more appropriate to model subcriteria and weights as T1 FSs, for example, as in the first column of Table 5.1.

As for the IWA, let

$$x_i \in [a_i, b_i] \qquad i = 1, ..., n \tag{5.13}$$

$$w_i \in [c_i, d_i] \qquad i = 1, ..., n \tag{5.14}$$

but, unlike the IWA, where the membership grade for each x_i and w_i is 1, now the membership grade for each $x_i = x_i'$ and $w_i = w_i'$ is $\mu_{X_i}(x_i')$ and $\mu_{W_i}(w_i')$, respectively. So, now, T1 FSs X_i and W_i and their MFs $\mu_{X_i}(x_i)$ and $\mu_{W_i}(w_i)$ are associated with equations (5.13) and (5.14), respectively.

Again, the WA in equation (5.1) is evaluated over the Cartesian product space

$$D_{X_1} \times D_{X_2} \times \cdots \times D_{X_n} \times D_{W_1} \times D_{W_2} \times \cdots \times D_{W_n}$$

making use of $\mu_{X1}(x_1)$, $\mu_{X2}(x_2)$, $\ldots$, $\mu_{Xn}(x_n)$ and $\mu_{W1}(w_1)$, $\mu_{W2}(w_2)$, $\ldots$, $\mu_{Wn}(w_n)$, the result being a specific numerical value, y, as well as a degree of membership, $\mu_{Y_{FWA}}(y)$. How to compute the latter will be explained in Section 5.4.3 below. The result of each pair of computations is the pair $(y, \mu_{Y_{FWA}}(y))$:

$$\{(x_1, \mu_{X_1}(x_1)), ..., (x_n, \mu_{X_n}(x_n)), (w_1, \mu_{W_1}(w_1)), ..., (w_n, \mu_{W_n}(w_n))\}$$
$$\rightarrow \left(y = \frac{\sum_{i=1}^{n} x_i w_i}{\sum_{i=1}^{n} w_i}, \mu_{Y_{FWA}}(y) \right) \tag{5.15}$$

When this is done for all elements in the Cartesian product space, the FWA, Y_{FWA}, is obtained. By this explanation, observe that Y_{FWA} is itself a T1 FS that is characterized by its MF $\mu_{Y_{FWA}}(y)$.

Of course, it is impossible to compute $\mu_{Y_{FWA}}(y)$ for all values of y as just described because to do so would require an uncountable number of computations. So, in the rest of this section, a practical algorithm is provided for computing $\mu_{Y_{FWA}}(y)$. To begin, a well-known novel decomposition of T1 FSs is introduced, and then how that decomposition can be used to compute functions of T1 FSs (which is what the FWA is) is explained.

5.4.1   α-cuts and a Decomposition Theorem

Definition 5.5 [Klir and Yuan (1995)]. The α-cut of T1 FS X, denoted $X(\alpha)$, is an interval of real numbers, defined as

$$X(\alpha) = \{x | \mu_X(x) \geq \alpha\} = [a(\alpha), b(\alpha)] \tag{5.16}$$

where $0 \leq \alpha \leq 1$.

An example of an α-cut is depicted in Fig. 5.2, and in this example, $X(\alpha) = [1.5, 5.5]$. Given a specific X, it is easy to obtain formulas for the end points of the α-cut (see Table 5.1). In order to obtain these formulas, such as the ones for the triangular distribution, solve the two equations $l(x) = \alpha$ for the left end point and $r(x) = \alpha$ for the right end point.

One of the major roles of α-cuts is their capability to represent a T1 FS. In order to do this, first the following *indicator function* is introduced:

$$I_{X(\alpha)}(x) = \begin{cases} 1, & \forall x \in X(\alpha) \\ 0, & \forall x \notin X(\alpha) \end{cases} \tag{5.17}$$

Associated with $I_{X(\alpha)}(x)$ is the following *square-well function:*

$$\mu_X(x|\alpha) = \alpha I_{X(\alpha)}(x) \tag{5.18}$$

This function, an example of which is depicted in Fig. 5.3, raises the α-cut $X(\alpha)$ off of the x-axis to height α.

Theorem 5.1 (Decomposition Theorem) [Klir and Yan (1995)]. A T1 FS X can be represented as

$$\mu_X(x) = \bigcup_{\alpha \in [0,1]} \mu_X(x|\alpha) \tag{5.19}$$

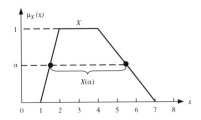

Figure 5.2. A trapezoidal T1 FS and an α-cut.

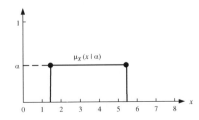

Figure 5.3. Square-well function $\mu_X(x|\alpha)$.

Table 5.1. Examples of T1 FSs and their α-cut formulas

T1 FS	α-cut formula
	$X(\alpha) = [m - a(1 - \alpha), m + b(1 - \alpha)]$
	$X(\alpha) = [m_1 - a(1 - \alpha), m_2 + b(1 - \alpha)]$

where $\mu_X(x|\alpha)$ is defined in equation (5.18) and $\cup$ (which is over all values of α) denotes the standard union operator, that is, the supremum (often the maximum) operator.

This theorem is called a "decomposition theorem" because X is decomposed into a collection of square-well functions that are then aggregated using the union operation.

An example of equation (5.19) is depicted in Fig. 5.4. When the dark circles at each α-level (e.g., α_3) are connected, $\mu_X(x|\alpha)$ is obtained. Because of the nonincreasing or nondecreasing nature of a T1 FS, the union operation picks up just the end points of the α-cuts, and when these points are connected, in the direction of increasing x, this provides $\mu_X(x)$. Note that greater resolution is obtained by including more α-cuts, and the calculation of new α-cuts does not affect previously calculated α-cuts.

5.4.2 Functions of T1 FSs

As stated above, the FWA is a function of T1 FSs. In order to compute any function of T1 FSs, some theory for doing this must be provided. This is done in Appendices 5A.1 and 5A.2. Appendix 5A.1 provides the *Extension Principle* for computing the

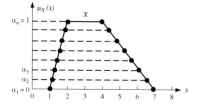

Figure 5.4. Example to illustrate the decomposition theorem when n α-cuts are used.

MF for a function of T1 FSs, and Appendix 5A.2 provides a practical way to compute such a MF, that is, a Decomposition Theorem for a function of T1 FSs using α-cuts (a *function decomposition theorem*), which is a direct application of Theorem 5.1, but subject to the Extension Principle. In words, the function decomposition theorem states:

> The MF for a function of T1 FSs equals the union (over all values of α) of the MFs for the same function applied to the α-cuts of the T1 FSs.

The importance of this decomposition is that it reduces all computations to interval computations because all α-cuts are intervals. The FWA is computed using this function decomposition theorem.

5.4.3 Computing the FWA

Because Appendices 5A.1 and 5A.2 are very technical, how to compute the FWA is explained here, assuming that the reader has either read those appendices or is willing to accept the truth of the above word statement of the function decomposition theorem (when it is extended from two variables to $2n$ variables).

There are three steps to computing the FWA:

1. For each $\alpha \in [0, 1]$, the corresponding α-cuts of the T1 FSs, X_i and W_i, must first be computed, that is, compute

$$X_i(\alpha) = [a_i(\alpha), b_i(\alpha)] \quad i = 1, ..., n \tag{5.20}$$

$$W_i(\alpha) = [c_i(\alpha), d_i(\alpha)] \quad i = 1, ..., n \tag{5.21}$$

2. For each $\alpha \in [0, 1]$, compute the α-cut of the FWA by recognizing that it is an IWA, that is, $Y_{FWA}(\alpha) = Y_{IWA}(\alpha)$, where

$$Y_{IWA}(\alpha) = [y_L(\alpha), y_R(\alpha)] \tag{5.22}$$

in which [see equations (5.6) and (5.7)]

$$y_L(\alpha) = \min_{\forall w_i(\alpha) \in [c_i(\alpha), d_i(\alpha)]} \frac{\sum_{i=1}^{n} a_i(\alpha) w_i(\alpha)}{\sum_{i=1}^{n} w_i(\alpha)} \tag{5.23}$$

$$y_R(\alpha) = \max_{\forall w_i(\alpha) \in [c_i(\alpha), d_i(\alpha)]} \frac{\sum_{i=1}^{n} b_i(\alpha) w_i(\alpha)}{\sum_{i=1}^{n} w_i(\alpha)} \tag{5.24}$$

where the notations under min and max in equations (5.23) and (5.24) mean i ranges from 1 to n, and each $w_i(\alpha)$ ranges from $c_i(\alpha)$ to $d_i(\alpha)$. From equations (5.8)–(5.11):

$$y_L(\alpha) = \frac{\sum_{i=1}^{L^*(\alpha)} a_i(\alpha) d_i(\alpha) + \sum_{i=L^*(\alpha)+1}^{n} a_i(\alpha) c_i(\alpha)}{\sum_{i=1}^{L^*(\alpha)} d_i(\alpha) + \sum_{i=L^*(\alpha)+1}^{n} c_i(\alpha)} \tag{5.25}$$

$$y_R(\alpha) = \frac{\sum_{i=1}^{R^*(\alpha)} b_i(\alpha)c_i(\alpha) + \sum_{i=R^*(\alpha)+1}^{n} b_i(\alpha)d_i(\alpha)}{\sum_{i=1}^{R^*(\alpha)} c_i(\alpha) + \sum_{i=R^*(\alpha)+1}^{n} d_i(\alpha)} \tag{5.26}$$

$$a_1(\alpha) \le a_2(\alpha) \le \cdots \le a_n(\alpha) \tag{5.27}$$

$$b_1(\alpha) \le b_2(\alpha) \le \cdots \le b_n(\alpha) \tag{5.28}$$

The KM or EKM Algorithms given in Tables 2.1 and 2.2 can be used to compute switch points $L^*(\alpha)$ and $R^*(\alpha)$. In practice, a finite number of α-cuts are used, so that $\alpha \in [0, 1] \rightarrow \{\alpha_1, \alpha_2, \ldots, \alpha_m\}$. If parallel processors are available, then all computations of this step can be done in parallel using $2m$ processors.

3. Connect all left coordinates $(y_L(\alpha), \alpha)$ and all right coordinates $(y_R(\alpha), \alpha)$ to form the T1 FS Y_{FWA}.

Example 5.2. This is a continuation of Example 5.1 in which each interval is assigned a symmetric triangular distribution that is centered at the midpoint (λ) of the interval, has distribution value equal to one at that point, and is zero at the interval end points ($\lambda - \delta$ and $\lambda + \delta$) (see Fig. 5.5). The FWA is depicted in Fig. 5.6(c). Although Y_{FWA} appears to be triangular, its sides are actually slightly curved.

The support of Y_{FWA} is [2.02, 6.36], which is the same as Y_{IWA} (see Example 5.1). This will always occur because the support of Y_{FWA} is the $\alpha = 0$ α-cut, and this is Y_{IWA}.

The centers of gravity of Y_{FWA} and Y_{IWA} are 4.15 and 4.19, respectively, and, though close, are not the same. The almost triangular distribution for Y_{FWA} indicates that more emphasis should be given to values of variable y that are closer to 4.15, whereas the uniform distribution for Y_{IWA} indicates that equal emphasis should be given to all values of variable y in its interval. The former reflects the propagation of the nonuniform uncertainties through the FWA, and can be used in future decisions.

Finally, the following is a very useful *expressive* way to summarize the FWA:

$$Y_{FWA} \equiv \frac{\sum_{i=1}^{n} X_i W_i}{\sum_{i=1}^{n} W_i} \tag{5.29}$$

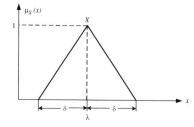

Figure 5.5. Illustration of a T1 FS used in Example 5.2.

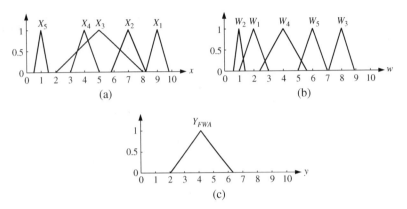

Figure 5.6. Example 5.2: (a) subcriteria, (b) weights, and, (c) Y_{FWA}.

where X_i and W_i are T1 FSs that are characterized by $\mu_{X_i}(x_i)$ and $\mu_{W_i}(w_i)$, respectively, and Y_{FWA} is also a T1 FS. Of course, in order to explain the right-hand side of this expressive equation, equations (5.15), (5.20)–(5.28), and their accompanying discussions are needed. Although the right-hand side of equations (5.29) and (5.12) look the same, it is the accompanying models for X_i and W_i that distinguish one from the other.

5.5   LINGUISTIC WEIGHTED AVERAGE

In the FWA, subcriteria and weights are modeled as T1 FSs. In some situations, it may be more appropriate to model subcriteria and weights as IT2 FSs. When equation (5.1) is computed using IT2 FSs for subcriteria and weights, then the result is the *linguistic weighted average* (LWA), $\tilde{Y}_{LWA}$ [Wu and Mendel (2007, 2008)]; see also Definition 5.4).

5.5.1   Introduction

As for the FWA, let

$$x_i \in [a_i, b_i] \quad i = 1, ..., n \tag{5.30}$$

$$w_i \in [c_i, d_i] \quad i = 1, ..., n \tag{5.31}$$

but, unlike the FWA, where the degree of membership for each $x_i = x_i'$ and $w_i = w_i'$ is $\mu_{X_i}(x_i')$ and $\mu_{W_i}(w_i')$, now the primary membership for each $x_i = x_i'$ and $w_i = w_i'$ is an interval $J_{x_i'}$ and $J_{w_i'}$, respectively [see equation (2.14)]. So, now, IT2 FSs $\tilde{X}_i$ and $\tilde{W}_i$ and their primary memberships J_{x_i} and J_{w_i} are associated with equations (5.30) and (5.31), respectively.

Now the WA in equation (5.1) is evaluated, but over the Cartesian product space

$$D_{\tilde{X}_1} \times D_{\tilde{X}_2} \times \cdots \times D_{\tilde{X}_n} \times D_{\tilde{W}_1} \times D_{\tilde{W}_2} \times \cdots \times D_{\tilde{W}_n}$$

making use of $J_{x1}, J_{x2}, \ldots, J_{xn}$ and $J_{w1}, J_{w2}, \ldots, J_{wn}$, the result being a specific numerical value, y, as well as the primary membership, J_y. Recall, from equation (2.14), that $J_{xi} = [\underline{\mu}_{\tilde{X}_i}(x_i), \overline{\mu}_{\tilde{X}_i}(x_i)]$ and $J_{wi} = [\underline{\mu}_{\tilde{W}_i}(w_i), \overline{\mu}_{\tilde{W}_i}(w_i)]$; consequently, $J_y = [\underline{\mu}_{\tilde{Y}_{LWA}}(y), \overline{\mu}_{\tilde{Y}_{LWA}}(y)]$. How to compute the latter interval of nonnegative real numbers will be explained below.[2] The result of each pair of computations is the pair (y, J_y):

$$\{(x_1, J_{x_1}), \ldots, (x_n, J_{x_n}), (w_1, J_{w_1}), \ldots, (w_n, J_{w_n})\}$$

$$\to \left(y = \frac{\sum_{i=1}^{n} x_i w_i}{\sum_{i=1}^{n} w_i}, J_y = [\underline{\mu}_{\tilde{Y}_{LWA}}(y), \overline{\mu}_{\tilde{Y}_{LWA}}(y)] \right) \tag{5.32}$$

When this is done for all elements in the Cartesian product space, $\tilde{Y}_{LWA}$ is obtained. By this explanation, observe that $\tilde{Y}_{LWA}$ is itself an IT2 FS that is characterized by its primary MF J_y, or equivalently by its FOU, $FOU(\tilde{Y}_{LWA})$:

$$FOU(\tilde{Y}_{LWA}) = \bigcup_{\forall y \in D_{\tilde{Y}_{LWA}}} J_y = \left[\underline{Y}_{LWA}, \overline{Y}_{LWA} \right] \tag{5.33}$$

where $D_{\tilde{Y}_{LWA}}$ is the domain of the primary variable, and $\underline{Y}_{LWA}$ and $\overline{Y}_{LWA}$ are the LMF and UMF of $\tilde{Y}_{LWA}$, respectively.

Similar to equation (5.29), the following is a very useful *expressive* way to summarize the LWA:

$$\tilde{Y}_{LWA} \equiv \frac{\sum_{i=1}^{n} \tilde{X}_i \tilde{W}_i}{\sum_{i=1}^{n} \tilde{W}_i} \tag{5.34}$$

where $\tilde{X}_i$ and $\tilde{W}_i$ are IT2 FSs that are characterized by their FOUs and $\tilde{Y}_{LWA}$ is also an IT2 FS.

Recall from the Wavy Slice Representation Theorem [equations (2.19) and (2.16)] that

$$\tilde{X}_i = 1/FOU(\tilde{X}_i) = 1/[\underline{X}_i, \overline{X}_i] \tag{5.35}$$

$$\tilde{W}_i = 1/FOU(\tilde{W}_i) = 1/[\underline{W}_i, \overline{W}_i] \tag{5.36}$$

as shown in Figs. 5.7 and 5.8. Because in equation (5.34) $\tilde{X}_i$ only appears in the numerator of $\tilde{Y}_{LWA}$, it follows that

---

[2] A different derivation, which uses the Wavy Slice Representation Theorem (Section 2.4) for an IT2 FS, is given in [Wu and Mendel (2007, 2008)]; however, the results are the same as those presented in this chapter.

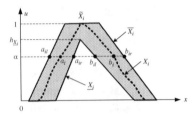

Figure 5.7. $\tilde{X}_i$ and an α-cut. The dashed curve is an embedded T1 FS of $\tilde{X}_i$.

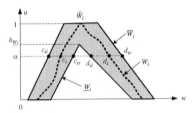

Figure 5.8. $\tilde{W}_i$ and an α-cut. The dashed curve is an embedded T1 FS of $\tilde{W}_i$.

$$\underline{Y}_{LWA} = \min_{\forall W_i \in [\underline{W}_i, \overline{W}_i]} \frac{\sum_{i=1}^n \underline{X}_i W_i}{\sum_{i=1}^n W_i} \tag{5.37}$$

$$\overline{Y}_{LWA} = \max_{\forall W_i \in [\underline{W}_i, \overline{W}_i]} \frac{\sum_{i=1}^n \overline{X}_i W_i}{\sum_{i=1}^n W_i} \tag{5.38}$$

By this preliminary approach to computing the LWA, it has been shown that it is only necessary to compute $\underline{Y}_{LWA}$ and $\overline{Y}_{LWA}$, as depicted in Fig. 5.9. One method is to compute the totality of all FWAs that can be formed from all of the embedded T1 FSs W_i; however, this is impractical because there can be infinite many W_i. In Section 5.5.2 an α-cut based approach is proposed; it eliminates the need to enumerate and evaluate all embedded T1 FSs.

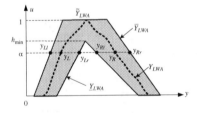

Figure 5.9. $\tilde{Y}_{LWA}$ and associated quantities. The dashed curve is an embedded T1 FS of $\tilde{Y}_{LWA}$.

Comment: One can (jokingly) think of the LWA as an FWA on steroids, that is, one can think of Fig. 5.9 as a fat version of Fig. 5.6(c). This actually is a very accurate explanation of the LWA and makes the derivations for $\underline{Y}_{LWA}$ and $\overline{Y}_{LWA}$ very easy to understand.

Detailed derivations of algorithms for computing $\underline{Y}_{LWA}$ and $\overline{Y}_{LWA}$ are given next. Once $\underline{Y}_{LWA}$ and $\overline{Y}_{LWA}$ are obtained, $\tilde{Y}_{LWA}$ is determined, i.e., $FOU(\tilde{Y}_{LWA})$ is the area between $\underline{Y}_{LWA}$ and $\overline{Y}_{LWA}$.

5.5.2 Computing the LWA

A typical $\tilde{Y}_{LWA}$ is depicted in Fig. 5.9, and a typical $\tilde{X}_i$ and $\tilde{W}_i$ are shown in Figs. 5.7 and 5.8, respectively. $\underline{Y}_{LWA}$ and $\overline{Y}_{LWA}$ will be computed by making use of the α-cut Decomposition Theorem (Theorem 5.3 in Appendix 5A.2); but, before they can be computed, their heights need to be determined. This is easy to do for $\overline{Y}_{LWA}$ because all UMFs are normal T1 FSs, but is less easy to do for $\underline{Y}_{LWA}$ because all LMFs are not normal T1 FSs.

Because all UMFs are normal T1 FSs, $h_{\overline{Y}_{LWA}} = 1$. Denote the height of $\underline{X}_i$ as $h_{\underline{X}_i}$ and the height of $\underline{W}_i$ as $h_{\underline{W}_i}$. Let

$$h_{\min} = \min\{\min_{\forall i} h_{\underline{X}_i}, \min_{\forall i} h_{\underline{W}_i}\} \tag{5.39}$$

where $h_{\min}$ is the smallest height of all FWAs computed from embedded T1 FSs of $\tilde{X}_i$ and $\tilde{W}_i$. Because $FOU(\tilde{Y}_{LWA})$ is the combination of all such FWAs, and $\underline{Y}_{LWA}$ is the lower bound of $FOU(\tilde{Y}_{LWA})$, it must hold that $h_{\underline{Y}_{LWA}} = h_{\min}$, as proved in Theorem 5.3.

Let $[a_i(\alpha), b_i(\alpha)]$ be an α-cut on an embedded T1 FS of $\tilde{X}_i$, and $[c_i(\alpha), d_i(\alpha)]$ be an α-cut on an embedded T1 FS of $\tilde{W}_i$. Observe in Fig. 5.7 that if the α-cut on $\underline{X}_i$ exists, then the interval $[a_{il}(\alpha), b_{ir}(\alpha)]$ is divided into three subintervals: $[a_{il}(\alpha), a_{ir}(\alpha)]$, $(a_{ir}(\alpha), b_{il}(\alpha))$, and $[b_{il}(\alpha), b_{ir}(\alpha)]$. In this case, $a_i(\alpha) \in [a_{il}(\alpha), a_{ir}(\alpha)]$ and $a_i(\alpha)$ cannot assume a value larger than $a_{ir}(\alpha)$. Similarly, $b_i(\alpha) \in [b_{il}(\alpha), b_{ir}(\alpha)]$ and $b_i(\alpha)$ cannot assume a value smaller than $b_{il}(\alpha)$. However, if the α-cut on $\underline{X}_i$ does not exist (e.g., $\alpha > h_{\underline{X}_i}$), then both $a_i(\alpha)$ and $b_i(\alpha)$ can assume values freely in the entire interval $[a_{il}(\alpha), b_{ir}(\alpha)]$:

$$a_i(\alpha) \in \begin{cases} [a_{il}(\alpha), a_{ir}(\alpha)], & \alpha \in [0, h_{\underline{X}_i}] \\ [a_{il}(\alpha), b_{ir}(\alpha)], & \alpha \in (h_{\underline{X}_i}, 1] \end{cases} \tag{5.40}$$

$$b_i(\alpha) \in \begin{cases} [b_{il}(\alpha), b_{ir}(\alpha)], & \alpha \in [0, h_{\underline{X}_i}] \\ [a_{il}(\alpha), b_{ir}(\alpha)], & \alpha \in (h_{\underline{X}_i}, 1] \end{cases} \tag{5.41}$$

Similarly, observe from Fig. 5.8 that

$$c_i(\alpha) \in \begin{cases} [c_{il}(\alpha), c_{ir}(\alpha)], & \alpha \in [0, h_{\underline{W}_i}] \\ [c_{il}(\alpha), d_{ir}(\alpha)], & \alpha \in (h_{\underline{W}_i}, 1] \end{cases} \tag{5.42}$$

$$d_i(\alpha) \in \begin{cases} [d_{il}(\alpha), d_{ir}(\alpha)], & \alpha \in [0, h_{\underline{W}_i}] \\ [c_{il}(\alpha), d_{ir}(\alpha)], & \alpha \in (h_{\underline{W}_i}, 1] \end{cases} \tag{5.43}$$

In equations (5.40)–(5.43), subscript i is the subcriterion or weight index, l means left, and r means right.

Using equations (5.40)–(5.43), let

$$a_{ir}(\alpha) \triangleq \begin{cases} a_{ir}(\alpha), & \alpha \leq h_{\underline{X}_i} \\ b_{ir}(\alpha), & \alpha > h_{\underline{X}_i} \end{cases} \tag{5.44}$$

$$b_{il}(\alpha) \triangleq \begin{cases} b_{il}(\alpha), & \alpha \leq h_{\underline{X}_i} \\ a_{il}(\alpha), & \alpha > h_{\underline{X}_i} \end{cases} \tag{5.45}$$

$$c_{ir}(\alpha) \triangleq \begin{cases} c_{ir}(\alpha), & \alpha \leq h_{\underline{W}_i} \\ d_{ir}(\alpha), & \alpha > h_{\underline{W}_i} \end{cases} \tag{5.46}$$

$$d_{il}(\alpha) \triangleq \begin{cases} d_{il}(\alpha), & \alpha \leq h_{\underline{W}_i} \\ c_{il}(\alpha), & \alpha > h_{\underline{W}_i} \end{cases} \tag{5.47}$$

Then

$$a_i(\alpha) \in [a_{il}(\alpha), a_{ir}(\alpha)], \forall \alpha \in [0, 1] \tag{5.48}$$

$$b_i(\alpha) \in [b_{il}(\alpha), b_{ir}(\alpha)], \forall \alpha \in [0, 1] \tag{5.49}$$

$$c_i(\alpha) \in [c_{il}(\alpha), c_{ir}(\alpha)], \forall \alpha \in [0, 1] \tag{5.50}$$

$$d_i(\alpha) \in [d_{il}(\alpha), d_{ir}(\alpha)], \forall \alpha \in [0, 1] \tag{5.51}$$

Note that in equations (5.23) and (5.24) for the FWA, $a_i(\alpha)$, $b_i(\alpha)$, $c_i(\alpha)$, and $d_i(\alpha)$ are crisp numbers; consequently, $y_L(\alpha)$ and $y_R(\alpha)$ computed from them are also crisp numbers; however, in the LWA, $a_i(\alpha)$, $b_i(\alpha)$, $c_i(\alpha)$, and $d_i(\alpha)$ can assume values continuously in their corresponding α-cut intervals. Numerous different combinations of $a_i(\alpha)$, $b_i(\alpha)$, $c_i(\alpha)$, and $d_i(\alpha)$ can be formed. $y_L(\alpha)$ and $y_R(\alpha)$ need to be computed for all the combinations. By collecting all $y_L(\alpha)$ a continuous interval $[y_{Ll}(\alpha), y_{Lr}(\alpha)]$ is obtained, and by collecting all $y_R(\alpha)$ a continuous interval $[y_{Rl}(\alpha), y_{Rr}(\alpha)]$ is also obtained (see Fig. 5.9):

$$\underline{Y}_{LWA}(\alpha) = [y_{Lr}(\alpha), y_{Rl}(\alpha)], \quad \alpha \in [0, h_{\min}] \tag{5.52}$$

and

$$\overline{Y}_{LWA}(\alpha) = [y_{Ll}(\alpha), y_{Rr}(\alpha)], \quad \alpha \in [0, 1] \tag{5.53}$$

where $y_{Lr}(\alpha)$, $y_{Rl}(\alpha)$, $y_{Ll}(\alpha)$, and $y_{Rr}(\alpha)$ are illustrated in Fig. 5.9. Clearly, to find $\underline{Y}_{LWA}(\alpha)$ and $\overline{Y}_{LWA}(\alpha)$, $y_{Ll}(\alpha)$, $y_{Lr}(\alpha)$, $y_{Rl}(\alpha)$, and $y_{Rr}(\alpha)$ need to be found.

Consider $y_{Ll}(\alpha)$ first. Note that it lies on $\overline{Y}_{LWA}$, and is the minimum of $y_L(\alpha)$, but now $a_i \in [a_{il}, a_{ir}]$, $c_i \in [c_{il}, c_{ir}]$, and $d_i \in [d_{il}, d_{ir}]$:

$$y_{Ll}(\alpha) = \min_{\substack{\forall a_i \in [a_{il}, a_{ir}] \\ \forall c_i \in [c_{il}, c_{ir}], \forall d_i \in [d_{il}, d_{ir}]}} y_L(\alpha) \tag{5.54}$$

Substituting $y_L(\alpha)$ from equation (5.25) into equation (5.54), it follows that

$$y_{Ll}(\alpha) \equiv \min_{\substack{\forall a_i \in [a_{il}, a_{ir}] \\ \forall c_i \in [c_{il}, c_{ir}], \forall d_i \in [d_{il}, d_{ir}]}} \frac{\sum_{i=1}^{L_1} a_i(\alpha)d_i(\alpha) + \sum_{i=L_1+1}^{n} a_i(\alpha)c_i(\alpha)}{\sum_{i=1}^{L_1} d_i(\alpha) + \sum_{i=L_1+1}^{n} c_i(\alpha)} \tag{5.55}$$

Observe that $a_i(\alpha)$ only appears in the numerator of equation (5.55); thus, $a_{il}(\alpha)$ should be used to calculate $y_{Ll}(\alpha)$:

$$y_{Ll}(\alpha) = \min_{\substack{\forall c_i \in [c_{il}, c_{ir}] \\ \forall d_i \in [d_{il}, d_{ir}]}} \frac{\sum_{i=1}^{L_1} a_{il}(\alpha)d_i(\alpha) + \sum_{i=L_1+1}^{n} a_{il}(\alpha)c_i(\alpha)}{\sum_{i=1}^{L_1} d_i(\alpha) + \sum_{i=L_1+1}^{n} c_i(\alpha)} \tag{5.56}$$

Following a similar line of reasoning, $y_{Lr}(\alpha)$, $y_{Rl}(\alpha)$, and $y_{Rr}(\alpha)$ can also be expressed as

$$y_{Lr}(\alpha) = \max_{\substack{\forall c_i \in [c_{il}, c_{ir}] \\ \forall d_i \in [d_{il}, d_{ir}]}} \frac{\sum_{i=1}^{L_2} a_{ir}(\alpha)d_i(\alpha) + \sum_{i=L_2+1}^{n} a_{ir}(\alpha)c_i(\alpha)}{\sum_{i=1}^{L_2} d_i(\alpha) + \sum_{i=L_2+1}^{n} c_i(\alpha)} \tag{5.57}$$

$$y_{Rl}(\alpha) = \min_{\substack{\forall c_i \in [c_{il}, c_{ir}] \\ \forall d_i \in [d_{il}, d_{ir}]}} \frac{\sum_{i=1}^{R_1} b_{il}(\alpha)c_i(\alpha) + \sum_{i=R_1+1}^{n} b_{il}(\alpha)d_i(\alpha)}{\sum_{i=1}^{R_1} c_i(\alpha) + \sum_{i=R_1+1}^{n} d_i(\alpha)} \tag{5.58}$$

$$y_{Rr}(\alpha) = \max_{\substack{\forall c_i \in [c_{il}, c_{ir}] \\ \forall d_i \in [d_{il}, d_{ir}]}} \frac{\sum_{i=1}^{R_2} b_{ir}(\alpha)c_i(\alpha) + \sum_{i=R_2+1}^{n} b_{ir}(\alpha)d_i(\alpha)}{\sum_{i=1}^{R_2} c_i(\alpha) + \sum_{i=R_2+1}^{n} d_i(\alpha)} \tag{5.59}$$

So far, only $a_i(\alpha)$ are fixed for $y_{Ll}(\alpha)$ and $y_{Lr}(\alpha)$, and $b_i(\alpha)$ are fixed for $y_{Rl}(\alpha)$ and $y_{Rr}(\alpha)$. As will be shown, it is also possible to fix $c_i(\alpha)$ and $d_i(\alpha)$ for $y_{Ll}(\alpha)$, $y_{Lr}(\alpha)$, $y_{Rl}(\alpha)$, and $y_{Rr}(\alpha)$; thus, there will be no need to enumerate and evaluate all of $\tilde{W}_i$'s embedded T1 FSs to find $\underline{Y}_{LWA}$ and $\overline{Y}_{LWA}$.

Theorem 5.2 [Wu and Mendel (2007, 2008)]. It is true that:

(a) $y_{Ll}(\alpha)$ in equation (5.56) can be specified as

$$y_{Ll}(\alpha) = \frac{\sum_{i=1}^{L_1^*} a_{il}(\alpha)d_{ir}(\alpha) + \sum_{i=L_1^*+1}^{n} a_{il}(\alpha)c_{il}(\alpha)}{\sum_{i=1}^{L_1^*} d_{ir}(\alpha) + \sum_{i=L_1^*+1}^{n} c_{il}(\alpha)}, \quad \alpha \in [0, 1] \tag{5.60}$$

(b) $y_{Lr}(\alpha)$ in equation (5.57) can be specified as

$$y_{Lr}(\alpha) = \frac{\sum_{i=1}^{L_r^*} a_{ir}(\alpha)d_{il}(\alpha) + \sum_{i=L_r^*+1}^{n} a_{ir}(\alpha)c_{ir}(\alpha)}{\sum_{i=1}^{L_r^*} d_{il}(\alpha) + \sum_{i=L_r^*+1}^{n} c_{ir}(\alpha)}, \quad \alpha \in [0, h_{\min}] \quad (5.61)$$

(c) $y_{Rl}(\alpha)$ in equation (5.58) can be specified as

$$y_{Rl}(\alpha) = \frac{\sum_{i=1}^{R_l^*} b_{il}(\alpha)c_{ir}(\alpha) + \sum_{i=R_l^*+1}^{n} b_{il}(\alpha)d_{il}(\alpha)}{\sum_{i=1}^{R_l^*} c_{ir}(\alpha) + \sum_{i=R_l^*+1}^{n} d_{il}(\alpha)}, \quad \alpha \in [0, h_{\min}] \quad (5.62)$$

(d) $y_{Rr}(\alpha)$ in equation (5.59) can be specified as

$$y_{Rr}(\alpha) = \frac{\sum_{i=1}^{R_r^*} b_{ir}(\alpha)c_{il}(\alpha) + \sum_{i=R_r^*+1}^{n} b_{ir}(\alpha)d_{ir}(\alpha)}{\sum_{i=1}^{R_r^*} c_{il}(\alpha) + \sum_{i=R_r^*+1}^{n} d_{ir}(\alpha)}, \quad \alpha \in [0, 1] \quad (5.63)$$

In these equations, L_l^*, L_r^*, R_l^*, and R_r^* are switch points that are computed using KM or EKM algorithms.

The proof is given in Appendix 5A.3.

Observe from equations (5.60) and (5.63) and Figs. 5.7 and 5.8 that $y_{Ll}(\alpha)$ and $y_{Rr}(\alpha)$ only depend on the UMFs of $\tilde{X}_i$ and $\tilde{W}_i$, that is, they are only computed from the corresponding α-cuts on the UMFs of $\tilde{X}_i$ and $\tilde{W}_i$; so (this is an expressive equation),

$$\overline{Y}_{LWA} = \frac{\sum_{i=1}^{n} \overline{X}_i \overline{W}_i}{\sum_{i=1}^{n} \overline{W}_i} \quad (5.64)$$

Because all $\overline{X}_i$ and $\overline{W}_i$ are normal T1 FSs, according to Theorem 5.3, $\overline{Y}_{LWA}$ is also normal.

Similarly, observe from equations (5.61) and (5.62) and Figs. 5.7 and 5.8 that $y_{Lr}(\alpha)$ and $y_{Rl}(\alpha)$ only depend on the LMFs of $\tilde{X}_i$ and $\tilde{W}_i$; hence (this is an expressive equation),

$$\underline{Y}_{LWA} = \frac{\sum_{i=1}^{n} \underline{X}_i \underline{W}_i}{\sum_{i=1}^{n} \underline{W}_i} \quad (5.65)$$

Unlike $\overline{Y}_{LWA}$, which is a normal T1 FS, the height of $\underline{Y}_{LWA}$ is $h_{\min}$, the minimum height of all $\underline{X}_i$ and $\underline{W}_i$.

5.5.3 Algorithms

It has been shown in the previous subsection that computing $\tilde{Y}_{LWA}$ is equivalent to computing two FWAs, $\overline{Y}_{LWA}$ and $\underline{Y}_{LWA}$. To compute $\overline{Y}_{LWA}$:

1. Select appropriate m α-cuts for $\overline{Y}_{LWA}$ (e.g., divide $[0, 1]$ into $m - 1$ intervals and set $\alpha_j = (j - 1)/(m - 1), j = 1, 2, \ldots, m)$.
2. Find the corresponding α-cuts on $\overline{X}_i$ and $\overline{W}_i$ $(i = 1, \ldots, n)$ for each α_j (Table 5.1); denote the end points of the α-cuts as $[a_{il}(\alpha_j), b_{ir}(\alpha_j)]$ and $[c_{il}(\alpha_j), d_{ir}(\alpha_j)]$, respectively.
3. Use a KM or EKM algorithm (Tables 2.1 and 2.2) to find $y_{Ll}(\alpha_j)$ in equation (5.60) and $y_{Rr}(\alpha_j)$ in equation (5.63).
4. Repeat Steps (2) and (3) for every α_j $(j = 1, \ldots, m)$.
5. Connect all left coordinates $(y_{Ll}(\alpha_j), \alpha_j)$ and all right coordinates $(y_{Rr}(\alpha_j), \alpha_j)$ to form the UMF $\overline{Y}_{LWA}$.

To compute $\underline{Y}_{LWA}$:

1. Determine $h_{\underline{X}_i}$ and $h_{\underline{W}_i}$, $i = 1, \ldots, n$, and $h_{\min}$ in equation (5.39).
2. Select appropriate p α-cuts for $\underline{Y}_{LWA}$ (e.g., divide $[0, h_{\min}]$ into $p - 1$ intervals and set $\alpha_j = h_{\min}(j - 1)/(p - 1), j = 1, 2, \ldots, p)$.
3. Find the corresponding α-cuts $[a_{ir}(\alpha_j), b_{il}(\alpha_j)]$ and $[c_{ir}(\alpha_j), d_{il}(\alpha_j)]$ on $\underline{X}_i$ and $\underline{W}_i$.
4. Use a KM or EKM algorithm to find $y_{Lr}(\alpha_j)$ in equation (5.61) and $y_{Rl}(\alpha_j)$ in equation (5.62).
5. Repeat Steps (3) and (4) for every $\alpha_j, j = 1, \ldots, p$.
6. Connect all left coordinates $(y_{Lr}(\alpha_j), \alpha_j)$ and all right coordinates $(y_{Rl}(\alpha_j), \alpha_j)$ to form the LMF $\underline{Y}_{LWA}$.

A flowchart for computing $\underline{Y}_{LWA}$ and $\overline{Y}_{LWA}$ is given in Fig. 5.10. For triangular or trapezoidal IT2 FSs, it is possible to reduce the number of α-cuts for both $\underline{Y}_{LWA}$ and $\overline{Y}_{LWA}$ by choosing them only at *turning points,* that is, points on the LMFs and UMFs of $\widetilde{X}_i$ and $\widetilde{W}_i$ $(i = 1, 2, \ldots, n)$ at which the slope of these functions changes.

Example 5.3. This is a continuation of Example 5.2, in which each subcriterion and weight is now assigned an FOU that is a 50% blurring of the T1 MF depicted in Fig. 5.5. The left half of each FOU (Fig. 5.11) has support on the $x(w)$-axis given by the interval of real numbers $[(\lambda - \delta) - 0.5\delta, (\lambda - \delta) + 0.5\delta]$ and the right half FOU (Fig. 5.11) has support on the x-axis given by the interval of real numbers $[(\lambda + \delta) - 0.5\delta, (\lambda + \delta) + 0.5\delta]$. The UMF is a triangle defined by the three points $(\lambda - \delta - 0.5\delta, 0)$, $(\lambda, 1)$, $(\lambda + \delta + 0.5\delta, 0)$, and the LMF is a triangle defined by the three points $(\lambda - \delta + 0.5\delta, 0)$, $(\lambda, 1)$, $(\lambda + \delta - 0.5\delta, 0)$. The resulting subcriterion and weight FOUs are depicted in Figs. 5.12(a) and 5.12(b), respectively, and $\widetilde{Y}_{LWA}$ is depicted in Fig. 5.12(c). Although $\widetilde{Y}_{LWA}$ appears to be symmetrical, it is not. The support of the left-hand side of $\widetilde{Y}_{LWA}$ is $[0.85, 3.10]$ and the support of the right-hand side of $\widetilde{Y}_{LWA}$ is $[5.22, 7.56]$; hence, the length of the support of the left-hand side of $\widetilde{Y}_{LWA}$ is 2.25, whereas the length of the support of the right-hand side of $\widetilde{Y}_{LWA}$ is 2.34. In addition, the centroid of $\widetilde{Y}_{LWA}$ is computed using the EKM algorithms (Table 2.2), and is *centroid*$(\widetilde{Y}_{LWA}) = C(\widetilde{Y}_{LWA}) = [3.38, 4.96]$, so that $avg[centroid(\widetilde{Y}_{LWA})] = c(\widetilde{Y}_{LWA}) = 4.17$.

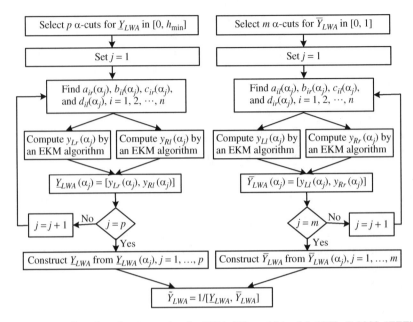

Figure 5.10. A flowchart for computing the LWA (Wu and Mendel, 2008; © 2008, IEEE).

Comparing Figs. 5.12(c) and 5.6(c), observe that $\tilde{Y}_{LWA}$ is spread out over a larger range of values than is Y_{FWA}, reflecting the additional uncertainties in the LWA due to the blurring of subcriteria and weights. This information can be used in future decisions.

Another way to interpret $\tilde{Y}_{LWA}$ is to associate values of y that have the largest vertical intervals (i.e., primary memberships) with values of greatest uncertainty; hence, there is no uncertainty at the three vertices of the UMF, and, for example, for the right half of $\tilde{Y}_{LWA}$ uncertainty increases from the apex of the UMF reaching its largest value at the right vertex of the LMF and then decreases to zero at the right vertex of the UMF.

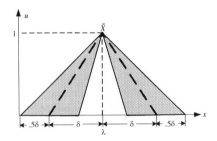

Figure 5.11. Illustration of an IT2 FS used in Example 5.3. The dashed lines indicate corresponding T1 FS used in Example 5.2.

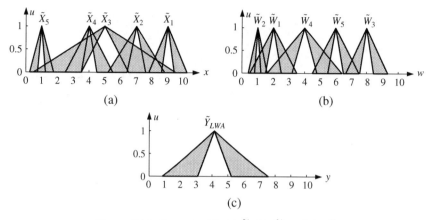

Figure 5.12. Example 5.3: (a) $\tilde{X}_i$, (b) $\tilde{W}_i$, and, (c) $\tilde{Y}_{LWA}$.

Example 5.4. In this example, we compute

$$\tilde{Y}_{LWA} = \frac{tiny \times small + little \times medium + sizeable \times large}{small + medium + large} \qquad (5.66)$$

where the word FOUs are contained in the 32-word vocabulary that is depicted in Fig. 3.18. For the convenience of the reader, these FOUs are repeated in Figs. 5.13(a) and 5.13(b). The corresponding $\tilde{Y}_{LWA}$ is shown in Fig. 5.13(c). Because in equation (5.66) larger weights are associated with larger subcriteria, it is expected that $\tilde{Y}_{LWA}$ should be larger than *little,* the median of the three subcriteria. This is verified by Fig. 5.13(c), that is, $\tilde{Y}_{LWA}$ extends to the right of *little* in Fig. 5.13(a).

Using the Jaccard similarity measure described in Chapter 4, $\tilde{Y}_{LWA}$ is mapped in the 32-word vocabulary to the word *some to moderate* [whose FOU is bounded by the dashed curve in Fig. 5.13(c)], because the similarity between $\tilde{Y}_{LWA}$ and FOU(*some to moderate*), which is 0.83, is the maximum of the similarities between $\tilde{Y}_{LWA}$ and the 32 word FOUs.

5.6 A SPECIAL CASE OF THE LWA

As shown in Fig. 5.1, there are many special cases of the general LWA introduced in the previous section, for example, the weights and/or subcriteria can be mixtures of numbers, intervals, T1 FSs, and IT2 FSs. The special case, in which all weights are numbers and all subcriteria are IT2 FSs, is of particular interest in this section because it is used in Chapter 6 for perceptual reasoning. Great simplifications of the LWA computations occur in this special case.

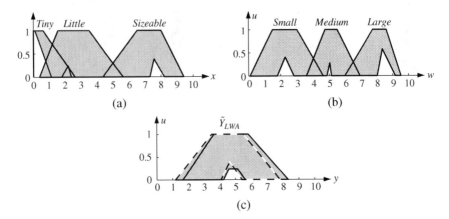

Figure 5.13. Example 5.4: (a) linguistic subcriteria, (b) linguistic weights, and, (c) $\tilde{Y}_{LWA}$ and the FOU for *some to moderate* (dashed curve).

Denote the crisp weights as w_i, $i = 1, \ldots, n$. Each w_i can still be interpreted as an IT2 FS $\tilde{W}_i$, where

$$\mu_{\underline{W}_i}(w) = \mu_{\overline{W}_i}(w) = \begin{cases} 1, & w = w_i \\ 0, & w \neq w_i \end{cases} \tag{5.67}$$

that is,

$$c_{il}(\alpha) = c_{ir}(\alpha) = d_{il}(\alpha) = d_{ir}(\alpha) = w_i, \quad \alpha \in [0, 1] \tag{5.68}$$

Substituting equation (5.68) into Theorem 5.2, equations (5.60)–(5.63) are simplified to

$$y_{Ll}(\alpha) = \frac{\sum_{i=1}^{n} a_{il}(\alpha)w_i}{\sum_{i=1}^{n} w_i}, \quad \alpha \in [0, 1] \tag{5.69}$$

$$y_{Rr}(\alpha) = \frac{\sum_{i=1}^{n} b_{ir}(\alpha)w_i}{\sum_{i=1}^{n} w_i}, \quad \alpha \in [0, 1] \tag{5.70}$$

$$y_{Lr}(\alpha) = \frac{\sum_{i=1}^{n} a_{ir}(\alpha)w_i}{\sum_{i=1}^{n} w_i}, \quad \alpha \in [0, h_{\min}] \tag{5.71}$$

$$y_{Rl}(\alpha) = \frac{\sum_{i=1}^{n} b_{il}(\alpha)w_i}{\sum_{i=1}^{n} w_i}, \quad \alpha \in [0, h_{\min}] \tag{5.72}$$

where

$$h_{\min} = \min_{\forall i} h_{\underline{X}_i} \tag{5.73}$$

Note that equations (5.69)–(5.72) are arithmetic weighted averages, so they are computed directly without using KM or EKM algorithms.

Example 5.5. This is a continuation of Example 5.3, in which the subcriteria are the same as those shown in Fig. 5.12(a) and weights are crisp numbers $\{w_i\}|_{i=1,\ldots,5} = \{2, 1, 8, 4, 6\}$, that is, they are the values of w that occur at the apexes of $\tilde{W}_i$ shown in Fig. 5.12(b). The resulting $\tilde{Y}_{LWA}$ is depicted in Fig. 5.14. Observe that it is more compact than $\tilde{Y}_{LWA}$ in Fig. 5.12(c), which is intuitive, because in this example the weights have less uncertainties than those in Example 5.3. In addition, unlike the unsymmetrical $\tilde{Y}_{LWA}$ in Fig. 5.12(c), $\tilde{Y}_{LWA}$ in Fig. 5.14 is symmetrical.[3] $C(\tilde{Y}_{LWA}) = [3.59, 4.69]$, which is inside the centroid of $\tilde{Y}_{LWA}$ in Fig. 5.12(c), and $c(\tilde{Y}_{LWA}) = 4.14$, which is the same[4] as y_{AWA} in Example 5.1.

5.7 FUZZY EXTENSIONS OF ORDERED WEIGHTED AVERAGES

The ordered weighted average (OWA) operator [Filev and Yager (1998), Liu (2007), Majlender (2005), Torra and Narukawa (2007), Yager (1988), Yager and Kacprzyk (1997)] was proposed by Yager to aggregate experts' opinions in decision making, as in Definition 5.6.

Definition 5.6. An OWA operator of dimension n is a mapping $y_{OWA} : R^n \to R$, which has an associated set of weights $w = \{w_1, \ldots, w_n\}$ for which $w_i \in [0, 1]$ and $\sum_{i=1}^n w_i = 1$, that is,

$$y_{OWA} = \sum_{i=1}^{n} w_i x_{\sigma(i)} \tag{5.74}$$

where $\sigma : \{1, \ldots, n\} \to \{1, \ldots, n\}$ is a permutation function such that $\{x_{\sigma(1)}, x_{\sigma(2)}, \ldots, x_{\sigma(n)}\}$ are in descending order.

Note that y_{OWA} is a nonlinear operator due to the permutation of x_i. The most attractive feature of the OWA operator is that it can implement different aggregation operators by choosing the weights differently [Filev and Yager (1998)], for example, by choosing $w_i = 1/n$ it implements the mean operator, by choosing $w_1 = 1$ and $w_i = 0$ $(i = 2, \ldots, n)$ it implements the maximum operator, and by choosing $w_i = 0$ $(i = 1, \ldots, n - 1)$ and $w_n = 1$ it implements the minimum operator.

Yager's (1988) original OWA operator considers only crisp numbers; however, experts may prefer to express their opinions in linguistic terms, which are modeled by FSs. Zhou et al. (2008a,b,c) were the first to extend OWAs to T1 and IT2 FSs;

---

[3]It can be shown that when all weights are crisp numbers, the resulting LWA from symmetrical $\tilde{X}_i$ is always symmetrical.

[4]Because $\tilde{Y}_{LWA}$ is symmetrical about y_{AWA}, according to Property 4 in Section 2.6.2, $c(\tilde{Y}_{LWA}) = y_{AWA}$.

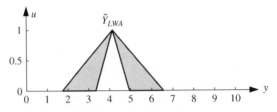

Figure 5.14. $\tilde{Y}_{LWA}$ for Example 5.5.

however, their extensions are different from ours, because they consider each α-cut of the FSs separately whereas we consider each FS in its entirety. In this section, we only consider fuzzy extensions of OWAs that build upon our NWAs.

5.7.1 Ordered Fuzzy Weighted Averages (OFWAs)

Definition 5.7. An ordered fuzzy weighted average (OFWA) is defined as

$$Y_{OFWA} = \frac{\sum_{i=1}^{n} W_i X_{\sigma(i)}}{\sum_{i=1}^{n} W_i} \tag{5.75}$$

where $\sigma : \{1, \ldots, n\} \to \{1, \ldots, n\}$ is a permutation function such that $\{X_{\sigma(1)}, X_{\sigma(2)}, \ldots, X_{\sigma(n)}\}$ are in descending order.

Definition 5.8. A group of T1 FSs $\{X_i\}_{i=1}^{n}$ are in descending order if $X_i \succcurlyeq X_j$ for $\forall i < j$ as determined by a ranking method.

Any T1 FS ranking method can be used to find σ. In this book, Yager's (1978) first method (see also Table 4A.2), which is a special case of the centroid-based ranking method (Section 4.3), is used. Once X_i are rank-ordered, Y_{OFWA} is computed by an FWA.

5.7.2 Ordered Linguistic Weighted Averages (OLWAs)

Definition 5.9. An ordered linguistic weighted average (OLWA) is defined as

$$\tilde{Y}_{OLWA} = \frac{\sum_{i=1}^{n} \tilde{W}_i \tilde{X}_{\sigma(i)}}{\sum_{i=1}^{n} \tilde{W}_i} \tag{5.76}$$

where $\sigma : \{1, \ldots, n\} \to \{1, \ldots, n\}$ is a permutation function such that $\{\tilde{X}_{\sigma(1)}, \tilde{X}_{\sigma(2)}, \ldots, \tilde{X}_{\sigma(n)}\}$ are in descending order.

Definition 5.10. A group of IT2 FSs $\{\tilde{X}_i\}_{i=1}^{n}$ are in descending order if $\tilde{X}_i \succcurlyeq \tilde{X}_j$ for $\forall i < j$ as determined by a ranking method.

The LWA algorithm can also be used to compute the OLWA, except that the centroid-based ranking method must first be used to sort $\tilde{X}_i$ in descending order.

APPENDIX 5A

This appendix briefly introduces the Extension Principle and the Decomposition Theorem of T1 FSs, and provides a proof for Theorem 5.2.

5A.1   Extension Principle

The Extension Principle was introduced by Zadeh (1975) and is an important tool in FS theory. It lets one extend mathematical relationships between nonfuzzy variables to fuzzy variables. Suppose, for example, one is given MFs for the FSs *small* and *light* and wants to determine the MF for the FS obtained by multiplying these FSs, i.e., *small* × *light*. The Extension Principle tells us how to determine the MF for *small* × *light* by making use of the nonfuzzy mathematical relationship $y = x_1 x_2$ in which the FS *small* plays the role of x_1 and the FS *light* plays the role of x_2.

Consider first a function of a single variable, $y = f(x)$, where $x \in D_X$ and $y \in D_Y$. A T1 FS X is given, whose universe of discourse is also D_X, and whose MF is $\mu_X(x)$, $\forall x \in D_X$. The Extension Principle [Jang et al. (1997)] states the image of X under the mapping $f(x)$ can be expressed as another T1 FS Y, by assigning $\mu_X(x)$ to the value of y where $y = f(x)$, that is,

$$\mu_Y(y) = \begin{cases} \mu_X(x), & \exists x \text{ s.t. } y = f(x) \\ 0, & \text{otherwise} \end{cases} \tag{5A.1}$$

The condition in equation (5A.1) that "$\mu_Y(y) = 0$, otherwise" means that if there are no values of x for which a specific value of y can be reached then the MF for that specific value of y is set equal to zero. Only those values of y that satisfy $y = f(x)$ can be reached.

The Extension Principle in equation (5A.1) is only valid if the mapping between y and x is one to one. It is quite possible that the same value of y can be obtained for different values of x—a many-to-one mapping (e.g., $y = x^2$)—in which case equation (5A.1) needs to be modified, for example, $f(x_1) = f(x_2) = y$, but $x_1 \neq x_2$ and $\mu_X(x_1) \neq \mu_X(x_2)$. To resolve this ambiguity, the larger of the two MF values is assigned to $\mu_Y(y)$. The general modification to equation (5A.1) is [Wang (1997)]:

$$\mu_Y(y) = \begin{cases} \max \mu_X(x), & \exists x \text{ s.t. } y = f(x) \\ 0, & \text{otherwise} \end{cases} \tag{5A.2}$$

So far, the Extension Principle has been stated just for a mapping of a single variable. Next, consider a function of two variables, $y = f(x_1, x_2)$, where $x_1 \in D_{X_1}$, $x_2 \in D_{X_2}$, $y \in D_Y$, and x_1 and x_2 are described by their respective MFs $\mu_{X_1}(x_1)$ and $\mu_{X_2}(x_2)$. It is of course possible for $y = f(x_1, x_2)$ to be many to one, just as it was in the single-variable case; so, the Extension Principle for the two-variable case needs to look something like equation (5A.2). The difference between the two-and the one-variable cases is that in the latter case there is only one MF that can be evaluated for each value of x, whereas in the former there are two MFs that can be evaluated, namely $\mu_{X_1}(x_1)$ and $\mu_{X_2}(x_2)$. In this case, the Extension Principle becomes:

$$\mu_Y(y) = \begin{cases} \sup \min \{\mu_{X_1}(x_1), \mu_{X_2}(x_2)\}, & \exists(x_1, x_2) \text{ s.t. } y = f(x_1, x_2) \\ 0, & \text{otherwise} \end{cases} \quad (5A.3)$$

For more than two variables, suppose that $y = f(x_1, x_2, \ldots, x_r)$, where $x_i \in D_{X_i}$ ($i = 1, \ldots, r$). Let $X_1, X_2, \ldots, X_r$ be T1 FSs in $D_{X_1}, D_{X_2}, \ldots, D_{X_r}$. Then, the Extension Principle lets us induce from the r T1 FSs $X_1, X_2, \ldots, X_r$ a T1 FS Y on D_Y, through f, that is, $Y = f(X_1, X_2, \ldots, X_r)$, such that

$$\mu_Y(y) = \begin{cases} \sup \min \{\mu_{X_1}(x_1), \ldots, \mu_{X_r}(x_r)\}, & \exists(x_1, \ldots, x_r) \text{ s.t. } y = f(x_1, \ldots, x_r) \\ 0, & \text{otherwise} \end{cases}$$
$$(5A.4)$$

In order to implement equation (5A.4), one must first find the values of $x_1, x_2, \ldots, x_r$ for which $y = f(x_1, x_2, \ldots, x_r)$, after which $\mu_{X_1}(x_1), \ldots, \mu_{X_r}(x_r)$ are computed at those values, and then min $\{\mu_{X_1}(x_1), \mu_{X_2}(x_2), \ldots, \mu_{X_r}(x_r)\}$ is computed. If more than one set of $x_1, x_2, \ldots, x_r$ satisfy $y = f(x_1, x_2, \ldots, x_r)$, then this is repeated for all of them and the largest of the minima is chosen as the choice for $\mu_Y(y)$. Usually, the evaluation of equation (5A.4) is very difficult, and the challenge is to find easier ways to do it than just described. The Function Decomposition Theorem that is given in Theorem 5.3 below is one such way.

Note, finally, that when it is necessary to extend an operation of the form $f(X_1, X_2, \ldots, X_r)$, where X_i are T1 FSs, the individual operations like addition, multiplication, division, and so on that are involved in f are not extended. Instead, the following is used [as derived from equation (5A.4)]:

$$f(X_1, X_2, \ldots, X_r) = \int_{x_1 \in D_{X_1}} \int_{x_2 \in D_{X_2}} \cdots \int_{x_r \in D_{X_r}} \mu_Y(y)/f(x_1, x_2, \ldots, x_r) \quad (5A.5)$$

where $\mu_Y(y)$ is defined in equation (5A.4).

For example, if $y = f(x_1, x_2) = (c_1 x_1 + c_2 x_2)/(x_1 + x_2)$, we write the extension of f to T1 FSs X_1 and X_2 as

$$f(X_1, X_2) = \int_{x_1 \in D_{X_1}} \int_{x_2 \in D_{X_2}} \mu_Y(y)/[(c_1 x_1 + c_2 x_2)/(x_1 + x_2)] \quad (5A.6)$$

where

$$\mu_Y(y) = \begin{cases} \sup\min\{\mu_{X_1}(x_1),\mu_{X_2}(x_2)\}, & \exists(x_1,x_2)\text{ s.t. } y = f(x_1,x_2) \\ 0, & \text{otherwise} \end{cases} \quad (5A.7)$$

If we write it as $Y = f(X_1, X_2) = (c_1X_1 + c_2X_2)/(X_1 + X_2)$, this does not mean that $f(X_1, X_2)$ is computed by adding and dividing the T1 FSs. It is merely an expressive equation computed by equation (5A.6).

5A.2   Decomposition of a Function of T1 FSs Using α-Cuts

The ultimate objective of this section is to show that a function of T1 FSs can be expressed as the union (over all values of α) of that function applied to the α-cuts of the T1 FSs. The original idea, stated as the α-cut Decomposition Theorem, is explained in [Klir and Yuan (1995)]. Though that theorem does not require the T1 FSs to be normal, it does not point out explicitly how subnormal T1 FSs should be handled. Because this theorem is so important, it is proved here for the convenience of the readers. Although the proof is very similar to that in [Klir and Yuan (1995)], it emphasizes subnormal cases because the LMFs in the LWA are generally subnormal.

We have just seen that the Extension Principle states that when the function $y = f(x_1, \ldots, x_r)$ is applied to T1 FSs X_i ($i = 1, \ldots, r$), the result is another T1 FS, Y, whose membership function is given by equation (5A.4). Because $\mu_Y(y)$ is a T1 FS, it can, therefore, be expressed in terms of its α-cuts as follows [see equations (5.16)–(5.19), where $Y(\alpha)$ plays the role of $X(\alpha)$]:

$$Y(\alpha) = \{y \,|\, \mu_Y(y) \geq \alpha\} \quad (5A.8)$$

$$I_{Y(\alpha)}(y) = \begin{cases} 1, & \forall y \in Y(\alpha) \\ 0, & \forall y \notin Y(\alpha) \end{cases} \quad (5A.9)$$

$$\mu_Y(y|\alpha) = \alpha I_{Y(\alpha)}(y) \quad (5A.10)$$

$$\mu_Y(y) = \bigcup_{\alpha \in [0,1]} \mu_Y(y|\alpha) \quad (5A.11)$$

In order to implement equations (5A.9)–(5A.11), a method is needed to compute $Y(\alpha)$, and this is provided in the following.

Theorem 5.3. (α-cuts Decomposition Theorem [Wu and Mendel (2007)]) Let $Y = f(X_1, \ldots, X_r)$ be an arbitrary (crisp) function, where X_i ($i = 1, \ldots, r$) is a T1 FS whose domain is D_{X_i} and α-cut is $X_i(\alpha)$. Then, under the Extension Principle:

$$Y(\alpha) = f(X_1(\alpha), \ldots, X_r(\alpha)) \quad (5A.12)$$

and the height of Y equals the minimum height of all X_i.

Equation (5A.12) shows that the α-cut of a function of T1 FSs equals that function applied to the α-cuts of those T1 FSs. Theorem 5.3 does not address how to compute $f(X_1(\alpha), \ldots, X_r(\alpha))$. Section 5.4 explains how to do this for the FWA.

Proof. For all $y \in D_Y$, from equation (5A.8) it follows that[5]

$$y \in Y(\alpha) \Leftrightarrow \mu_Y(y) \geq \alpha \tag{5A.13}$$

Under the Extension Principle in equation (5A.4),

$$\mu_Y(y) \geq \alpha \Leftrightarrow \sup_{(x_1,\ldots,x_r)|y=f(x_1,\ldots,x_r)} \min\{\mu_{X_1}(x_1),\ldots,\mu_{X_r}(x_r)\} \geq \alpha \tag{5A.14}$$

It follows that:

$$\sup_{(x_1,\ldots,x_r)|y=f(x_1,\ldots,x_r)} \min\{\mu_{X_1}(x_1),\ldots,\mu_{X_r}(x_r)\} \geq \alpha$$

$\Leftrightarrow (\exists x_{10} \in D_{X_1}$ and $\cdots$ and $x_{r0} \in D_{X_r})$

s.t. $(y = f(x_{10},\ldots,x_{r0})$ and $\min\{\mu_{X_1}(x_{10}),\ldots,\mu_{X_r}(x_{r0})\} \geq \alpha)$

$\Leftrightarrow (\exists x_{10} \in D_{X_1}$ and $\cdots$ and $x_{r0} \in D_{X_r})$

s.t. $(y = f(x_{10},\ldots,x_{r0})$ and $[\mu_{X_1}(x_{10}) \geq \alpha$ and $\cdots$ and $\mu_{X_r}(x_{r0}) \geq \alpha])$

$\Leftrightarrow (\exists x_{10} \in D_{X_1}$ and $\cdots$ and $x_{r0} \in D_{X_r})$

s.t. $(y = f(x_{10},\ldots,x_{r0})$ and $[x_{10} \in X_1(\alpha)$ and $\cdots$ and $x_{r0} \in X_r(\alpha)])$

$\Leftrightarrow y \in f(X_1(\alpha),\ldots,X_r(\alpha)) \tag{5A.15}$

Hence, from the last line of equations (5A.15) and (5A.14),

$$\mu_Y(y) \geq \alpha \Leftrightarrow y \in f(X_1(\alpha),\ldots,X_r(\alpha)) \tag{5A.16}$$

which means that

$$Y(\alpha) = f(X_1(\alpha),\ldots,X_r(\alpha)) \tag{5A.17}$$

Because the right-hand side of equation (5A.14) (read from right to the left) indicates that α cannot exceed the minimum height of all $\mu_{X_i}(x_i)$ (otherwise there is no α-cut on one or more X_i), the height of Y must equal the minimum height of all X_i.

---

[5]The results in Theorem 5.3 are adapted from [Klir and Yuan (1995)], Theorem 2.9, where they are stated and proved only for a function of a single variable. Even so, our proof of Theorem 5.3 follows the proof of their Theorem 2.9 very closely.

5A.3 Proof of Theorem 5.2

Because the proofs of Parts (b)–(d) of Theorem 5.2 are quite similar to the proof of Part (a), only the proof of Part (a) is given here.

Let

$$g_{LI}(\mathbf{c}(\alpha_j), \mathbf{d}(\alpha_j)) \equiv \frac{\sum_{i=1}^{L_1} a_{il}(\alpha_j)d_i(\alpha_j) + \sum_{i=L_1+1}^{n} a_{il}(\alpha_j)c_i(\alpha_j)}{\sum_{i=1}^{L_1} d_i(\alpha_j) + \sum_{i=L_1+1}^{n} c_i(\alpha_j)} \qquad (5A.18)$$

where $\mathbf{c}(\alpha_j) \equiv [c_{L1+1}(\alpha_j), c_{L1+2}(\alpha_j), \ldots, c_n(\alpha_j)]^T$, $\mathbf{d}(\alpha_j) \equiv [d_1(\alpha_j), d_2(\alpha_j), \ldots, d_{L1}(\alpha_j)]^T$, $c_i(\alpha_j) \in [c_{il}(\alpha_j), c_{ir}(\alpha_j)]$, and $d_i(\alpha_j) \in [d_{il}(\alpha_j), d_{ir}(\alpha_j)]$. Then $y_{LI}(\alpha_j)$ in equation (5.56) can be found by:

1. Enumerating all possible combinations of $(c_{L1+1}(\alpha_j), \ldots, c_n(\alpha_j), d_1(\alpha_j), \ldots, d_{L1}(\alpha_j))$ for $c_i(\alpha_j) \in [c_{il}(\alpha_j), c_{ir}(\alpha_j)]$ and $d_i(\alpha_j) \in [d_{il}(\alpha_j), d_{ir}(\alpha_j)]$
2. Computing $g_{LI}(\mathbf{c}(\alpha_j), \mathbf{d}(\alpha_j))$ in equation (5A.18) for each combination
3. Setting $y_{LI}(\alpha_j)$ to the smallest $g_{LI}(\mathbf{c}(\alpha_j), \mathbf{d}(\alpha_j))$

Note that L_1, corresponding to the smallest $g_{LI}(\mathbf{c}(\alpha_j), \mathbf{d}(\alpha_j))$ in Step (3), is L_l^* in Theorem 5.2. In the following proof, the fact that there always exists such a L_l^* is used.

Equation (5.56) can be expressed as

$$y_{LI}(\alpha_j) = \min_{\substack{\forall c_i \in [c_{il}, c_{ir}] \\ \forall d_i \in [d_{il}, d_{ir}]}} g_{LI}(\mathbf{c}(\alpha_j), \mathbf{d}(\alpha_j)) \qquad (5A.19)$$

In Liu and Mendel (2008) it is proved that $y_{LI}(\alpha_j)$ has a value in the interval $[a_{L_l^*,I}(\alpha_j), a_{L_l^*+1,I}(\alpha_j)]$; hence, at least one $g_{LI}(\mathbf{c}(\alpha_j), \mathbf{d}(\alpha_j))$ must assume a value in this interval. In general there can be numerous $g_{LI}(\mathbf{c}(\alpha_j), \mathbf{d}(\alpha_j))$ satisfying

$$a_{L_l^*,I}(\alpha_j) \le g_{LI}(\mathbf{c}(\alpha_j), \mathbf{d}(\alpha_j)) \le a_{L_l^*+1,I}(\alpha_j) \qquad (5A.20)$$

The remaining $g_{LI}(\mathbf{c}(\alpha_j), \mathbf{d}(\alpha_j))$ must be larger than $a_{L_l^*+1,I}(\alpha_j)$, that is, they must assume values in one of the intervals $(a_{L_l^*+1,I}(\alpha_j), a_{L_l^*+2,I}(\alpha_j)]$, $(a_{L_l^*+2,I}(\alpha_j), a_{L_l^*+3,I}(\alpha_j)]$, and so on. Because the minimum of $g_{LI}(\mathbf{c}(\alpha_j), \mathbf{d}(\alpha_j))$ is of interest, only those $g_{LI}(\mathbf{c}(\alpha_j), \mathbf{d}(\alpha_j))$ satisfying equation (5A.20) will be considered in this proof.

Next it is shown that when $g_{LI}(\mathbf{c}(\alpha_j), \mathbf{d}(\alpha_j))$ achieves its minimum, (i) $d_i(\alpha_j) = d_{ir}(\alpha_j)$ for $i \le L_l^*$, and (ii) $c_i(\alpha_j) = c_{il}(\alpha_j)$ for $i \ge L_l^* + 1$.

i. When $i \le L_l^*$, it is straightforward to show that the derivative of $g_{LI}(\mathbf{c}(\alpha_j), \mathbf{d}(\alpha_j))$ with respect to $d_i(\alpha_j)$, computed from equation (5A.18), is

$$\frac{\partial g_{LI}(\mathbf{c}(\alpha_j), \mathbf{d}(\alpha_j))}{\partial d_i(\alpha_j)} = \frac{a_{il}(\alpha_j) - g_{LI}(\mathbf{c}(\alpha_j), \mathbf{d}(\alpha_j))}{\sum_{i=1}^{L_l^*} d_i(\alpha_j) + \sum_{i=L_l^*+1}^{n} c_i(\alpha_j)} \qquad (5A.21)$$

Using the left-hand side of equation (5A.20), it follows that

$$-g_{LI}\left(\mathbf{c}(\alpha_j), \mathbf{d}(\alpha_j)\right) \le - a_{L_j^*, l}(\alpha_j) \tag{5A.22}$$

Hence, in the numerator of equation (5A.21),

$$a_{il}(\alpha_j) - g_{LI}\left(\mathbf{c}(\alpha_j), \mathbf{d}(\alpha_j)\right) \le a_{il}(\alpha_j) - a_{L_j^*, l}(\alpha_j) \le 0 \tag{5A.23}$$

In obtaining the last inequality in equation (5A.23) the fact that $a_{il}(\alpha_j) \le a_{LI*, l}(\alpha_j)$ when $i \le L_j^*$ [due to the a priori increased ordering of the $a_{il}(\alpha_j)$] was used. Consequently, using equation (5A.23) in equation (5A.21), it follows that

$$\frac{\partial g_{LI}\left(\mathbf{c}(\alpha_j), \mathbf{d}(\alpha_j)\right)}{\partial d_i(\alpha_j)} \le \frac{a_{il}(\alpha_j) - a_{L_j^*, l}(\alpha_j)}{\sum_{i=1}^{L_j^*} d_i(\alpha_j) + \sum_{i=L_j^*+1}^{n} c_i(\alpha_j)} \le 0 \tag{5A.24}$$

Equation (5A.24) indicates that the first derivative of $g_{LI}(\mathbf{c}(\alpha_j), \mathbf{d}(\alpha_j))$ with respect to $d_i(\alpha_j)$ $(i \le L_j^*)$ is negative; thus, $g_{LI}(\mathbf{c}(\alpha_j), \mathbf{d}(\alpha_j))$ decreases when $d_i(\alpha_j)$ $(i \le L_j^*)$ increases. Consequently, the minimum of $g_{LI}(\mathbf{c}(\alpha_j), \mathbf{d}(\alpha_j))$ must use the maximum possible $d_i(\alpha_j)$ for $i \le L_j^*$, that is, $d_i(\alpha_j) = d_{ir}(\alpha_j)$ for $i \le L_j^*$, as stated in equation (5.60).

ii. When $i \ge L_j^*$, it is straightforward to show that the derivative of $g_{LI}(\mathbf{c}(\alpha_j), \mathbf{d}(\alpha_j))$ with respect to $c_i(\alpha_j)$, computed from equation (5A.18), is

$$\frac{\partial g_{LI}\left(\mathbf{c}(\alpha_j), \mathbf{d}(\alpha_j)\right)}{\partial c_i(\alpha_j)} = \frac{a_{il}(\alpha_j) - g_{LI}\left(\mathbf{c}(\alpha_j), \mathbf{d}(\alpha_j)\right)}{\sum_{i=1}^{L_j^*} d_i(\alpha_j) + \sum_{i=L_j^*+1}^{n} c_i(\alpha_j)} \tag{5A.25}$$

Using the right-hand side of equation (5A.20), it follows that

$$-g_{LI}\left(\mathbf{c}(\alpha_j), \mathbf{d}(\alpha_j)\right) \ge - a_{L_j^*+1, l}(\alpha_j) \tag{5A.26}$$

Hence, in the numerator of equation (5A.25),

$$a_{il}(\alpha_j) - g_{LI}\left(\mathbf{c}(\alpha_j), \mathbf{d}(\alpha_j)\right) \ge a_{il}(\alpha_j) - a_{L_j^*+1, l}(\alpha_j) \ge 0 \tag{5A.27}$$

In obtaining the last inequality in equation (5A.27) the fact that $a_{il}(\alpha_j) \ge a_{L_j^*+1, l}(\alpha_j)$ when $i \ge L_j^* + 1$ [due to the a priori increased ordering of the $a_{il}(\alpha_j)$] was used. Consequently, using equation (5A.27) in equation (5A.25), it follows that

$$\frac{\partial g_{LI}\left(\mathbf{c}(\alpha_j), \mathbf{d}(\alpha_j)\right)}{\partial c_i(\alpha_j)} \ge \frac{a_{il}(\alpha_j) - a_{L_j^*+1, l}(\alpha_j)}{\sum_{i=1}^{L_j^*} d_i(\alpha_j) + \sum_{i=L_j^*+1}^{n} c_i(\alpha_j)} \ge 0 \tag{5A.28}$$

Equation (5A.28) indicates that the first derivative of $g_{LI}(\mathbf{c}(\alpha_j), \mathbf{d}(\alpha_j))$ with respect to $c_i(\alpha_j)(i \ge L_j^* + 1)$ is positive; thus, $g_{LI}(\mathbf{c}(\alpha_j), \mathbf{d}(\alpha_j))$ decreases when $c_i(\alpha_j)(i \ge L_j^* + 1)$ decreases. Consequently, the minimum of $g_{LI}(\mathbf{c}(\alpha_j), \mathbf{d}(\alpha_j))$ must use the minimum possible $c_i(\alpha_j)$ for $i \ge L_j^* + 1$, that is, $c_i(\alpha_j) = c_{il}(\alpha_j)$ for $i \ge L_j^* + 1$, as stated in equation (5.60).

REFERENCES

D. Filev and R. Yager, "On the issue of obtaining OWA operator weights," *Fuzzy Sets and Systems,* vol. 94, pp. 157–169, 1998.

J.-S. R. Jang, C.-T. Sun, and E. Mizutani, *Neuro-Fuzzy and Soft-Computing.* Upper Saddle River, NJ: Prentice-Hall, 1997.

G. J. Klir and B. Yuan, *Fuzzy Sets and Fuzzy Logic: Theory and Applications.* Upper Saddle River, NJ: Prentice-Hall, 1995.

X. Liu, "The solution equivalence of minimax disparity and minimum variance problems for OWA operators," *International Journal of Approximate Reasoning,* vol. 45, pp. 68–81, 2007.

F. Liu and J. M. Mendel, "Aggregation using the fuzzy weighted average, as computed using the Karnik-Mendel Algorithms," *IEEE Trans. on Fuzzy Systems,* vol. 12, no. 1, pp. 1–12, 2008.

P. Majlender, "OWA operators with maximal Renya entropy," *Fuzzy Sets and Systems,* vol. 155, pp. 340–360, 2005.

V. Torra and Y. Narukawa, *Modeling Decisions: Information Fusion and Aggregation Operators.* Berlin: Springer, 2007.

L.-X. Wang, *A Course in Fuzzy Systems and Control.* Upper Saddle River, NJ: Prentice-Hall, 1997.

D. Wu and J. M. Mendel, "Aggregation using the linguistic weighted average and interval type-2 fuzzy sets," *IEEE Trans. on Fuzzy Systems,* vol. 15, no. 6, pp. 1145–1161, 2007.

D. Wu and J. M. Mendel, "Corrections to 'Aggregation using the linguistic weighted average and interval type-2 fuzzy sets'," *IEEE Trans. on Fuzzy Systems,* vol. 16, no. 6, pp. 1664–1666, 2008.

R. Yager, "Ranking fuzzy subsets over the unit interval," in *Proc. IEEE Conf. on Decision and Control,* vol. 17, 1978, pp. 1435–1437.

R. Yager, "On ordered weighted averaging aggregation operators in multi-criteria decision making," *IEEE Trans. on Systems, Man, and Cybernetics,* vol. 18, pp. 183–190, 1988.

R. Yager and J. Kacprzyk, *The Ordered Weighted Averaging Operators: Theory and Applications.* Norwell, MA: Kluwer, 1997.

L. A. Zadeh, "The concept of a linguistic variable and its application to approximate reasoning-1," *Information Sciences,* vol. 8, pp. 199–249, 1975.

S.-M. Zhou, F. Chiclana, R. I. John, and J. M. Garibaldi, "A practical approach to type-1 OWA operation for soft decision making," in *Proceedings of the 8th International FLINS Conference on Computational Intelligence in Decision and Control,* Madrid, Spain, 2008a, pp. 507–512.

S.-M. Zhou, F. Chiclana, R. I. John, and J. M. Garibaldi, "Type-1 OWA operators for aggregating uncertain information with uncertain weights induced by type-2 linguistic quantifiers," *Fuzzy Sets and Systems,* vol. 159, no. 24, pp. 3281–3296, 2008b.

S.-M. Zhou, F. Chiclana, R. I. John, and J. M. Garibaldi, "Type-2 OWA operators—aggregating type-2 fuzzy sets in soft decision making," in *Proceedings of FUZZ-IEEE,* Hong Kong, June 2008c, pp. 625–630.

CHAPTER 6

IF–THEN Rules as a CWW Engine— Perceptual Reasoning

6.1 INTRODUCTION

One of the most popular CWW engines uses if–then rules. This chapter is about such rules and how they are processed within a CWW engine so that their outputs can be mapped into a word-recommendation by the decoder.

There are many methods to construct if–then rules from data [Guillame (2001), Jamei et al. (2004), Mendel (2001), Mitra and Hayashi (2000), Nozaki et al. (1997), Sudkamp (1993), Wang and Qiu (2003), Wang and Mendel (1992), Yager and Filev (1994b)] or from people [Koeppel et al. (1993), Mendel (2001), Mendel et al. (1999)]; however, rule construction is not the focus of this book, and only one method to mine the rules from experts, using a survey, is introduced in Chapter 8.

The use of if–then rules in Per-C is quite different from their use in most engineering applications of rule-based systems—fuzzy logic systems (FLSs)—because in a FLS the output almost always is a number, whereas the output of the Per-C is a recommendation. This distinction has some very interesting ramifications and they are also covered in this chapter.

By a rule, we mean an if–then statement, such as:

$$R^i : \text{ IF } x_1 \text{ is } F_1^i \text{ and } x_2 \text{ is } F_2^i, \text{ THEN } y \text{ is } G^i \quad i = 1, ..., N \qquad (6.1)$$

where x_1 and x_2 are called *antecedents* and y is called the *consequent*. A concrete example of such a two-antecedent rule is:

IF touching (x_1) is low (F_1) and eye contact (x_2) is moderate (F_2), THEN flirtation (y) is moderate (G).

A generic rule with multiple antecedents is represented as:

$$R^i : \text{ IF } x_1 \text{ is } F_1^i \text{ and } \cdots \text{ and } x_p \text{ is } F_p^i, \text{ THEN } y \text{ is } G^i \quad i = 1, ..., N \qquad (6.2)$$

Perceptual Computing. By Jerry M. Mendel and Dongrui Wu

In logic, equation (6.2) is also called an *implication,* where in:

- *Crisp logic, F_j^i* is a crisp set with characteristic value $\mu_{F_j^i}$ that only has two elements: 1 when x_j is exactly the same as F_j^i, and 0 when x_j differs from F_j^i
- *Type-1 fuzzy logic, F_j^i* is a T1 FS with membership $\mu_{F_j^i}(x_j)$, so that x_j does not have to be exactly the same as F_j^i, and $\mu_{F_j^i}(x_j)$ provides the crisp degree of membership of x_j to F_j^i
- *Type-2 fuzzy logic, F_j^i* is a T2 FS $\tilde{F}_j^i$ with membership $\mu_{\tilde{F}_j^i}(x_j)$, so that x_j not only does not have to be exactly the same as $\tilde{F}_j^i$, but $\mu_{\tilde{F}_j^i}(x_j)$ provides a fuzzy degree of membership of x_j to $\tilde{F}_j^i$

When F_j^i in equation (6.2) is either a T1 or T2 FS then (6.2) will be called a *fuzzy implication.*

There are many mathematical models for a fuzzy implication that appear under the rubric of *approximate reasoning,* for example, Table 11.1 in [Klir and Yuan (1995)] lists 14. Each of these models has the property that it reduces to the truth table of material implication (Table 6.1) when fuzziness disappears.

Following is a quote from [Chater et al. (2003)] that we have found to be very illuminating:

> *Rational calculation* is the view that the mind works by carrying out probabilistic, logical, or decision-theoretic operations. Rational calculation is explicitly avowed by relatively few theorists, though it has clear advocates with respect to logical inference. Mental logicians propose that much of cognition is a matter of carrying out logical calculations [e.g., Brain (1978), Inhelder and Piaget (1958), Rips (1994)]. *Rational description,* by contrast, is the view that behavior can be approximately described as conforming with the results that would be obtained by some rational calculation. This view does not assume (though it does not rule out) that the thought processes underlying behavior involves any rational calculation.

For perceptual computing, logical reasoning will not be implemented as prescribed by the truth table of material implication; instead, rational description will be subscribed to.

Rational description has already been very widely used in rule-based FLSs, where material implication has been replaced by Mamdani implication, for example, Jang (1997), Mamdani (1974), Mendel (2001), Wang (1997), Yager and Filev (1994a), and Yen and Langari (1999). In those FLSs the final output is almost always a number and is not a linguistic recommendation.

Table 6.1. Truth table for material implication

p	q	$p \rightarrow q$
T	T	T
T	F	F
F	T	T
F	F	T

6.2   A BRIEF OVERVIEW OF INTERVAL TYPE-2 FUZZY LOGIC SYSTEMS

An IT2 FLS is depicted in Fig. 6.1. For an IT2 FLS each input is fuzzified into an IT2 FS, after which these FSs activate a subset of rules. The output of each activated rule is obtained by using an extended sup-star composition [Mendel (2001)]. First, a firing interval is computed and then a fired-rule output FOU is computed. Then all of the fired-rule output FOUs are blended in some way and reduced from IT2 FSs to a number. The latter is accomplished in two steps: type reduction, which projects an IT2 FS into an interval-valued set, and defuzzification, which takes the average of the interval's two end points.

6.2.1   Firing Interval

The first step in this chain of computations is to compute a *firing interval*. This can be a very complicated calculation, especially when the inputs are fuzzified into IT2 FSs, as they would be when the inputs are words. For the minimum t-norm,[1] this calculation requires computing the sup-min operation between the LMFs of the FOUs of each input and its corresponding antecedent, as well as the UMFs of these FOUs. The firing interval propagates the uncertainties from all of the inputs through their respective antecedents. Note that when all of the uncertainties disappear, the firing interval becomes a crisp value, a *firing level*.

An example of computing the firing interval when the inputs are singletons (not words)[2] is depicted in the left-hand part of Fig. 6.2 for a rule that has two antecedents.[3] When $x_1 = x_1'$, the vertical line at x_1' intersects $FOU(\tilde{F}_1)$ everywhere in the interval $[\mu_{\tilde{F}_1}(x_1'), \overline{\mu}_{\tilde{F}_1}(x_1')]$; and, when $x_2 = x_2'$, the vertical line at x_2' intersects $FOU(\tilde{F}_2)$ everywhere in the interval $[\mu_{\tilde{F}_2}(x_2'), \overline{\mu}_{\tilde{F}_2}(x_2')]$. Two firing levels are then computed, a lower firing level, $\underline{f}(\mathbf{x}')$, and an upper firing level, $\overline{f}(\mathbf{x}')$, where $\underline{f}(\mathbf{x}') = \min[\mu_{\tilde{F}_1}(x_1'), \mu_{\tilde{F}_2}(x_2')]$ and $\overline{f}(\mathbf{x}') = \min[\overline{\mu}_{\tilde{F}_1}(x_1'), \overline{\mu}_{\tilde{F}_2}(x_2')]$. The main thing to observe from this figure is that the result of input and antecedent operations is an interval—the firing interval $F(\mathbf{x}')$, where $F(\mathbf{x}') = [\underline{f}(\mathbf{x}'), \overline{f}(\mathbf{x}')]$.

A firing interval is also obtained when the inputs are words (i.e., IT2 FSs), but in that case the calculations of $\underline{f}(\mathbf{x}')$ and $\overline{f}(\mathbf{x}')$ are more complicated [Mendel and Wu (2008)] than the ones in Fig. 6.2. Fortunately, for a given vocabulary, $\underline{f}(\mathbf{x}')$ and $\overline{f}(\mathbf{x}')$ can be precomputed (because all the word FOUs are known ahead of time) and stored in a table, and, hence, the online computation of firing intervals reduces to a table look-up. This is unique to the Per-C, because the input words can only be selected from a prespecified vocabulary.

---

[1]The same conclusions in Section 6.2.5 can be reached when the product t-norm is used.
[2]In the figures of this chapter, it is to be understood that the IT2 FS $\tilde{A}$ is synonymous with its FOU, $FOU(\tilde{A})$.
[3]A mathematical derivation of the firing interval that uses T1 FS mathematics is found in Mendel et al. (2006).

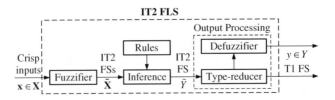

Figure 6.1. An IT2 FLS (Mendel, 2001; © 2001, Prentice-Hall).

6.2.2   Fired-Rule Output FOU

If one abides strictly by the extended sup-star composition, then the next computation after the firing interval computation is[4] the meet operation between the firing interval and its consequent FOU, the result being a fired-rule output FOU.

An example of computing the meet operation between the firing interval and its consequent FOU is depicted in the right-hand part of Fig. 6.2. $f(\mathbf{x'})$ is t-normed with $\underline{G}$ and $\overline{f}(\mathbf{x'})$ is t-normed with $\overline{G}$. When $FOU(\tilde{G})$ is triangular, and the t-norm is minimum, the resulting *fired-rule output FOU* ($\tilde{B}$) is the filled-in trapezoidal FOU. Observe that $\underline{B}$ and $\overline{B}$ are clipped versions of $\underline{G}$ and $\overline{G}$, respectively, which is a characteristic property of using the minimum t-norm.

6.2.3   Aggregation of Fired-Rule Output FOUs

There is no unique way to aggregate fired-rule output FOUs. One way to do this is to use the union operation, the result being yet another FOU.

An example of aggregating two fired-rule output FOUs that uses the union operation is depicted in Fig. 6.3. Recall from Chapter 2 that the union of two IT2 FSs is another IT2 FS whose LMF is the union of the LMFs of the two inputs, and whose UMF is the union of the UMFs of the two inputs. Part (a) of Fig. 6.3 shows the fired-rule output sets for two fired rules, and Part (b) shows the union of those two IT2 FSs. Observe that the union tends to spread out the domain over which nonzero values of the output occur, and that $FOU(\tilde{B})$ does not have the appearance of either $FOU(\tilde{B}^1)$ or $FOU(\tilde{B}^2)$.

6.2.4   Type Reduction and Defuzzification

Referring to Fig. 6.1, the aggregated FOU in Fig. 6.3 is then type reduced, that is, the centroid (see Section 2.6) of the IT2 FS $\tilde{B}$ is computed. The result is an interval-valued set, which is defuzzified by taking the average of the interval's two endpoints.

---

[4]A mathematical derivation of the fired rule output FOU that uses T1 FS mathematics is also found in Mendel et al. (2006).

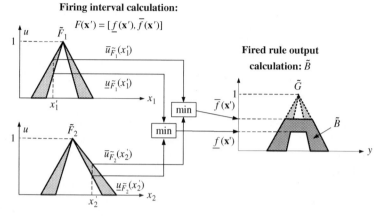

Figure 6.2. IT2 FLS inference: from firing interval to fired-rule output FOU (Mendel, 2007; © 2007, IEEE).

6.2.5 Observations

Two points about this chain of computations are worth emphasizing:

1. Each fired-rule output FOU does not resemble the FOU of a word in the Per-C codebook (Chapter 3). This is, as we have already seen, because the meet operation between the firing interval and its consequent FOU results in an

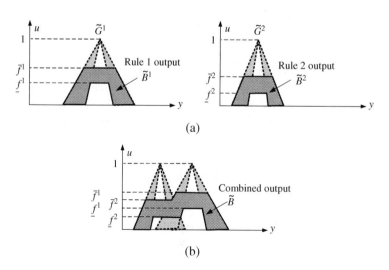

Figure 6.3. Pictorial descriptions of (a) fired-rule output FOUs for two fired rules, and (b) combined fired output FOU for the two fired rules in (a).

FOU whose lower and upper MFs are clipped versions of the respective lower and upper MFs of a consequent FOU.

2. The aggregated fired-rule output FOU also does not resemble the FOU of a word in the Per-C codebook. This is, as we also have already seen, because when the union operator is applied to all of the fired rule output FOUs it further distorts those already-distorted FOUs.

The reason these two points are being restated here is that for CWW we believe that the result of combining fired rules should lead to an FOU that resembles the three kinds of FOUs in a CWW codebook. This is in the spirit of the Chapter 3 requirement that words must mean similar things to different people.

Abiding strictly to the extended sup-star composition does not let us satisfy this requirement; hence, we turn to an alternative that is widely used by practitioners of FLSs, one that blends attributes about the fired rule consequent IT2 FSs with the firing quantities.

6.2.6   A Different Way to Aggregate Fired Rules by Blending Attributes

Attributes of a fired rule consequent IT2 FS include its centroid and the point of symmetry of its FOU (if the FOU is symmetrical). The blending is accomplished directly by the kind of type reduction that is chosen, for example, center-of-sets type reduction makes use of the centroids of the consequents, whereas height type reduction makes use of the point of symmetry of each consequent FOU. Regardless of the details of this kind of type reduction blending,[5] the type-reduced result is an interval-valued set after which that interval is defuzzified as before by taking the average of the interval's two end points.

It is worth noting that by taking this alternative approach there is no associated FOU for either each fired rule or all of the fired rules; hence, there is no FOU obtained from this approach that can be compared with the FOUs in the codebook. Consequently, using this alternative to abiding strictly to the extended sup-star composition also does not let us satisfy the requirement that the result of combining fired rules should lead to an FOU that resembles the three kinds of FOUs in a CWW codebook.

By these lines of reasoning we have ruled out the two usual ways in which rules are fired and combined for use by the Per-C.

6.3   PERCEPTUAL REASONING: COMPUTATIONS

A new fuzzy reasoning model is now proposed [Mendel and Wu (2007, 2008), Wu and Mendel (2008, 2009)]—*perceptual reasoning*[6] (PR)—that not only fits the concept of rational description, but also satisfies the following:

---

[5]More details about type reduction can be found in Mendel (2001).

[6]Perceptual Reasoning is a term coined in Mendel and Wu (2008) because it is used by the Per-C when the CWW engine consists of if–then rules. In Mendel and Wu (2008) firing intervals are used to combine

Requirement: The result of combining fired rules should lead to an FOU that resembles the three kinds of FOUs in a CWW codebook.

This requirement cannot be assumed to be satisfied a priori but must be demonstrated through analysis, something that is done in Section 6.4. "Resemblance" in this requirement means that: (1) the output of the CWW engine should resemble the *nature* of the FOUs in a CWW codebook, that is, the CWW engine should be able to output left-shoulder, right-shoulder, and interior FOUs; and, (2) the output of the CWW engine should resemble the *shape* of FOUs in the codebook, that is, it should have high similarity with at least one FOU in the codebook.

Let $\tilde{\mathbf{X}}'$ denote an $N \times 1$ vector of IT2 FSs that are the inputs to a collection of N rules, as would be the case when such inputs are words. $f^i(\tilde{\mathbf{X}}')$ denotes the firing level for the ith rule, and it is computed only for the $n \leq N$ number of fired rules, that is, the rules whose firing levels do not equal zero. In PR, the fired rules are combined using a linguistic weighted average (LWA). Denote the output IT2 FS of PR as $\tilde{Y}_{PR}$. Then, $\tilde{Y}_{PR}$ can be written in the following expressive[7] way:

$$\tilde{Y}_{PR} = \frac{\sum_{i=1}^{n} f^i(\tilde{\mathbf{X}}')\tilde{G}^i}{\sum_{i=1}^{n} f^i(\tilde{\mathbf{X}}')} \tag{6.3}$$

This LWA is a special case of the more general LWA (Section 5.5) in which both $\tilde{G}^i$ and $f^i(\tilde{\mathbf{X}}')$ were IT2 FSs.

Observe that PR consists of two steps:

1. A *firing level* is computed for each rule.
2. The IT2 FS consequents of the fired rules are combined using an LWA in which the "weights" are the firing levels and the "subcriteria" are the IT2 FS consequents.

6.3.1 Computing Firing Levels

Similarity is frequently used in approximate reasoning to compute the firing levels [Bustince (2000), Raha et al. (2002), Zeung and Tsang (1997)], and it can also be used in PR to do this.

Let the p inputs that activate a collection of N rules be denoted $\tilde{\mathbf{X}}'$. The result of the input and antecedent operations for the ith fired rule is the firing level $f^i(\tilde{\mathbf{X}}')$, where

$$f^i(\tilde{\mathbf{X}}') = sm_J(\tilde{X}'_1, \tilde{F}^i_1) \star \cdots \star sm_J(\tilde{X}'_p, \tilde{F}^i_p) \equiv f^i \tag{6.4}$$

where $sm_J(\tilde{X}'_j, \tilde{F}^i_j)$ is the Jaccard's similarity measure for IT2 FSs [see equation (4.6)], and $\star$ denotes a *t*-norm. The minimum *t*-norm is used in equation (6.4).

---

the rules; however, firing levels are used in this book because, as shown in Wu and Mendel (2009), they give an output FOU which more closely resembles the word FOUs in a codebook.

[7]As in Section 5.5.1, equation (6.3) is referred to as "expressive" because it is not computed using multiplications, additions and divisions, as expressed by it. Instead, $\underline{Y}_{PR}$ and $\overline{Y}_{PR}$ are computed separately using α-cuts, as explained in Section 6.3.2.

Comment. To use PR, we need a codebook[8] consisting of words and their associated FOUs so that a user can choose inputs from it. Once this codebook is obtained, the similarities between the input words and the antecedent words of the rules (i.e., sm_J $(\tilde{X}_j', \tilde{F}_j^i), j = 1, \ldots, p, i = 1, \ldots, N$) can be precomputed and stored in a table (e.g., the similarity matrix shown in Table 4.1), so that $sm_J (\tilde{X}_j', \tilde{F}_j^i)$ can be retrieved on-line to save computational cost.

6.3.2 Computing $\tilde{Y}_{PR}$

$\tilde{Y}_{PR}$ in equation (6.3) is a special case of the more general LWA introduced in Chapter 5. The formulas for this special case have been presented in Section 5.6, except that different notations were used. Because PR is widely used in the rest of this book, these formulas are repeated here using the notations in this chapter.

An interior FOU for rule consequent $\tilde{G}^i$ is depicted in Fig. 6.4(a), in which the height of $\underline{G}_i$ is denoted h_{Gi}, the α-cut on $\underline{G}_i$ is denoted $[a_{il}(\alpha), b_{il}(\alpha)]$, $\alpha \in [0, h_{Gi}]$, and the α-cut on $\overline{G}_i$ is denoted $[a_{ir}(\alpha), b_{ir}(\alpha)]$, $\alpha \in [0, 1]$. For the left shoulder $\tilde{G}^i$ depicted in Fig. 6.4(b), $h_{Gi} = 1$ and $a_{il}(\alpha) = a_{ir}(\alpha) = 0$ for $\forall \alpha \in [0, 1]$. For the right-shoulder $\tilde{G}^i$ depicted in Fig. 6.4(c), $h_{Gi} = 1$ and $b_{il}(\alpha) = b_{ir}(\alpha) = M$ for $\forall \alpha \in [0, 1]$.

Because the output of PR must resemble the three kinds of FOUs in a codebook, $\tilde{Y}_{PR}$ can also be an interior, left-shoulder or right-shoulder FOU, as shown in Fig. 6.5 (this is actually proved in Section 6.4.2). The α-cut on $\overline{Y}_{PR}$ is $[y_{Ll}(\alpha), y_{Rr}(\alpha)]$ and the α-cut on $\underline{Y}_{PR}$ is $[y_{Lr}(\alpha), y_{Rl}(\alpha)]$, where, as explained in Section 5.6, the end points of these α-cuts are computed for equation (6.3) as:

$$y_{Ll}(\alpha) = \frac{\sum_{i=1}^{n} a_{il}(\alpha) f^i}{\sum_{i=1}^{n} f^i}, \quad \alpha \in [0, 1] \tag{6.5}$$

$$y_{Rr}(\alpha) = \frac{\sum_{i=1}^{n} b_{ir}(\alpha) f^i}{\sum_{i=1}^{n} f^i}, \quad \alpha \in [0, 1] \tag{6.6}$$

$$y_{Lr}(\alpha) = \frac{\sum_{i=1}^{n} a_{ir}(\alpha) f^i}{\sum_{i=1}^{n} f^i}, \quad \alpha \in [0, h_{\underline{Y}_{PR}}] \tag{6.7}$$

$$y_{Rl}(\alpha) = \frac{\sum_{i=1}^{n} b_{il}(\alpha) f^i}{\sum_{i=1}^{n} f^i}, \quad \alpha \in [0, h_{\underline{Y}_{PR}}] \tag{6.8}$$

where

$$h_{\underline{Y}_{PR}} = \min_i h_{\underline{G}^i} \tag{6.9}$$

---

[8]The words used in the antecedents of the rules, as will the words that excite the rules, are always included in this codebook.

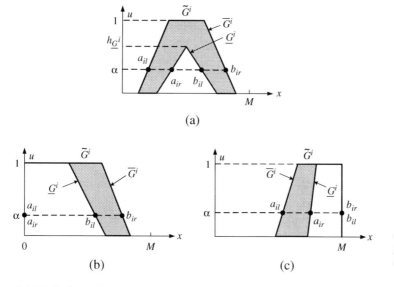

Figure 6.4. Typical word FOUs and an α-cut. (a) Interior, (b) left-shoulder, and (c) right-shoulder FOUs (Mendel and Wu, 2008; © 2008, IEEE).

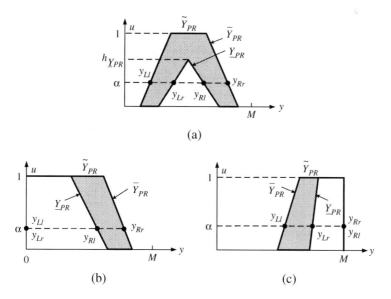

Figure 6.5. PR FOUs and α-cuts on (a) interior, (b) left-shoulder, and (c) right-shoulder FOUs. [Fig. 6.5(a): Mendel and Wu, 2008; © 2008, IEEE.]

Note that equations (6.5)–(6.8) are arithmetic weighted averages, so they are computed directly without using KM or EKM algorithms.

Observe from equations (6.5) and (6.6) that $\overline{Y}_{PR}$, characterized by $[y_{Ll}(\alpha), y_{Rr}(\alpha)]$, is completely determined by $\overline{G}^i$, because it depends only on $a_{il}(\alpha)$ and $b_{ir}(\alpha)$, and from equations (6.7) and (6.8) that $\underline{Y}_{PR}$, characterized by $[y_{Lr}(\alpha), y_{Rl}(\alpha)]$, is completely determined by $\underline{G}_i$, because it depends only on $a_{ir}(\alpha)$ and $b_{il}(\alpha)$. Observe also, from equations (6.5) and (6.6), that $\widetilde{Y}_{PR}$ is always normal, that is, its $\alpha = 1$ α-cut can always be computed. This is different from many other approximate reasoning methods, whose aggregated fired-rule output sets are not normal, for example, the Mamdani-inference-based method. For the latter, even if only one rule is fired (see Fig. 6.2), unless the firing level is one, the output is a clipped or scaled version[9] of the consequent IT2 FS instead of a normal IT2 FS. This may cause problems when the output is mapped to a word in the codebook.

In summary, knowing the firing levels f^i, $i = 1, \ldots, n$, $\overline{Y}_{PR}$ is computed, according to Section 5.5.3, in the following way:

1. Select m appropriate α-cuts for $\overline{Y}_{PR}$ (e.g., divide $[0, 1]$ into $m-1$ intervals and set $\alpha_j = (j-1)/(m-1), j = 1, 2, \ldots, m$).
2. Find the α_j α-cut on $\overline{G}^i$ ($i = 1, \ldots, n$); denote the end points of its interval as $[a_{il}(\alpha_j), b_{ir}(\alpha_j)]$, respectively.
3. Compute $y_{Ll}(\alpha_j)$ in equation (6.5) and $y_{Rr}(\alpha_j)$ in equation (6.6).
4. Repeat steps (2) and (3) for every α_j ($j = 1, \ldots, m$).
5. Connect all left coordinates $(y_{Ll}(\alpha_j), \alpha_j)$ and all right coordinates $(y_{Rr}(\alpha_j), \alpha_j)$ to form the UMF $\overline{Y}_{PR}$.

Similarly, to compute $\underline{Y}_{PR}$:

1. Determine $h_{\underline{G}^i}$, $i = 1, \ldots, n$, and $h_{\underline{Y}_{PR}}$ in equation (6.9).
2. Select appropriate p α-cuts for $\underline{Y}_{PR}$ (e.g., divide $[0, h_{\underline{Y}_{PR}}]$ into $p-1$ intervals and set $\alpha_j = h_{\underline{Y}_{PR}} (j-1)/(p-1), j = 1, 2, \ldots, p$).
3. Find the α_j α-cut on $\underline{G}^i$ ($i = 1, \ldots, n$).
4. Compute $y_{Lr}(\alpha_j)$ in equation (6.7) and $y_{Rl}(\alpha_j)$ in equation (6.8).
5. Repeat steps (3) and (4) for every α_j ($j = 1, \ldots, p$).
6. Connect all left coordinates $(y_{Lr}(\alpha_j), \alpha_j)$ and all right coordinates $(y_{Rl}(\alpha_j), \alpha_j)$ to form the LMF $\underline{Y}_{PR}$.

6.4   PERCEPTUAL REASONING: PROPERTIES

Properties of PR are presented in this section. All of them help demonstrate the requirement for PR, namely, the result of combining fired rules using PR leads to an

---

[9]A scaled version of the consequent IT2 FS occurs when the product t-norm is used to combine the firing level and the consequent IT2 FS.

IT2 FS that resembles the three kinds of FOUs in a CWW codebook. Readers who are not interested in theorems about this requirement can skip to Section 6.5. The proofs for all theorems in this section are given in the Appendix.

6.4.1 General Properties About the Shape of $\tilde{Y}_{PR}$

In this section, some general properties are provided that are about the shape of $\tilde{Y}_{PR}$.

Theorem 6.1. When all fired rules have the same consequent $\tilde{G}$, $\tilde{Y}_{PR}$, defined in equation (6.3), is the same as $\tilde{G}$.

Although Theorem 6.1 is true regardless of how many rules are fired, its most interesting application occurs when only one rule is fired, in which case the output from PR is the consequent FS, $\tilde{G}$, and $\tilde{G}$ resides in the codebook. On the other hand, when one rule fires, the output from Mamdani inferencing is a clipped version of $\tilde{G}$, $\tilde{B}$, as depicted in Fig. 6.2, and $\tilde{B}$ does not reside in the codebook.

Theorem 6.2. $\tilde{Y}_{PR}$ is constrained by the consequents of the fired rules:

$$\min_i a_{il}(\alpha) \leq y_{Ll}(\alpha) \leq \max_i a_{il}(\alpha) \tag{6.10}$$

$$\min_i a_{ir}(\alpha) \leq y_{Lr}(\alpha) \leq \max_i a_{ir}(\alpha) \tag{6.11}$$

$$\min_i b_{il}(\alpha) \leq y_{Rl}(\alpha) \leq \max_i b_{il}(\alpha) \tag{6.12}$$

$$\min_i b_{ir}(\alpha) \leq y_{Rr}(\alpha) \leq \max_i b_{ir}(\alpha) \tag{6.13}$$

where $a_{il}(\alpha)$, $a_{ir}(\alpha)$, $b_{il}(\alpha)$, and $b_{ir}(\alpha)$ are defined for three kinds of consequent FOUs in Fig. 6.4.

The equalities in equations (6.10)–(6.13) hold simultaneously if and only if all n fired rules have the same consequent. A graphical illustration of Theorem 6.2 is shown in Fig. 6.6. Assume only two rules are fired and $\tilde{G}^1$ lies to the left of $\tilde{G}^2$; then, $\tilde{Y}_{PR}$ lies between $\tilde{G}^1$ and $\tilde{G}^2$.

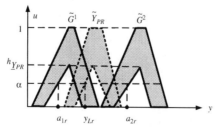

Figure 6.6. A graphical illustration of Theorems 6.2 and 6.4, when only two rules fire.

Theorem 6.2 is about the location of $\tilde{Y}_{PR}$. Theorem 6.3 below is about the span of $\tilde{Y}_{PR}$; but first, the span of an IT2 FS is defined.

Definition 6.1. The span of the IT2 FS $\tilde{G}^i$ is $b_{ir}(0) - \underline{a}_{il}(0)$, where $a_{il}(0)$ and $b_{ir}(0)$ are the left and right end points of the $\alpha = 0$ α-cut on $\overline{G}^i$, respectively.

It is well known from interval arithmetic that operations (e.g., $+$, $-$, and $\times$) on intervals usually spread out the resulting interval; however, this is not true for PR, as indicated by the following:

Theorem 6.3. The span of $\tilde{Y}_{PR}$, $y_{Rr}(0) - y_{Ll}(0)$, is constrained by the spans of the consequents of the fired rules:

$$\min_i (b_{ir}(0) - a_{il}(0)) \leq y_{Rr}(0) - y_{Ll}(0) \leq \max_i (b_{ir}(0) - a_{il}(0)) \quad (6.14)$$

Both equalities in equation (6.14) hold simultaneously if and only if all n fired rules have the same span.

The following two definitions are about the shape of a T1 FS, and they are used in proving properties about the shape of $\tilde{Y}_{PR}$.

Definition 6.2. Let A be a T1 FS and h_A be its height. Then, A is trapezoidal-looking if its $\alpha = h_A$ α-cut is an interval instead of a single point.

$\overline{Y}_{PR}$ in Fig. 6.5(a) is trapezoidal-looking.

Definition 6.3. Let A be a T1 FS and h_A be its height. Then, A is triangular-looking if its $\alpha = h_A$ α-cut consists of a single point.

$\underline{Y}_{PR}$ in Fig. 6.5(a) is triangular-looking.

Theorem 6.4. Generally, $\underline{Y}_{PR}$ is trapezoidal-looking; however, $\underline{Y}_{PR}$ is triangular-looking if and only if all $\underline{G}^i$ are triangles with the same height.

An illustration of Theorem 6.4 is shown in Fig. 6.6.

Theorem 6.5. Generally, $\overline{Y}_{PR}$ is trapezoidal-looking; however, $\overline{Y}_{PR}$ is triangular-looking when all $\overline{G}^i$ are normal triangles.

6.4.2 Properties of $\tilde{Y}_{PR}$ FOUs

In this subsection, it is shown that $\tilde{Y}_{PR}$ computed from equation (6.3), which uses firing levels, resembles the three kinds of FOUs in a CWW codebook. But first, three definitions about the nature of $\tilde{Y}_{PR}$ FOUs are introduced.

Definition 6.4. An IT2 FS $\tilde{Y}_{PR}$ is a left-shoulder FOU [see Fig. 6.5(b)] if and only if $h_{\underline{Y}_{PR}} = 1$, and $y_{Ll}(\alpha) = 0$ and $y_{Lr}(\alpha) = 0$ for $\forall \alpha \in [0, 1]$.

Definition 6.5. An IT2 FS $\tilde{Y}_{PR}$ is a right-shoulder FOU [see Fig. 6.5(c)] if and only if $h_{\tilde{Y}_{PR}} = 1$, and $y_{Rl}(\alpha) = M$ and $y_{Rr}(\alpha) = M$ for $\forall \alpha \in [0, 1]$.

Definition 6.6. An IT2 FS $\tilde{Y}_{PR}$ is an interior FOU [see Fig. 6.5(a)] if and only if it is neither a left-shoulder FOU nor a right-shoulder FOU.

Theorem 6.6. Let $\tilde{Y}_{PR}$ be expressed as in equation (6.3). Then, $\tilde{Y}_{PR}$ is a left-shoulder FOU if and only if all $\tilde{G}^i$ are left-shoulder FOUs.

Theorem 6.7. Let $\tilde{Y}_{PR}$ be expressed as in equation (6.3). Then, $\tilde{Y}_{PR}$ is a right-shoulder FOU if and only if all $\tilde{G}^i$ are right-shoulder FOUs.

Theorem 6.8. Let $\tilde{Y}_{PR}$ be expressed as in equation (6.3). Then, $\tilde{Y}_{PR}$ is an interior FOU if and only if one of the following conditions is satisfied:

1. $\{\tilde{G}^i | i = 1, 2, \ldots, n\}$ is a mixture of both left and right shoulders.
2. At least one $\tilde{G}^i$ is an interior FOU.

Theorems 6.6–6.8 are important because they show that the output of PR is a normal IT2 FS and is similar to the word FOUs in a codebook[10] (see Fig. 3.17). So, a similarity measure (Chapter 4) can be used to map $\tilde{Y}_{PR}$ to a word in the codebook. On the other hand, it is less intuitive to map a clipped FOU (see $\tilde{B}$ in Fig. 6.2), as obtained from a Mamdani inference mechanism, to a normal IT2 FS word FOU in the codebook.

6.5 EXAMPLES

Two examples are given in this section to illustrate PR. Each of them uses a subset of the 25 rules from Social Judgment Advisor 3 in Chapter 8. FOUs for the nine-word vocabulary used by both examples are shown in Fig. 6.7.

Example 6.1. This example focuses only on the following four rules:

R^1: If touching is *NVL* and eye contact is *NVL*, then flirtation is $\tilde{Y}^1$.
R^2: If touching is *NVL* and eye contact is *S*, then flirtation is $\tilde{Y}^2$.
R^3: If touching is *S* and eye contact is *NVL*, then flirtation is $\tilde{Y}^3$.
R^4: If touching is *S* and eye contact is *S*, then flirtation is $\tilde{Y}^4$.

The FOUs for $\tilde{Y}^i$ that were computed from survey histograms, as explained in Chapter 8, are depicted in Fig. 6.8. Observe from the rules, that as either touching or

---

[10]A small difference is that the LMFs of interior codebook word FOUs are always triangular, whereas the LMFs of interior $\tilde{Y}_{PR}$ are usually trapezoidal.

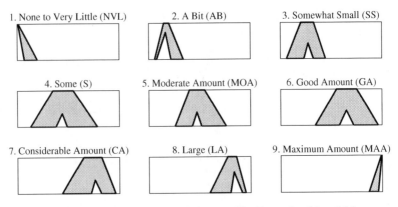

Figure 6.7. The nine-word vocabulary used by Examples 6.1 and 6.2.

eye contact increases, the flirtation consequent also increases, that is, the rules implement a monotonic mapping, as one would expect for the social judgment of flirtation.

The input words used to activate the four rules in this example are *A Bit* (AB) and *Somewhat Small* (SS). Their FOUs are also depicted in Fig. 6.7. Four combinations of these input words are considered for the two indicators of flirtation and the resulting flirtation levels are shown in Fig. 6.9. For example, when touching is *AB* and eye contact is *AB*, $\tilde{Y}_{PR}$ is shown in Fig. 6.9(a) as the dashed FOU. This FOU is mapped into the word *AB* in the nine-word vocabulary, whose FOU is also shown in Fig. 6.9(a) as the solid curve. Recall that to map $\tilde{Y}_{PR}$ into a word in the vocabulary, the similarities between $\tilde{Y}_{PR}$ and the nine words in Fig. 6.7 are computed and then

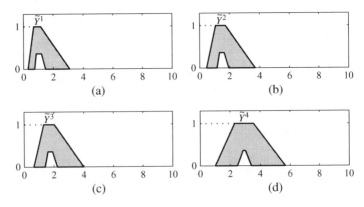

Figure 6.8. Consequent FOUs for the four rules.

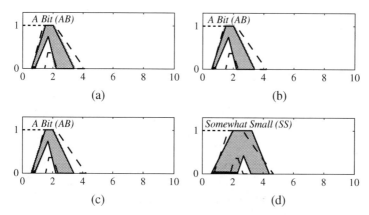

Figure 6.9. $\tilde{Y}_{PR}$ (dashed curve) and its mapped word in the nine-word vocabulary (solid curve). (a) Touching is *AB* and eye contact is *AB*; (b) touching is *AB* and eye contact is *SS*; (c) touching is *SS* and eye contact is *AB*; and, (d) touching is *SS* and eye contact is *SS*.

the word with the maximum similarity is chosen. Because a linguistic level of flirtation must be provided using just the nine-word vocabulary in Fig. 6.7, one of those words must be chosen; so, even though $\tilde{Y}_{PR}$ and *FOU(AB)* do not look so similar, "*A bit (of flirtation)*" is that word.

Observe from Fig. 6.9 that as either input increases, $\tilde{Y}_{PR}$ also increases, which is reasonable; however, the linguistic description of flirtation is the same in the first three cases.

Example 6.2. This example focuses only on the following four rules:

R^1: If touching is *MOA* and eye contact is *MOA*, then flirtation is $\tilde{Y}^1$.
R^2: If touching is *MOA* and eye contact is *LA*, then flirtation is $\tilde{Y}^2$.
R^3: If touching is *LA* and eye contact is *MOA*, then flirtation is $\tilde{Y}^3$.
R^4: If touching is *LA* and eye contact is *LA*, then flirtation is $\tilde{Y}^4$.

The FOUs for $\tilde{Y}^i$, which were computed from survey histograms, are depicted in Fig. 6.10. Observe again that the rules implement a monotonic mapping, as one would expect for the social judgment of flirtation.

The input words used to activate the four rules in this example are *Good amount* (GA) and *Considerable amount* (CA). Their FOUs are also depicted in Fig. 6.7. Four combinations of these input words are considered for the two indicators of flirtation and the resulting flirtation levels are shown in Fig. 6.11. For example, when touching is *GA* and eye contact is *GA*, $\tilde{Y}_{PR}$ is shown in Fig. 6.11(a) as the dashed FOU. This FOU is mapped into the word *CA* in the nine-word vocabulary, whose FOU is also shown in Fig. 6.11(a) as the solid curve.

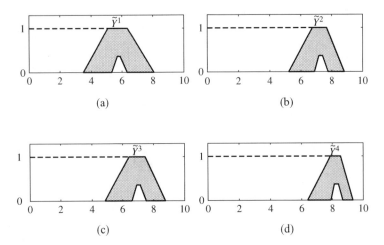

Figure 6.10. Consequent FOUs for the four rules.

Again, observe from Fig. 6.11 that as either input increases, $\tilde{Y}_{PR}$ also increases, which is reasonable; however, because the increase is small and a limited number of words are used in the codebook, all four $\tilde{Y}_{PR}$ are mapped into the same word CA in the codebook. Observe, also, that the higher levels of touching and eye contact in this example (as compared with the levels of these indicators in Example 6.1) lead to higher levels of flirtation.

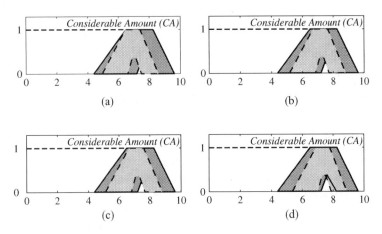

Figure 6.11. $\tilde{Y}_{PR}$ (dashed curve) and its mapped word in the nine-word vocabulary (solid curve). (a) Touching is GA and eye contact is GA; (b) touching is GA and eye contact is CA; (c) touching is CA and eye contact is GA; and, (d) touching is CA and eye contact is CA.

APPENDIX 6A

6A.1   Proof of Theorem 6.1

When all fired rules have the same consequent $\tilde{G}$, equation (6.3) simplifies to

$$\tilde{Y}_{PR} = \frac{\sum_{i=1}^{n} f^i \tilde{G}}{\sum_{i=1}^{n} f^i} = \tilde{G}\left(\frac{\sum_{i=1}^{n} f^i}{\sum_{i=1}^{n} f^i}\right) = \tilde{G} \qquad (6A.1)$$

That is, when all fired rules have the same consequent $\tilde{G}$, $\tilde{Y}_{PR}$ defined in equation (6.3) is the same as $\tilde{G}$.

6A.2   Proof of Theorem 6.2

Theorem 6.2 is obvious because each of $y_{Ll}(\alpha)$, $y_{Lr}(\alpha)$, $y_{Rl}(\alpha)$, and $y_{Rr}(\alpha)$ is an arithmetic weighted average of the corresponding quantities on $\tilde{G}^i$. So, for example, from equation (6.5), observe that

$$y_{Ll}(\alpha) = \frac{\sum_{i=1}^{n} a_{il}(\alpha)f^i}{\sum_{i=1}^{n} f^i} \geq \frac{\min_i a_{il}(\alpha) \cdot \sum_{i=1}^{n} f^i}{\sum_{i=1}^{n} f^i} = \min_i a_{il}(\alpha) \qquad (6A.2)$$

$$y_{Ll}(\alpha) = \frac{\sum_{i=1}^{n} a_{il}(\alpha)f^i}{\sum_{i=1}^{n} f^i} \leq \frac{\max_i a_{il}(\alpha) \cdot \sum_{i=1}^{n} f^i}{\sum_{i=1}^{n} f^i} = \max_i a_{il}(\alpha) \qquad (6A.3)$$

6A.3   Proof of Theorem 6.3

It follows from equations (6.5) and (6.6) that

$$\begin{aligned}
y_{Rr}(0) - y_{Ll}(0) &= \frac{\sum_{i=1}^{n} (b_{ir}(0) - a_{il}(0))f^i}{\sum_{i=1}^{n} f^i} \\
&\geq \frac{\min_i (b_{ir}(0) - a_{il}(0)) \cdot \sum_{i=1}^{n} f^i}{\sum_{i=1}^{n} f^i} \\
&= \min_i (b_{ir}(0) - a_{il}(0)) \qquad (6A.4)
\end{aligned}$$

$$\begin{aligned}
y_{Rr}(0) - y_{Ll}(0) &= \frac{\sum_{i=1}^{n} (b_{ir}(0) - a_{il}(0))f^i}{\sum_{i=1}^{n} f^i} \\
&\leq \frac{\max_i (b_{ir}(0) - a_{il}(0)) \cdot \sum_{i=1}^{n} f^i}{\sum_{i=1}^{n} f^i} \\
&= \max_i (b_{ir}(0) - a_{il}(0)) \qquad (6A.5)
\end{aligned}$$

6A.4 Proof of Theorem 6.4

Because $a_{ir}(\alpha) \le b_{il}(\alpha)$ [see Fig. 6.4(a)], it follows from equations (6.7) and (6.8) that, for $\forall \alpha \in [0, h_{\underline{Y}_{PR}}]$,

$$y_{Lr}(h_{\underline{Y}_{PR}}) = \frac{\sum_{i=1}^{n} a_{ir}(h_{\underline{Y}_{PR}})f^{i}}{\sum_{i=1}^{n} f^{i}} \le \frac{\sum_{i=1}^{n} b_{il}(h_{\underline{Y}_{PR}})f^{i}}{\sum_{i=1}^{n} f^{i}} = y_{Rl}(h_{\underline{Y}_{PR}}) \qquad (6A.6)$$

that is, $y_{Lr}(h_{\underline{Y}_{PR}}) \le y_{Rl}(h_{\underline{Y}_{PR}})$. The equality holds if and only if $a_{ir}(h_{\underline{Y}_{PR}}) = b_{il}(h_{\underline{Y}_{PR}})$ for $\forall i = 1, \ldots, n$, that is, when all $\underline{G}^{i}$ are triangles with the same height $h_{\underline{Y}_{PR}} = \min_{i} h_{\underline{G}^{i}}$. In this case, according to Definition 6.3, $\underline{Y}_{PR}$ is triangle-looking. Otherwise, $y_{Lr}(h_{\underline{Y}_{PR}}) < y_{Rl}(h_{\underline{Y}_{PR}})$, and according to Definition 6.2, $\underline{Y}_{PR}$ is trapezoidal-looking.

6A.5 Proof of Theorem 6.5

Because $a_{il}(\alpha) \le b_{ir}(\alpha)$ [see Fig. 6.4(a)], it follows from equations (6.5) and (6.6) that, for $\forall \alpha \in [0, 1]$,

$$y_{Ll}(1) = \frac{\sum_{i=1}^{n} a_{il}(1)f^{i}}{\sum_{i=1}^{n} f^{i}} \le \frac{\sum_{i=1}^{n} b_{ir}(1)f^{i}}{\sum_{i=1}^{n} f^{i}} = y_{Rr}(1) \qquad (6A.7)$$

that is, $y_{Ll}(1) \le y_{Rr}(1)$. The equality holds if and only if $a_{il}(1) = b_{ir}(1)$ for $\forall i = 1, \ldots, n$, i.e., when all $\bar{G}^{i}$ are normal triangles. In this case, $\bar{Y}_{PR}$ is triangular-looking according to Definition 6.3. Otherwise, $y_{Ll}(1) < y_{Rr}(1)$ and, hence, $\bar{Y}_{PR}$ is trapezoidal-looking according to Definition 6.2.

6A.6 Proof of Theorem 6.6

A Lemma is introduced before Theorem 6.6 is proved.

Lemma 6A.1. An IT2 FS $\tilde{Y}_{PR}$ is a left-shoulder FOU if and only if $h_{\underline{Y}_{PR}} = 1$ and $y_{Lr}(1) = 0$.

Proof. According to Definition 6.4, one only needs to show that "$y_{Lr}(1) = 0$" and "$y_{Ll}(\alpha) = 0$ and $y_{Lr}(\alpha) = 0$ for $\forall \alpha \in [0, 1]$" are equivalent. When $h_{\underline{Y}_{PR}} = 1$, $y_{Ll}(\alpha) \le y_{Lr}(\alpha)$ holds for $\forall \alpha \in [0, 1]$ for an arbitrary FOU [e.g., see Fig. 6.12]; hence, one only needs to show that "$y_{Lr}(1) = 0$" and "$y_{Lr}(\alpha) = 0$ for $\forall \alpha \in [0, 1]$" are equivalent. Because only convex IT2 FSs are used in PR, $y_{Lr}(\alpha) \le y_{Lr}(1)$ for $\forall \alpha \in [0, 1]$ [e.g., see again Fig. 6.12]; hence, $y_{Lr}(1) = 0$ is equivalent to $y_{Lr}(\alpha) = 0$ for $\forall \alpha \in [0, 1]$.

Next we prove Theorem 6.6.

From Lemma 6A.1, $\tilde{Y}_{PR}$ is a left-shoulder FOU if and only if $h_{\underline{Y}_{PR}} = 1$ and $y_{Lr}(1) = 0$, and, similarly, all $\tilde{G}^{i}$ are left-shoulder FOUs if and only if $h_{\underline{G}^{i}} = 1$ and $a_{ir}(1) = 0$ for $\forall i$. To prove Theorem 6.6, one needs to show (1) "$h_{\underline{Y}_{PR}} = 1$" and "$h_{\underline{G}^{i}} = 1$ for $\forall i$" are equivalent, and (2) "$y_{Lr}(1) = 0$" and "$a_{ir}(1) = 0$ for $\forall i$" are equivalent.

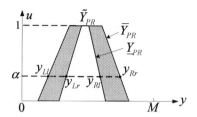

Figure 6.12. An IT2 FS with $h_{\tilde{Y}_{PR}} = 1$.

The first requirement is obvious from equation (6.9). For the second requirement, it follows from equation (6.7) that

$$y_{Lr}(1) = \frac{\sum_{i=1}^{n} a_{ir}(1)f^i}{\sum_{i=1}^{n} f^i} \tag{6A.8}$$

Because all $f^i > 0$, $y_{Lr}(1) = 0$ if and only if all $a_{ir}(1) = 0$.

6A.7 Proof of Theorem 6.7

A Lemma is introduced before Theorem 6.7 is proved.

Lemma 6A.2. An IT2 FS $\tilde{Y}_{PR}$ is a right-shoulder FOU if and only if $h_{\tilde{Y}_{PR}} = 1$ and $y_{Rl}(1) = M$.

Proof. According to Definition 6.5, one only needs to show that "$y_{Rl}(1) = M$" and "$y_{Rl}(\alpha) = M$ and $y_{Rr}(\alpha) = M$ for $\forall \alpha \in [0, 1]$" are equivalent. When $h_{\tilde{Y}_{PR}} = 1$, $y_{Rr}(\alpha) \geq y_{Rl}(\alpha)$ holds for $\forall \alpha \in [0, 1]$ [e.g., see Fig. 6.12]; hence, one only needs to show that "$y_{Rl}(1) = M$" and "$y_{Rl}(\alpha) = M$ for $\forall \alpha \in [0, 1]$" are equivalent. Because only convex IT2 FSs are used in PR, $y_{Rl}(\alpha) \geq y_{Rl}(1)$ for $\forall \alpha \in [0, 1]$ [e.g., see again Fig. 6.12]; hence, $y_{Rl}(1) = M$ is equivalent to $y_{Rl}(\alpha) = M$ for $\forall \alpha \in [0, 1]$.

Next we prove Theorem 6.7.

From Lemma 6A.2, $\tilde{Y}_{PR}$ is a right-shoulder FOU if and only if $h_{\tilde{Y}_{PR}} = 1$ and $y_{Rl}(1) = M$, and similarly all $\tilde{G}^i$ are right-shoulder FOUs, if and only if $h_{\tilde{G}^i} = 1$ and $b_{il}(1) = M$ for $\forall i$. To prove Theorem 6.7, one only needs to show that (1) "$h_{\tilde{Y}_{PR}} = 1$" and "$h_{\tilde{G}^i} = 1$ for $\forall i$" are equivalent, and, (2) "$y_{Rl}(1) = M$" and "$b_{il}(1) = M$ for $\forall i$" are equivalent.

The first requirement is obvious from equation (6.9). For the second requirement, it follows from equation (6.8) that

$$y_{Rl}(1) = \frac{\sum_{i=1}^{n} b_{il}(1)f^i}{\sum_{i=1}^{n} f^i} \tag{6A.9}$$

Because all $f^i > 0$, $y_{Rl}(1) = M$ if and only if all $b_{il}(1) = M$.

6A.8   Proof of Theorem 6.8

A Lemma is introduced before Theorem 6.8 is proved.

Lemma 6A.3. An IT2 FS $\tilde{Y}_{PR}$ is an interior FOU if and only if:

(1) $h_{\underline{Y}_{PR}} < 1$, or (2) $h_{\underline{Y}_{PR}} = 1$, $y_{Lr}(1) > 0$, and $y_{Rl}(1) < M$.

Proof. (1) Because both left-shoulder and right-shoulder FOUs require $h_{\underline{Y}_{PR}} = 1$ (see Lemmas 6A.1 and 6A.2), $\tilde{Y}_{PR}$ must be an interior FOU when $h_{\underline{Y}_{PR}} < 1$.

(2) When $h_{\underline{Y}_{PR}} = 1$ and $y_{Lr}(1) > 0$, $\tilde{Y}_{PR}$ is not a left-shoulder FOU by Lemma 6A.1. When $h_{\underline{Y}_{PR}} = 1$ and $y_{Rl}(1) < M$, $\tilde{Y}_{PR}$ is not a right-shoulder FOU by Lemma 6A.2. Consequently, $\tilde{Y}_{PR}$ must be an interior FOU.

Next we prove Theorem 6.8.

The sufficiency is proved first. Consider first condition (1). Since all shoulders have height 1, it follows from equation (6.9) that $h_{\underline{Y}_{PR}} = 1$. Without loss of generality, assume $\{\tilde{G}^i | i = 1, \ldots, n_1\}$ are left-shoulder FOUs and $\{\tilde{G}^i | i = n_1 + 1, \ldots, n\}$ are right-shoulder FOUs, where $1 \leq n_1 \leq n - 1$. For each left-shoulder FOU $\tilde{G}^i$, it is true that [see Fig. 6.4(b)] $a_{ir}(1) = 0$ and[11] $b_{il}(1) < M$. For each right-shoulder $\tilde{G}^i$, it is true that[12] [see Fig. 6.4(c)] $a_{ir}(1) > 0$ and $b_{il}(1) = M$. In summary,

$$a_{ir}(1) \begin{cases} = 0, & i = 1, \ldots, n_1 \\ > 0, & i = n_1 + 1, \ldots, n \end{cases} \tag{6A.10}$$

$$b_{il}(1) \begin{cases} < M, & i = 1, \ldots, n_1 \\ = M, & i = n_1 + 1, \ldots, n \end{cases} \tag{6A.11}$$

It follows that

$$y_{Lr}(1) = \frac{\sum_{i=1}^{n} a_{ir}(1)f^i}{\sum_{i=1}^{n} f^i} = \frac{\sum_{i=n_1}^{n} a_{ir}(1)f^i}{\sum_{i=1}^{n} f^i} > 0 \tag{6A.12}$$

$$y_{Rl}(1) = \frac{\sum_{i=1}^{n} b_{il}(1)f^i}{\sum_{i=1}^{n} f^i} < \frac{\sum_{i=1}^{n} Mf^i}{\sum_{i=1}^{n} f^i} = M \tag{6A.13}$$

hence, $\tilde{Y}_{PR}$ is an interior FOU according to Part (2) of Lemma 6A.3.

Next consider condition (2). Without loss of generality, assume only $\tilde{G}^1$ is an interior FOU, $\{\tilde{G}^i | i = 2, \ldots, n_2\}$ are left-shoulder FOUs, and $\{\tilde{G}^i | i = n_2 + 1, \ldots, n\}$ are right-shoulder FOUs, where $2 \leq n_2 \leq n - 1$. Two subcases are considered:

---

[11]$b_{il}(1)$ for a left shoulder cannot be M, because otherwise according to Lemma 6A.2, $\tilde{G}^i$ would be a right-shoulder FOU.

[12]$a_{ir}(1)$ for a right-shoulder FOU cannot be 0, because otherwise according to Lemma 6A.1, $\tilde{G}^i$ would be a left-shoulder FOU.

1. When $h_{G^1} < 1$, according to equation (6.9), $h_{Y_{PR}} = h_{G^1} < 1$ and, hence, $\tilde{Y}_{PR}$ is an interior FOU according to Part (1) of Lemma 6A.3.

2. When $h_{G^1} = 1$, it follows from equation (6.9) that $h_{Y_{PR}} = 1$ and, from condition 2 of Lemma 6A.3 applied to $\tilde{G}^1$, that $a_{ir}(1) > 0$ and $b_{il}(1) < M$:

$$a_{ir}(1) \begin{cases} = 0, & i = 2, \ldots, n_2 \\ > 0, & i = 1, n_2 + 1, \ldots, n \end{cases} \tag{6A.14}$$

$$b_{il}(1) \begin{cases} < M, & i = 1, 2, \ldots, n_2 \\ = M, & i = n_2 + 1, \ldots, n \end{cases} \tag{6A.15}$$

Consequently,

$$y_{Lr}(1) = \frac{\sum_{i=1}^{n} a_{ir}(1) f^i}{\sum_{i=1}^{n} f^i} = \frac{a_{1r}(1) f^1 + \sum_{i=n_2+1}^{n} a_{ir}(1) f^i}{\sum_{i=1}^{n} f^i} > 0 \tag{6A.16}$$

$$y_{Rl}(1) = \frac{\sum_{i=1}^{n} b_{il}(1) f^i}{\sum_{i=1}^{n} f^i} < \frac{\sum_{i=1}^{n} M f^i}{\sum_{i=1}^{n} f^i} = M \tag{6A.17}$$

Again, $\tilde{Y}_{PR}$ is an interior FOU according to Part (2) of Lemma 6A.3.

Next consider the necessity. $\{\tilde{G}^i | i = 1, 2, \ldots, n\}$ can only take the following four forms:

1. All $\tilde{G}^i$ are left-shoulder FOUs.
2. All $\tilde{G}^i$ are right-shoulder FOUs.
3. $\{\tilde{G}^i | i = 1, 2, \ldots, n\}$ is a mixture of both left- and right-shoulder FOUs.
4. At least one $\tilde{G}^i$ is an interior FOU.

Assume $\tilde{Y}_{PR}$ is an interior FOU, whereas $\{\tilde{G}^i | i = 1, 2, \ldots, n\}$ is not in forms (3) and (4). Then, $\{\tilde{G}^i | i = 1, 2, \ldots, n\}$ must be in form (1) or (2). When $\{\tilde{G}^i | i = 1, 2, \ldots, n\}$ is in form (1) (i.e., all $\tilde{G}^i$ are left-shoulder FOUs), according to Theorem 6.6, $\tilde{Y}_{PR}$ must also be a left-shoulder FOU, which violates the assumption that $\tilde{Y}_{PR}$ is an interior FOU. Similarly, when $\{\tilde{G}^i | i = 1, 2, \ldots, n\}$ is in form (2) (i.e., all $\tilde{G}^i$ are right-shoulder FOUs), according to Theorem 6.7, $\tilde{Y}_{PR}$ must be a right-shoulder FOU, which also violates the assumption. Hence, when $\tilde{Y}_{PR}$ is an interior FOU, $\{\tilde{G}^i | i = 1, 2, \ldots, n\}$ must be a mixture of both left- and right-shoulder FOUs, or at least one $\tilde{G}^i$ is an interior FOU.

REFERENCES

M. D. S. Brain, "On the relation between the natural logic of reasoning and standard logic," *Psychological Review*, vol. 85, pp. 1–21, 1978.

H. Bustince, "Indicator of inclusion grade for interval-valued fuzzy sets. Application to approximate reasoning based on interval-valued fuzzy sets," *Int. Journal of Approximate Reasoning,* vol. 23, no. 3, pp. 137–209, 2000.

N. Chater, M. Oaksford, R. Nakisa, and M. Redington, "Fast, frugal and rational: How rational norms explain behavior," *Organizational Behaviour and Human Decision Processes,* vol. 90, no. 1, pp. 63–86, 2003.

S. Guillaume, "Designing fuzzy inference systems from data: An interpretability-oriented review," *IEEE Trans. on Fuzzy Systems,* vol. 9, no. 3, pp. 426–443, 2001.

B. Inhelder and J. Piaget, *The Growth of Logical Thinking From Childhood to Adolescence.* New York: Basic Books, 1958.

M. Jamei, M. Mahfouf, and D. A. Linkens, "Elicitation and fine-tuning of fuzzy control rules using symbiotic evolution," *Fuzzy Sets and Systems,* vol. 147, no. 1, pp. 57–74, October 2004.

J.-S. R. Jang, C.-T. Sun, and E. Mizutani, *Neuro-Fuzzy and Soft-Computing.* Upper Saddle River, NJ: Prentice-Hall, 1997.

G. J. Klir and B. Yuan, *Fuzzy Sets and Fuzzy Logic: Theory and Applications.* Upper Saddle River, NJ: Prentice-Hall, 1995.

L. B. Koeppel, Y. Montagne-Miller, D. O'Hair, and M. J. Cody, "Friendly? flirting? wrong?" in P. J. Kalbfleisch (Ed.), *Interpersonal Communication: Evolving Interpersonal Relationship,* Hillsdale, NJ: Erlbaum, 1993, pp. 13–32.

E. H. Mamdani, "Application of fuzzy algorithms for control of simple dynamic plant," *Proc. IEE,* vol. 121, no. 12, pp. 1585–1588, 1974.

J. M. Mendel, *Uncertain Rule-Based Fuzzy Logic Systems: Introduction and New Directions.* Upper Saddle River, NJ: Prentice-Hall, 2001.

J. M. Mendel, "Type-2 fuzzy sets and systems: An overview," *IEEE Computational Intelligence Magazine,* vol. 2, no. 1, pp. 20–29, 2007.

J. M. Mendel, R. I. John, and F. Liu, "Interval type-2 fuzzy logic systems made simple," *IEEE Trans. on Fuzzy Systems,* vol. 14, no. 6, pp. 808–821, 2006.

J. M. Mendel, S. Murphy, L. C. Miller, M. Martin, and N. Karnik, "The fuzzy logic advisor for social judgments," in L. A. Zadeh and J. Kacprzyk (Eds.), *Computing with Words in Information/Intelligent Systems,* Physica-Verlag, 1999, pp. 459–483.

J. M. Mendel and D. Wu, "Perceptual reasoning: A new computing with words engine," in *Proceedings of IEEE International Conference on Granular Computing,* Silicon Valley, CA, November 2007, pp. 446–451.

J. M. Mendel and D. Wu, "Perceptual reasoning for perceptual computing," *IEEE Trans. on Fuzzy Systems,* vol. 16, no. 6, pp. 1550–1564, 2008.

S. Mitra and Y. Hayashi, "Neuro-fuzzy rule generation: Survey in soft computing framework," *IEEE Trans. on Neural Networks,* vol. 11, no. 3, pp. 748–768, 2000.

K. Nozaki, H. Ishibuchi, and H. Tanaka, "A simple but powerful heuristic method for generating fuzzy rules from numerical data," *Fuzzy Sets and Systems,* vol. 86, no. 3, pp. 251–270, 1997.

S. Raha, N. Pal, and K. Ray, "Similarity-based approximate reasoning: Methodology and application," *IEEE Trans. on Systems, Man, and Cybernetics-A,* vol. 32, no. 4, pp. 541–547, 2002.

L. J. Rips, *The Psychology of Proof.* Cambridge, MA: MIT Press, 1994.

T. Sudkamp, "Similarity, interpolation, and fuzzy rule construction," *Fuzzy Sets and Systems,* vol. 58, no. 1, pp. 73–86, 1993.

H. Wang and D. Qiu, "Computing with words via Turing machines: A formal approach," *IEEE Trans. on Fuzzy Systems,* vol. 11, no. 6, pp. 742–753, 2003.

L.-X. Wang and J. M. Mendel, "Generating fuzzy rules by learning from examples," *IEEE Trans. on Systems, Man, and Cybernetics,* vol. 22, no. 2, pp. 1414–1427, 1992.

L.-X. Wang, *A Course in Fuzzy Systems and Control.* Upper Saddle River, NJ: Prentice Hall, 1997.

D. Wu and J. M. Mendel, "Perceptual reasoning using interval type-2 fuzzy sets: Properties," in *Proceedings of IEEE International Conference on Fuzzy Systems,* Hong Kong, June 2008, pp. 1219–1226.

D. Wu and J. M. Mendel, "Perceptual reasoning for perceptual computing: A similarity-based approach," *IEEE Trans. on Fuzzy Systems,* vol. 17, no. 6, pp. 1397–1411, 2009.

R. Yager and D. Filev, *Essentials of Fuzzy Modeling and Control.* New York: Wiley, 1994a.

R. R. Yager and D. P. Filev, "Generation of fuzzy rules by mountain clustering," *Journal of Intelligent and Fuzzy Systems,* vol. 2, pp. 209–219, 1994b.

J. Yen and R. Langari, *Fuzzy Logic: Intelligence, Control, and Information.* Upper Saddle River, NJ: Prentice Hall, 1999.

D. S. Yeung and E. C. C. Tsang, "A comparative study on similarity-based fuzzy reasoning methods," *IEEE Trans. on Systems, Man, and Cybernetics-B,* vol. 27, pp. 216–227, 1997.

CHAPTER 7

Assisting in Making Investment Choices—Investment Judgment Advisor (IJA)[1]

7.1 INTRODUCTION

Recall, from Chapter 1, Tong and Bonissone's (1980) investment decision example:

A private citizen has a moderately large amount of capital that he wishes to invest to his best advantage. He has selected five possible investment areas $\{a_1, a_2, a_3, a_4, a_5\}$ and has four investment criteria $\{c_1, c_2, c_3, c_4\}$ by which to judge them. These are:

- a_1, the commodity market; a_2, the stock market; a_3, gold[2]; a_4, real estate[3]; and a_5, long-term bonds
- c_1, the risk of losing the capital sum; c_2, the vulnerability of the capital sum to modification by inflation; c_3, the amount of interest[4] (profit) received; and c_4, the cash realizeability of the capital sum [liquidity]

The investor's goal is to decide which investments he should partake in. In order to arrive at his decisions,[5] the individual must first rate each of the five alternative investment areas for each of the four criteria. To do this requires that he either knows about the investments or becomes knowledgeable about them. His ratings use words and, therefore, are linguistic ratings. In order to illustrate what the linguistic ratings might look like, the ones used by Tong and Bonissone are provided in the investment alternatives/investment criteria array in Table 7.1. For example,

---

[1]This chapter was written with the assistance of Ms. Jhiin Joo, a Ph. D. student working under the supervision of the authors.

[2]Tong and Bonissone called this "gold and/or diamonds." In this chapter, this is simplified to "gold."

[3]The term *real estate* is somewhat ambiguous because it could mean individual properties, ranging from residential to commercial, or investment vehicles that focus exclusively on real estate, such as a real estate investment trust (REIT) or a real estate mutual fund. In this chapter, real estate is interpreted to mean the latter two.

[4]By *interest* is meant the profit percent from the capital invested; so, in this chapter the term *profit* is used.

[5]In order to make this chapter self-contained, some of the material in the rest of this section is repeated from Section 1.2.1.

Perceptual Computing. By Jerry M. Mendel and Dongrui Wu

Table 7.1. Investment alternatives/investment criteria array. Example of the linguistic ratings of investment alternatives for investment criteria, provided by an individual[a]

Investment alternatives	Investment Criteria			
	c_1 (Risk of losing capital)	c_2 (Vulnerability to inflation)	c_3 (Amount of profit received)	c_4 (Liquidity)
a_1 (commodities)	High	More or less high	Very high	Fair
a_2 (stocks)	Fair	Fair	Fair	More or less good
a_3 (gold)	Low	From fair to more or less low	Fair	Good
a_4 (real estate)	Low	Very low	More or less high	Bad
a_5 (long-term bonds)	Very low	High	More or less low	Very good

[a]An individual fills in this table by completing the following statements: To me, the risk of losing my capital in investment alternative a_j seems to be _____? To me, the vulnerability of investment alternative a_j to inflation seems to be_____? To me, the amount of profit that I would receive from investment alternative a_j seems to be _____? To me, the liquidity of investment alternative a_j seems to be_____?

the individual's linguistic ratings about commodities are that there is a high risk of losing his capital sum from investing in commodities, commodities have a more or less high vulnerability to inflation, the amount of profit received from commodities is very high, and commodities are fairly liquid.

What makes the individual's investment choices challenging is that his knowledge about the investments is uncertain; hence, his linguistic ratings are uncertain. Additionally, each individual does not necessarily consider each criterion to be equally important. So, he must also assign a linguistic weight to each of them. The weights chosen by Tong and Bonissone are given in Table 7.2. This individual views the risk of losing his capital as moderately important, the vulnerability to inflation as more or less important, the amount of profit received as very important, and liquidity as more or less unimportant. Although common weights are used for

Table 7.2. Example of the linguistic weights for the investment criteria, provided by an individual[a]

c_1 (Risk of losing capital)	c_2 (Vulnerability to inflation)	c_3 (Amount of profit received)	c_4 (Liquidity)
Moderately important	More or less important	Very important	More or less unimportant

[a]An individual fills in this table by completing the following statement: The importance that I attach to the investment criterion c_i is _____?

all five investment alternatives, they could be chosen separately for each of the alternatives.

The problem facing the individual investor is how to aggregate the linguistic information in Tables 7.1 and 7.2 so as to arrive at his preferential ranking of the five investments (Fig. 7.1). Clearly, the results will be very subjective because these tables are filled with words and not numbers. The investor may also want to play "what–if" games, meaning that he may want to see what the effects are of changing the words in one or both of the tables on the preferential rankings.

The preferential ranking of the five investment alternatives can be used to establish the components of an investor's portfolio; for example, if the investor only wants three of the five alternatives in his portfolio, then the preferential ranking of the five alternatives will lead to those three alternatives. How much money should then be allocated to those alternatives is another study that is beyond the scope of this chapter.[6]

The Per-C that is associated with this application is called an *investment judgment advisor* (IJA), and its design is studied in detail in this chapter. One of the interesting features of this application is that any person, such as the reader of this book, can fill in Tables 7.1 and 7.2, and immediately find out his/her preferential rankings of the five investments.

The following are some additional important points made by Tong and Bonissone (1980), as well as our comments about them:

- The main feature, and advantage, of our approach is that it generates a linguistic assessment of the decision, thus making explicit the subjective nature of any choice that is made using fuzzy information.

We believe that an investor not only needs a linguistic assessment of the decision but also some data (Chapter 1, Section 1.1); hence, our IJA will have both linguistic and numerical outputs.

- In any decision problem in which there is uncertainty in the data, there must be uncertainty in the decision itself. Obviously, one of the alternatives has to be selected, but we should be aware of the consequences of fuzzifying the problem.

We handle uncertainty in the data by using interval type-2 fuzzy set models for all words, and uncertainty in the decision making by using the linguistic weighted average (LWA) and the centroid that provides a measure of the uncertainty for the LWA.

- What is required is some way of actually ranking the dominant alternatives. It would be better to treat this final ranking as a separate problem.

[6]The investor may want to allocate his resources among the portfolio alternatives so as to maximize wealth or to minimize risk, or a mixture of both [Magoc, et al. (2008)].

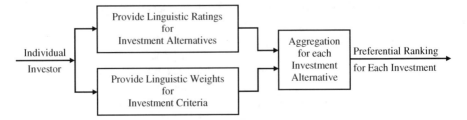

Figure 7.1. Investment judgment advisor.

Not only will we perform ranking of the alternatives, but we will also provide the similarities of the alternatives to each other; both will be done by our decoder, and, as suggested by Tong and Bonissone, the decoder is indeed a separate block in the Per-C IJA.

- To be of maximum value, our technique has to be implemented as an interactive computer system.

An interactive software tool, developed by the authors and Ms. Jhiin Joo, is discussed in Section 7.7.

In the rest of this chapter, we describe the encoder, CWW engine, and decoder used by the IJA. Additionally, examples are provided that illustrate the IJA.

7.2   ENCODER FOR THE IJA

As always, the encoder leads to a codebook for an application, and it requires two steps: (1) establish a vocabulary for the application, and (2) establish word FOUs using the IA (Chapter 3). In this section, details are provided for both of these steps.

7.2.1   Vocabulary

Table 7.1, which has been taken from Tong and Bonissone (1980), seems to use the same set of words to rate risk of losing capital, vulnerability to inflation, and amount of profit received, and (except for the word "fair") another set of words to rate liquidity. Consequently, the following 15 words were chosen to rate the investment criteria *risk of losing capital, vulnerability to inflation,* and *amount of profit received*: none to very little, extremely low, very low, more or less low, somewhat low, moderately low, low, from low to more or less fair, from fair to more or less high, somewhat high, moderately high, more or less high, high, very high, and extremely high. Each of these words flows naturally when an investor states, "To me the risk of losing capital, the vulnerability to inflation, or the amount of profit received for this investment alternative is _____."

The following 11 words were chosen to rate *liquidity*: very bad, more or less bad, somewhat bad, bad, somewhat fair, fair, very fair, more or less good, somewhat good, good, and very good. Each of these words flows naturally when an investor states, "To me the liquidity of this investment alternative seems to be _____."

Finally, the following six words were chosen for the weighting that an investor assigns to each of the four investment criteria: unimportant, moderately unimportant, more or less unimportant, moderately important, more or less important, and very important. Each of these words flows naturally when an investor states, "To me this criterion is _____."

Although an investor could use any of these six words for the importance of *risk of losing capital, the vulnerability to inflation,* and *liquidity,* he would only use the following subset of three words for the importance of *amount of profit* received: moderately important, more or less important, or very important. The reason for omitting the other three words should be obvious to any investor, but if it is not, then, as an example, if you as an investor chose, "To me the importance of *amount of profit* received is *moderately unimportant,*" then why are you investing? People invest to make a profit so as to increase their wealth.

7.2.2 Word FOUs and Codebooks

During the first four months of 2008, a word survey was conducted and data were collected from 40 adult (male and female) subjects. The survey was in three parts:

1. The first part of the survey had the 15 words (listed above) and they were randomized. The subjects were told:

   Each of the 15 words describes an interval or a "range" that falls somewhere between 0 and 10. For each word, please tell us where this range would start and where it would stop. (In other words, please tell us how much of the distance from 0 to 10 this range would cover.) For example, the range of "The risk/vulnerability/profit to me is *somewhat low*" might start at 2.1 and end at 4.3. It is important to note that not all the ranges are the same size, and overlapping the ranges is okay.

2. The second part of the survey had the 11 words (listed above), also randomized. The subjects were told:

   Each of the 11 words describes an interval or a "range" that falls somewhere between 0 and 10. For each word, please tell us where this range would start and where it would stop. (In other words, please tell us how much of the distance from 0 to 10 this range would cover.) Zero denotes your worst assessment of liquidity whereas 10 denotes your best assessment of liquidity. For example, the range "liquidity of this investment is *fair*" might start at 4 and end at 7.5. It is important to note that not all the ranges are the same size, and overlapping the ranges is okay.

3. The third part of the survey had the six words (listed above), also randomized. The subjects were told:

   Each of the six words describes an interval or a "range" that falls somewhere between 0 and 10. For each word, please tell us where this range would start and where it would stop. (In other words, please tell us how much of the distance from 0 to 10 this range would cover.) For example, the range "for a given investment choice, this specified criterion to me is *moderately important*" might start at 5.3 and end at 7.6. It is important to note that not all the ranges are the same size, and overlapping the ranges is okay.

The IA (Chapter 3) was applied separately to the data collected from the three surveys. Tables 7.3–7.8 summarize the results for the three vocabularies and their codebooks. Pictures of the FOUs for the three vocabularies are given in Figs. 7.2–7.4.

7.3 REDUCTION OF THE CODEBOOKS TO USER-FRIENDLY CODEBOOKS

In our first design of the IJA, we observed that when an individual was given the opportunity to choose a word from the full 15-word, 11-word and six-word codebooks, and then changed the words to the ones either to the left or to the right of them, there was almost no change in the outputs of the IJA. The individuals who tested the IJA did not like this because they were expecting to see changes when they changed the words. This made the IJA not "user-friendly." This "human factor" was surprising to us because we have always advocated providing the individ-

Table 7.3. Remaining data intervals and their end-point statistics for m^* data intervals and the 15-word vocabulary[a]

Word	Preprocessing				FS part	Left-end statistic		Right-end statistic	
	Stage 1 n'	Stage 2 m'	Stage 3 m''	Stage 4 m	m^*	m_l	s_l	m_r	s_r
None to very little	40	34	32	30	30	0	0	1.3233	0.5591
Extremely low	40	34	28	25	25	0.012	0.0596	1.344	0.4285
Very low	40	35	34	27	27	0.4593	0.4976	2.2519	0.5316
More or less low	40	32	29	25	25	2.232	0.6428	4.166	0.441
Somewhat low	40	35	32	15	15	2.4533	0.5142	4.0667	0.496
Moderately low	40	35	32	22	22	2.3591	0.5798	4.125	0.6423
Low	40	35	33	24	16	1.05	0.8368	3.3896	0.5236
From low to more or less fair	40	33	31	28	28	2.4571	0.6700	4.9732	0.8063
From fair to more or less high	40	35	33	26	26	4.8158	0.7259	7.5362	0.5271
Somewhat high	40	36	34	23	23	6.5196	0.5782	8.3522	0.5143
Moderately high	40	33	31	23	23	6.6022	0.4433	8.1674	0.4654
More or less high	40	37	36	27	26	6.5019	0.6425	8.3741	0.6273
High	40	35	33	27	27	7.2778	0.6326	9.7222	0.4312
Very high	40	35	32	27	27	8.2926	0.5880	9.8922	0.2086
Extremely high	40	33	33	31	31	8.8984	0.5430	10	0.0002

[a]The words in this table are in the order of the list that is in Section 7.2.1.

Table 7.4. FOU data for the 15 words (based on $m*$ data intervals)—the 15-word codebook.[a] Each UMF and LMF is represented as a trapezoid (see Fig. 4.5). The fifth parameter for the LMF is its height.

Word	LMF	UMF	Centroid	Mean of centroid
None to very little	(0, 0, 0.02, 0.33, 1)	(0, 0, 0.22, 3.16)	[0.11, 1.53]	0.820
Extremely low	(0, 0, 0.06, 0.92, 1)	(0, 0, 0.46, 2.63)	[0.30, 1.00]	0.650
Very low	(0, 0, 0.14, 1.82, 1)	(0, 0, 1.37, 3.95)	[0.60, 1.54]	1.070
Low	(1.90, 2.24, 2.24, 0.31, 2.51)	(0.38, 1.63, 3.00, 4.62)	[1.26, 3.55]	2.404
More or less low	(2.99, 3.31, 3.31, 0.32, 3.81)	(0.38, 2.25, 4.00, 5.92)	[1.72, 4.67]	3.196
Somewhat low	(2.79, 3.30, 3.30, 0.42, 3.71)	(0.98, 2.75, 4.00, 5.46)	[2.26, 4.27]	3.261
Moderately low	(2.95, 3.18, 3.18, 0.15, 3.30)	(0.38, 2.50, 4.50, 6.62)	[1.24, 5.67]	3.457
From low to more or less fair	(3.29, 3.75, 3.75, 0.31, 4.21)	(0.17, 2.73, 4.80, 7.91)	[1.79, 6.09]	3.936
From fair to more or less high	(5.79, 6.31, 6.31, 0.43, 7.21)	(2.33, 5.11, 7.00, 9.59)	[4.47, 7.75]	6.113
More or less high	(6.90, 7.21, 7.21, 0.29, 7.60)	(4.38, 6.25, 8.00, 9.62)	[5.61, 8.53]	7.072
Somewhat high	(6.81, 7.27, 7.27, 0.35, 7.81)	(4.48, 6.25, 8.15, 9.52)	[5.87, 8.37]	7.115
Moderately high	(6.79, 7.30, 7.30, 0.42, 7.71)	(5.59, 6.75, 8.00, 9.56)	[6.57, 8.32]	7.444
High	(7.68, 9.82, 10, 10, 1)	(4.73, 8.82, 10, 10)	[8.04, 9.23]	8.636
Very high	(8.71, 9.91, 10, 10, 1)	(6.05, 9.36, 10, 10)	[8.50, 9.57]	9.034
Extremely high	(9.74, 9.98, 10, 10, 1)	(7.10, 9.80, 10, 10)	[8.55, 9.91]	9.232

[a]The words in this table have been ordered according to the rank of the mean of the centroid of their FOUs, except that None to very little and Extremely low have been interchanged.

Table 7.5. Remaining data intervals and their end-point statistics for $m*$ data intervals—the 11-word codebook[a]

Word	Preprocessing				FS part	Left-end statistic		Right-end statistic	
	Stage 1	Stage 2	Stage 3	Stage 4					
	n'	m'	m''	m	$m*$	m_l	s_l	m_r	s_r
Very bad	40	36	34	26	26	0.0481	0.117	1.8846	0.6870
More or less bad	40	36	34	12	12	2.4583	0.6142	4.1917	0.5389
Somewhat bad	40	39	35	21	21	2.4048	0.4741	4.1548	0.3334
Bad	40	37	35	20	14	1.05	0.7973	3.425	0.5928
Somewhat fair	40	35	34	23	23	4.2283	0.5545	6.2739	0.6396
Fair	40	36	35	25	25	4.252	0.5304	6.244	0.5869
Very fair	40	36	35	25	25	4.614	0.6388	6.48	0.6367
More or less good	40	37	34	22	22	5.6977	0.4833	7.5614	0.5520
Somewhat good	40	39	36	18	18	5.7278	0.4747	7.5083	0.5486
Good	40	39	36	20	17	6.365	0.5926	8.4225	0.767
Very good	40	39	36	25	25	7.606	0.5293	9.444	0.5915

[a]The words in this table are in the order of the list that is in Section 7.2.1.

Table 7.6. FOU data for the 11 words (based on m^* data intervals)—the 11-word codebook.[a] Each UMF and LMF is represented as a trapezoid (see Fig. 4.5). The fifth parameter for the LMF is its height.

Word	LMF	UMF	Centroid	Mean of centroid
Very bad	(0, 0, 0.09, 1.32,1)	(0, 0, 0.59, 3.95)	[0.44, 1.49]	0.965
Bad	(1.79, 2.37, 2.37, 0.48, 2.71)	(0.28, 2.00, 3.00, 5.22)	[1.49, 3.64]	2.568
More or less bad	(2.79, 3.22, 3.22, 0.35, 3.67)	(0.98, 2.40, 4.00, 5.41)	[2.12. 4.29]	3.207
Somewhat bad	(2.79, 3.30, 3.30, 0.42, 3.71)	(0.98, 2.75, 4.00, 5.41)	[2.26, 4.24]	3.251
Fair	(4.79, 5.12, 5.12, 0.27, 5.35)	(2.38, 4.50, 6.00, 8.18)	[3.52, 6.96]	5.240
Somewhat fair	(4.79, 5.33, 5.33, 0.31, 5.71)	(2.38, 4.50, 6.50, 8.62)	[3.78, 7.12]	5.450
Very fair	(5.19, 5.63, 5.63, 0.34, 6.21)	(2.38, 4.50, 6.50, 8.62)	[3.94, 7.15]	5.542
Somewhat good	(5.89, 6.34, 6.34, 0.40, 6.81)	(4.02, 5.65, 7.00, 8.41)	[5.27, 7.28]	6.276
More or less good	(6.23, 6.73, 6.73, 0.39, 7.21)	(4.38, 6.00, 7.50, 9.62)	[5.64, 8.12]	6.880
Good	(6.79, 7.25, 7.25, 0.47, 7.91)	(4.38, 6.50, 7.75, 9.62)	[6.02, 8.23]	7.122
Very good	(7.66, 9.82,10, 10, 1)	(5.21, 8.27, 10, 10)	[8.14, 9.22]	8.679

[a]The words in this table have been ordered according to the rank of the mean of the centroid of their FOUs.

ual who will interact with the Per-C a large vocabulary in order to make this interaction "user-friendly." In this application, it is important to provide an individual with vocabularies in each of the three codebooks that contain *sufficiently dissimilar* words so that when a change is made from one word to another there is a noticeable change in the output of the IJA.

G. A. Miller (1965) conjectured that there is an upper limit on one's capacity to process information on simultaneously interacting elements (e.g., words in a vocab-

Table 7.7. Remaining data intervals and their end-point statistics for m^* data intervals—the six-word codebook[a]

Word	Preprocessing				FS part	Left-end statistic		Right-end statistic	
	Stage 1 n'	Stage 2 m'	Stage 3 m''	Stage 4 m	m^*	m_l	s_l	m_r	s_r
Unimportant	40	35	30	23	23	0.0217	0.1001	1.717	0.742
Moderately unimportant	40	36	34	23	23	2.6587	0.4465	4.2457	0.5447
More or less unimportant	40	38	34	19	19	2.2358	0.6440	4.0184	0.4482
Moderately important	40	38	37	20	20	5.935	0.3842	7.605	0.4568
More or less important	40	37	36	18	18	5.5111	0.6671	7.3333	0.4985
very important	40	32	30	25	25	8.144	0.3018	9.976	0.0979

[a]The words in this table are in the order of the list that is in Section 7.2.1.

Table 7.8. FOU data for the six words (based on m^* data intervals)—the six-word codebook.[a] Each UMF and LMF is represented as a trapezoid (see Fig. 4.5). The fifth parameter for the LMF is its height.

Word	LMF	UMF	Centroid	Mean of centroid
Unimportant	(0, 0, 0.09, 1.15, 1)	(0, 0, 0.55, 4.61)	[0.38, 1.83]	1.103
More or less unimportant	(2.79, 3.21, 3.21, 0.34, 3.71)	(0.42, 2.25, 4.00, 5.41)	[1.78, 4.29]	3.036
Moderately unimportant	(2.79, 3.34, 3.34, 0.35, 3.67)	(1.59, 2.75, 4.35, 6.26)	[2.52, 4.85]	3.684
More or less important	(5.79, 6.28, 6.28, 0.33, 6.67)	(3.38, 5.50, 7.25, 9.02)	[4.77, 7.71]	6.241
Moderately important	(6.29, 6.67, 6.67, 0.39, 7.17)	(4.59, 5.90, 7.25, 8.50)	[5.70, 7.49]	6.597
Very important	(8.68, 9.91, 10, 10, 1)	(7.37, 9.36, 10, 10)	[9.02, 9.57]	9.295

[a]The words in this table have been ordered according to the rank of the mean of the centroid of their FOUs.

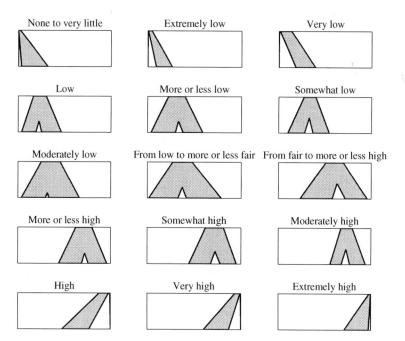

Figure 7.2. FOUs for the 15-word vocabulary. Start at the top row and proceed downward, scanning from left to right. Note that *None to very little* has been relocated to the left of *Extremely low*.

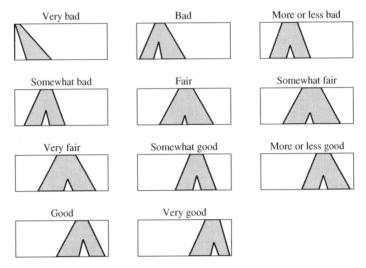

Figure 7.3. FOUs for the 11-word vocabulary. Start at the top row and proceed downward, scanning from left to right.

ulary) with reliable accuracy and with validity. He conjectured that people are only able to deal with five to nine elements at one time. Cowan (2001) argues that people can successfully deal with only two to six elements at one time. Saaty and Ozdemir (2003) support Miller's conjecture for making preference judgments on pairs of elements in a group, as is done in the analytical hierarchy process (AHP). So, when we provide a person with a vocabulary from which they have to make a choice for investment criteria or their weights, it seems it should contain from five (or maybe fewer, according to Cowan) to nine words.

In order to accomplish this, the similarity matrices for the three codebooks were computed using the Jaccard similarity measure that is described in Chapter 4. Those matrices are in Tables 7.9–7.11. Next, the phrase "sufficiently dissimilar words"

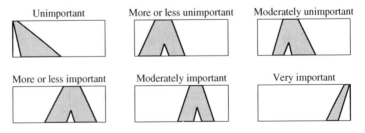

Figure 7.4. FOUs for the six-word vocabulary. Start at the top row and proceed downward, scanning from left to right.

Table 7.9. Similarity matrix for the 15-word vocabulary

Word	NVL	EL	VL	L	MLL	SL	ML	LMLF	FMLH	MLH	SH	MH	H	VH	EH
None to very little (NVL)	1.00	0.76	0.51	0.24	0.17	0.11	0.15	0.13	0.01	0.00	0.00	0.00	0.00	0.00	0.00
Extremely low (EL)	0.76	1.00	0.56	0.18	0.12	0.07	0.11	0.10	0.00	0.00	0.00	0.00	0.00	0.00	0.00
Very low (VL)	0.51	0.56	1.00	0.34	0.24	0.18	0.21	0.19	0.03	0.00	0.00	0.00	0.00	0.00	0.00
Low (L)	0.24	0.18	0.34	1.00	0.60	0.48	0.51	0.42	0.08	0.00	0.00	0.00	0.00	0.00	0.00
More or less low (MLL)	0.17	0.12	0.24	0.60	1.00	0.78	0.81	0.67	0.19	0.04	0.04	0.00	0.01	0.00	0.00
Somewhat low (SL)	0.11	0.07	0.18	0.48	0.78	1.00	0.67	0.56	0.17	0.03	0.02	0.00	0.01	0.00	0.00
Moderately low (ML)	0.15	0.11	0.21	0.51	0.81	0.67	1.00	0.79	0.26	0.09	0.08	0.02	0.03	0.00	0.00
From low to more or less fair (LMLF)	0.13	0.10	0.19	0.42	0.67	0.56	0.79	1.00	0.36	0.17	0.16	0.09	0.08	0.03	0.01
From fair to more or less high (FMLH)	0.01	0.00	0.03	0.08	0.19	0.17	0.26	0.36	1.00	0.55	0.53	0.39	0.23	0.16	0.10
More or less high (MLH)	0.00	0.00	0.00	0.00	0.04	0.03	0.09	0.17	0.55	1.00	0.95	0.74	0.35	0.25	0.16
Somewhat high (SH)	0.00	0.00	0.00	0.00	0.04	0.02	0.08	0.16	0.53	0.95	1.00	0.75	0.35	0.24	0.16
Moderately high (MH)	0.00	0.00	0.00	0.00	0.00	0.00	0.02	0.09	0.39	0.74	0.75	1.00	0.36	0.28	0.19
High (H)	0.00	0.00	0.00	0.00	0.01	0.01	0.03	0.08	0.23	0.35	0.35	0.36	1.00	0.66	0.37
Very high (VH)	0.00	0.00	0.00	0.00	0.00	0.00	0.00	0.03	0.16	0.25	0.24	0.28	0.66	1.00	0.56
Extremely high (EH)	0.00	0.00	0.00	0.00	0.00	0.00	0.00	0.01	0.10	0.16	0.16	0.19	0.37	0.56	1.00

Table 7.10. Similarity matrix for the 11-word vocabulary

Word	VB	B	MLB	SB	F	SF	VF	SG	MLG	G	VG
Very bad (VB)	1.00	0.28	0.18	0.17	0.04	0.03	0.03	0.00	0.00	0.00	0.00
Bad (B)	0.28	1.00	0.61	0.56	0.16	0.14	0.14	0.03	0.01	0.01	0.00
More or less bad (MLB)	0.18	0.61	1.00	0.93	0.23	0.21	0.21	0.05	0.03	0.02	0.00
Somewhat bad (SB)	0.17	0.56	0.93	1.00	0.24	0.22	0.22	0.06	0.03	0.02	0.00
Fair (F)	0.04	0.16	0.23	0.24	1.00	0.87	0.84	0.50	0.35	0.30	0.11
Somewhat fair (SF)	0.03	0.14	0.21	0.22	0.87	1.00	0.95	0.58	0.43	0.38	0.15
Very fair (VF)	0.03	0.14	0.21	0.22	0.84	0.95	1.00	0.58	0.43	0.37	0.15
Somewhat good (SG)	0.00	0.03	0.05	0.06	0.50	0.58	0.58	1.00	0.64	0.53	0.18
More or less good (MLG)	0.00	0.01	0.03	0.03	0.35	0.43	0.43	0.64	1.00	0.81	0.30
Good (G)	0.00	0.01	0.02	0.02	0.30	0.38	0.37	0.53	0.81	1.00	0.33
Very good (VG)	0.00	0.00	0.00	0.00	0.11	0.15	0.15	0.18	0.30	0.33	1.00

Table 7.11. Similarity matrix for the six-word vocabulary

Word	U	MLU	MU	MLI	MI	VI
Unimportant (U)	1.00	0.29	0.16	0.02	0.00	0.00
More or less unimportant (MLU)	0.29	1.00	0.65	0.09	0.02	0.00
Moderately unimportant (MU)	0.16	0.65	1.00	0.17	0.08	0.00
More or less important (MLI)	0.02	0.09	0.17	1.00	0.67	0.06
Moderately important (MI)	0.00	0.02	0.08	0.67	1.00	0.04
Very important (VI)	0.00	0.00	0.00	0.06	0.04	1.00

has to be interpreted in order to find such words. Clearly, this phrase means different things to different people and so there can be many ways to proceed.

Our approach was to set a similarity threshold at 0.6, meaning that words that have similarity values greater than 0.6 are considered "too similar" and need to be eliminated from a codebook—but how? Again, there is no unique way to do this.

Our approach for each word was to start from the left column of a similarity matrix and to remove all of the words to which it is similar to degree greater than 0.6. This process is summarized in Table 7.12. Beginning with None to very little, observe that it is similar to Extremely low to degree 0.76; hence, Extremely low is eliminated. There are no other words in the row for None to very little for which the similarity is > 0.6; hence, no other words are eliminated, None to very little is kept in the user-friendly codebook, and we move next to the word, Very low. Focusing on the elements on the right-hand side of the diagonal element in the row for Very low, observe that Very low is not similar to any other words to degree > 0.6; hence, no words are eliminated, Very low is kept in the user-friendly codebook, and we move next to the word, Low. Focusing on the elements on the right-hand side of the diagonal element in the row for Low, we observe that it is also not similar to any other words to degree > 0.6; hence, no words are eliminated, Low is kept in the user-friendly codebook, and we move to the word, More or less low. Focusing on the elements on the right-hand side of the diagonal element in the row for More or less low, we observe that it is similar to Somewhat low, Moderately low, and From low to More or less fair to degree > 0.6; hence, More or less low is kept in the user-friendly codebook, but Somewhat low, Moderately low, and From low to More or less fair are not. Proceeding in this way through the rest of the similarity matrix, a user-friendly codebook that has eight words is arrived at, namely: none to very little, very low, low, more or less low, from fair to more or less high, more or less high, high, extremely high. Table 7.13, which is extracted from Table 7.4, provides the FOU data for these eight words, and their FOUs are depicted in Fig. 7.5.

Instead of starting with the left-column word, we could have started with the right-most-column word Extremely high and proceeded in a very similar fashion, but going from right to left, instead of from left to right. A somewhat different user-friendly vocabulary would have been obtained. Either user-friendly vocabulary can be used. Our choice was to use the first one.

Table 7.12. Similarity matrix for the 15-word vocabulary showing the words that are similar to degree > 0.6 underlined, starting from the left-most word NVL

Word	NVL	EL	VL	L	MLL	SL	ML	LMLF	FMLH	MLH	SH	MH	H	VH	EH
None to very little (NVL)	1.00	0.76	0.51	0.24	0.17	0.11	0.15	0.13	0.01	0.00	0.00	0.00	0.00	0.00	0.00
Extremely low (EL)	0.76	1.00	0.56	0.18	0.12	0.07	0.11	0.10	0.00	0.00	0.00	0.00	0.00	0.00	0.00
Very low (VL)	0.51	0.56	1.00	0.34	0.24	0.18	0.21	0.19	0.03	0.00	0.00	0.00	0.00	0.00	0.00
Low (L)	0.24	0.18	0.34	1.00	0.60	0.48	0.51	0.42	0.08	0.00	0.00	0.00	0.00	0.00	0.00
More or less low (MLL)	0.17	0.12	0.24	0.60	1.00	0.78	0.81	0.67	0.19	0.04	0.04	0.00	0.01	0.00	0.00
Somewhat low (SL)	0.11	0.07	0.18	0.48	0.78	1.00	0.67	0.56	0.17	0.03	0.02	0.00	0.01	0.00	0.00
Moderately low (ML)	0.15	0.11	0.21	0.51	0.81	0.67	1.00	0.79	0.26	0.09	0.08	0.02	0.03	0.00	0.00
From low to more or less fair (LMLF)	0.13	0.10	0.19	0.42	0.67	0.56	0.79	1.00	0.36	0.17	0.16	0.09	0.08	0.03	0.01
From fair to more or less high (FMLH)	0.01	0.00	0.03	0.08	0.19	0.17	0.26	0.36	1.00	0.55	0.53	0.39	0.23	0.16	0.10
More or less high (MLH)	0.00	0.00	0.00	0.00	0.04	0.03	0.09	0.17	0.55	1.00	0.95	0.74	0.35	0.25	0.16
Somewhat high (SH)	0.00	0.00	0.00	0.00	0.04	0.02	0.08	0.16	0.53	0.95	1.00	0.75	0.35	0.24	0.16
Moderately high (MH)	0.00	0.00	0.00	0.00	0.00	0.00	0.02	0.09	0.39	0.74	0.75	1.00	0.36	0.28	0.19
High (H)	0.00	0.00	0.00	0.00	0.01	0.01	0.03	0.08	0.23	0.35	0.35	0.36	1.00	0.66	0.37
Very high (VH)	0.00	0.00	0.00	0.00	0.00	0.00	0.00	0.03	0.16	0.25	0.24	0.28	0.66	1.00	0.56
Extremely high (EH)	0.00	0.00	0.00	0.00	0.00	0.00	0.00	0.01	0.10	0.16	0.16	0.19	0.37	0.56	1.00

Table 7.13. FOU data for the eight words—the user-friendly codebook for the first survey. Each UMF and LMF is represented as a trapezoid (see Fig. 4.5). The fifth parameter for the LMF is its height. The parenthetical word acronyms are used in the examples.

Word	LMF	UMF	Centroid	Mean of centroid
None to very little (NVL)	(0, 0, 0.02, 0.33, 1)	(0, 0, 0.22, 3.16)	[0.11, 1.53]	0.820
Very low (VL)	(0, 0, 0.14, 1.82, 1)	(0, 0, 1.37, 3.95)	[0.60, 1.54]	1.070
Low (L)	(1.90, 2.24, 2.24, 0.31, 2.51)	(0.38, 1.63, 3.00, 4.62)	[1.26, 3.55]	2.404
More or less low (MLL)	(2.99, 3.31, 3.31, 0.32, 3.81)	(0.38, 2.25, 4.00, 5.92)	[1.72, 4.67]	3.196
From fair to more or less high (FMLH)	(5.79, 6.31, 6.31, 0.43, 7.21)	(2.33, 5.11, 7.00, 9.59)	[4.47, 7.75]	6.113
More or less high (MLH)	(6.90, 7.21, 7.21, 0.29, 7.60)	(4.38, 6.25, 8.00, 9.62)	[5.61, 8.53]	7.072
High (H)	(7.68, 9.82, 10, 10, 1)	(4.73, 8.82, 10, 10)	[8.04, 9.23]	8.636
Extremely high (EH)	(9.74, 9.98, 10, 10, 1)	(7.10, 9.80, 10, 10)	[8.55, 9.91]	9.232

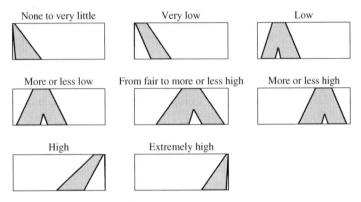

Figure 7.5. FOUs for the user-friendly eight-word vocabulary. Start at the top row and proceed downward, scanning from left to right.

Proceeding in a similar manner for the words in Table 7.10, one arrives at a user-friendly codebook that has seven words, namely: very bad, bad, somewhat bad, fair, somewhat good, good, and very good. Table 7.14, which is extracted from Table 7.6, provides the FOU data for these eight words, and their FOUs are depicted in Fig. 7.6.

Proceeding in a similar manner for the words in Table 7.11, one arrives at a user-friendly codebook that has four words, namely: unimportant, more or less unimportant, more or less important, and very important. Table 7.15, which is extracted from Table 7.8, provides the FOU data for these four words, and their FOUs are depicted in Fig. 7.7.

Each of the three user-friendly codebooks has significantly fewer words in it than the original codebooks. The user-friendly words were not chosen ahead of time

Table 7.14. FOU data for the seven words—the user-friendly codebook for the second survey. Each UMF and LMF is represented as a trapezoid (see Fig. 4.5). The fifth parameter for the LMF is its height. The parenthetical word acronyms are used in the examples.

Word	LMF	UMF	Centroid	Mean of centroid
Very bad (VB)	(0, 0, 0.09, 1.32, 1)	(0, 0, 0.59, 3.95)	[0.44, 1.49]	0.965
Bad (B)	(1.79, 2.37, 2.37, 0.48, 2.71)	(0.28, 2.00, 3.00, 5.22)	[1.49, 3.64]	2.568
Somewhat bad (SB)	(2.79, 3.30, 3.30, 0.42, 3.71)	(0.98, 2.75, 4.00, 5.41)	[2.26, 4.24]	3.251
Fair (F)	(4.79, 5.12, 5.12, 0.27, 5.35)	(2.38, 4.50, 6.00, 8.18)	[3.52, 6.96]	5.240
Somewhat good (SG)	(5.89, 6.34, 6.34, 0.40, 6.81)	(4.02, 5.65, 7.00, 8.41)	[5.27, 7.28]	6.276
Good (G)	(6.79, 7.25, 7.25, 0.47, 7.91)	(4.38, 6.50, 7.75, 9.62)	[6.02, 8.23]	7.122
Very good (VG)	(7.66, 9.82, 10, 10, 1)	(5.21, 8.27, 10, 10)	[8.14, 9.22]	8.679

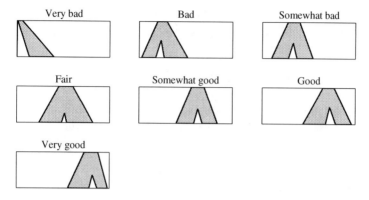

Figure 7.6. FOUs for the user-friendly seven-word vocabulary. Start at the top row and proceed downward, scanning from left to right.

Table 7.15. FOU data for the four words—the user-friendly codebook for the third survey. Each UMF and LMF is represented as a trapezoid (see Fig. 4.5). The fifth parameter for the LMF is its height. The parenthetical word acronyms are used in the examples.

Word	LMF	UMF	Centroid	Mean of centroid
Unimportant (U)	(0, 0, 0.09, 1.15, 1)	(0, 0, 0.55, 4.61)	[0.38, 1.83]	1.103
More or less unimportant (MLU)	(2.79, 3.21, 3.21, 0.34, 3.71)	(0.42, 2.25, 4.00, 5.41)	[1.78, 4.29]	3.036
More or less important (MLI)	(5.79, 6.28, 6.28, 0.33, 6.67)	(3.38, 5.50, 7.25, 9.02)	[4.77, 7.71]	6.241
Very important (VI)	(8.68, 9.91, 10, 10, 1)	(7.37, 9.36, 10, 10)	[9.02, 9.57]	9.295

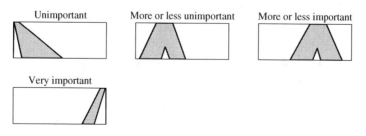

Figure 7.7. FOUs for the user-friendly four-word vocabulary. Start at the top row and proceed downward, scanning from left to right.

in some arbitrary manner, but instead were a result of further processing of the data that were collected from the 40 subjects. Our IJA uses the user-friendly codebooks.

7.4   CWW ENGINE FOR THE IJA

The IJA uses an LWA (Chapter 5) to aggregate the results for each of the rows in Table 7.1. The structure of each of the five LWAs is [see equation (5.38)][7]:

$$
\tilde{Y}_{LWA(a_i)} = \frac{\sum_{j=1}^{4} \tilde{X}_{ij} \tilde{W}_j}{\sum_{j=1}^{4} \tilde{W}_j} \quad i = 1,...,5 \tag{7.1}
$$

where $\tilde{X}_{ij}$ are IT2 FSs *related to* the linguistic ratings of the investment alternative a_i, and $\tilde{W}_j$ are the linguistic weights for the investment criteria. Whereas $\tilde{W}_j$ are the same for all five investment alternatives, as is apparent from Table 7.2, in which there is only one row, $\tilde{X}_{ij}$ can be and usually are different for all five investment alternatives, as is apparent from Table 7.1.

Observe that the phrase "$\tilde{X}_{ij}$ are IT2 FSs *related to* the linguistic ratings of the investment alternative a_i," has just been used instead of the phrase "$\tilde{X}_{ij}$ are IT2 FSs *for* the linguistic ratings of the investment alternative a_i." This is because two of the investment criteria have a positive connotation—amount of profit received and liquidity—and two have a negative connotation—risk of losing capital and vulnerability to inflation. "Positive connotation" means that an investor generally thinks positively about amount of profit received and liquidity (i.e., the more the better), whereas "negative connotation" means that an investor generally thinks negatively about risk of losing capital and vulnerability to inflation (i.e., the less the better). So, to correctly handle negative connotations in the LWA, a small-sounding word for them should be replaced by a large-sounding word, and a large-sounding word for them should be replaced by a small-sounding word. This kind of word replacement is essentially the idea of an *antonym*[8] [De Soto (1996), De Soto and Trillas (1999), Kim et al. (2000), Novaka (2001), Trillas and Guadarrama (2005), and Zadeh (2005)].

Though there are several different definitions of the antonym of a T1 FS, in this book the most basic one is used [Kim et al. (2000) and Zadeh (2005)]:

$$
\mu_{10-A}(x) = \mu_A(10-x), \quad \forall x \tag{7.2}
$$

where $10 - A$ is the antonym of the T1 FS A, and 10 is the right end of the domain of all FSs used in this book. The definition in equation (7.2) can easily be extended to IT2 FSs:

---

[7]Recall (Chapter 5) that equation (7.1) is an expressive equation and does *not* mean that IT2 FSs are multiplied, added and divided. How to compute equation (7.1) is explained in Chapter 5.

[8]An antonym is a word of directly contrary significance to another (e.g., large is an antonym of small); it is the opposite of a synonym, which is a word having the same signification.

$$\mu_{10-\tilde{A}}(x) = \mu_{\tilde{A}}(10-x), \quad \forall x \tag{7.3}$$

where $10 - \tilde{A}$ is the antonym of the IT2 FS $\tilde{A}$. Because an IT2 FS is completely characterized by its LMF and UMF, each of which is a T1 FS, $\mu_{10-\tilde{A}}(x)$ in (7.3) is obtained by applying equation (7.2) to both $LMF(\tilde{A})$ and $UMF(\tilde{A})$.

Note that an antonym and not a complement is used because an antonym maps a large (small) normal convex FS into a small (large) one, and the result is still a normal convex FS that can be mapped into a word in the vocabulary, whereas usually the complement is not convex; for example, in Fig. 7.8 the complement of the word Large, Not large, is quite different from the word FOUs introduced in Chapter 3.

In summary, the FOUs in the codebook of Table 7.13 are used as is for amount of interest received and the FOUs in the codebook of Table 7.14 are used as is for liquidity; however, the antonyms of the FOUs in the codebook of Table 7.13 are used for both risk of losing capital and vulnerability to inflation, that is, $(i = 1, \ldots,$ 5):

$$\tilde{X}_{i1} = Antonym[FOU(\text{risk of losing capital for investment } a_i)] \tag{7.4}$$

$$\tilde{X}_{i2} = Antonym[FOU(\text{vulnerability to inflation for investment } a_i)] \tag{7.5}$$

$$\tilde{X}_{i3} = FOU(\text{amount of interest received for investment } a_i) \tag{7.6}$$

$$\tilde{X}_{i4} = FOU(\text{liquidity of investment } a_i) \tag{7.7}$$

7.5 DECODER FOR THE IJA

The IJA decoder provides a linguistic ranking (first, second, $\ldots$, fifth) as well as a numerical ranking band for the five investment alternatives. It also provides similarities between those alternatives, the centroid of each $FOU(\tilde{Y}_{LWA(ai)})$ and a *risk band* for each alternative.

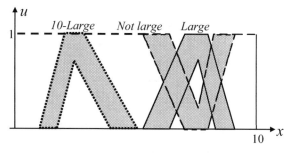

Figure 7.8. An illustration of the word *Large*, its antonym *10-Large*, and complement *Not large*.

Ranking is obtained using the centroid-based ranking method that is described in Section 4.3.2; similarities are obtained using the Jaccard similarity measure that is described in Section 4.2.7; the centroid of $FOU(\tilde{Y}_{LWA(a_i)})$ is computed using the EKM that is described in Appendix 2B; and a risk band is computed as described below.

Recall that the centroid is a measure of the uncertainty of an IT2 FS; hence, the centroid, which is an interval, is used by us as a *ranking band* for each alternative. The amount of overlap of the ranking bands is another indicator of how similar the investment alternatives are.

The antonym of the ranking band is used to provide a risk band, that is, high rank implies low risk,[9] and vice versa; hence,

$$risk\ band(a_i) = Antonym(rank\ band(a_i)) \qquad (7.8)$$

$$risk\ band\ (a_i) \equiv 10 - \text{Centroid}(\tilde{Y}_{LWA(a_i)}) = [10 - c_r(\tilde{Y}_{LWA(a_i)}),\ 10 - c_l(\tilde{Y}_{LWA(a_i)})] \quad (7.9)$$

Frequently, an investor is asked to provide a numerical value of the risk that he/she associates with an investment alternative, so that optimal allocations can be determined for the investments that are in the investor's portfolio in order to, for example, minimize risk while achieving a prescribed level of profit (return). Such numerical values of risk are usually quite uncertain and may, therefore, be unreliable. One of the very interesting by-products of the IJA is a numerical risk band; hence, by using the IJA it will no longer be necessary to ask an investor for a numerical value of the risk that he/she associates with an investment alternative. Additionally, optimal allocations can now be performed using risk bands instead of risk values, so that the uncertainties about the risk bands flow through the calculations of the optimal allocations.

7.6 EXAMPLES

In this section, some examples are provided that illustrate the IJA for different kinds of investors.

7.6.1 Example 1: Comparisons for Three Kinds of Investors

In this example, results are obtained from the IJA for speculative, conservative, and in-between investors. A speculative investor is one who is willing to take large risks in order to maximize his/her wealth. A conservative investor is one who is more interested in protecting his/her capital and making a reasonable profit, and is not willing to take large risks. An in-between investor is someone who is in between the speculative and conservative investors. Intuition suggests that the portfolio of a

---

[9]Note, for example, that even though commodities may be generally viewed as a risky investment, if they are ranked as the number one alternative by an investor, then that person does not view them as risky; so, the high ranking of commodities translates into a low risk investment, but only for that specific person.

speculative investor would be preferentially ranked[10] as commodities, stocks, real estate, gold, and long-term bonds, whereas the portfolio of a conservative investor would be preferentially ranked as long-term bonds, gold, real estate, stocks, and commodities, and the portfolio of the in-between investor would be preferentially ranked as some kind of a mixture of the rankings of the speculative and conservative investors.

Table 7.16 depicts the linguistic ratings and the linguistics weights of the five investment alternatives and four investment criteria for the three kinds of investors. What distinguishes the three kinds of investors the most are the linguistic weights they have assigned to the four investment criteria. The speculative investor has indicated that the risk of losing capital is unimportant, the vulnerability to inflation is more or less unimportant, the amount of profit received is very important, and liquidity is more or less unimportant. The conservative investor has indicated that the risk of losing capital is very important, the vulnerability to inflation is more or less important, the amount of profit received is very important, and liquidity is more or less important. The in-between investor has indicated that the risk of losing capital is more or less important, the vulnerability to inflation is more or less important, the amount of profit received is very important, and liquidity is more or less important. The entries in each of the linguistic rating arrays are merely representative for each kind of investor and were chosen by them one row at a time.

It seems clear to us that each of the tables in Table 7.16 is very difficult to interpret—each is a muddle of symbols. Can the reader determine the preferential ranking of the five alternatives from these tables?

Figure 7.9 depicts the resulting five IJA LWA FOUs for the three kinds of investors. These FOUs have been ranked for each of the investors in order of decreasing importance; hence, the preferential ranking of the investment alternatives—which are now easy to visualize—for the speculative investor is commodities, stocks, real estate, gold, and long-term bonds, which is in exact agreement with our earlier stated intuition. The preferential ranking of the investment alternatives for the conservative investor is long-term bonds, gold, real estate, stocks, and commodities, which is also in exact agreement with our earlier stated intuition. The preferential ranking of the investment alternatives for the in-between investor is stocks, real estate, long-term bonds, gold, and commodities. This ranking was not anticipated by us ahead of time, but has instead been revealed to us by the IJA.

Although it may be very informative for someone who is knowledgeable about IT2 FSs to view pictures of the LWA FOUs for the five investment alternatives, we have found that these pictures are not meaningful to individual investors who are not knowledgeable about IT2 FSs. So, our decoder for the IJA has taken this observation into consideration and, as explained next, provides data that are more informative to any kind of investor.

Figure 7.10 depicts average centroids and ranking bands for the three kinds of investors. The average centroids are stated numerically after the slash mark for

---

[10]These rankings are for illustrative purposes only and are not meant to suggest that they are the only rankings of the five investment alternatives for the different kinds of investors.

Table 7.16. Linguistic ratings and weights of the five investment alternatives and four investment criteria for three kinds of investors. See Tables 7.13–7.15 for definitions of the word acronyms.[a]

Linguistic ratings	Speculative investor				Conservative investor				In-between investor			
	(c_1)	(c_2)	(c_3)	(c_4)	(c_1)	(c_2)	(c_3)	(c_4)	(c_1)	(c_2)	(c_3)	(c_4)
(a_1)	FMLH	FMLH	EH	G	EH	MLH	MLL	F	H	H	MLH	SB
(a_2)	MLH	FMLH	H	SG	H	H	MLH	SG	FMLH	FMLH	H	VG
(a_3)	VL	L	VL	SB	MLL	FMLH	FMLH	F	L	MLL	MLL	SB
(a_4)	MLL	MLH	MLH	SG	MLH	MLH	H	F	FMLH	FMLH	H	SG
(a_5)	NVL	MLL	VL	VB	NVL	MLL	MLH	SG	L	L	L	F
Linguistic weights	U	MLU	VI	MLU	VI	MLI	VI	MLI	MLI	MLI	VI	MLI

[a]Alternatives: (a_1) Commodities, (a_2) Stocks, (a_3) Gold, (a_4) Real Estate, (a_5) Long-term Bonds. Criteria: (c_1) Risk of Losing Capital, (c_2) Vulnerability to Inflation, (c_3) Amount of profit received, (c_4) Liquidity.

each of the investment alternatives and are also shown by the larger filled-in diamonds. The investment alternatives have been preferentially ranked for each investor according to the locations of the average centroids. It is easy for anyone to follow the flow of the average centroids from the first-ranked investment to the fifth-ranked investment, because the ranking is always from top right to lower left. Observe that there can be significant overlap of ranking bands for some of the investment alternatives; for example, for the speculative investor, the ranking bands for gold and long-term bonds have a huge amount of overlap, indicating that the rankings of gold and long-term bonds as fourth and fifth could just as well have been reversed.

Another way to capture overlap of the ranking bands is to examine the similarities of the LWA FOUs for each of the investors. Table 7.17 depicts similarity arrays[11] for the three kinds of investors. Observe that for the speculative investor, the degree of similarity between commodities and stocks is 0.76, which is pretty high, and the similarity between gold and long-term bonds is 0.79, which is also pretty high. Comparable conclusions can be observed from the similarity arrays for the conservative and in-between investors. Investors can use this information to modify the investment choices made for their portfolios.

Finally, Fig. 7.11 depicts the risk bands for the three kinds of investors in the order of least risky to the most risky. This figure was obtained by applying equation (7.9) to each of the ranking bands in Fig. 7.10. Observe that the risk bands always flow in an opposite direction to the flow of the ranking bands, that is, they flow from the upper left to the lower right.

Using the results of this example, it is now possible to define the portfolios for each of the three kinds of investors. For example, if each portfolio is limited to the three most highly ranked investment alternatives, the portfolios are:

[11]The words "array" and "matrix" are used interchangeably by us; however, a nontechnical investor is more likely to understand the word "array" than the word "matrix," which is why "array" is used in this section.

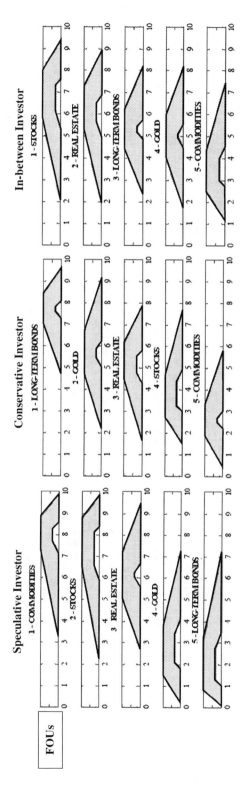

Figure 7.9. Five LWA FOUs for the three kinds of investors.

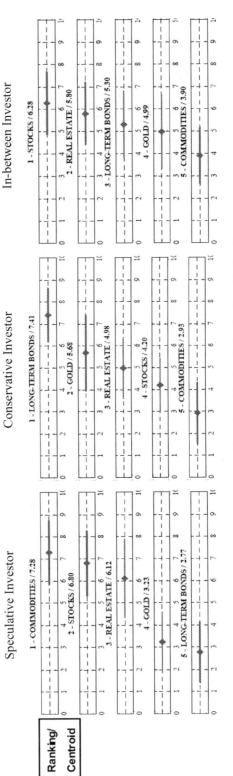

Figure 7.10. Average centroids and ranking bands for the three kinds of investors.

Table 7.17. Similarity arrays for three kinds of investors. The orderings of the rows and columns are in agreement with the orderings of the FOUs in Fig. 7.9. C, S, RE, G, and LTB are short for commodities, stocks, real estate, gold, and long-term bonds.

Similarity rmatrix	Speculative investor					Conservative investor					In-between investor				
	C	S	RE	G	LTB	LTB	G	RE	S	C	S	RE	LTB	G	C
	1	0.76	0.51	0.12	0.11	1	0.35	0.20	0.12	0.02	1	0.77	0.54	0.48	0.27
	0.76	1	0.64	0.18	0.16	0.35	1	0.70	0.42	0.19	0.77	1	0.68	0.60	0.33
	0.51	0.64	1	0.22	0.19	0.20	0.70	1	0.57	0.26	0.54	0.68	1	0.83	0.42
	0.12	0.18	0.22	1	0.79	0.12	0.42	0.57	1	0.43	0.48	0.60	0.83	1	0.52
	0.11	0.16	0.19	0.79	1	0.02	0.19	0.26	0.43	1	0.27	0.33	0.42	0.52	1

- *Speculative investor:* Commodities, stocks, and real estate
- *Conservative investor:* Long-term bonds, gold, and real estate
- *In-between investor:* Stocks, real estate, and long-term bonds

7.6.2 Example 2: Sensitivity of IJA to the Linguistic Ratings

In the previous example, although it was not stated explicitly, the three kinds of investors were all knowledgeable about the five investment alternatives and had a pretty good understanding about the linguistic ratings and weights for the alternatives and the weights of the four investment criteria. This example is about a naïve investor, one who is a bit fearful about investing and really does not have a good understanding about the five investment alternatives or the four investment criteria. After completing the linguistic ratings and linguistics weights arrays, he realizes that he needs some financial counseling and so he goes to an advisor who examines his arrays and suggests some changes but only to the linguistic ratings array. No changes are made to the linguistics weights array because its entries represent the investor's gut feelings and concerns about the four investment criteria, and the advisor only wants to advise the investor to consider changing things that are based on corrected knowledge about an investment. After some changes are made to the investor's linguistic ratings array, a final tuning is made to that array based on a second meeting between the investor and his advisor.

Table 7.18 depicts the linguistic ratings and the linguistics weights of the five investment alternatives and four investment criteria for the three situations. Focusing first on the array that is labeled "naïve investor," observe that seven of its entries are shaded. Those are the ones that were changed at the first meeting of the investor and his advisor, leading to the middle array in Table 7.18, labeled "naïve investor + advice." Only one entry of the middle array was changed at the second meeting of the investor and his advisor, leading to the right-hand array in Table 7.18, labeled "final tuning."

Examining the array of linguistic weights, observe that for this investor the risk of losing his capital (c_1) is *very important* to him, the vulnerability of an investment to inflation (c_2) is *more or less unimportant* to him, and both the amount of profit

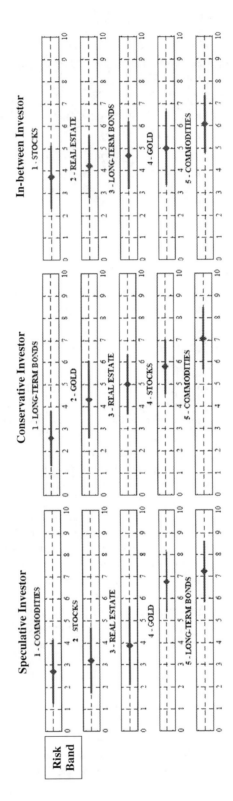

Figure 7.11. Risk bands for the three kinds of investors.

Table 7.18. Linguistic ratings and weights of the five investment alternatives and four investment criteria for a naïve investor and three situations. See Tables 7.13–7.15 for definitions of the word acronyms.[a]

Linguistic ratings	Naïve investor				Naïve investor + advice				Final tuning			
	(c_1)	(c_2)	(c_3)	(c_4)	(c_1)	(c_2)	(c_3)	(c_4)	(c_1)	(c_2)	(c_3)	(c_4)
(a_1)	H	MLH	FMLH	SG	H	MLH	FMLH	SB	H	MLH	FMLH	SB
(a_2)	EH	H	L	F	FMLH	H	H	G	FMLH	H	H	G
(a_3)	VL	MLL	MLL	F	VL	MLL	MLL	F	VL	MLL	MLL	F
(a_4)	MLH	L	FMLH	SG	L	L	FMLH	G	FMLH	L	FMLH	G
(a_5)	NVL	VL	MLH	B	NVL	VL	MLH	G	NVL	VL	MLH	G
Linguistic weights	VI	MLU	MLI	MLI	VI	MLU	MLI	MLI	VI	MLU	MLI	MLI

[a]Alternatives: (a_1) Commodities, (a_2) Stocks, (a_3) Gold, (a_4) Real Estate, (a_5) Long-term Bonds. Criteria: (c_1) Risk of Losing Capital, (c_2) Vulnerability to Inflation, (c_3) Amount of profit received, (c_4) Liquidity.

received from an investment (c_3) and the liquidity of an investment (c_4) are *more or less important* to him. This investor was very worried about losing his money in an investment, a concern that was related to his father having lost a lot of money in the stock market that greatly affected the entire family.

When the investor went to his advisor, the advisor examined each entry of the linguistic ratings array and explained to him that[12]:

- The liquidity of commodities was not Somewhat good (SG) and suggested he change his linguistic rating. Together they looked at the codebook words in Table 7.13 and the investor chose Somewhat bad (SB).

- The risk of losing his capital in stocks was not Extremely high (EH) and suggested he change his linguistic rating. Colored by his father's bad experience in the stock market, the investor and advisor examined the words in Table 7.13 and the investor backed off from Extremely high to From fair to more or less high (FMLH). He would not go above that rating.

- The amount of profit received from stocks was not Low (L) (again, this rating was colored by his father's bad experience in the stock market) and suggested he significantly change his linguistic rating. Together, they looked at the codebook words in Table 7.13 and the investor chose High (H).

- The liquidity of investing in stocks was not Fair (F) (one call to his stockbroker and he could cash out immediately, although it could take some time to actually receive the money from the cash out). Together they looked at the codebook words in Table 7.14 and the investor chose Good (G).

---

[12]The authors are playing the role of a financial advisor and do not claim to have such expertise, so, if the reader does not agree with any or all of the advice, he/she may change (or may not) the entries in any way that he/she so chooses.

- This process continues for the remaining three shaded entries in the "naïve investor" array.[13]

Upon further reflection, the investor felt that his linguistic rating for the risk of losing capital on real estate was incorrect, and so he changed it from Low to From fair to more or less high. No other changes were made to the linguistic ratings in the "naïve investor + advice" array, the result being the "final tuning" array.

Figure 7.12 depicts the five IJA LWA FOUs for the three situations. As in the previous example, these FOUs have been preferentially ranked for each of the situations in order of decreasing importance; hence, the preferential ranking of the investment alternatives for the "naïve investor" is long-term bonds, gold, real estate, commodities, and stocks. Observe that the investor's father having lost a lot of money in the stock market has led to stocks appearing at the very bottom of his investment alternatives. The preferential ranking of the investment alternatives for the "naïve investor + advice" is long-term bonds, real estate, gold, stocks, and commodities, and the preferential ranking of the investment alternatives for the "final tuning" is long-term bonds, gold, real estate, stocks and commodities. It is very interesting to observe that if this investor were to create a portfolio of the three most highly ranked investment alternatives, his portfolio would contain long-term bonds, gold, and real estate, and that these three alternatives are in the top three in all three situations. It is only the relative ranking of the three alternatives that has changed, and they are exactly the same in the "final tuning" and "naïve investor" arrays. If, however, the investor wants the four most highly ranked investment alternatives in his portfolio, then commodities (which appears in the "naïve investor" array) would be replaced by stocks (which appears in the "final tuning" array).

Figures 7.13 and 7.14 and Table 7.19 provide the average centroids and ranking bands, risk bands, and similarity arrays for the three situations. Observe from the "final tuning" similarity array in Table 7.19 that the similarities of long-term bonds to the four other investment alternatives are below 0.5, whereas the similarities of gold to real estate and stocks are above 0.6, and the similarity of real estate to stocks is above 0.9. This suggests that, even in a three-investment portfolio, stocks could be swapped with real estate, demonstrating that the two meetings with the advisor had a very significant effect on the investor toward his perceptions about stocks.

In conclusion, this example demonstrates how the IJA might be used in an interactive way, and that it leads to very reasonable results.

---

[13]The authors have purposely made some changes to the "naïve investor array" that are controversial, so that the reader can make whatever changes they feel are better ones and then compute the results of doing that. For example, advising this investor that the risk of losing capital in real estate is *low* rather than *more or less high* may be very poor advice to anyone who has lived through some of the major declines in real estate (e.g., 2006–2009); however, recall that in this chapter real estate means a REIT or a real estate mutual fund. This is also why the investor was advised that the liquidity of real estate is better than *somewhat good*.

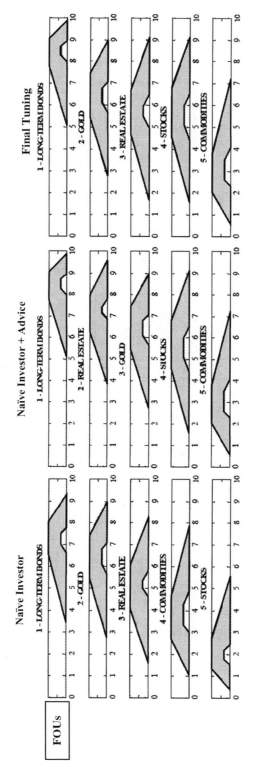

Figure 7.12. Five LWA FOUs for a naïve investor and three situations.

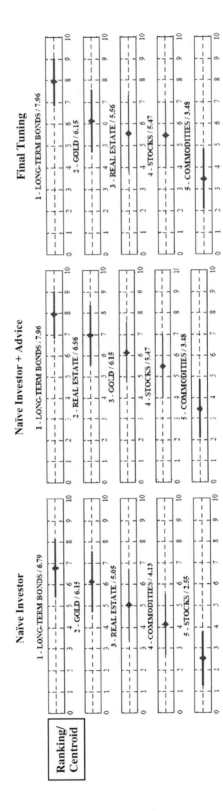

Figure 7.13. Average centroids and ranking bands for a naïve investor and three situations.

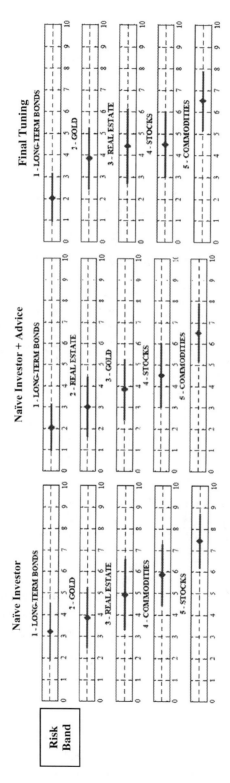

Figure 7.14. Risk bands for a naïve investor and three situations.

Table 7.19. Similarity arrays for a naïve investor and three situations. The orderings of the rows and columns are in agreement with the orderings of the FOUs in Fig. 7.12. C, S, RE, G, and LTB are short for commodities, stocks, real estate, gold, and long-term bonds.

Similarity rmatrix	Naïve investor					Naïve investor + advice					Final tuning				
	LTB	G	RE	C	S	LTB	RE	G	S	C	LTB	G	RE	S	C
	1	0.65	0.35	0.21	0.05	1	0.49	0.31	0.23	0.05	1	0.31	0.24	0.23	0.05
	0.65	1	0.52	0.31	0.10	0.49	1	0.62	0.45	0.13	0.31	1	0.71	0.68	0.22
	0.35	0.52	1	0.58	0.23	0.31	0.62	1	0.68	0.22	0.24	0.71	1	0.93	0.33
	0.21	0.31	0.58	1	0.38	0.23	0.45	0.68	1	0.33	0.23	0.68	0.93	1	0.33
	0.05	0.10	0.23	0.38	1	0.05	0.13	0.22	0.33	1	0.05	0.22	0.33	0.33	1

7.7   INTERACTIVE SOFTWARE FOR THE IJA

Software that implements the IJA is on-line at http://sipi.usc.edu/~mendel/software. It lets the investor choose linguistic ratings for the investment-alternatives/investment-criteria array by using pull-down menus, one investment alternative at a time. It also lets the investor choose linguistic weights for the investment criteria by using pull-down menus. It then displays the two arrays on one screen (Fig. 7.15) and provides the investor with an opportunity to make changes to the two arrays. Using one click on "Get the Result," the IJA LWA FOUs, average centroids and ranking bands, risk bands, and similarity array are computed for the five investment alternatives. LWA FOUs are not displayed to the investor. What is displayed are (Fig. 7.16): a summary of the two arrays in Fig. 7.15, a ranking/centroid figure, a risk band figure, and a similarity array.

The investor can play "what–if" games by making changes to the linguistic entries using pull-down menus on the summary of the two arrays in Fig. 7.16, after which, again using one click on "Change," the modified IJA LWA FOUs, average centroids and ranking bands, risk bands, and similarity matrix are computed. The figures for the newly computed ranking/centroid and risk band, as well as the modified arrays and the table for the newly computed similarity array are displayed on a new screen to the right of the previously displayed figures (Fig. 7.17) so that it is easy for the investor to make side-by-side comparisons, in order to see what the effects are of the changes he/she has made to the two arrays. Changes that were made to the first pair of arrays appear in a different color in the second pair of arrays. This can be repeated up to 10 times; however, the screen that displays the figures and table will only display up to three sets of them side-by-side (Fig. 7.18), with the most recent changes displayed in the right-most figures and table. It is possible, however, for previous results to be recalled and redisplayed in groups of three.

7.8   CONCLUSIONS

The IJA is a very interesting and enlightening application of the Per-C. During its design, the concepts of an antonym and a user-friendly codebook were needed, and

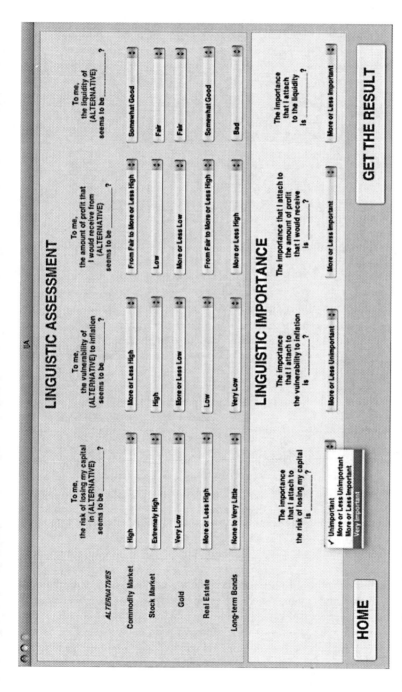

Figure 7.15. Screen shot of two arrays, one for linguistic ratings for the investment alternatives/investment criteria and the other for linguistic weights for the investment criteria. Pull-down menus let the investor choose the linguistic ratings and linguistic weights. One of these is shown for the weights.

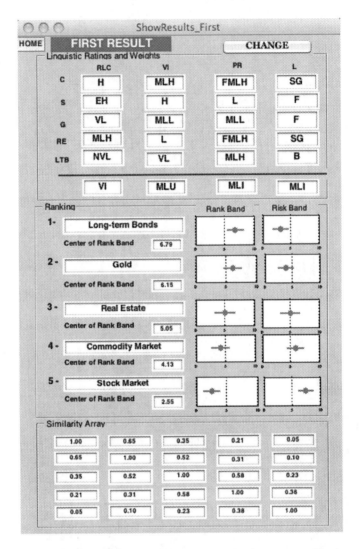

Figure 7.16. Screen shot of a summary of the two arrays in Fig. 7.15: a ranking/centroid figure, a risk band figure, and a similarity array.

word data had to be collected for three vocabularies, each of which was chosen to fit the needs of this application. Without the LWA, it would not have been possible to do what the IJA has been able to do.

Someone may argue that all of this could have been done using T1 FSs. Our counterargument, as explained in Chapter 1, is that to do so would be scientifically incorrect. Additionally, the ranking and risk bands that have been computed very naturally within the framework of IT2 FSs do not exist naturally within the framework of T1 FSs.

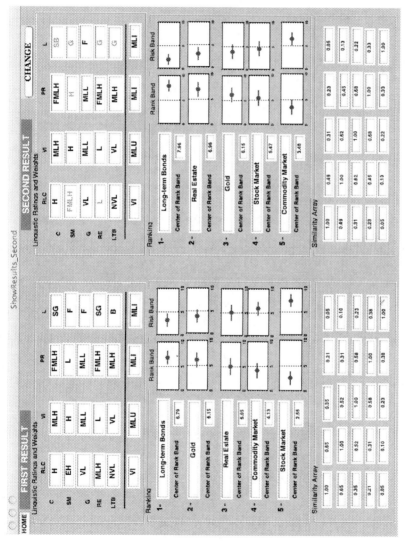

Figure 7.17. Screen shot of the figures for the newly computed ranking/centroid and risk band, as well as the modified arrays and the table for the newly computed similarity array. The new figures are displayed to the right of the previously displayed figures.

231

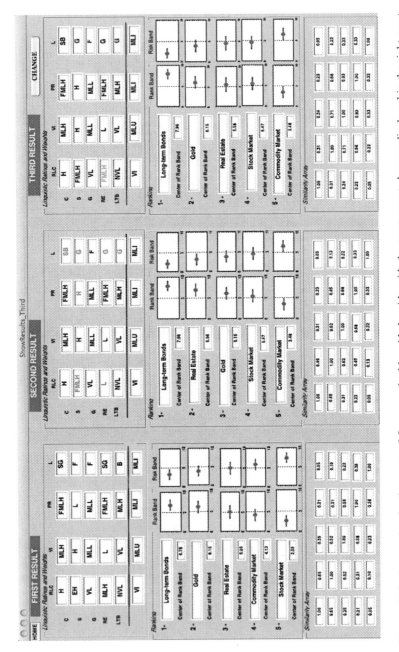

Figure 7.18. Screen shot for three sets of figures and tables side by side with the most recent changes displayed in the right-most figures and table.

REFERENCES

N. Cowan, "The magical number 4 in short-term memory: A reconsideration of mental storage capacity," *Behavioral and Brain Sciences,* vol. 24, pp. 87–105, 2001.

A.R. De Soto, "On automorphism, synonyms and antonyms in fuzzy set theory," in *Proceedings of International Conference on Intelligent Technologies in Human-Related Science,* vol. 1, pp, 217–221, Leon, Spain, 1996.

A.R. De Soto and E. Trillas, "Second thoughts on linguistic variables," in *18th International Conference of the North American Fuzzy Information Processing Society,* pp. 37–41, New York, July 1999.

A.R. De Soto and E. Trillas, "On Antonym and Negate in Fuzzy Logic," *International Journal of Intelligent Systems,* Vol. 14, pp. 295–303, 1999.

C. S. Kim, D. S. Kim, and J. S. Park, "A new fuzzy resolution principle based on the antonym," *Fuzzy Sets and Systems,* vol. 113, pp. 299–307, 2000.

T. Magoc, F. Modavve, M. Ceberio, and V. Kreinovich, "Computational methods for investment portfolio: The use of fuzzy measures and constraint programming for risk management," in A.-E. Hassanien and A. Abraham (Eds.), *Foundations of Computational Intelligence,* vol. 2, pp. 133–173, Springer-Verlag, 2009.

G. A. Miller, "The magical number seven plus or minus two: Some limits on the capacity for processing information," *Psychological Review,* vol. 63, no. 2, pp. 81–97, 1956.

V. Novaka, "Antonyms and linguistic quantifiers in fuzzy logic," *Fuzzy Sets and Systems,* vol. 124, pp. 335–351, 2001.

T. Saaty and M. Ozdemir, "Why the magic number seven plus or minus two," *Mathematical and Computer Modeling,* vol. 38, no. 3, pp. 233–244, 2003.

R. M. Tong and P. P. Bonissone, "A linguistic approach to decision making with fuzzy sets," *IEEE Trans. on Systems, Man, and Cybernetics,* vol. 10, pp. 716–723, 1980.

E. Trillas and S. Guadarrama, "What about fuzzy logic's linguistic soundness?" *Fuzzy Sets and Systems,* vol. 156, pp. 334–340, 2005.

L. A. Zadeh, "Toward a generalized theory of uncertainty (GTU)—An outline," *Information Sciences,* vol. 172, pp. 1–40, 2005.

CHAPTER 8

Assisting in Making Social Judgments—Social Judgment Advisor (SJA)

8.1 INTRODUCTION

In this chapter, the perceptual computer (Per-C) is designed as an aid for making social judgments. The result is called a *social judgment advisor* (SJA). By "judgment" is meant an assessment of the *level* of a variable of interest. For example, in everyday social interaction, each of us is called upon to make judgments about the meaning of another's behavior (e.g., kindness, generosity, flirtation, or harassment). Such judgments are far from trivial, since they often affect the nature and direction of the subsequent social interaction and communications. Although a variety of factors may enter into our decision, behavior (e.g., touching, or eye contact) is apt to play a critical role in assessing the level of the variable of interest.

In this chapter, an SJA is developed for flirtation judgments [Luscombe (2008)] based on if–then rules that are obtained from people, the result being an *FL flirtation advisor*. Flirtation judgments offer a fertile starting place for developing an SJA for a variety of reasons. First, many behavioral indicators associated with flirtation have been well established [Koeppel et al. (1993)]. Second, the indicators (e.g., smiling, touching, and eye contact) are often ambiguous by themselves and along with a changing level of the behavior (along with other cues) the meaning of the behavior is apt to shift from one inference (e.g., friendly) to another (e.g., flirtatious, seductive, or harassing). Third, participants are apt to have had a great deal of experience with flirtation judgments and, therefore, be apt to easily make them. Finally, inferences made about the meaning of these behaviors are often sensitive to both the gender of the perceiver and the gender of the interactants [Koeppel et al. (1993)].

Earlier works on the SJA are Mendel et al. (1999) and Mendel (2001). The former is limited to type-1 FS SJAs whereas the latter does provide both T1 and IT2 SJAs, however, it is limited by the way in which multiple-fired rules are combined and to numerical inputs and outputs. All of these limitations are overcome using the methodology of the Per-C, as will be seen below.

8.2 DESIGN AN SJA

In this section, the complete procedure for designing an SJA is described. Although the focus is on flirtation judgment as an example of a social judgment, we believe that the methodology can also be applied to engineering judgments such as global warming, environmental impact, water quality, audio quality, toxicity, and so on.

8.2.1   Methodology

In developing an SJA for social variables, it is useful to adopt the following methodology[1] [Mendel (2001), Mendel et al. (1999)]:

1. *Identify the behavior of interest.* This step, although obvious, is highly application dependent. As mentioned in the Introduction, our focus is on the behavior of flirtation.

2. *Determine the indicators of the behavior of interest.* This requires:

   (a) Establishing a list of candidate indicators (e.g., for flirtation [Mendel et al. (1999)], six candidate indicators are touching, eye contact, acting witty, primping, smiling, and complementing).

   (b) Conducting a survey in which a representative population is asked to rank order in importance the indicators on the list of candidate indicators. In some applications, it may already be known what the relative importance of the indicators are, in which case a survey is not necessary.

   (c) Choosing a meaningful subset of the indicators, because not all of them may be important. In Step 6, where people are asked to provide consequents for a collection of if–then rules by means of a survey, the survey must be kept manageable, because most people do not like to answer lots of questions; hence, it is very important to focus on the truly significant indicators. The analytic hierarchy process [Saaty (1980)] and factor analysis [Gorsuch (1983)] from statistics can be used to help establish the relative significance of indicators.

3. *Establish scales for each indicator and the behavior of interest.* If an indicator is a physically measurable quantity (e.g., temperature or pressure), then the scale is associated with the expected range between the minimum and maximum values for that quantity. On the other hand, many social judgment indicators as well as the behavior of interest are not measurable by means of instrumentation (e.g., touching, eye contact, flirtation, etc.). Such indicators and behaviors need to have a scale associated with them, or else it will not be possible to design or activate an SJA. Commonly used scales are 1 through 5, 0 through 5, 0 through 10, and so on. We shall use the scale 0 through 10.

4. *Establish names and collect interval data for each of the indicator's FSs and behavior of interest's FSs.* The issues here are:

   (a) What vocabulary should be used and what should its size be so that the FOUs for the vocabulary completely cover the 0–10 scale and provide the user of the SJA with a user-friendly interface?

   (b) What is the smallest number of FSs that should be used for each indicator and behavior of interest for establishing rules?

---

[1]The material in this section is taken from Section 4.3.1 of [Mendel (2001)].

This is the encoding problem and the IA of Chapter 3 can be used to find the FOU word models once a satisfactory vocabulary has been established and word data have been collected from a group of subjects using surveys.

5. *Establish the rules.* Rules are the heart of the SJA; they link the indicators of a behavior of interest to that behavior. The following issues need to be addressed:

   (a) How many antecedents will the rules have? As mentioned earlier, people generally do not like to answer complicated questions; so, we advocate using rules that have either one or two antecedents. An interesting (nonengineering) interpretation for a two-antecedent rule is that it provides the *correlation* effect that exists in the mind of the survey respondent between the two antecedents. Psychologists have told us that it is just about impossible for humans to correlate more than two antecedents (indicators) at a time, and that even correlating two antecedents at a time is difficult. Using only one or two antecedents does not mean that a person does not use more than this number of indicators to make a judgment; it means that a person uses the indicators one or two at a time (this should be viewed as a *conjecture*). This suggests the overall architecture for the SJA should be parallel or hierarchical (see Section 8.3.4).

   (b) How many rule bases need to be established? Each rule base has its own SJA. When there is more than one rule base, each of the advisors is a social judgment subadvisor, and the outputs of these subadvisors can be combined to create the structure of the overall SJA. If, for example, it has been established that four indicators are equally important for the judgment of flirtation, then there would be up to four single-antecedent rule bases as well as six two-antecedent rule bases. These rule bases can be rank ordered in importance by means of another survey in which the respondents are asked to do this. Later, when the outputs of the different rule bases are combined, they can be weighted using the results of this step.

   There is a very important reason for using subadvisors for an SJA. Even though the number of important indicators has been established for the social judgment, it is very unlikely that they will all occur at the same time in a social judgment situation. If, for example, touching, eye contact, acting witty, and primping have been established as the four most important indicators for flirtation, it is very unlikely that in a new flirtation scenario all four will occur simultaneously. From your own experiences in flirting, can you recall a situation when someone was simultaneously touching you, made eye contact with you, was acting witty, and was also primping? Not very likely! Note that a missing observation is not the same as an observation of zero value; hence, even if it were possible to create four antecedent rules, none of those rules could be activated if one or more of the indicators had a missing observation. It is, therefore, very important to have subadvisors that will be activated when one or two of these indicators are occurring.

   More discussions about this are in Section 8.3.4.

6. *Survey people (experts) to provide consequents for the rules.* If, for example, a single antecedent has five FSs associated with it, then respondents would be asked five questions. For two-antecedent rules, where each antecedent is again described by five FSs, there would be 25 questions. The order of the questions should be randomized so that respondents do not correlate their answers from one question to the next. In Step 4 above, the names of the consequent FSs were established. Each single-antecedent rule is associated with a question of the form:

> IF the antecedent is (<u>state one of the antecedent's FSs</u>),
> THEN there is (<u>state one of the consequent's FSs</u>) of the behavior.

Each two-antecedent rule is associated with a question of the form:

> IF antecedent 1 is (<u>state one of antecedent 1's FSs</u>)
> and antecedent 2 is (<u>state one of antecedent 2's FSs</u>),
> THEN there is (<u>state one of the consequent's FSs</u>) of the behavior.

The respondent is asked to choose one of the given names for the consequent's FSs. The rule base surveys will lead to rule consequent histograms, because everyone will not answer a question the same way.

8.2.2 Some Survey Results

The following nine terms, shown in Fig. 8.1, are taken from the 32-word vocabulary[2] in Fig. 3.18 and are used as the codebook for the SJA: none to very little (NVL), a bit (AB), somewhat small (SS), some (S), moderate amount (MOA), good amount (GA), considerable amount (CA), large (LA), and maximum amount (MAA). Table 8.1, which has been extracted from Table 3.6, summarizes the FOUs and centroids of these words. These FOUs are being used only to illustrate our SJA methodology. In actual practice, word survey data would have to be collected from a group of subjects, using the words in the context of flirtation.

Our SJA was limited to rulebases for one-and two-antecedent rules, in which x_1 and x_2 denote touching and eye contact, respectively, and y denotes flirtation level. Section 8.3.4 explains how to deduce the output for multiple antecedents using rule bases consisting of only one or two antecedents. For all of the rules, the following five-word subset of the codebook was used for both their antecedents and consequents: none to very little, some, moderate amount, large, and maximum amount. It is easy to see from Fig. 8.1 that these words cover the interval [0, 10]. Tables 8.2–8.4, which are taken from Mendel et al. (1999) and Chapter 4 of Mendel (2001), provide the data collected from 47 respondents to the Step 6 surveys.

8.2.3 Data Preprocessing

Inevitably, there are bad responses and outliers in the survey histograms that need to be removed before the histograms are used.

---

[2]They are selected in such a way that they are distributed somewhat uniformly in [0, 10].

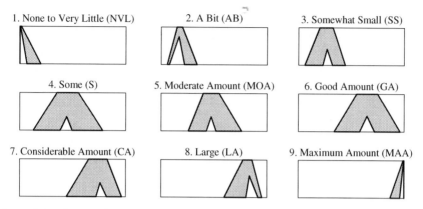

Figure 8.1. Nine word FOUs ranked by their centers of centroid. Words 1, 4, 5, 8, and 9 were used in the Step 6 survey.

Data preprocessing consists of three steps: (1) bad data processing, (2) outlier processing, and, (3) tolerance limit processing, which are quite similar to the preprocessing steps used in Chapter 3. Rule 2 in Table 8.2 is used below as an example to illustrate the details of these three steps.

8.2.3.1 Bad Data Processing. This removes gaps (a zero between two nonzero values) in a group of subject's responses. In Table 8.2, for the question "IF

Table 8.1. FOU data for the nine-word codebook. All numerical values are from Table 3.6. Each UMF and LMF is represented as a trapezoid (see Fig. 4.5). The fifth parameter for the LMF is its height.

Word	UMF	LMF	Centroid	Center of centroid
1. None to very little	[0, 0, 0.14, 1.97]	[0, 0, 0.05, 0.66, 1]	[0.22, 0.73]	0.48
2. A bit	[0.59, 1.50, 2.00, 3.41]	[0.79, 1.68, 1.68, 2.21, 0.74]	[1.42, 2.08]	1.75
3. Somewhat small	[0.59, 2.00, 3.25, 4.41]	[2.29, 2.70, 2.70, 3.21, 0.42]	[1.76, 3.43]	2.59
4. Some	[1.28, 3.50, 5.50, 7.83]	[3.79, 4.41, 4.41, 4.91, 0.36]	[2.87, 6.13]	4.50
5. Moderate amount	[2.59, 4.00, 5.50, 7.62]	[4.29, 4.75, 4.75, 5.21, 0.38]	[3.74, 6.16]	4.95
6. Good amount	[3.38, 5.50, 7.50, 9.62]	[5.79, 6.50, 6.50, 7.21, 0.41]	[5.11, 7.89]	6.50
7. Considerable amount	[4.38, 6.50, 8.25, 9.62]	[7.19, 7.58, 0.37, 8.21]	[5.97, 8.52]	7.25
8. Large	[5.98, 7.75, 8.60, 9.52]	[8.03, 8.37, 0.57, 9.17]	[7.50, 8.75]	8.13
9. Maximum amount	[8.68, 9.91, 10, 10]	[9.61, 9.97, 10, 10, 1]	[9.50, 9.87]	9.68

Table 8.2. Histogram of survey responses for single-antecedent rules between indicator x_1 = touching level and consequent y = flirtation level. Entries denote the number of respondents out of 47 that chose the consequent

	Flirtation				
Touching	NVL	S	MOA	LA	MAA
1. NVL	42	3	2	0	0
2. S	33	12	0	2	0
3. MOA	12	16	15	3	1
4. LA	3	6	11	25	2
5. MAA	3	6	8	22	8

Source: Adapted from Mendel, 2001; © 2001, Prentice-Hall.

there is some touching, THEN there is _____ flirtation," three different consequents were obtained: *none to very little, some,* and *large.* Observe that 33 respondents selected *none to very little,* 12 selected *some,* only two selected *large,* and no respondent selected *moderate amount* between *some* and *large;* hence, a gap exists between *some* and *large.* Let G_1 = {*none to very little, some*} and G_2 = {*large*}. Because G_1 has more responses than G_2, it is passed to the next step of data preprocessing and G_2 is discarded. The remaining responses after bad data processing are shown in the second row of Table 8.5.

8.2.3.2 *Outlier Processing.* Outlier processing uses a Box and Whisker test [Walpole et al. (2007)]. As explained in Chapter 3, outliers are points that are unusually too large or too small. A Box and Whisker test is usually stated in terms of first and third quartiles and an interquartile range. The first and third quartiles, $Q(0.25)$ and $Q(0.75)$, contain 25% and 75% of the data, respectively. The interquartile range, *IQR,* is the difference between the third and first quartiles; hence, *IQR* contains 50% of the data between the first and third quartiles. Any datum that is more than 1.5 IQR above the third quartile or more than 1.5 *IQR* below the first quartile is considered to be an outlier [Walpole et al. (2007)].

Table 8.3. Histogram of survey responses for single-antecedent rules between indicator x_2 = eye contact level and consequent y = flirtation level. Entries denote the number of respondents out of 47 that chose the consequent

	Flirtation				
Eye contact	NVL	S	MOA	LA	MAA
1. NVL	36	7	4	0	0
2. S	26	17	4	0	0
3. MOA	2	16	27	2	0
4. LA	1	3	11	22	10
5. MAA	0	3	7	17	20

Source: Adapted from Mendel, 2001; © 2001, Prentice-Hall.

Table 8.4. Histogram of survey responses for two-antecedent rules between indicators $x_1 =$ touching and $x_2 =$ eye contact, and consequent $y =$ flirtation level

Touching/Eye contact	Flirtation[a]				
	NVL	S	MOA	LA	MAA
1. NVL/NVL	38	7	2	0	0
2. NVL/S	33	11	3	0	0
3. NVL/MOA	6	21	16	4	0
4. NVL/LA	0	12	26	8	1
5. NVL/MAA	0	9	16	19	3
6. S/NVL	31	11	4	1	0
7. S/S	17	23	7	0	0
8. S/MOA	0	19	19	8	1
9. S/LA	1	8	23	13	2
10. S/MAA	0	7	17	21	2
11. MOA/NVL	7	23	16	1	0
12. MOA/S	5	22	20	0	0
13. MOA/MOA	2	7	22	15	1
14. MOA/LA	1	4	13	17	12
15. MOA/MAA	0	4	12	24	7
16. LA/NVL	7	13	21	6	0
17. LA/S	3	11	23	10	0
18. LA/MOA	0	3	18	18	8
19. LA/LA	0	1	9	17	20
20. LA/MAA	1	2	6	11	27
21. MAA/NVL	2	16	18	11	0
22. MAA/S	2	9	22	13	1
23. MAA/MOA	0	3	15	18	11
24. MAA/LA	0	1	7	17	22
25. MAA/MAA	0	2	3	12	30

[a]Entries denote the number of respondents out of 47 that chose the consequent (adapted from Mendel, 2001, © 2001, Prentice-Hall).

Rule consequents are words modeled by IT2 FSs; hence, the Box and Whisker test cannot be directly applied to them. In our approach, the Box and Whisker test is applied to the set of centers of centroids formed by the centers of centroids of the rule consequents. Focusing again on the rule in Table 8.5, the centers of centroids of the consequent IT2 FSs *NVL, S, MOA, LA,* and *MAA* are first computed (see the last column of Table 8.1), and are 0.48, 4.50, 4.95, 8.13, and 9.68, respectively. Then the set of centers of centroids is

$$\{\underbrace{0.48, \cdots, 0.48}_{33}, \underbrace{4.50, \cdots, 4.50}_{12}\} \tag{8.1}$$

where each center of centroid is repeated a certain number of times according to the number of respondents in Table 8.2. The Box and Whisker test is then applied to this crisp set, where $Q(0.25) = 0.48$, $Q(0.75) = 4.50$, and $1.5 \, IQR = 6.03$. For Rule 2, no data are removed in this step. On the other hand, for Rule 1, the three responses to *some* and the two responses to *moderate amount* are removed.

8.2.3.3 *Tolerance Limit Processing.* Let m and σ be the mean and standard deviation of the remaining histogram data after outlier processing. If a datum lies in the tolerance interval $[m - k\sigma, m + k\sigma]$, then it is accepted; otherwise, it is rejected [Walpole et al. (2007)]. k is determined such that one is 95% confident that the given limits contain at least 95% of the available data (see also Section 3.3.2, especially Table 3.2).

For the rule in Table 8.5, tolerance limit processing is performed on the set of centers of centroids in equation (8.1), for which $m = 1.55$, $\sigma = 1.80$, and $k = 2.41$. No word is removed for this particular example; so, two consequents, *none to very little* and *some,* are accepted for this rule.

The final preprocessed responses for the histograms in Tables 8.2, 8.3, and 8.4 are given in Tables 8.6, 8.7, and 8.8, respectively. Comparing each pair of tables, observe that most responses have been preserved.

8.2.4 Rule Base Generation

Observe from Tables 8.6, 8.7, and 8.8 that the survey and data preprocessing lead to rule-consequent histograms, but how the histograms should be used is an open question. In Mendel (2001), three possibilities were proposed:

1. Keep the response chosen by the largest number of respondents.
2. Find a weighted average of the rule consequents for each rule.
3. Preserve the distributions of the expert responses for each rule.

Clearly, the disadvantage of keeping the response chosen by the largest number of respondents is that this ignores all the other responses. The second method was studied in detail in Mendel (2001). Using that method, when T1 FSs were used [see Chapter 5 of Mendel (2001)], the consequent for each rule was a crisp number, c, where

$$c = \frac{\sum_{m=1}^{5} c_m \, w_m}{\sum_{m=1}^{5} w_m} \tag{8.2}$$

Table 8.5. Data preprocessing results for the 47 responses to the question "IF there is some touching, THEN there is _____ flirtation"

Number of responses	NVL	S	MOA	LA	MAA
Before preprocessing	33	12	0	2	0
After bad data processing	33	12	0	0	0
After outlier processing	33	12	0	0	0
After tolerance limit processing	33	12	0	0	0

Table 8.6. Preprocessed histograms of Table 8.2

Touching	Flirtation				
	NVL	S	MOA	LA	MAA
1. NVL	42	0	0	0	0
2. S	33	12	0	0	0
3. MOA	12	16	15	3	0
4. LA	0	6	11	25	2
5. MAA	0	6	8	22	8

in which c_m is the centroid [Mendel (2001)] of the mth T1 consequent FS, and w_m is the number of respondents for the mth consequent. When IT2 FSs were used [see Chapter 10 of Mendel (2001)], the consequent for each rule was an interval, C, where

$$C = \frac{\sum_{m=1}^{5} C_m w_m}{\sum_{m=1}^{5} w_m} \tag{8.3}$$

in which C_m is the centroid of the mth IT2 consequent FS.

The disadvantages of using equations (8.2) or (8.3) are: (1) there is information lost when converting the T1 or IT2 consequent FSs into their centroids, and (2) it is difficult to describe the aggregated rule consequents (c or C) linguistically.

Our approach is to preserve the distributions of the expert responses for each rule by using a different weighted average to obtain the rule consequents, as illustrated by the following example.

Example 8.1. Observe from Table 8.6 that when the antecedent is *some* (S) there are two valid consequents, so that the following two rules will be fired:

R_1^2: If touching is *some*, then flirtation is *none to very little*.
R_2^2: If touching is *some*, then flirtation is *some*.

These two rules should not be considered of equal importance because they have been selected by different numbers of respondents. An intuitive way to handle this

Table 8.7. Preprocessed histograms of Table 8.3

Eye contact	Flirtation				
	NVL	S	MOA	LA	MAA
1. NVL	36	0	0	0	0
2. S	26	17	4	0	0
3. MOA	0	16	27	0	0
4. LA	0	3	11	22	10
5. MAA	0	0	0	17	20

Table 8.8. Preprocessed histograms of Table 8.4

Touching/Eye contact	Flirtation				
	NVL	S	MOA	LA	MAA
1. NVL/NVL	38	0	0	0	0
2. NVL/S	33	11	3	0	0
3. NVL/MOA	0	21	16	0	0
4. NVL/LA	0	12	28	0	0
5. NVL/MAA	0	9	16	19	3
6. S/NVL	31	11	4	1	0
7. S/S	17	23	7	0	0
8. S/MOA	0	19	19	0	0
9. S/LA	0	8	23	13	2
10. S/MAA	0	7	17	21	2
11. MOA/NVL	0	23	16	0	0
12. MOA/S	0	22	20	0	0
13. MOA/MOA	0	7	22	15	1
14. MOA/LA	0	4	13	17	12
15. MOA/MAA	0	4	12	24	7
16. LA/NVL	0	13	21	0	0
17. LA/S	0	11	23	0	0
18. LA/MOA	0	3	18	18	8
19. LA/LA	0	0	0	17	20
20. LA/MAA	0	0	0	11	27
21. MAA/NVL	0	16	18	11	0
22. MAA/S	0	9	22	13	1
23. MAA/MOA	0	3	15	18	11
24. MAA/LA	0	0	0	17	22
25. MAA/MAA	0	0	0	12	30

is to assign weights to the two rules, where the weights are proportional to the number of responses, for example, the weight for R_1^2 is $33/45 = 0.73$, and the weight for R_2^2 is $12/45 = 0.27$. The aggregated consequent $\tilde{Y}^2$ for R_1^2 and R_2^2 is

$$\tilde{Y}^2 = \frac{33 NVL + 12 S}{33 + 12} \tag{8.4}$$

$\tilde{Y}^2$ is computed by the algorithm introduced in Section 5.6. The result is shown in Fig. 8.2.

Without loss of generality, assume there are N different combinations of antecedents (e.g., $N = 5$ for the single-antecedent rules in Tables 8.6 and 8.7, and $N = 25$ for the two-antecedent rules in Table 8.8), and each combination has M possible different consequents (e.g., $M = 5$ for the rules in Tables 8.6–8.8); hence, there can be as many as MN rules. Denote the mth consequent of the ith combination of the

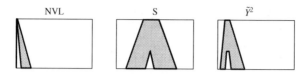

Figure 8.2. $\tilde{Y}^2$ obtained by aggregating the consequents of R_1^2 (NVL) and R_2^2 (S).

antecedents as $\tilde{Y}_m^i$ ($m = 1, 2, \ldots, M, i = 1, 2, \ldots, N$), and the number of responses to $\tilde{Y}_m^i$ as w_m^i. For each i, all M $\tilde{Y}_m^i$ can be combined first into a single IT2 FS by a special LWA (computed by the algorithm introduced in Section 5.6):

$$\tilde{Y}^i = \frac{\sum_{m=1}^{M} w_m^i \tilde{Y}_m^i}{\sum_{m=1}^{M} w_m^i} \tag{8.5}$$

$\tilde{Y}^i$ then acts as the (new) consequent for the ith rule. By doing this, the distribution of the expert responses has been preserved for each rule. Examples of $\tilde{Y}^i$ for single-antecedent and two-antecedent rules are depicted in Figs. 8.4(a), 8.6(a), and 8.7.

8.2.5 Computing the Output of the SJA

The previous section described how a simplified rulebase can be generated from a survey. In this subsection, we explain how PR is used to compute an output of the SJA for a new input $\tilde{X}$.

First consider single-antecedent rules of the form

$$R^i : \text{IF } x \text{ is } \tilde{F}^i, \text{ THEN } y \text{ is } \tilde{Y}^i \qquad i = 1, \ldots, N \tag{8.6}$$

where $\tilde{Y}^i$ are computed by equation (8.5). In PR, the Jaccard similarity measure (Section 6.4) is used to compute the firing levels of the rules ($i = 1, \ldots, N$),

$$f^i = sm_j(\tilde{X}, \tilde{F}^i) = \frac{\int_X \min(\overline{X}(x), \overline{F}^i(x))dx + \int_X \min(\underline{X}(x), \underline{F}^i(x))dx}{\int_X \max(\overline{X}(x), \overline{F}^i(x))dx + \int_X \max(\underline{X}(x), \underline{F}^i(x))dx} \tag{8.7}$$

where $\overline{X}$ and $\overline{F}^i$ are the UMFs of $\tilde{X}$ and $\tilde{F}^i$, and $\underline{X}$ and $\underline{F}^i$ are the corresponding LMFs. Once f^i are computed, the output FOU of the SJA is computed as

$$\tilde{Y}_C = \frac{\sum_{i=1}^{N} f^i \tilde{Y}^i}{\sum_{i=1}^{N} f^i} \tag{8.8}$$

The subscript C in $\tilde{Y}_C$ stands for *consensus* because $\tilde{Y}_C$ is obtained by aggregating the survey results from a population of people, and the resulting SJA is called a *consensus SJA*. Because only the nine words in Fig. 8.1 are used in the SJAs, the simi-

Table 8.9. Similarities among the nine words used in the SJAs. Taken from Table 4.1.

	NVL	AB	SS	S	MOA	GA	CA	LA	MAA
None to very little (NVL)	1	0.11	0.08	0.01	0	0	0	0	0
A bit (AB)	0.11	1	0.40	0.10	0.02	0	0	0	0
Somewhat small (SS)	0.08	0.40	1	0.25	0.12	0.02	0	0	0
Some (S)	0.01	0.10	0.25	1	0.73	0.33	0.20	0.06	0
Moderate amount (MOA)	0	0.02	0.12	0.73	1	0.37	0.21	0.06	0
Good amount (GA)	0	0	0.02	0.33	0.37	1	0.63	0.32	0.03
Considerable amount (CA)	0	0	0	0.20	0.21	0.63	1	0.50	0.04
Large (LA)	0	0	0	0.06	0.06	0.32	0.50	1	0.05
Maximum amount (MAA)	0	0	0	0	0	0.03	0.04	0.05	1

larities among them can be precomputed, and f^i in equation (8.8) can be retrieved from Table 8.9. Finally, $\tilde{Y}_C$ is mapped into a word in the Fig. 8.1 vocabulary also using the Jaccard similarity measure.[3]

Next consider two-antecedent rules of the form

$$R^i : \text{ IF } x_1 \text{ is } \tilde{F}_1^i \text{ and } x_2 \text{ is } \tilde{F}_2^i, \text{ THEN } y \text{ is } \tilde{Y}^i \qquad i = 1, \ldots, N \qquad (8.9)$$

The firing levels are computed as

$$f^i = sm_j(\tilde{X}_1, \tilde{F}_1^i) \star sm_j(\tilde{X}_2, \tilde{F}_2^i) \qquad i = 1, \ldots, N \qquad (8.10)$$

where in this book $\star$ is the minimum t-norm. Again, $sm_j(\tilde{X}_1, \tilde{F}_1^i)$ and $sm_j(\tilde{X}_2, \tilde{F}_2^i)$ can be obtained from the precomputed similarities in Table 8.9. When all f^i are obtained, the output FOU is computed again using equation (8.8) and mapped back into a word in the Fig. 8.1 vocabulary using the Jaccard similarity measure.

8.3   USING AN SJA

As mentioned above [see equation (8.8)], each SJA that is designed from a survey is referred to as a *consensus SJA*, because it is obtained by using survey results from a group of people. Figure 8.3 depicts[4] one way to use an SJA to advise (counsel) an individual about a social judgment. An individual is given a questionnaire similar to the one used in Step 6 of the knowledge mining process, and his/her responses are obtained for all the words in the vocabulary. These responses can then be compared with the outputs of the consensus SJA. If some or all of the individual's responses are "far" from those of the consensus SJA, then some action could be taken to sen-

---

[3]The Jaccard similarity measure is used here instead of the average subsethood (see Section 4.4) because $\tilde{Y}_C$ and the mapped word belong to the same domain (vocabulary), that is, both of them represent the level of flirtation.

[4]The material in this paragraph is similar to Section 4.3.4 in Mendel (2001).

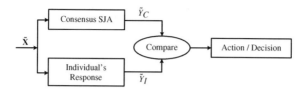

Figure 8.3. One way to use the SJA for a social judgment.

sitize the individual about these differences. More details about this are give in this section.

8.3.1 Single-Antecedent Rules: Touching and Flirtation

In this subsection, the single-antecedent SJA, which describes the relationship between touching and flirtation, is studied; it is denoted SJA_1. A consensus SJA_1 is constructed from Table 8.6, and is compared with an individual SJA.

When equation (8.5) is used to combine the different responses for each antecedent into a single consequent for the rule data in Table 8.6, one obtains the rule consequents depicted in Fig. 8.4(a). As a comparison, the rule consequents obtained from the original rule data in Table 8.2 are depicted in Fig. 8.4(b). Observe that:

1. The consequent for *none to very little* (NVL) touching is a left-shoulder FOU in Fig. 8.4(a), whereas it is an interior FOU in Fig. 8.4(b). The former seems more reasonable to us.

2. The consequent for *some* (S) touching in Fig. 8.4(a) is similar to that in Fig. 8.4(b), except that it is shifted a little to the left. This is because the two largest responses [*large* (LA)] in Table 8.2 are removed in preprocessing.

3. The consequent for *moderate amount* (MOA) touching in Fig. 8.4(a) is similar to that in Fig. 8.4(b), except that it is shifted a little to the left. This is be-

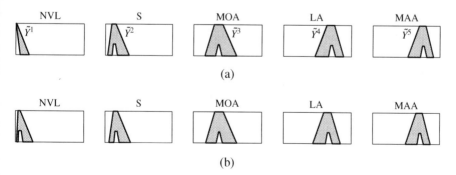

Figure 8.4. Flirtation-level consequents of the five rules for the single-antecedent *touching* SJA_1: (a) with data preprocessing and (b) without data preprocessing. The level of touching is indicated at the top of each figure.

cause the largest response [*maximum amount* (MAA)] in Table 8.2 is removed in preprocessing.

4. The consequent for *large* (LA) is similar to that in Fig. 8.4(b), except that it is shifted a little to the right. This is because the three smallest responses [*none to very little* (NVL)] in Table 8.2 are removed in preprocessing.

5. The consequent for *maximum amount* (MAA) is similar to those in Fig. 8.4(b), except that it is shifted a little to the right. This is because the three smallest responses [*none to very little* (NVL)] in Table 8.2 are removed in preprocessing.

The consequents $\tilde{Y}_1$–$\tilde{Y}_5$ shown in Fig. 8.4(a) are used in the rest of this section for the consensus SJA1. Its five-rule rule base is

R^1: If touching is *NVL*, then flirtation is $\tilde{Y}^1$.
R^2: If touching is *S*, then flirtation is $\tilde{Y}^2$.
R^3: If touching is *MOA*, then flirtation is $\tilde{Y}^3$.
R^4: If touching is *LA*, then flirtation is $\tilde{Y}^4$.
R^5: If touching is *MAA*, then flirtation is $\tilde{Y}^5$.

For an input-touching level, the output of SJA_1 can easily be computed by PR, as illustrated by the following example.

Example 8.2. Let observed touching be *considerable amount* (CA). From the seventh row of Table 8.9 the following firing levels of the five rules are obtained:

$f^1 = sm_J(CA, NVL) = 0$
$f^2 = sm_J(CA, S) = 0.20$
$f^3 = sm_J(CA, MOA) = 0.21$
$f^4 = sm_J(CA, LA) = 0.50$
$f^5 = sm_J(CA, MAA) = 0.04$

The resulting $\tilde{Y}_C$ computed from equation (8.8) is depicted in Fig. 8.5 as the dashed curve. The similarities between $\tilde{Y}_C$ and the nine words in the Fig. 8.1 vocabulary are computed to be

$sm_J(\tilde{Y}_C, NVL) = 0$ $sm_J(\tilde{Y}_C, AB) = 0$ $sm_J(\tilde{Y}_C, SS) = 0.07$
$sm_J(\tilde{Y}_C, S) = 0.55$ $sm_J(\tilde{Y}_C, MOA) = \mathbf{0.73}$ $sm_J(\tilde{Y}_C, GA) = 0.37$
$sm_J(\tilde{Y}_C, CA) = 0.19$ $sm_J(\tilde{Y}_C, LA) = 0.04$ $sm_J(\tilde{Y}_C, MAA) = 0$

Because $\tilde{Y}_C$ and *MOA* have the largest similarity, $\tilde{Y}_C$ is mapped into the word *MOA*.

When PR is used to combine the rules and any of the nine words in Fig. 8.1 are used as inputs, the outputs of the consensus SJA_1 are mapped to words shown in the

MOA

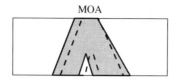

Figure 8.5. $\tilde{Y}_C$ (dashed curve) and the mapped word (MOA, solid curve) when the input is *considerable amount* of touching.

second column of Table 8.10. Observe that, generally, the flirtation level increases as touching increases, as one would expect.

Next, assume that for the nine codebook words an individual gives the responses[5] shown in the third column of Table 8.10. Observe that this individual's responses are generally the same as or higher than $\tilde{Y}_C$. This means that this individual may overreact to touching.

The similarities between the consensus outputs $\tilde{Y}_C$ and the individual's responses $\tilde{Y}_I$ are shown in the fourth column of Table 8.10. $\tilde{Y}_I$ and $\tilde{Y}_C$ are said to be "significantly different" if $sm_J(\tilde{Y}_C, \tilde{Y}_I)$ is smaller than a threshold θ. Let $\theta = 0.5$. Then, except for the first two inputs (NVL and AB), $\tilde{Y}_I$ and $\tilde{Y}_C$ are significantly different. Some action could be taken to sensitize the individual about these differences.

8.3.2 Single-Antecedent Rules: Eye Contact and Flirtation

In this subsection, another single-antecedent SJA, which describes the relationship between eye contact and flirtation, is studied; it is denoted SJA$_2$. A consensus SJA$_2$ is constructed from Table 8.7 and is compared with an individual SJA.

When equation (8.5) is used to combine the different responses for each antecedent into a single consequent for the rule data in Table 8.7, one obtains the rule consequents depicted in Fig. 8.6(a). As a comparison, the rule consequents obtained from the original rule data in Table 8.3 are depicted in Fig. 8.6(b). The rule consequents for *NVL, MOA, LA,* and *MAA* are different in these two figures. The consequents in Fig. 8.6(a) are used by SJA$_2$.

When PR is used to combine the rules and any of the nine words in Fig. 8.1 are used as inputs, the outputs of the consensus SJA$_2$ are mapped to words shown in the second column of Table 8.11. Observe that generally the flirtation level increases as eye contact increases, as one would expect.

Assume that for the nine codebook words an individual gives the responses shown in the third column of Table 8.11. Observe that this individual's responses are generally the same as or lower than those from the consensus SJA$_2$. This means that this individual may underreact to eye contact.

The similarities between the consensus outputs $\tilde{Y}_C$ and the individual's responses $\tilde{Y}_I$ are shown in the fourth column of Table 8.11. Again, let the threshold be $\theta = 0.5$.

---

[5]The individual is asked the following question for each of the nine codebook words: "If there is (one of the nine codebook words) touching, then what is the level of flirtation?" and the answer must also be a word from the nine-word codebook.

Table 8.10. A comparison between the consensus SJA_1 outputs and an individual's responses

Touching	Flirtation level		
	Consensus ($\tilde{Y}_C$)	Individual ($\tilde{Y}_I$)	Similarity $sm_J(\tilde{Y}_C, \tilde{Y}_I)$
None to very little (NVL)	NVL	NVL	1
A bit (AB)	AB	AB	1
Somewhat small (SS)	AB	SS	0.40
Some (S)	SS	MOA	0.12
Moderate amount (MOA)	SS	MOA	0.12
Good amount (GA)	S	LA	0.06
Considerable amount (CA)	MOA	LA	0.06
Large (LA)	GA	LA	0.32
Maximum amount (MAA)	CA	MAA	0.04

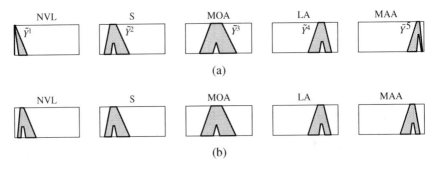

Figure 8.6. Flirtation-level consequents of the five rules for the single-antecedent *eye contact* SJA_2: (a) with data preprocessing and (b) without data preprocessing. The level of eye contact is indicated at the top of each figure.

Table 8.11. A comparison between the consensus SJA_2 outputs and an individual's responses

Eye contact	Flirtation level		
	Consensus ($\tilde{Y}_C$)	Individual ($\tilde{Y}_I$)	Similarity $sm_J(\tilde{Y}_C, \tilde{Y}_I)$
None to very little (NVL)	NVL	NVL	1
A bit (AB)	AB	NVL	0.11
Somewhat small (SS)	SS	AB	0.40
Some (S)	S	AB	0.10
Moderate amount (MOA)	S	SS	0.25
Good amount (GA)	MOA	S	0.73
Considerable amount (CA)	GA	MOA	0.37
Large (LA)	CA	GA	0.63
Maximum amount (MAA)	LA	GA	0.32

Then, when eye contact is $\{AB, SS, S, MOA, CA, MAA\}$, $\tilde{Y}_I$ and $\tilde{Y}_C$ are significantly different. Some action could be taken to sensitize the individual about these differences.

8.3.3 Two-Antecedent Rules: Touching/Eye Contact and Flirtation

The previous two subsections have considered single-antecedent rules. This subsection considers two-antecedent (touching and eye contact) rules, whose corresponding SJA is denoted SJA_3.

When equation (8.5) is used to combine the different responses for each pair of antecedents into a single consequent for the rule data in Table 8.8, one obtains the 25 rule consequents $\tilde{Y}^{1,1}$–$\tilde{Y}^{5,5}$ depicted in Fig. 8.7. Observe that the rule consequent becomes larger (i.e., moves towards the right in the [0,10] interval) as either input increases, which is intuitive.

The 25-rule rulebase of SJA_3 is

$R^{1,1}$: IF touching is *NVL* and eye contact is *NVL*, THEN flirtation is $\tilde{Y}^{1,1}$.

$\vdots$

$R^{1,5}$: IF touching is *NVL* and eye contact is *MAA*, THEN flirtation is $\tilde{Y}^{1,5}$.

$\vdots$

$R^{5,1}$: IF touching is *MAA* and eye contact is *NVL*, THEN flirtation is $\tilde{Y}^{5,1}$.

$\vdots$

$R^{5,5}$: IF touching is *MAA* and eye contact is *MAA*, THEN flirtation is $\tilde{Y}^{5,5}$.

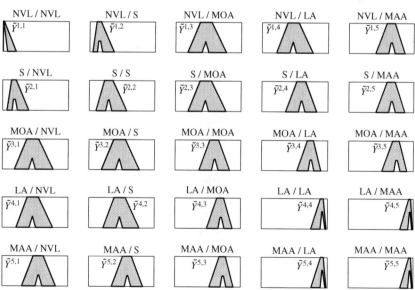

Figure 8.7. Flirtation-level consequents of the 25 rules for the two-antecedent consensus SJA_3 with data preprocessing. The levels of touching and eye contact are indicated at the top of each figure.

For input touching and eye contact levels, the output of SJA_3 can easily be computed by PR, as illustrated by the following example.

Example 8.3. Let observed touching be *considerable amount* (CA) and observed eye contact be *a bit* (AB). Only 12 of the possible 25 firing levels are nonzero, and they are obtained from the seventh and the second rows of Table 8.9, as

$$f^{2,1} = \min\{sm_f(CA, S), sm_f(AB, NVL)\} = \min(0.20, 0.11) = 0.11$$
$$f^{2,2} = \min\{sm_f(CA, S), sm_f(AB, S)\} = \min(0.20, 0.10) = 0.10$$
$$f^{2,3} = \min\{sm_f(CA, S), sm_f(AB, MOA)\} = \min(0.20, 0.02) = 0.02$$
$$f^{3,1} = \min\{sm_f(CA, MOA), sm_f(AB, NVL)\} = \min(0.21, 0.11) = 0.11$$
$$f^{3,2} = \min\{sm_f(CA, MOA), sm_f(AB, S)\} = \min(0.21, 0.10) = 0.10$$
$$f^{3,3} = \min\{sm_f(CA, MOA), sm_f(AB, MOA)\} = \min(0.21, 0.02) = 0.02$$
$$f^{4,1} = \min\{sm_f(CA, LA), sm_f(AB, NVL)\} = \min(0.50, 0.11) = 0.11$$
$$f^{4,2} = \min\{sm_f(CA, LA), sm_f(AB, S)\} = \min(0.50, 0.10) = 0.10$$
$$f^{4,3} = \min\{sm_f(CA, LA), sm_f(AB, MOA)\} = \min(0.50, 0.02) = 0.02$$
$$f^{5,1} = \min\{sm_f(CA, MAA), sm_f(AB, NVL)\} = \min(0.04, 0.11) = 0.04$$
$$f^{5,2} = \min\{sm_f(CA, MAA), sm_f(AB, S)\} = \min(0.04, 0.10) = 0.04$$
$$f^{5,3} = \min\{sm_f(CA, MAA), sm_f(AB, MOA)\} = \min(0.04, 0.02) = 0.02$$

The resulting $\tilde{Y}_C$ computed from equation (8.8) is depicted in Fig. 8.8 as the dashed curve. The similarities between $\tilde{Y}_C$ and the nine words in the Fig. 8.1 vocabulary are computed to be

$sm_f(\tilde{Y}_C, NVL) = 0$	$sm_f(\tilde{Y}_C, AB) = 0.06$	$sm_f(\tilde{Y}_C, SS) = 0.21$
$sm_f(\tilde{Y}_C, S) = \mathbf{0.76}$	$sm_f(\tilde{Y}_C, MOA) = 0.68$	$sm_f(\tilde{Y}_C, GA) = 0.26$
$sm_f(\tilde{Y}_C, CA) = 0.14$	$sm_f(\tilde{Y}_C, LA) = 0.03$	$sm_f(\tilde{Y}_C, MAA) = 0$

Because $\tilde{Y}_C$ and *some* (S) have the largest similarity, $\tilde{Y}_C$ is mapped into the word *some* (S).

When PR is used to combine the rules, and any pair of the nine words in Fig. 8.1 are used as observed inputs for touching and eye contact, there are a total of 81 combinations of these two inputs. The 81 SJA outputs and the words that are most

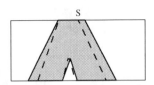

Figure 8.8. $\tilde{Y}_C$ (dashed curve) and the mapped word (S, solid curve) when touching is *considerable amount* (CA) and eye contact is *a bit* (AB).

similar to them are shown in Fig. 8.9. Observe that, generally, the flirtation level increases as either one or both inputs increase, as one would expect.

Once the consensus SJA_3 is constructed, one can again check an individual's responses against it, as he or she did for SJA_1 and SJA_2. The procedures are quite similar, so they are not repeated here.

8.3.4 On Multiple Indicators

Generally, people have difficulties in answering questions with more than two antecedents. So, in the survey each rule consists of only one or two antecedents; however, in practice an individual may observe one indicator or more than one indicators. An interesting problem is how to deduce the output for multiple antecedents sing rule bases consisting of only one or two antecedents.

For the sake of this discussion, assume there are four indicators of flirtation, *touching, eye contact, acting witty,* and *primping,* and that the following ten SJAs have been created:

SJA_1: IF *touching* is _____, THEN flirtation is _____.

SJA_2: IF *eye contact* is _____, THEN flirtation is _____.

SJA_3: IF *acting witty* is _____, THEN flirtation is _____.

SJA_4: IF *primping* is _____, THEN flirtation is _____.

SJA_5: IF *touching* is _____ and *eye contact* is _____, THEN flirtation is _____.

SJA_6: IF *touching* is _____ and *acting witty* is _____, THEN flirtation is _____.

SJA_7: IF *touching* is _____ and *primping* is _____, THEN flirtation is _____.

SJA_8: IF *eye contact* is _____ and *acting witty* is _____, THEN flirtation is _____.

SJA_9: IF *eye contact* is _____ and *primping* is _____, THEN flirtation is _____.

SJA_{10}: IF *acting witty* is _____ and *primping* is _____, THEN flirtation is _____.

These ten SJAs can be used as follows:

1. When only one indicator is observed, only one single-antecedent SJA from SJA_1–SJA_4 is activated.
2. When only two indicators are observed, only one two-antecedent SJA from SJA_5–SJA_{10} is activated.
3. When more than two indicators are observed, the output is computed by aggregating the outputs of the activated two-antecedent SJAs.[6] For example, when the observed indicators are *touching, eye contact,* and *primping,* three

---

[6]Some of the four single-antecedent SJAs, SJA_1–SJA_4, are also fired; however, they are not used because they do not fit the inputs as well as two-antecedent SJAs, since the latter account for the correlation between two antecedents, whereas the former do not.

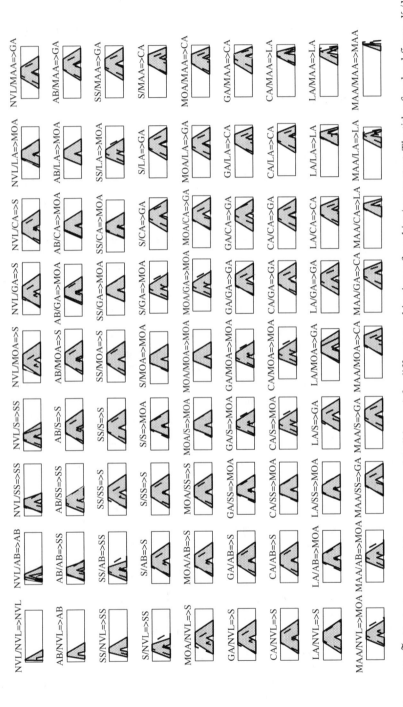

Figure 8.9. $\widetilde{Y}_C$ (dashed curve) and the mapped word (solid curve) for different combinations of touching/eye contact. The title of each subfigure, X_1/X_2 $\Rightarrow Y$ means that "when touching is X_1 and eye contact is X_2, the flirtation level is Y." Scan this figure horizontally from left to right to see the effect of varying eye contact on flirtation. Scan it vertically from top to bottom to see the effect of varying touching on flirtation. Scan it diagonally from top-left to bottom-right to see the simultaneous effects of varying eye contact and touching on flirtation.

two-antecedent SJAs—SJA_5, SJA_7, and SJA_9—are activated, and each one gives a flirtation level. The final output is some kind of aggregation of the results from these three SJAs. There are different aggregation operators, such as mean, linguistic weighted average, and maximum. An intuitive approach is to survey the subjects about the relative importance of the four indicators and then determine the linguistic relative importance of SJA_5–SJA_{10}. These relative importance words can then be used as the weights for SJA_5–SJA_{10}, and the final flirtation level can then be computed by a linguistic weighted average.

A diagram of the proposed SJA architecture for different numbers of indicators is shown in Fig. 8.10.

8.3.5 On First and Succeeding Encounters

In a social judgment situation, one may have to distinguish between a "first encounter" and "succeeding encounters." In a first encounter one has no memory about the social judgment for an individual; for example, when A meets B for the first time in a flirtation situation, A has no memory of B's "flirtation status." When A meets B in succeeding flirtation situations A brings his memory of B's previous flirtation status into his social judgment. So, different SJAs may be used to distinguish between a first encounter and succeeding encounters; however, exactly how to do this is an open question.

8.4 DISCUSSION

A prevailing paradigm for examining social judgments would be to examine the influence of various factors on the variable of interest using linear approaches, for example, linear regression. Unfortunately, perceptions regarding the variable of interest may not be linear but, rather, step-like. A linear model is unable to capture such nonlinear changes, whereas the Per-C is able to do this because of its nonlinear nature. In summary, the main differences between linear approaches and an SJA are:

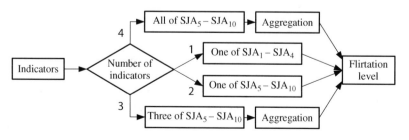

Figure 8.10. An SJA architecture for one to four indicators.

1. The former are determined only from numerical data (e.g., regression coefficients are fitted to numerical data) whereas the SJA is determined from linguistic information, that is, a collection of if–then rules that are provided by people.

2. The rules, when properly collected, convey the details of a *nonlinear* relationship between the antecedents of the rule and the consequent of the rule.

3. An SJA can directly quantify a linguistic rule and can provide a linguistic output; a regression model cannot do this.

4. Regression models can, however, include nonlinear regressors (e.g., interaction terms), which make them also nonlinear functions of their inputs. However, the structure of the nonlinearities in the SJA is not prespecified, as it must be for a regression model; it is a direct result of the mathematics of the SJA.

5. An SJA is a *variable structure model,* in that it simultaneously provides excellent local and global approximations to social judgments, whereas a regression model can only provide global approximations to social judgments. By "variable structure model" is meant that only a (usually) small subset of the rules are fired for a given set of inputs, and when the inputs change, so does the subset of fired rules, and this happens automatically because of the mathematics of the SJA.

6. The way in which uncertainty is dealt with. Typically, in a linear regression model individuals are forced to translate their assessment into absolute numbers, for example, 1, 2, 3, 4. In contrast a person can interact with the SJA using normal linguistic phrases, for example, about eye contact (one of the indicators of flirtation), such as "eye contact is moderate."

7. Finally, if determining the level of flirtation were easy, we would all be experts; but it is not, and we are not. In fact, many times we get "mixed signals." Fuzzy logic leads to an explanation and potential resolution of "mixed signals," through the simultaneous firing of more than one rule, each of which may have a different consequent. So the SJA also provides us with *insight* into why determining whether or not we are being flirted with is often difficult. The same should also be true for other social judgments. We do not believe that this is possible using a regression model.

8.5 CONCLUSIONS

An application of the Per-C to a social judgment has been introduced in this chapter. First, histograms are obtained from surveys. Three preprocessing steps are then used to remove bad responses and outliers. Because for each combination of inputs there may be several different consequents, PR is used to combine these consequents into a single one; hence, the rule base is greatly simplified. PR is also used to infer the output FOU for input words that are not used in the survey. Finally, the output FOU is mapped back into a word in the codebook using the Jaccard similarity measure. So, from a user's point of view, he or she is interacting with the Per-C using only words from a vocabulary.

The techniques introduced in this chapter should be applicable to many situations in which rule-based decision making is needed, and inputs and outputs are words.

REFERENCES

R. L. Gorsuch, *Factor Analysis.* Hillsdale, NJ: Lawrence Erlbaum, 1983.

L. B. Koeppel, Y. Montagne-Miller, D. O'Hair, and M. J. Cody, "Friendly? flirting? wrong?" in P. J. Kalbfleisch (Ed.), *Interpersonal communication: Evolving interpersonal relationship,* Hillsdale, NJ: Lawrence Erlbaum, 1993, pp. 13–32.

B. Luscombe, "Why we flirt," *Time Magazine,* vol. 171, no. 4, pp. 62–65, 2008.

J. M. Mendel, *Uncertain Rule-Based Fuzzy Logic Systems: Introduction and New Directions.* Upper Saddle River, NJ: Prentice-Hall, 2001.

J. M. Mendel, S. Murphy, L. C. Miller, M. Martin, and N. Karnik, "The fuzzy logic advisor for social judgments," in L. A. Zadeh and J. Kacprzyk (Eds.), *Computing with Words in Information/intelligent Systems,* Physica-Verlag, 1999, pp. 459–483.

T. L. Saaty, *The Analytic Hierarchy Process: Planning, Priority Setting, Resource Allocation.* New York: McGraw-Hill, 1980.

R. W. Walpole, R. H. Myers, A. Myers, and K. Ye, *Probability and Statistics for Engineers and Scientists,* 8th ed. Upper Saddle River, NJ: Prentice-Hall, 2007.

CHAPTER 9

Assisting in Hierarchical Decision Making—Procurement Judgment Advisor (PJA)

9.1 INTRODUCTION

Recall from Chapter 1 that by "hierarchical decision making" is meant decision making by a single individual, group, or organization that is based on comparing the performance of competing alternatives, such as an individual's performance in an athletic, dancing, or cooking competition, a group or individual's proposal for solving a problem or building a product, product selection (e.g., which car should I purchase?), where each alternative is first evaluated or scored (this process may itself involve a hierarchical process involving criteria and subcriteria), after which the evaluations or scores are compared at a higher level to arrive at either a single winning competitor or a subset of winners. What can make this challenging is that the evaluations or scores of the subcriteria and criteria can use numbers, or intervals, or T1 FSs, or even words modeled by IT2 FSs.

This chapter is directed at the following hierarchical multicriteria missile evaluation problem [Mon et al. (1994)]. A contractor has to decide which of three companies is going to get the final mass production contract for the missile. The contractor uses five criteria to base his/her final decision, namely: tactics, technology, maintenance, economy, and advancement. Each of these criteria has some associated technical subcriteria; for example, for tactics the subcriteria are effective range, flight height, flight velocity, reliability, firing accuracy, destruction rate, and kill radius, whereas for economy the subcriteria are system cost, system life, and material limitation.

The contractor creates a performance evaluation table in order to assist in choosing the winning system. Table 9.1 is an example of such a table.[1] Contained within this table are three columns, one for each of the three competing systems. The rows of the table are partitioned into the five criteria, and each of the partitions has additional rows, one for each of its subcriteria. Entries into this table for the three systems are evaluations of the subcriteria. Additionally, weights are assigned to all of

[1]The weights and subcriteria performance evaluation data are the same as in Tables I and II of Chen (1996b).

Copyright © 2010 the Institute of Electrical and Electronics Engineers, Inc.

the subcriteria, because they are not of equal importance. These weights are fuzzy numbers, for example, around seven, around five, and so on. The subcriteria evaluations range from numbers to words.

Somehow, the contractor has to aggregate this disparate information, and this is even more difficult because the five criteria are themselves not of equal importance and have their own fuzzy weights assigned to them. This chapter demonstrates how NWAs can be used to assist the contractor in making a final decision. The result is a *procurement judgment advisor* (PJA).

To begin, Section 9.2 provides a very complete description of the missile evaluation problem. Section 9.3 introduces a Per-C approach for missile evaluation. Section 9.4 provides examples that demonstrate the use and results of Per-C. Section 9.5 summarizes a number of prior approaches that have been taken to this hierarchical decision making problem that use T1 FSs and compares them with Per-C. Section 9.6 draws conclusions. The Appendix summarizes some other hierarchical multicriteria decision making applications in which the Per-C can be used to assist in making a final decision.

9.2 MISSILE EVALUATION PROBLEM STATEMENT

The missile evaluation problem is summarized in Fig. 9.1, a figure that is adopted from [Mon et al. (1994)] where it first appeared. It is very clear from this figure that this is a multicriteria and two-level decision making problem. At the first level, each of the three systems (A, B, and C) is evaluated for its performance on five criteria: tactics, technology, maintenance, economy, and advancement. The lines emanating from each of the systems to these criteria indicate these evaluations, each of which involves a number of important (but not shown) subcriteria and their weighted aggregations that are described below. The second level in this hierarchical decision making problem involves a weighted aggregation of the five criteria for each of the three systems.

Table 9.1, which is a performance evaluation table, summarizes all of the information about this problem. Observe the following:

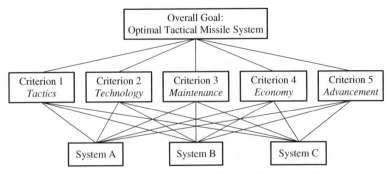

Figure 9.1. Structure of evaluating competing tactical missile systems from three companies [Mon et al. (1994)].

Table 9.1. Performance evaluation table. Criteria with their weights, subcriteria with their weights, and subcriteria performance valuation data for the three systems

Item	Weighting	System A	System B	System C
Criterion 1: Tactics	$\tilde{9}$			
1. Effective range (km)	$\tilde{7}$	43	36	38
2. Flight height (m)	$\tilde{1}$	25	20	23
3. Flight velocity (M. No)	$\tilde{9}$	0.72	0.80	0.75
4. Reliability (%)	$\tilde{9}$	80	83	76
5. Firing accuracy (%)	$\tilde{9}$	67	70	63
6. Destruction rate (%)	$\tilde{7}$	84	88	86
7. Kill radius (m)	$\tilde{6}$	15	12	18
Criterion 2: Technology	$\tilde{3}$			
8. Missile scale (cm) (l × d – span)	$\tilde{4}$	521 × 35 – 135	381 × 34 – 105	445 × 35 – 120
9. Reaction time (min)	$\tilde{9}$	1.2	1.5	1.3
10. Fire rate (round/min)	$\tilde{9}$	0.6	0.6	0.7
11. Antijam (%)	$\tilde{8}$	68	75	70
12. Combat capability	$\tilde{9}$	Very Good	Good	Good
Criterion 3: Maintenance	$\tilde{1}$			
13. Operation condition requirement	$\tilde{5}$	High	Low	Low
14. Safety	$\tilde{6}$	Very Good	Good	Good
15. Defilade[a]	$\tilde{2}$	Good	Very Good	Good
16. Simplicity	$\tilde{3}$	Good	Good	Good
17. Assembly	$\tilde{3}$	Good	Good	Poor
Criterion 4: Economy	$\tilde{5}$			
18. System cost (10,000)	$\tilde{8}$	800	755	785
19. System life (years)	$\tilde{8}$	7	7	5
20. Material limitation	$\tilde{5}$	High	Low	Low
Criterion 5: Advancement	$\tilde{7}$			
21. Modularization	$\tilde{5}$	Average[b]	Good	Average[b]
22. Mobility	$\tilde{7}$	Poor	Very Good	Good
23. Standardization	$\tilde{3}$	Good	Good	Very Good

[a]*Defilade* means to surround by defensive works so as to protect the interior when in danger of being command-ed by an enemy's guns.
[b]The word *general* used in Cheng (1999) has been replaced by the word *average*, because it was not clear to us what *general* meant.

1. The major criteria are not equally weighted, but instead are weighted using fuzzy numbers[2] (T1 FSs, as depicted in Fig. 9.2 and Table 9.2) in the follow-ing order of importance: tactics, advancement, economy, technology, and maintenance. These weightings were established ahead of time by the con-tractor and not by the companies.

[2]It is common practice to use a tilde overmark to denote a fuzzy number that is modeled using a T1 FS. Even though it is also common practice to use such a tilde overmark to denote an IT2 FS, we shall not change this common practice for a fuzzy number in this chapter. Instead, we shall indicate in the text when the fuzzy number $\tilde{n}$ is modeled either as a T1 FS or as an IT2 FS.

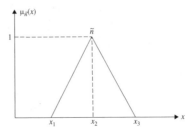

Figure 9.2. Membership function (MF) for a fuzzy number $\tilde{n}$ (see Table 9.2).

2. *Tactics* has seven subcriteria, *technology* and *maintenance* each have five subcriteria, and *economy* and *advancement* each have three subcriteria; hence, there are 23 subcriteria all of which were established ahead of time by the contractor and not by the companies.

3. All of the subcriteria are weighted using fuzzy numbers. These weightings have also been established ahead of time by the contractor and not by the companies, and have been established separately within each of the five criteria and not simultaneously across all of the 23 subcriteria.

4. The performance evaluations for all 23 subcriteria are shown for the three systems, and are either numbers or words. It is assumed that each company designed, built, and tested a small number of its missiles after which they were able to fill in the numerical performance scores. It is not clear how the linguistic scores were obtained, so it is speculated that the contractor provided them based on other evidence and perhaps on some subjective rules.

5. How to aggregate all of this data seems like a daunting task, especially since it involves numbers, fuzzy numbers for the weights, and words.

6. Finally, we believe there should be an uncertainty band for each numerical score because the numbers correspond to measurements of physical properties obtained from an ensemble of test missiles. Those bands have not been

Table 9.2. Fuzzy numbers and their corresponding MFs

Fuzzy numbers[a]	(x_1, x_2, x_3)
$\tilde{1}$	$(1, 1, 2)$
$\tilde{2}$	$(1, 2, 3)$
$\tilde{3}$	$(2, 3, 4)$
$\tilde{4}$	$(3, 4, 5)$
$\tilde{5}$	$(4, 5, 6)$
$\tilde{6}$	$(5, 6, 7)$
$\tilde{7}$	$(6, 7, 8)$
$\tilde{8}$	$(7, 8, 9)$
$\tilde{9}$	$(8, 9, 9)$

Source: Chen (1996a).
[a]Observe that $\tilde{1}$ and $\tilde{9}$ are left- and right-shoulder MFs, respectively.

provided, but will be assumed in this chapter to inject some additional realism into this application.

9.3 PER-C FOR MISSILE EVALUATION: DESIGN

Recall that the Per-C has three components: encoder, CWW engine, and decoder. When perceptual computing is used for the missile evaluation problem, each of these components must be considered.

9.3.1 Encoder

In this application, mixed data are used—crisp numbers, T1 fuzzy numbers, and words. The codebook contains the crisp numbers, the T1 fuzzy numbers with their associated T1 FS models (Fig. 9.2 and Table 9.2), and the words and their IT2 FS models.

To ensure that NWAs would not be unduly influenced by large numbers, all of the Table 9.1 numbers were mapped into [0, 10]. Let x_1, x_2, and x_3 denote the raw numbers for Systems A, B, and C, respectively. For the 13 subcriteria whose inputs are numbers, those raw numbers were transformed into

$$x_i \rightarrow x_i' = \frac{10x_i}{\max(x_1, x_2, x_3)} \tag{9.1}$$

Examining Table 9.1, observe that the words used for the remaining 10 subcriteria are {*low, high*} and {*poor, average, good, very good*}. Because this application is being used merely to illustrate how a Per-C can be used for missile system evaluation, and we do not have access to domain experts, interval end-point data were not collected for these words in the context of this application. Instead, the codebook from Table 3.6 [see also Liu and Mendel (2008)] is used. Unfortunately, none of the six words that are actually used in this application appear in that codebook. So, each word was mapped into a word that was felt to be a synonym for it. The mappings are:

$$
\begin{aligned}
Low &\;\rightarrow\; Low\ Amount \\
High &\;\rightarrow\; High\ Amount
\end{aligned}
\tag{9.2}
$$

$$
\left.
\begin{aligned}
Poor &\;\rightarrow\; Small \\
Average &\;\rightarrow\; Medium \\
Good &\;\rightarrow\; Large \\
Very\ Good &\;\rightarrow\; Very\ Large
\end{aligned}
\right\}
\tag{9.3}
$$

The IT2 FS models of the six words are shown in Fig. 9.3.

As in Chapter 7, where it was first observed that some subcriteria may have a positive connotation and others may have a negative connotation, a similar situation

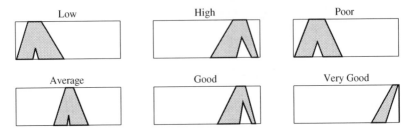

Figure 9.3. IT2 FS models for the six words used in missile evaluation.

occurs here. Observe from Table 9.1 that the following six subcriteria have a negative connotation:

1. *Flight height.* The lower the flight height, the better, because it is then more difficult for a missile to be detected by radar.
2. *Missile scale.* A smaller missile is harder to detect by radar.
3. *Reaction time.* A missile with shorter reaction time can respond more quickly.
4. *System cost.* The cheaper the better.
5. *Operation condition requirement.* A missile with a lower operation condition require-ment can be deployed more easily and widely.
6. *Material limitation.* A missile with a lower material limitation can be produced more easily, especially during wartime.

The first four of these subcriteria have numbers as their inputs. For them, a pre-processing step is needed to convert a large x_i' into a small number x_i^* and a small x_i' into a large number x_i^*, that is

$$x_i \rightarrow x_i^* = 1/x_i \tag{9.4}$$

and then equation (9.1) is applied to x_i^*:

$$x_i^* \rightarrow x_i' = \frac{10x_i^*}{\max(x_1^*, x_2^*, x_3^*)} \tag{9.5}$$

Equations (9.4) and (9.5) can be summarized by one equation:

$$x_i \rightarrow x' = \frac{10\min(x_1, x_2, x_3)}{x_i} \tag{9.6}$$

Example 9.1. Suppose that $x_1 = 3$, $x_2 = 4$, and $x_3 = 5$. Then when these numbers are mapped into [0, 10] using equation (9.1) they become $x_1' = 10(3/5) = 6$, $x_2' = 10(4/5) = 8$, and $x_3' = 10(5/5) = 10$. On the other hand, for subcriteria with negative connotation, these numbers are mapped into [0, 10] using equation (9.6), and they become $x'_1 = 10(3/3) = 10$, $x'_2 = 10(3/4) = 7.5$, and $x'_3 = 10(3/5) = 6$.

For the other two subcriteria with a negative connotation (operation condition requirement and material limitation), *antonyms* [Kim et al. (2000), Novák (2001), Soto and Trillas (1999), Zadeh (2005)] are used for the words in equations (9.2) and (9.3):

$$\mu_{10-A}(x) = \mu_A(10 - x), \ \forall x \tag{9.7}$$

where $10 - A$ is the antonym of a T1 FS A, and 10 is the right end of the domain of all FSs used in this chapter. The definition in equation (9.7) can easily be extended to IT2 FSs:

$$\mu_{10-\tilde{A}}(x) = \mu_{\tilde{A}}(10 - x), \ \forall x \tag{9.8}$$

where $10 - \tilde{A}$ is the antonym of an IT2 FS $\tilde{A}$. Because an IT2 FS is completely characterized by its LMF and UMF, each of which is a T1 FS, $\mu_{10-\tilde{A}}(x)$ in equation (9.8) is obtained by applying equation (9.7) to both $\underline{A}$ and $\overline{A}$.

Comment: Using these mappings, the highest score for the numerical subcriteria that have a positive connotation is always assigned the value 10, and the lowest score for the numerical subcriteria that have a negative connotation is also always assigned the value 10. What if such scores are not actually "good" scores? Assigning it our highest value does not then seem to be correct.

In this type of procurement competition, the contractor often sets specifications on numerical performance subcriteria. Unfortunately, such specifications do not appear in any of the published articles about this application, so we have had to do the best we can without them. If, for example, the contractor had set a specification for *reliability* as at least 85%, then (see Table 9.1) no company should get a 10. A different kind of normalization would then have to be used.

9.3.2 CWW Engine

NWAs are used as our CWW engine. Each major criterion has an NWA computed for it. Consider System A as an example. Examining Table 9.1, observe that the NWA for *Tactics* ($\tilde{Y}_{A1}$) is a FWA (because the weights are T1 FSs and the subcriteria evaluations are numbers), whereas the NWAs for *Technology* ($\tilde{Y}_{A2}$), *Maintenance* ($\tilde{Y}_{A3}$), *Economy* ($\tilde{Y}_{A4}$), and *Advancement* ($\tilde{Y}_{A5}$) are LWAs (because at least one subcriterion evaluation is a word modeled by an IT2 FS). More specifically:

$$\tilde{Y}_{A1} = \frac{\sum_{i=1}^{7} X_{Ai} W_i}{\sum_{i=1}^{7} W_i} \tag{9.9}$$

$$\tilde{Y}_{A2} = \frac{\sum_{i=8}^{12} \tilde{X}_{Ai} \tilde{W}_i}{\sum_{i=8}^{12} \tilde{W}_i} \tag{9.10}$$

$$\tilde{Y}_{A3} = \frac{\sum_{i=13}^{17} \tilde{X}_{Ai} \tilde{W}_i}{\sum_{i=13}^{17} \tilde{W}_i} \tag{9.11}$$

$$\tilde{Y}_{A4} = \frac{\sum_{i=18}^{20} \tilde{X}_{Ai} \tilde{W}_i}{\sum_{i=18}^{20} \tilde{W}_i} \tag{9.12}$$

$$\tilde{Y}_{A5} = \frac{\sum_{i=21}^{23} \tilde{X}_{Ai} \tilde{W}_i}{\sum_{i=21}^{23} \tilde{W}_i} \tag{9.13}$$

These five NWAs are then aggregated by another NWA to obtain the overall performance of System A, $\tilde{Y}_A$, as follows:

$$\tilde{Y}_A = \frac{\tilde{9}\tilde{Y}_{A1} + \tilde{3}\tilde{Y}_{A2} + \tilde{1}\tilde{Y}_{A3} + \tilde{5}\tilde{Y}_{A4} + \tilde{7}\tilde{Y}_{A5}}{\tilde{9} + \tilde{3} + \tilde{1} + \tilde{5} + \tilde{7}} \tag{9.14}$$

As a reminder to the reader, when $i = \{2, 8, 9, 18\}$, equation (9.4) must be used, and when $i = \{13, 20\}$, the antonyms of the corresponding word-IT2 FSs must be used. For all other values of i, the numbers or word-IT2 FSs are used directly.

9.3.3 Decoder

The decoder computes ranking, similarity, and centroid. Rankings of the three systems are obtained for the six NWA results in equations (9.9)–(9.14) using the centroid-based ranking method introduced in Section 4.3.3.

Similarity is computed only for the three systems' overall performances $\tilde{Y}_A$, $\tilde{Y}_B$, and $\tilde{Y}_C$ so that one can observe how similar the overall performances are for them.

Centroids are also computed for the three systems' $\tilde{Y}_A$, $\tilde{Y}_B$, and $\tilde{Y}_C$, and provide a measure of uncertainty for each system's overall ranking, since $\tilde{Y}_A$, $\tilde{Y}_B$, and $\tilde{Y}_C$ have propagated both numerical and linguistic uncertainties through their calculations.

9.4 PER-C FOR MISSILE EVALUATION: EXAMPLES

This section contains examples that illustrate the missile evaluation results for different scenarios. Example 9.2 uses the data that are in Table 9.1 as is. Examples 9.4 and 9.5 use intervals for all numerical values (Example 9.3 explains how such intervals can be normalized); for example, in Example 9.4 each numerical value x (except Missile scale) is changed to the interval $[x - 10\%x, x + 10\%x]$ for all three companies, and in Example 9.5 x is changed to $[x - 10\%x, x + 10\%x]$ for System A, $[x - 20\%x, x + 20\%x]$ for System B, and $[x - 5\%x, x + 5\%x]$ for System C. Using more realistic data intervals instead of numbers is something that was mentioned earlier at the end of Section 9.2 in Item 6.

Example 9.2. As just mentioned, this example uses the data that are in Table 9.1 as is. In all figures, System A is represented by the solid curve, System B is represented by the dashed curve, and System C is represented by the dotted curve. In order to simplify the notation in the figures, the notations $\tilde{Y}_{Aj}$, $\tilde{Y}_{Bj}$, and $\tilde{Y}_{Cj}$ are used for aggregated results for Criterion j and for Systems A, B, and C, respectively. The caption of each figure indicates the name of Criterion j ($j = 1, 2, \ldots, 5$) and the numbering of the criteria corresponds to their numbering in Table 9.1.

FOUs for *Tactics, Technology, Maintenance, Economy,* and *Advancement* are depicted in Figs. 9.4(a)–(e), respectively. FOUs for *Overall Performance* are depicted in Fig. 9.4(f). Observe from Fig. 9.4(f) that not only is $FOU(\tilde{Y}_B)$ visually well to the right of the other two FOUs, but its average centroid (which is on the horizontal axis) is also well to the right of those for Systems A and C. So, based on ranking alone, System B would be declared the winner. This happens because System B ranks first in *Maintenance, Economy,* and *Advancement* by significant amounts. Although it ranks last for *Tactics* and *Technology*, its FOUs for these two criteria are very close to those of Systems A and C.

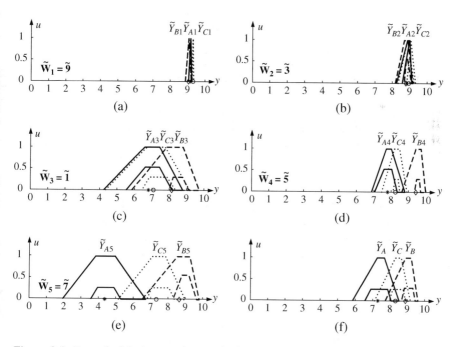

Figure 9.4. Example 9.2. Aggregation results for (a) Criterion 1: Tactics; (b) Criterion 2: Technology; (c) Criterion 3: Maintenance; (d) Criterion 4: Economy; (e) Criterion 5: Advancement; and, (f) Overall performances of the three systems. The average centroids for Systems A, B, and C are shown in all figures by *, ◊, and ○, respectively. The FOUs in (b)–(f) are not filled in so that the three IT2 FSs can be distinguished more easily.

Table 9.3 summarizes the similarities between $\tilde{Y}_A$, $\tilde{Y}_B$, and $\tilde{Y}_C$. Observe that $\tilde{Y}_B$ is not very similar to either $\tilde{Y}_A$ or $\tilde{Y}_C$, so choosing System B as the winner is further reinforced, that is, it is not a close call.

Finally, the centroids of $\tilde{Y}_A$, $\tilde{Y}_B$, and $\tilde{Y}_C$ (Table 9.4) are $C_A = [6.92, 7.67]$, $C_B = [8.59, 9.19]$, and $C_C = [7.99, 8.65]$. Let the numerical rankings be the average centroids. It follows that $c_A = 7.30$, $c_B = 8.89$, and $c_C = 8.32$.

Define

$$\delta_A = \frac{c_{A,r} - c_{A,l}}{2} \tag{9.15}$$

where $c_{A,l}$ and $c_{A,r}$ are the left and right endpoints of C_A, respectively. Similarly, define δ_B and δ_C as

$$\delta_B = \frac{c_{B,r} - c_{B,l}}{2} \tag{9.16}$$

$$\delta_C = \frac{c_{C,r} - c_{C,l}}{2} \tag{9.17}$$

Then, $\delta_A = 0.37$, $\delta_B = 0.30$, and $\delta_C = 0.33$. One way to use these half-lengths is to summarize the rankings as $r = c \pm \delta$, that is, $r_B = 8.89 \pm 0.30$, $r_C = 8.32 \pm 0.33$, and $r_A = 7.30 \pm 0.37$. Note that the centroids can also be interpreted as ranking bands and that there is no or little overlap of these bands in this example. All these results are summarized in Table 9.4.

Not only does System B have the largest ranking but it also has the smallest uncertainty band about that ranking and $\tilde{Y}_B$ is not very similar to either $\tilde{Y}_A$ or $\tilde{Y}_C$. Choosing System B as the winner seems the right thing to do. This decision is also consistent with those obtained in [Chen (1996a, 1996b), Chen (1999), and Mon et al. (1994)].

As we have explained in Item 6 of Section 9.2, in reality there are uncertainties about each of the numbers in Table 9.1 except Missile scale, which is fixed once the missile design is finished. In the remaining examples, uncertainty intervals are assigned to each of these numbers, except Missile scale, so that the effects of such uncertainties on the overall performances of the three companies can be studied.

Table 9.3. Similarities of $\tilde{Y}$ in Example 9.2 for the three companies

System	$\tilde{Y}_A$	$\tilde{Y}_B$	$\tilde{Y}_C$
$\tilde{Y}_A$	1	0.05	0.18
$\tilde{Y}_B$	0.05	1	0.31
$\tilde{Y}_C$	0.18	0.31	1

Table 9.4. Centroids, centers of centroid, and ranking bands of $\tilde{Y}$ for various uncertainties

System		0% for all three systems, Example 9.2	±10% for all three systems, Example 9.4	±10% for System A, ±20% for System B, and ±5% for System C, Example 9.5
A	C_A	[6.92, 7.67]	[6.59, 7.53]	[6.48, 7.42]
	c_A	7.30	7.06	6.95
	r_A	7.30 ± 0.37	7.06 ± 0.47	6.95 ± 0.47
B	C_B	[8.59, 9.19]	[8.24, 8.99]	[7.93, 8.83]
	c_B	8.89	8.61	8.38
	r_B	8.89 ± 0.30	8.61 ± 0.37	8.38 ± 0.45
C	C_C	[7.99, 8.65]	[7.70, 8.58]	[7.66, 8.42]
	c_C	8.32	8.14	8.04
	r_C	8.32 ± 0.33	8.14 ± 0.44	8.04 ± 0.38

For the 10 subcriteria that have a positive connotation, the uncertainty intervals are

$$x_i \to [x_i - v\%x_i, \min(x_i + v\%x_i, \max(x_1, x_2, x_3))] \equiv [\alpha_i, \beta_i], \quad i = 1, 2, 3 \quad (9.18)$$

Note that $\max(x_1, x_2, x_3)$ is used as an upper limit so that the converted number is not larger than 10 [see equation (9.19)]. The specific choice(s) made for v are explained in the examples. Equation (9.1) is then used for the two end-points in equation (9.18), i.e.,

$$[\alpha_i, \beta_i] \to \left[\frac{10\alpha_i}{\max(\beta_1, \beta_2, \beta_3)}, \frac{10\beta_i}{\max(\beta_1, \beta_2, \beta_3)} \right] \quad (9.19)$$

For the two subcriteria (Flight height and Reaction time) that have a negative connotation, the uncertainty intervals are

$$x_i \to [\max(x_i - v\%x_i, \min(x_1, x_2, x_3)), x_i + v\%x_i)] \equiv [\alpha_i', \beta_i'], \quad i = 1, 2, 3 \quad (9.20)$$

Note that $\min(x_1, x_2, x_3)$ is used as a lower limit so that the converted number is not larger than 10 [see equation (9.21)]. Equation (9.6) is then used for the two end points in equation (9.20), so that

$$[\alpha_i', \beta_i'] \to \left[\frac{10\min(\alpha_1', \alpha_2', \alpha_3')}{\beta_i'}, \frac{10\min(\alpha_1', \alpha_2', \alpha_3')}{\alpha_i'} \right] \quad (9.21)$$

The following example illustrates equations (9.18)–(9.21).

Example 9.3. As in Example 9.1, suppose that $x_1 = 3$, $x_2 = 4$, and $x_3 = 5$. Let $v = 10$. For a subcriterion with positive connotation, it follows from equation (9.18) that $x_1 \to [2.7, 3.3]$, $x_2 \to [3.6, 4.4]$, and $x_3 \to [4.5, 5]$. Using (9.19), one finds that

$$[2.7, 3.3] \rightarrow [10(2.7/5), 10(3.3/5)] = [5.4, 6.6]$$

$$[3.6, 4.4] \rightarrow [10(3.6/5), 10(4.4/5)] = [7.2, 8.8]$$

$$[4.5, 5] \rightarrow [10(4.5/5), 10(5/5)] = [9, 10];$$

For a subcriterion with negative connotation, it follows from equation (9.20) that $x_1 \rightarrow [3, 3.3]$, $x_2 \rightarrow [3.6, 4.4]$, and $x_3 \rightarrow [4.5, 5.5]$. Using equation (9.21), one finds that

$$[3, 3.3] \rightarrow [10(3/3.3), 10(3/3)] = [9.1, 10]$$

$$[3.6, 4.4] \rightarrow [10(3/4.4), 10(3/3.6)] = [6.8, 8.3]$$

$$[4.5, 5.5] \rightarrow [10(3/5.5), 10(3/4.5)] = [5.5, 6.7].$$

Example 9.4. In this example each numerical value x in Table 9.1 except Missile scale is changed by the same percentage amount to the interval $[x - 10\%x, x + 10\%x]$. We are interested to learn if such uncertainty intervals change the rankings of the three companies. FOUs for *Tactics, Technology, Maintenance, Economy,* and *Advancement* are depicted in Figs. 9.5(a)–(e), respectively. The overall performances of the three systems are depicted in Fig. 9.5(f). System B still appears to be the winning system.

Comparing the results in Fig. 9.5 with their counterparts in Fig. 9.4, observe that generally the FOUs have larger support. Particularly, the T1 FSs in Fig. 9.4(a) are triangular whereas the T1 FSs in Fig. 9.5(a) are trapezoidal. This is because in Fig. 9.4(a) the inputs to the subcriteria are numbers and the weights are triangular T1 FSs and, hence, the $\alpha = 1$ α-cut on $\tilde{Y}_{A1}$ ($\tilde{Y}_{B1}$, or $\tilde{Y}_{C1}$) is an AWA, whereas in Fig. 9.5(a) the inputs to the subcriteria are intervals and the weights are triangular T1 FSs and, hence, the $\alpha = 1$ α-cut on $\tilde{Y}_{A1}$ ($\tilde{Y}_{B1}$, or $\tilde{Y}_{C1}$) is an IWA.

Table 9.5 summarizes the similarities between $\tilde{Y}_A$, $\tilde{Y}_B$, and $\tilde{Y}_C$. Observe that $\tilde{Y}_C$ is much more similar to $\tilde{Y}_B$ in this example than it was in Example 9.2. Consequently, one may be less certain about choosing System B as the winner when there is ±10% uncertainty on all of the numbers in Table 9.1 than when there is no uncertainty on those numbers.

The centroids, centers of centroids, and the ranking bands of $\tilde{Y}_A$, $\tilde{Y}_B$, and $\tilde{Y}_C$ are shown in Table 9.4. Observe that not only does System B still have the largest ranking but it still has the smallest uncertainty band about that ranking. However, when there is ±10% uncertainty on all of the numbers in Table 9.1, not only do the numerical rankings for the three companies shift to the left (to lower values) but the uncertainty bands about those rankings increase. The overlap between the ranking bands of Systems B and C also increases.

In short, even though System B could still be declared the winner, one is less certain about doing this when there is ±10% uncertainty on all of the numbers in Table 9.1.

Example 9.5. In this example each numerical value x in Table 9.1 is changed to $[x - 10\%x, x + 10\%x]$ for System A, $[x - 20\%x, x + 20\%x]$ for System B and $[x - 5\%x, x$

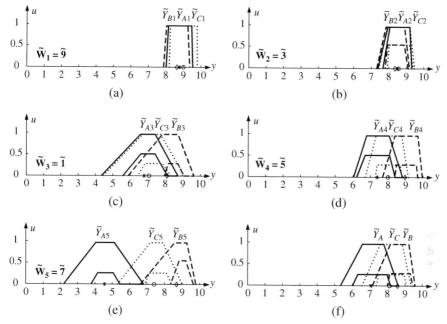

Figure 9.5. Example 9.4. Aggregation results for (a) Criterion 1: Tactics; (b) Criterion 2: Technology; (c) Criterion 3: Maintenance; (d) Criterion 4: Economy; (e) Criterion 5: Advancement; and, (f) Overall performances of the three systems. The average centroids for Systems A, B, and C are shown in all figures by $*$, $\diamond$, and $\circ$, respectively.

+ 5%x] for System C. FOUs for *Tactics, Technology, Maintenance, Economy,* and *Advancement* are depicted in Figs. 9.6(a)–(e), respectively. The overall performances of the three systems are depicted in Fig. 9.6(f). Observe that the UMF (LMF) of $\tilde{Y}_C$ is completely inside the UMF (LFM) of $\tilde{Y}_B$; so, it is difficult to declare System B the winner.

Table 9.6 summarizes the similarities between $\tilde{Y}_A$, $\tilde{Y}_B$, and $\tilde{Y}_C$. Observe that $\tilde{Y}_C$ is more similar to $\tilde{Y}_B$ in this example than in Example 9.4, so one may be less certain about choosing System B as the winner in this case.

Table 9.5. Similarities of $\tilde{Y}$ in Example 9.4 for the three companies

System	$\tilde{Y}_A$	$\tilde{Y}_B$	$\tilde{Y}_C$
$\tilde{Y}_A$	1	0.14	0.33
$\tilde{Y}_B$	0.14	1	0.59
$\tilde{Y}_C$	0.33	0.59	1

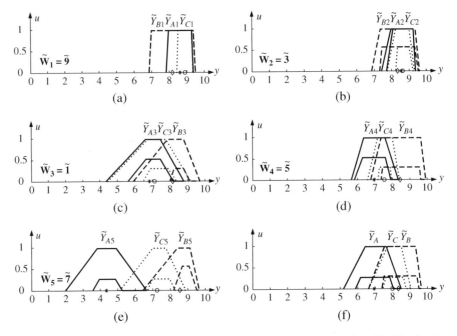

Figure 9.6. Example 9.5. Aggregation results for (a) Criterion 1: Tactics; (b) Criterion 2: Technology; (c) Criterion 3: Maintenance; (d) Criterion 4: Economy; (e) Criterion 5: Advancement; and, (f) Overall performances of the three systems. The average centroids for Systems A, B, and C are shown in all figures by ∗, ◇, and ○, respectively.

The centroids, centers of centroids, and the ranking bands of $\tilde{Y}_A$, $\tilde{Y}_B$, and $\tilde{Y}_C$ are shown in Table 9.4. Now the ranking bands for Systems B and C overlap a lot, which is why it is difficult to declare System B the winner.

This example clearly demonstrates that providing only average values for the subcriteria in Table 9.1 can lead to misleading conclusions. Uncertainty bands about those average values can change conclusions dramatically.

In summary, our Per-C approach can consider scenarios with different levels of uncertainties and, hence, evaluate the robustness of the final decision, for example, the numerical rankings of the three companies (c) when v [see equations (9.18) and

Table 9.6. Similarities of $\tilde{Y}$ in Example 9.5 for the three companies

System	$\tilde{Y}_A$	$\tilde{Y}_B$	$\tilde{Y}_C$
$\tilde{Y}_A$	1	0.24	0.27
$\tilde{Y}_B$	0.24	1	0.64
$\tilde{Y}_C$	0.27	0.64	1

(9.20)] changes by the same amount for all three systems from 0 to 20, are shown in Fig. 9.7(a), and the corresponding δ [see equations (9.15)–(9.17)] are shown in Fig. 9.7(b). Observe that System B is always the best choice, but as v increases, c decreases and δ increases, which means that the ranking band overlap between $\tilde{Y}_B$ and $\tilde{Y}_C$ increases and, hence, the lead of System B over System C decreases.

9.5 COMPARISONS WITH PREVIOUS APPROACHES

In this section, the results from our Per-C approach are compared with results from three previous approaches to the missile evaluation problem. We are only able to do this for the 0% situation of Example 9.2, because none of the previous methods were developed to handle intervals of numbers for the subcriteria.

9.5.1 Comparison with Mon et al.'s Approach

Mon et al. (1994) appear to be the first to work on "performance evaluation and optimal design of weapon systems [as] multiple criteria decision making problems" using FSs. They perform the following steps (we comment on some of these steps below):

1. Convert each subcriterion entry in Table 9.1 into either 1 if the (contractor's specified) subcriterion is satisfied or 0.5 or 0 if the subcriterion is not satisfied.[3]
2. Aggregate the subcriteria crisp scores by first adding them (implying that they are given the same weight) to provide a total score, and then mapping it into a fuzzy number. The fuzzy numbers are then put into a 3 × 5 *fuzzy judgment matrix X*. An example of computing the total scores for Tactics and Maintenance, based on the entries in Table 9.1, is shown in Table 9.7 and[4] the fuzzy judgment matrix is given in equation (9.22):

$$
X = \begin{array}{c} \\ A \\ B \\ C \end{array}
\begin{array}{ccccc}
\text{Tactics} & \text{Technology} & \text{Maintenance} & \text{Economy} & \text{Advancement} \\
\left[\begin{array}{ccccc}
\tilde{5} & \tilde{1} & \tilde{7} & \tilde{3} & \tilde{1} \\
\tilde{7} & \tilde{5} & \tilde{5} & \tilde{5} & \tilde{7} \\
\tilde{1} & \tilde{3} & \tilde{1} & \tilde{1} & \tilde{5}
\end{array}\right]
\end{array} \quad (9.22)
$$

---

[3]For Tactics, the following specifications are given [Mon et al. (1994)]: "If the *effective range* is further than 40 km, the *flight height* is smaller than 20 m, the *flight velocity* is greater than 0.8 Mach number, *reliability* is greater than 80%, *firing accuracy* is greater than 65%, *destruction rate* is greater than 85%, and *kill radius* is greater than 15 m, then the corresponding score of the [each] subcriterion is 1; otherwise, the score is 0.5." For Maintenance, the following specifications are given [Mon et al. (1994)]: "If the subcriteria are *good* or higher, their scores are 1; if they are *poor* the score is 0; otherwise, the scores are 0.5." Specifications are not provided in [Mon et al. (1994)] for Technology, Economy, and Advancement.

[4]There is no obvious connection between the total scores in Table 9.7 and their fuzzy counterparts in equation (9.22), something that we comment upon later in this section.

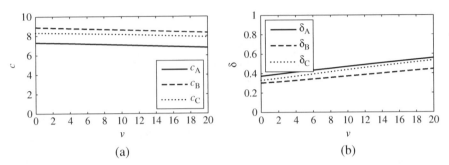

Figure 9.7. (a) Ranking of the three systems, c, and (b) half-length of ranking band, δ, when v changes from 0 to 20.

3. Assign fuzzy importance weights (fuzzy numbers) to each of the five criteria. These weights are indicated in Table 9.1.

4. Compute a *total fuzzy judgment matrix* Y by multiplying each element of X by its fuzzy weight:

$$Y = \begin{matrix} & \text{Tactics} & \text{Technology} & \text{Maintenance} & \text{Economy} & \text{Advancement} \\ A & \tilde{5} \times \tilde{9} & \tilde{1} \times \tilde{3} & \tilde{7} \times \tilde{1} & \tilde{3} \times \tilde{5} & \tilde{1} \times \tilde{7} \\ B & \tilde{7} \times \tilde{9} & \tilde{5} \times \tilde{3} & \tilde{5} \times \tilde{1} & \tilde{5} \times \tilde{5} & \tilde{7} \times \tilde{7} \\ C & \tilde{1} \times \tilde{9} & \tilde{3} \times \tilde{3} & \tilde{1} \times \tilde{1} & \tilde{1} \times \tilde{5} & \tilde{5} \times \tilde{7} \end{matrix} \qquad (9.23)$$

The multiplications are performed using α-cuts, for many values of α, the result for each α being Y_α, where:

Table 9.7. Mon et al.'s (1994) scores and total scores for the tactics and maintenance criteria for the three missile systems

System	Tactics			System	Maintenance		
	A	B	C		A	B	C
Effective range	1	0.5	0.5	Operation	1	0.5	0.5
Flight height	0.5	1	0.5	condition			
Flight velocity	0.5	1	0.5	requirement			
Reliability	1	1	0.5	Safety	1	0.5	0.5
Firing accuracy	1	1	0.5	Defilade	0.5	1	0.5
Destruction rate	0.5	1	1	Simplicity	0.5	0.5	0.5
Kill radius	1	0.5	1	Assembly	0.5	0.5	0
Total score	5.5	6	4.5	Total score	3.5	3	2

$$Y_\alpha = \begin{array}{c} A \\ B \\ C \end{array} \begin{bmatrix} (\tilde{5} \times \tilde{9})_\alpha & (\tilde{1} \times \tilde{3})_\alpha & (\tilde{7} \times \tilde{1})_\alpha & (\tilde{3} \times \tilde{5})_\alpha & (\tilde{1} \times \tilde{7})_\alpha \\ (\tilde{7} \times \tilde{9})_\alpha & (\tilde{5} \times \tilde{3})_\alpha & (\tilde{5} \times \tilde{1})_\alpha & (\tilde{5} \times \tilde{5})_\alpha & (\tilde{7} \times \tilde{7})_\alpha \\ (\tilde{1} \times \tilde{9})_\alpha & (\tilde{3} \times \tilde{3})_\alpha & (\tilde{1} \times \tilde{1})_\alpha & (\tilde{1} \times \tilde{5})_\alpha & (\tilde{5} \times \tilde{7})_\alpha \end{bmatrix} \quad (9.24)$$

$$\begin{array}{ccccc} \text{Tactics} & \text{Technology} & \text{Maintenance} & \text{Economy} & \text{Advancement} \end{array}$$

Each element of Y_α is an interval $(y_{il})_\alpha = [(y_{il}^l)_\alpha, (y_{il}^r)_\alpha]$ ($i = 1, 2, 3$ and $l = 1, \ldots, 5$).

5. Construct a *crisp judgment matrix* $J(\alpha) = \{j_{ik}(\alpha)\}_{i=1,2,3,k=1,2,\ldots,5}$, where

$$j_{ik}(\alpha) = \lambda y_{ik}^l(\alpha) + (1 - \lambda) y_{ik}^r(\alpha) \quad (9.25)$$

in which $\lambda \in [0, 1]$ is called an *index of optimism* and $j_{ik}(\alpha)$ is called the *degree of satisfaction*. When $j_{ik}(\alpha)$ is 0 or ½ or 1 the decision maker is called *pessimistic, moderate,* or *optimistic,* respectively. In Mon et al. (1994) results are provide for these three values of λ.

6. Compute the *entropy, e_i,* for each system, as

$$e_i = - \sum_{k=1}^{5} f_{ik} \log_2(f_{ik}), \quad i = 1, 2, 3 \quad (9.26)$$

where

$$f_{ik} = \frac{j_{ik}(\alpha)}{\max_k j_{ik}(\alpha)} \quad (9.27)$$

7. Normalize the three entropies by diving each entropy number by the sum of the three entropy numbers, leading to three entropy weights, one for each company. This is done for sampled values of $\alpha \in [0, 1]$ and for specified values of λ.
8. Choose the winning company as the one that has the largest entropy.

Mon et al. (1994) demonstrate that System B is the winner (which agrees with our results) and System A is better than System C (which does not agree with our results; see Table 9.4, column 3) for the three values of λ mentioned in Step 5, and for all values of α. Note that in their approach:

1. Words are not modeled (probably because they did not know how to do this); instead, they are ranked in an ad hoc manner using the crisp numbers 0, 0.5, and 1.
2. When a numerical subcriterion is not satisfied, a company is assigned a score of 0.5 (or 0) regardless of how far away its score is from its specification; hence, useful information is lost.
3. Each subcriterion is weighted the same when the total score is computed, which is counterintuitive, and is very different from the weightings that are used in Table 9.1.

4. How the "total score" is converted into a fuzzy number is not explained and seems very strange and inconsistent (e.g., for Tactics, $5.5 \rightarrow \tilde{5}$, $6 \rightarrow \tilde{7}$, and $4.5 \rightarrow \tilde{1}$, and for Maintenance, $3.5 \rightarrow \tilde{7}$, $3 \rightarrow \tilde{5}$, and $2 \rightarrow \tilde{1}$). Information is lost when this is done.

5. Step 6 is controversial since entropy is a measure of uncertainty rather than a measure of overall performance of a system.

6. Their procedure has to be repeated for many values of α and λ. Although the same result was obtained in Mon et al. (1994) for all values of α and λ, there is no guarantee that results could not depend on both α and λ, in which case conflicting conclusions could be reached.

9.5.2   Comparison with Chen's First Approach

Chen has published two approaches (1996a, 1996b) for the same missile evaluation problem. In Chen (1996a), he:

1. Converts each subcriterion entry in Table 9.1 into either 1 if the (contractor's specified) subcriterion is satisfied or 2 or 3 if the subcriterion is not satisfied.

2. Aggregates the subcriteria crisp scores by first adding them (implying that they are given the same weight) to provide a total score, and then mapping it into a fuzzy number. The fuzzy numbers are then put into a 3×5 fuzzy rank score matrix[5] X. An example for computing the total scores of Tactics and Maintenance, based on the entries in Table 9.1, is shown in Table 9.8 and the fuzzy rank score matrix is given in equation (9.28). Observe that Table 9.8 is quite similar to Table 9.7, except that scores 0, 0.5, and 1 have been replaced by 3, 2, and 1, respectively, and equation (9.28) is analogous to equation (9.22):

$$
X = \begin{array}{c} \\ A \\ B \\ C \end{array}
\begin{array}{ccccc}
\text{Tactics} & \text{Technology} & \text{Maintenance} & \text{Economy} & \text{Advancement} \\
\left[\begin{array}{ccccc}
\tilde{1}0 & \tilde{9} & \tilde{8} & \tilde{5} & \tilde{7} \\
\tilde{9} & \tilde{7} & \tilde{9} & \tilde{4} & \tilde{4} \\
\tilde{1}2 & \tilde{8} & \tilde{1}1 & \tilde{6} & \tilde{5}
\end{array}\right]
\end{array} \quad (9.28)
$$

3. Assigns fuzzy importance weights (fuzzy numbers) to each of the five criteria. These weights are indicated in Table 9.1.

4. Multiplies each element of X by its fuzzy importance weight, and then adds the resulting five fuzzy numbers for each company to obtain three (triangle) fuzzy numbers,[6] R_A, R_B, and R_C. For triangle and trapezoidal fuzzy numbers (as in Table 9.2) Chen explains how to do this without having to use α-cuts. His results are:

---

[5]This term is synonymous with Mon et al.'s (1994) "fuzzy judgment matrix."
[6]Recall that a triangle fuzzy number can be specified as (a, b, c), where a and c are its base end points and b is its apex location.

Table 9.8. Chen's (1996a) scores and total scores for the tactics and maintenance criteria for the three missile systems

	Tactics				Maintenance		
System	A	B	C	System	A	B	C
Effective range	1	2	2	Operation	1	2	2
Flight height	2	1	2	condition			
Flight velocity	2	1	2	requirement			
Reliability	1	1	2	Safety	1	2	2
Firing accuracy	1	1	2	Defilade	2	1	2
Destruction rate	2	1	1	Simplicity	2	2	2
Kill radius	1	2	1	Assembly	2	2	3
Total score	10	9	12	Total score	8	9	11

$$R_A = (140, 199, 257), \quad R_B = (106, 159, 222), \quad R_C = (146, 208, 290) \qquad (9.29)$$

5. Defuzzifies each of these fuzzy numbers to obtain the rank of the three companies, namely:

$$\overline{R}_A = 198.75, \quad \overline{R}_B = 161.5, \quad \overline{R}_C = 210.5 \qquad (9.30)$$

6. Chooses the winning company as the one that has the smallest rank. The smallest number is the winner because in Chen (1996a) 1 is of higher rank than 2 or 3.

By this method, Chen arrives at the same results as Mon et al., namely System B is the winner and System A is better than System C.

Comparing Chen's first approach with Mon et al.'s, we see that:

1. Words are still not modeled; instead, they are ranked in an ad hoc manner using the crisp numbers 3, 2, and 1.
2. It appears that Chen started with Mon et al.'s scores and mapped 1 into 1, 0.5 into 2, and 0 into 3, regardless of how far away a score is from its specification hence, again useful information is lost.
3. Each subcriterion is weighted the same when the total score is computed, which again is counterintuitive and very different from the weightings that are used in Table 9.1.
4. How the "total score" is converted into a fuzzy number is now transparent, for example, $9 \to \tilde{9}$, which overcomes one of our objections to Mon et al.'s approach.
5. Chen's first approach only has to be performed one time since it does not depend on α-cuts nor does it use a (variable) index of optimism, which overcomes another one of our objections to Mon et al.'s approach.

9.5.3 Comparison with Chen's Second Approach

In Chen (1996b), Chen uses the index of optimism introduced in Mon et al.'s (1994) approach, that is, he:

1. Assigns (for the first time) a *fuzzy importance number* to each of the subcriteria.
2. Ranks the subcriteria by using fuzzy ranking ($\tilde{1}$, $\tilde{2}$, or $\tilde{3}$), where now $\tilde{3}$ is the highest rank and $\tilde{1}$ is the lowest rank. An example of this ranking for Tactics and Maintenance, based on the entries in Table 9.1 that is consistent with those entries, is shown in Table 9.9.
3. Computes a *fuzzy score* for each company by multiplying each subcriterion's fuzzy importance number by its fuzzy ranking and then adding all of these products to obtain three (triangle) fuzzy numbers, T_A, T_B, and T_C. His results are:

$$T_A = (134, 234, 418), \quad T_B = (174, 276, 467), \quad T_C = (125, 226, 412) \quad (9.31)$$

4. Computes the α-cuts of T_A, T_B, and T_C, for many values of α, where the α-cuts of T_A, T_B, and T_C are denoted $[a_1^{(\alpha)}, a_2^{(\alpha)}]$, $[b_1^{(\alpha)}, b_2^{(\alpha)}]$ and $[c_1^{(\alpha)}, c_2^{(\alpha)}]$, respectively.
5. Lets $\lambda \in [0, 1]$ be an *index of optimism* and constructs the following three *crisp scores*:

$$\begin{cases} D_a^\lambda(A|\alpha) = \lambda a_1^{(\alpha)} + (1 - \lambda)a_2^{(\alpha)} \\ D_b^\lambda(B|\alpha) = \lambda b_1^{(\alpha)} + (1 - \lambda)b_2^{(\alpha)} \\ D_c^\lambda(C|\alpha) = \lambda c_1^{(\alpha)} + (1 - \lambda)c_2^{(\alpha)} \end{cases} \quad (9.32)$$

6. Normalizes these crisp scores to obtain:

$$\begin{cases} N_a^\lambda(A|\alpha) = D_a^\lambda(A|\alpha)/[D_a^\lambda(A|\alpha) + D_b^\lambda(B|\alpha) + D_c^\lambda(C|\alpha)] \\ N_b^\lambda(A|\alpha) = D_b^\lambda(A|\alpha)/[D_a^\lambda(A|\alpha) + D_b^\lambda(B|\alpha) + D_c^\lambda(C|\alpha)] \\ N_c^\lambda(A|\alpha) = D_c^\lambda(A|\alpha)/[D_a^\lambda(A|\alpha) + D_b^\lambda(B|\alpha) + D_c^\lambda(C|\alpha)] \end{cases} \quad (9.33)$$

Table 9.9. Chen's (1996b) scores for the tactics and maintenance criteria for the three missile systems

	Tactics				Maintenance		
System	A	B	C	System	A	B	C
Effective range	$\tilde{3}$	$\tilde{1}$	$\tilde{2}$	Operation	$\tilde{3}$	$\tilde{1}$	$\tilde{1}$
Flight height	$\tilde{1}$	$\tilde{3}$	$\tilde{2}$	condition			
Flight velocity	$\tilde{1}$	$\tilde{3}$	$\tilde{2}$	requirement			
Reliability	$\tilde{2}$	$\tilde{3}$	$\tilde{1}$	Safety	$\tilde{2}$	$\tilde{1}$	$\tilde{1}$
Firing accuracy	$\tilde{2}$	$\tilde{3}$	$\tilde{1}$	Defilade	$\tilde{1}$	$\tilde{2}$	$\tilde{1}$
Destruction rate	$\tilde{1}$	$\tilde{3}$	$\tilde{2}$	Simplicity	$\tilde{1}$	$\tilde{1}$	$\tilde{1}$
Kill radius	$\tilde{2}$	$\tilde{1}$	$\tilde{3}$	Assembly	$\tilde{2}$	$\tilde{2}$	$\tilde{1}$

7. Choose the winning company as the one that has the largest normalized crisp score.

Chen (1996b) demonstrates that System B is again the winner and System A is again better than System C for $\lambda = 0$, 0.5 and 1, and for all values of α.

Comparing Chen's second approach with his first approach and with Mon et al.'s approach, we see that:

1. By assigning a fuzzy importance number to each subcriterion, Chen not only overcomes the objection to Mon et al.'s method and his first approach, that every subcriterion is weighted the same, but also introduces some uncertainty into the importance of each subcriterion; however, he is still losing information by first assigning a fuzzy importance number to each subcriterion and then processing the ranked subcriteria.

2. Chen's rankings are now consistent with the entries in Table 9.1.

3. Unlike Mon et al. (1994) and Chen (1996a), who used the fuzzy importance weights that are shown in Table 9.1 for the main criteria, Chen does not use them in his Step 3. In effect, this means that he is weighting each of the five main criteria the same, which does not agree with the two previous studies. Most likely, this was done because Chen did not know how to perform hierarchical aggregation involving fuzzy numbers.

4. As in Mon et al.'s approach (1994), Chen's second approach has to be repeated for many values of α and λ; and, although the same result was obtained in Chen (1996b) for all values of α and λ, there is no guarantee that results could not depend on both α and λ, in which case conflicting conclusions could again be reached.

9.5.4 Discussion

Cheng (1999) has pointed out that because the fuzzy scores in Chen's second approach (1996b) are not normalized, each score may be unduly influenced by one large fuzzy number. He introduces a normalization method that "uses the fuzzy numbers $\tilde{1}, \tilde{3}, \tilde{5}, \tilde{7}$, and $\tilde{9}$ to indicate the relative contribution or impact of each element on each governing objective or criterion . . . the fuzzy numbers are assigned through comparison of the performance scores in the same criterion."[7] The actual implementation of this is subjective, that is, it is possible for different people to choose different fuzzy numbers.

Cheng obtains the results that System B is still the winner (which agrees with our result), but now System C is better than System A (which also agrees with our result).

By this time, the reader will have noticed that each of the above approaches contains questionable steps. The Per-C approach avoids all of them because of its dis-

---

[7]Here $\tilde{1}$ denotes *almost equal importance*, $\tilde{3}$ denotes *moderate importance* of one over another, $\tilde{5}$ denotes *strong importance,* $\tilde{7}$ denotes *very strong importance,* and $\tilde{9}$ denotes *extreme importance.* These scales are similar to those used in Saaty's analytic hierarchy process (AHP) [Saaty (1980, 1982)], except that in AHP crisp numbers instead of fuzzy numbers are used.

tinguishing features, which are listed below in the Conclusions section. Because the Per-C uses a NWA that includes a normalization of the subcriterion weights, it is able to automatically overcome Cheng's objection to Chen's second approach without having to introduce another subjective step.

9.6   CONCLUSIONS

This chapter has shown how the Per-C can be applied to a missile evaluation problem, which is a hierarchical multicriteria decision making problem, in which a contractor has to decide which of three companies will be awarded a contract to manufacture a missile weapon system. It is representative of a class of procurement judgment applications. Distinguishing features of our approach are:

1. No preprocessing of the subcriteria scores (e.g., by ranking) is done and, therefore, no information is lost.
2. A wide range of mixed data can be used, from numbers to words. By not having to convert words into a preprocessed rank, information is again not lost.
3. Uncertainties about the subcriteria scores as well as their weights flow through all NWA calculations, so that our final company-performance FOUs not only contain ranking and similarity information but also uncertainty information. No other existing method contains such uncertainty information.
4. Normalization automatically occurs in a NWA.

APPENDIX 9A: SOME HIERARCHICAL MULTICRITERIA DECISION-MAKING APPLICATIONS

A fuzzy multiobjective transportation selection problem [Tzeng and Teng (1993)] has already been described in Chapter 1. In this appendix, brief descriptions are provided for six other hierarchical multicriteria decision-making applications in which FSs have already been used. These applications are a sampling of the applications in which FSs have been used and others can be found in the literature.

- *Tool Steel Material Selection.* Wang and Chang (1995) considered FS based multiple-criteria decision making in a manufacturing application, for example, to select the most suitable tool steel materials for die design. Linguistic terms, which were represented by T1 FSs, were used to describe the material suitability ratings of various alternatives under different criteria and also for the weights of the criteria. After a weighted aggregation, a ranking method was used to find the most suitable tool steel material.
- *New Product Screening* [Zadeh (2005)]. New product development is both complex and risky. It requires between six to seven ideas to generate a successful product, and it is important to eliminate inferior products as soon as

possible. Since most new product evaluation criteria ratings and their importance are described subjectively by linguistic terms, the FWA was used to aggregate them into a fuzzy-possible-success rating (FPSR) of the product. Then, the FPSR was translated back into linguistic terms to assist in decision making. Compared with crisp-number-based approaches, the FWA approach coped better with ambiguity and was also more user friendly.

- *Network Security Systems Evaluation* [Chang and Hung (2005)]. This application is very similar to the missile systems evaluation application. The aim was to select the best alternative from three different information technology companies who provide alternatives of network security systems for the military. A team of experts from the military decided on the ratings for the criteria and their importance. Since the ratings and importance were vague and expressed by linguistic terms, the evaluation was carried out by the FWA. The aggregated results were ranked to provide decision references.

- *Competitiveness of Manufacturing Firms Evaluation* [Kao and Liu (1999)]. In this application, competitiveness indices were computed for 15 firms selected from the 74 largest machinery firms in Taiwan. Two main criteria—technology and management—were used in the evaluation. Each criterion also consisted of several subcriteria. Since the ratings for and the importance of the subcriteria and criteria were represented by linguistic terms, FWAs were used in the aggregation process.

- *Damage Assessment of Existing Transmission Towers.* Hathout (1993) introduced a transmission structure damage assessment model that can be used for fuzzy inferences made by an expert system about the overall stability of the structure. In the proposed model, a transmission tower was decomposed into six major components that were ranked by their importance to the overall stability of the tower. The FWA was used to combine the fuzzy condition ratings of the structural components. In this way, the inherent human bias and subjective judgment that prevail during visual inspection of existing transmission structures were incorporated into the transmission structure damage assessment model.

- *Engineering Design Evaluation.* According to Vanegas and Labib (2001), "engineering design evaluation is characterized by imprecise (vague) importance and satisfaction levels of criteria, which are better treated as fuzzy variables rather than as subjective crisp variables." In this case study, steel, polymer composite, and an aluminum alloy were compared for bumper beam material using three criteria. Ratings to and the importance of the three criteria were represented by linguistic terms. After FWA aggregation, the centroids were used to rank the candidates.

Note that none of the preceding applications have used IT2 FSs nor have they collected data from a group of subjects in order to obtain the FSs that are used to model their linguistic terms; hence, no further details are provided for them herein.

REFERENCES

P.-T. Chang and K.-C. Hung, "Applying the fuzzy-weighted-average approach to evaluate network security systems," *Computers and Mathematics with Applications,* vol. 49, pp. 1797–1814, 2005.

S.-M. Chen, "Evaluating weapon systems using fuzzy arithmetic operations," *Fuzzy Sets and Systems,* vol. 77, pp. 265–276, 1996a.

S.-M. Chen, "A new method for evaluating weapon systems using fuzzy set theory," *IEEE Trans. on Systems, Man, and Cybernetics-A,* vol. 26, pp. 493–497, 1996b.

C.-H. Cheng, "Evaluating weapon systems using ranking fuzzy numbers," *Fuzzy Sets and Systems,* vol. 107, pp. 25–35, 1999.

I. Hathout, "Damage assessment of existing transmission towers using fuzzy weighted averages," in *Proceedings of 2nd International Symposium on Uncertainty Modeling and Analysis,* College Park, MD, USA, April 1993, pp. 573–580.

C. Kao and S.-T. Liu, "Competitiveness of manufacturing firms: An application of fuzzy weighted average," *IEEE Trans. on Systems, Man, and Cybernetics-A,* vol. 29, no. 6, pp. 661–667, 1999.

C. S. Kim, D. S. Kim, and J. S. Park, "A new fuzzy resolution principle based on the antonym," *Fuzzy Sets and Systems,* vol. 113, pp. 299–307, 2000.

C.-T. Lin and C.-T. Chen, "A fuzzy-logic-based approach for new product Go/NoGo decision at the front end," *IEEE Transactions on Systems, Man, and Cybernetics-A,* vol. 34, no. 1, pp. 132–142, 2004.

F. Liu and J. M. Mendel, "Encoding words into interval type-2 fuzzy sets using an *interval approach*," *IEEE Trans. on Fuzzy Systems,* vol. 16, no. 6, pp. 1503–1521, 2008.

D.-L. Mon, C.-H. Cheng, and J.-L. Lin, "Evaluating weapon system using fuzzy analytic hierarchy process based on entropy weight," *Fuzzy Sets and Systems,* vol. 62, pp. 127–134, 1994.

V. Novák, "Antonyms and linguistic quantifiers in fuzzy logic," *Fuzzy Sets and Systems,* vol. 124, pp. 335–351, 2001.

T. L. Saaty, *The Analytic Hierarchy Process: Planning, Priority Setting, Resource Allocation,* New York: McGraw-Hill, 1980.

T. L. Saaty, *Decision Making for Leaders: The Analytical Hierarchy Process for Decisions in a Complex World.* Lifetime Learning Publications, 1982.

A. D. Soto and E. Trillas, "On antonym and negate in fuzzy logic," *International Journal of Intelligent Systems,* vol. 14, pp. 295–303, 1999.

G.-H. Tzeng and J.-Y. Teng, "Transportation investment project selection with fuzzy multi-objectives," *Transportation Planning Technology,* vol. 17, pp. 91–112, 1993.

L. V. Vanegas and A. W. Labib, "Application of new fuzzy-weighted average (NFWA) method to engineering design evaluation," *International Journal of Production Research,* vol. 39, no. 6, pp. 1147–1162, 2001.

M.-J. J. Wang and T.-C. Chang, "Tool steel materials selection under fuzzy environment," *Fuzzy Sets and Systems,* vol. 72, no. 3, pp. 263–270, 1995.

L. A. Zadeh, "Toward a generalized theory of uncertainty (GTU)—An outline," *Information Sciences,* vol. 172, pp. 1–40, 2005.

Assisting in Hierarchical and Distributed Decision Making— Journal Publication Judgment Advisor (JPJA)

10.1 INTRODUCTION

Recall from Chapter 1 that by "hierarchical and distributed decision making" is meant decision making that is ultimately made by a single individual, group or organization, but is based on aggregating independently made recommendations about an object from other individuals, groups or organizations (i.e., judges). An object could be a person being considered for a job, an article being reviewed for publication in a journal, a military objective, and so on. It is the independent nature of the recommendations that leads to this being called "distributed," and it is the aggregation of the distributed recommendations at a higher level that leads to this being called "hierarchical."

There can be multiple levels of hierarchy in this process, because each of the independent recommendations may also involve a hierarchical decision making process, as described in Chapter 9. Additionally, the individuals, groups, or organizations making their independent recommendations may not be of equal expertise, so a weight has to be assigned to each of them when they are aggregated. The independent recommendations can involve aggregating numbers, intervals, T1 FSs, and words modeled by IT2 FSs. The final recommendation (or decision) is made by a decision maker who not only uses an aggregated recommendation that is made across all of the judges but may also use the aggregated recommendation from each of the judges.

In this chapter, our attention is directed to the hierarchical and distributed journal publication judgment advisor (JPJA) in which, for the first time, only words are used at every level. This application is representative of other distributed and hierarchical decision-making applications, so its results should be extendable to them.

The rest of this chapter is organized as follows: Section 10.2 introduces the traditional journal paper review process, Section 10.3 describes how the Per-C is used to construct the JPJA, Section 10.4 illustrates the performance of the JPJA using several examples, and, finally, Section 10.5 draws conclusions.

10.2   THE JOURNAL PUBLICATION JUDGMENT ADVISOR (JPJA)

When an author submits a paper to a journal [Wu and Mendel (2007)], the Editor usually assigns its review to an Associate Editor (AE), who then sends it to at least three reviewers. The reviewers send their reviews back to the AE who then makes a publication recommendation to the Editor based on these reviews. The Editor uses this publication recommendation to assist in making a final decision about the paper.

In addition to the "comments for the author(s)," each reviewer usually has to complete a form similar to the one shown in Table 10.1 in which the reviewer has to evaluate the paper based on two major criteria, Technical Merit and Presentation. Technical Merit has three subcriteria: Importance, Content, and Depth; and Presentation has four subcriteria, Style, Organization, Clarity, and References. Observe that each subcriterion has an assessment level that is characterized by a starting word and an ending word (e.g., *Valuable* is the starting word for Importance and *Useless* is its ending word) and there are five boxes between them. A reviewer chooses one assessment level by checking-off one of the five boxes. This is very subjective because no one knows what words are associated with the middle three boxes. Usually, the reviewer is also asked to give an overall evaluation of the paper and make a recommendation to the AE. The AE then makes a final decision based on the opinions of the three reviewers.

The distributed and hierarchical nature of the decision-making process is shown in Fig. 10.1. Observe that there are three levels in the hierarchy: (1) aggregation of

Table 10.1. Paper review form for a generic journal

Technical Merit:							
Importance	Valuable	○	○	○	○	○	Useless
Content	Original	○	○	○	○	○	Derivative
Depth	Deep	○	○	○	○	○	Shallow
Presentation:							
Style	Readable	○	○	○	○	○	Incoherent
Organization	Precise	○	○	○	○	○	Ambiguous
Clarity	Clear	○	○	○	○	○	Confusing
References	Complete	○	○	○	○	○	Incomplete
Overall:							
Overall Evaluation	Excellent	○	○	○	○	○	Dreadful
Recommendation:							
○	ACCEPT: as written (editorial corrections as noted are necessary)						
○	REWRITE: needs substantial changes and rereview						
○	REJECT: material is unsuitable for publication in this journal						
○	TRANSFER: more suitable for publication in _____						

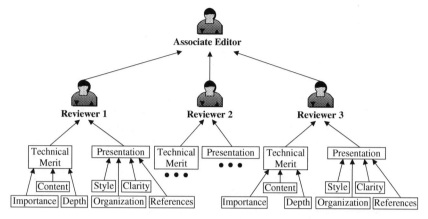

Figure 10.1. The paper review process. (Wu and Mendel, 2007; © 2007, IEEE.)

the subcriteria for the two major criteria, (2) aggregation of the two major criteria, and (3) aggregation of the three reviewers' recommendations.

Sometimes, a reviewer may feel it is difficult to give an overall evaluation of a paper because it gets high assessment levels on some of the subcriteria but does poorly on the others. In that case, the reviewer may give an evaluation based on the reputation of the author(s) or randomly choose an evaluation from several comparable evaluations. A similar situation may occur at the AE level; for example, if one reviewer suggests rejection of the paper, another suggests a revision of the paper, and a third reviewer suggests acceptance of the paper, what should the final decision be?

Because this evaluation process is often difficult and subjective, it may be better to leave it to a computer, that is, each reviewer should only be asked to provide a subjective evaluation of a paper for each of the seven subcriteria [as well as the "Comments for the author(s)"], after which linguistic weighted averages (LWAs) would automatically compute the reviewer's overall judgment of the paper. Once the opinion of all the reviewers are obtained, another LWA would compute an overall aggregated opinion for the AE. This automatic process has the potential to relieve much of the burden of the reviewers and the AE, and, moreover, it may be more accurate and less subjective.

10.3 PER-C FOR THE JPJA

This section explains how a Per-C can be used as a JPJA.

10.3.1 Modified Paper Review Form

To begin, a modified version of the Table 10.1 paper review form is needed, one that removes the uncertainty about the words that are associated with the three middle boxes for each subcriterion, and that asks each reviewer to indicate their level of expertise for reviewing the paper. The modified paper review form (for a generic journal) is depicted in Table 10.2.

Comparing the review forms in Tables 10.1 and 10.2, observe that:

1. The same words are now used for all seven subcriteria: Poor, Marginal, Adequate, Good, and Excellent. These five words are linguistically appropriate for each of the seven subcriteria. Of course, fewer or more than five words could be used, and different words could be used for each subcriterion.
2. Three words are used for a reviewer's level of expertise: Low, Moderate, and High. While it is doubtful that fewer than three words should be used, it is possible that more than three words could be used.
3. A reviewer is no longer asked to provide a recommendation.

When perceptual computing is used for the JPJA, each of the three components of a Per-C—encoder, CWW engine, and decoder—must be considered.

10.3.2 Encoder

Two codebooks are needed, one for the words that will be used by a reviewer and the other for weights, and each of these codebooks has subcodebooks, as explained next.

10.3.2.1 Codebook Words Used by a Reviewer. The reviewer codebook has two subcodebooks:

1. *Subcodebook R1.* This codebook contains the five words (Poor, Marginal, Adequate, Good, and Excellent) and their FOUs that are used to assess the seven subcriteria. FOUs for these words are depicted in Fig. 10.2. They were

Table 10.2. Modified paper review form for a generic journal

	Poor	Marginal	Adequate	Good	Excellent
Technical Merit:					
Importance	○	○	○	○	○
Content	○	○	○	○	○
Depth	○	○	○	○	○
Presentation:					
Style	○	○	○	○	○
Organization	○	○	○	○	○
Clarity	○	○	○	○	○
References	○	○	○	○	○
Expertise:	Low		Moderate		High
Your Expertise	○		○		○

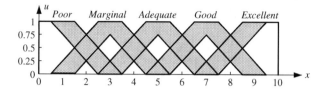

Figure 10.2. FOUs for the five-word Subcodebook R1.

not obtained by collecting data from a group of subjects,[1] for example, AEs and reviewers, but instead were generated by the authors. Consequently, all of the results that are in this chapter are synthetic. In order to get more accurate results, a pool of knowledgeable AEs and reviewers should be surveyed and then their data intervals should be mapped into word FOUs using the IA introduced in Chapter 3.

2. *Subcodebook R2.* This codebook contains the three words (Low, Moderate, and High) and their FOUs that describe a reviewer's level of expertise. FOUs for these words are depicted in Fig. 10.3. They also were not obtained by collecting data from a group of subjects, but instead were generated by the authors; so the admonition just given for the FOUs in Subcodebook R1 applies here as well.

10.3.2.2 Codebook for the Weights. The weights codebook has three sub-codebooks, each of which is described next. A major difference between the weights subcodebooks and the two reviewer subcodebooks is that for the latter each FOU has a word associated with it, whereas for the weight subcodebooks each FOU is associated with a weight that has no word associated with it. The weight FOUs are only used in LWAs and are not available to a reviewer; hence, they are assigned symbols rather than words.

1. *Subcodebook W1.* This codebook contains labels and FOUs for the relative weighting of the three subcriteria that are associated with the criterion of Technical Merit. FOUs for these weights are depicted in Fig. 10.4. These FOUs were also generated by the authors; however, the relative orderings of the three subcriteria were first established (in 2007) with the help of Dr. Nikhil Pal (Editor-in-Chief of the *IEEE Transactions on Fuzzy Systems*). That ordering is: Content (Co) is more important than Importance (I) which in turn is more important that Depth (D); hence, $\tilde{W}_{Co} > \tilde{W}_I > \tilde{W}_D$.

---

[1]Intervals could be collected from a group of subjects by stating:

> You are to assign an interval or a "range" of numbers that falls somewhere between 0 and 10 to each of following three subcriteria that are associated with judging the Technical Merit of a journal article submission: Content, Importance, and Depth. The interval corresponds to a linguistic weighting that you assign to each subcriterion. It is important to note that not all ranges have to be the same and ranges can overlap. Subjects are then asked a question like: "Where on a scale of 0–10 would you locate the end points of an interval that you assign to Content (Importance, Depth) is Poor?"

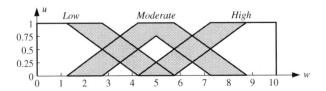

Figure 10.3. FOUs for the three-word Subcodebook R2.

2. *Subcodebook W2.* This codebook contains labels and FOUs for the relative weighting of the four subcriteria that are associated with the criterion of Presentation. FOUs for these weights are depicted in Fig. 10.5. Again, with the help of Dr. Nikhil Pal, it was decided that Organization (O) and References (R) were indistinguishable, as were Style (S) and Clarity (C), and the Style and Clarity are more important than Organization and References; hence, $\tilde{W}_S = \tilde{W}_{Cl} > \tilde{W}_O = \tilde{W}_D$.

3. *Subcodebook W3.* This codebook contains labels and FOUs for the relative weighting of the two criteria Technical Merit and Presentation. Clearly Technical Merit (T) is more important than Presentation (P), that is, $\tilde{W}_T > \tilde{W}_P$. Again, with the help of Dr. Nikhil Pal, it was decided that the FOUs for these weights should be located as depicted in Fig. 10.6.

If interval data are collected from AEs and reviewers for subcodebooks W1, W2 and W3, and the FOUs are determined using the IA, then the shapes of the FOUs as well as the amount that they overlap will be different from the ones in Figs. 10.4-10.6. Those details, while important for the application of the JPJA to a specific journal, do not change the methodology of the JPJA that is further explained below.

10.3.3 CWW Engine

For the CWW Engine of the JPJA, LWAs are used because one of the unique features of this application is that all assessments and weights are words (or FOUs). To begin, each of the two major criteria (Technical Merit and Presentation) has an LWA computed for it, that is, ($j = 1, 2, \ldots, n_R$):

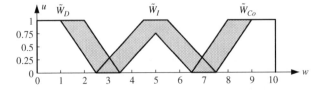

Figure 10.4. FOUs for the three-word Subcodebook W1. Weights correspond to Importance ($\tilde{W}_I$), Content ($\tilde{W}_{Co}$), and Depth ($\tilde{W}_D$).

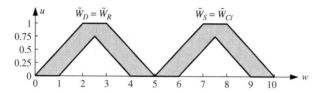

Figure 10.5. FOUs for the four-word Subcodebook W2. Weights correspond to Style ($\tilde{W}_S$), Organization ($\tilde{W}_O$), Clarity ($\tilde{W}_{Cl}$), and Reference ($\tilde{W}_R$).

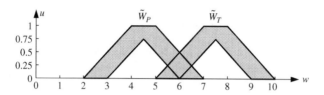

Figure 10.6. FOUs for the two-word Subcodebook W3. Weights correspond to Technical Merit ($\tilde{W}_T$) and Presentation ($\tilde{W}_P$).

$$\tilde{Y}_{jT} = \frac{\tilde{X}_{jI}\,\tilde{W}_I + \tilde{X}_{jC_o}\,\tilde{W}_{C_o} + \tilde{X}_{jD}\,\tilde{W}_D}{\tilde{W}_I + \tilde{W}_{C_o} + \tilde{W}_D} \tag{10.1}$$

$$\tilde{Y}_{jP} = \frac{\tilde{X}_{jS}\,\tilde{W}_S + \tilde{X}_{jO}\,\tilde{W}_O + \tilde{X}_{jCl}\,\tilde{W}_{Cl} + \tilde{X}_{jR}\,\tilde{W}_R}{\tilde{W}_S + \tilde{W}_O + \tilde{W}_{Cl} + \tilde{W}_R} \tag{10.2}$$

where n_R is the number of reviewers,[2] $\tilde{Y}_{jT}$ is the LWA for Technical Merit in which $\tilde{X}_{jI}$, $\tilde{X}_{jC_o}$, and $\tilde{X}_{jD}$ are the linguistic assessments provided by Reviewer j for Importance, Content, and Depth, respectively, and $\tilde{Y}_{jP}$ is the LWA for Presentation in which $\tilde{X}_{jS}$, $\tilde{X}_{jO}$, $\tilde{X}_{jCl}$, and $\tilde{X}_{jR}$ are the linguistic assessments provided by Reviewer j for Style, Organization, Clarity, and References, respectively.

Next, $\tilde{Y}_{jT}$ and $\tilde{Y}_{jP}$ are aggregated using the following Reviewer LWAs, $\tilde{Y}_{Rj}$ ($j = 1$, $2, \ldots, n_R$):

$$\tilde{Y}_{Rj} = \frac{\tilde{Y}_{jT}\,\tilde{W}_T + \tilde{Y}_{jP}\,\tilde{W}_P}{\tilde{W}_T + \tilde{W}_P} \tag{10.3}$$

Finally, the n_R Reviewer LWAs are aggregated using the following AE LWA:

$$\tilde{Y}_{AE} = \frac{\sum_{j=1}^{n_R} \tilde{Y}_{Rj}\,\tilde{W}_{Rj}}{\sum_{j=1}^{n_R} \tilde{W}_{Rj}} \tag{10.4}$$

in which $\tilde{W}_{Rj} \in \{\text{Low, Moderate, High}\}$.

---

[2]Although Fig. 10.1 shows three reviewers, the number of reviewers is treated here as a variable.

10.3.4 Decoder

The decoder for the JPJA is actually a classifier, that is, it classifies the overall quality of a paper, $\tilde{Y}_{AE}$, into one of three classes: Accept, Rewrite, or Reject. A decoding codebook is needed to store the FOUs for these three words. Two approaches for constructing such a codebook are described next, as well as our preferred method for decoding.

10.3.4.1 Construct the Decoding Codebook Using a Survey. In this approach, AEs are surveyed using a statement and question like:

> A reviewer of a journal submission must score the submission using a number between 0 and 10, where 0 is the lowest score and 10 is the highest score. The reviewer's score must then be mapped into one of three classes—Accept, Rewrite, or Reject. Where on the scale of 0–10 would you locate the ends points of an interval that you assign to Accept (Rewrite, Reject)?

The IA (Chapter 3) can then be used to map the crisp intervals into IT2 FS FOUs for Accept, Rewrite, and Reject.

10.3.4.2 Construct the Decoding Codebook Using Training Examples. A training dataset is a collection of training examples, each of which consists of n_R reviewers' completed review forms, the AE's FOU for a specific journal submission, and the final recommendation made for the paper by the Editor-in-Chief (Accept, Rewrite, or Reject). For instance, for the kth submission ($k = 1, \ldots, N_T$) in the training dataset, a training example is

$$\{(\tilde{X}_{jI}^{k}, \tilde{X}_{jCo}^{k}, \tilde{X}_{jD}^{k}, \tilde{X}_{jS}^{k}, \tilde{X}_{jO}^{k}, \tilde{X}_{jCl}^{k}, \tilde{X}_{jR}^{k}, \tilde{W}_{Rj}^{k}),\ j = 1, \ldots, n_R;$$

$$\tilde{Y}_{AE}^{k},\ Final\ Recommendation(k)\}$$

Instead of prespecifying the FOUs for Accept, Rewrite, and Reject, their shapes are chosen like the ones in Fig. 10.7 but their specific parameters that completely define each FOU are not fixed ahead of time. Instead, the FOU parameters are tuned using search algorithms to minimize the errors between the given Final Recommendation and an Estimated Recommendation for all N_T elements in the training dataset. The Estimated Recommendation for each training example is obtained as

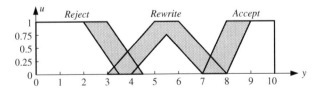

Figure 10.7. FOUs for the three-classes decoding codebook.

follows: (1) FOU parameters for Accept, Rewrite, and Reject are specified (or updated using an optimization algorithm); (2) the average subsethoods of $\tilde{Y}_{AE}^k$ in Accept, Rewrite, and Reject are computed; and (3) the paper is assigned to the class with the maximum average subsethood.

10.3.4.3 Remarks. In principle, either approach could be used; however, because the generic review form in Table 10.2 has yet to be used, no training examples are available. So, for the present, only the approach described in Section 10.3.4.1 can be used for constructing the decoding codebook.

Because we did not have access to a pool of AEs and reviewers, the decoding codebook used in this chapter is shown in Fig. 10.7. Its FOUs were synthesized with the help of Dr. Nikhil Pal.

10.3.4.4 Decoding. Vlachos and Sergiadis's IT2FS subsethood measure (Section 4.4.4) is computed between $\tilde{Y}_{AE}$ and Accept, Rewrite, and Reject, namely, $ss_{VS}(\tilde{Y}_{AE}, \text{Accept})$, $ss_{VS}(\tilde{Y}_{AE}, \text{Rewrite})$, and $ss_{VS}(\tilde{Y}_{AE}, \text{Reject})$, after which the decoder recommends to the AE the publication class of maximum subsethood. The decoder also provides $\tilde{Y}_{AE}$ and the values of the three subsethoods to the AE, because the AE may want to make some subjective adjustments to the publication class when two subsethoods are very close.

10.4 EXAMPLES

This section contains some examples that illustrate the automatic paper review process. First the different levels of aggregation are examined to demonstrate that reasonable results are obtained, and then three complete paper reviews are provided.

10.4.1 Aggregation of Technical Merit Subcriteria

To consider all possible combinations of the inputs to the criterion of Technical Merit, one would need to examine a total of $5^3 = 125$ cases, because each of its three subcriteria has five possible linguistic terms (Fig. 10.2) that can be chosen by a reviewer. This is impractical for us to do so, instead, our focus is on whether or not Content dominates the other subcriteria of Importance and Depth as it should, since in equation (10.1) and Subcodebook W1 it has already been established that $\tilde{W}_{Co} > \tilde{W}_I > \tilde{W}_D$. To do this, 15 of the 125 possible cases are studied. In all cases, $\tilde{Y}_T$ in equation (10.1) is computed for the three weight FOUs that are depicted in Fig. 10.4, and only $\tilde{X}_I$, $\tilde{X}_{Co}$, and $\tilde{X}_D$ are varied. If Content dominates the other subcriteria of Importance and Depth, then regardless of the words chosen for Importance and Depth, one expects to see $\tilde{Y}_T$ move from left to right as $\tilde{X}_{Co}$ moves from left to right.

10.4.1.1 Importance is Good, Depth is Excellent, and Content Varies from Poor to Excellent. The FOUs of $\tilde{Y}_T$ for these five cases are depicted in the

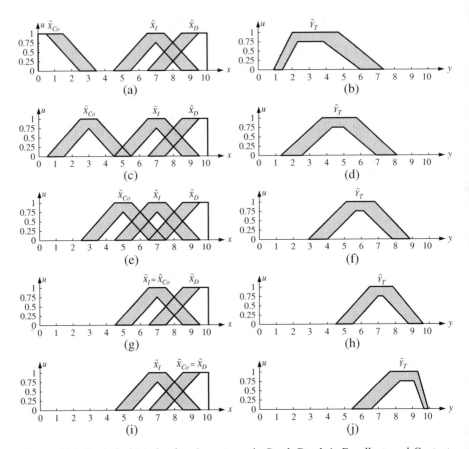

Figure 10.8. Technical Merit when Importance is Good, Depth is Excellent, and Content varies. (a), (c), (e), (g), (i): Input FOUs when a reviewer's response to Content changes from Poor to Excellent; (b), (d), (f), (h), (j): Output $\tilde{Y}_T$ when a reviewer's response to Content changes from Poor to Excellent. The corresponding weights for the three subcriteria are shown in Fig. 10.4.

right-hand figures of Fig. 10.8. Each of the left-hand figures in Fig. 10.8 depicts the respective FOUs for $\tilde{X}_I$, $\tilde{X}_{Co}$, and $\tilde{X}_D$. Note that $\tilde{X}_I$ = Good and $\tilde{X}_D$ = Excellent are the ones in Fig. 10.2. Only $\tilde{X}_{Co}$ changes in the left-hand figures, and its FOUs match the ones in Fig. 10.2 for all five words.

Observe that as the reviewer's response to Content varies from Poor to Excellent, $\tilde{Y}_T$ does move from left to right toward the maximal score of 10, which supports our expectation that Content dominates.

10.4.1.2 Importance is Poor, Depth is Excellent, and Content Varies from Poor to Excellent. Starting with the choices that were made for

Importance, Depth, and Content in Fig. 10.8, Importance is changed from Good to Poor, and everything else is kept the same. The FOUs of $\tilde{Y}_T$ for the present five cases are depicted in the right-hand figures of Fig. 10.9. Each of the left-hand figures in Fig. 10.9 depicts the respective FOUs for $\tilde{X}_I$, $\tilde{X}_{Co}$, and $\tilde{X}_D$. Note that $\tilde{X}_I =$ Poor and $\tilde{X}_D =$ Excellent are the ones in Fig. 10.2. As in Fig. 10.8, only $\tilde{X}_{Co}$ changes in the left-hand figures, and its FOUs match the ones in Fig. 10.2 for all five words.

Observe that as the reviewer's response to the subcriterion Content varies from Poor to Excellent, $\tilde{Y}_T$ moves from left to right toward the maximal score of 10

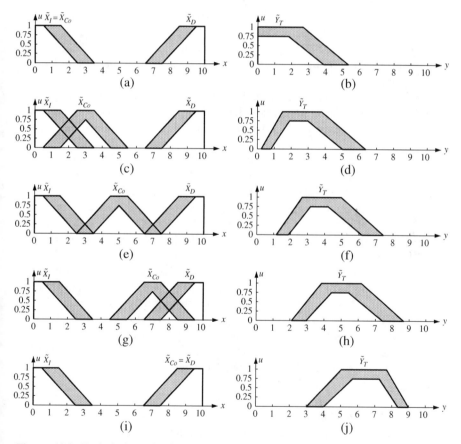

Figure 10.9. Technical Merit when Importance is Poor, Depth is Excellent, and Content varies. (a), (c), (e), (g), (i): Input FOUs when a reviewer's response to Content changes from Poor to Excellent; (b), (d), (f), (h), (j): Output $\tilde{Y}_T$ when a reviewer's response to Content changes from Poor to Excellent. The corresponding weights for the three subcriteria are shown in Fig. 10.4.

(but never reaches it), which again supports our expectation that Content dominates.

By comparing each line of the two sets of right-hand figures in Figs. 10.8 and 10.9, observe that each of the FOUs of $\tilde{Y}_T$ for when Importance is Good lies farther to the right of its respective FOU for when Importance is Poor. This also agrees with our expectation, because improving the assessment of Importance should improve $\tilde{Y}_T$, that is, move $\tilde{Y}_T$ further to the right.

10.4.1.3 *Importance is Poor, Depth is Marginal, and Content Varies from Poor to Excellent.* Starting with the choices that were made for Importance, Depth, and Content in Fig. 10.9, Depth is changed from Excellent to Marginal, and everything else is kept the same. The FOUs of $\tilde{Y}_T$ for the present five cases are depicted in the right-hand figures of Fig. 10.10. Each of the left-hand figures in Fig. 10.10 depicts the respective FOUs for $\tilde{X}_I$, $\tilde{X}_{Co}$, and $\tilde{X}_D$. Note that $\tilde{X}_I = $ Poor and $\tilde{X}_D = $ Marginal are the ones in Fig. 10.2. As in Figs. 10.8 and 10.9, only $\tilde{X}_{Co}$ changes in the left-hand figures, and its FOUs again match the ones in Fig. 10.2 for all five words.

Observe again that as the reviewer's response to the subcriterion Content varies from Poor to Excellent, $\tilde{Y}_T$ moves from left to right toward the maximal score of 10 (which, again, it never reaches), which again supports our expectation that Content dominates.

By comparing each line of the two sets of right-hand figures in Figs. 10.9 and 10.10, observe that each of the FOUs of $\tilde{X}_T$ for when Depth is Excellent lies farther to the right of its respective FOU for when Depth is Marginal. This also agrees with our expectation, because improving the assessment of Depth should improve $\tilde{Y}_T$, that is, move $\tilde{Y}_T$ further to the right.

Finally, observe that the five cases in Fig. 10.9 represent a deterioration of the respective cases in Fig. 10.8, and the five cases in Fig. 10.10 represent an even greater deterioration of those cases. These deteriorations (which correspond to poorer reviews within the criterion of Technical Merit) are evident in all respective right-hand figure FOUs in Figs. 10.8–10.10 by their moving toward the left. For example, comparing Fig. (j) in these figures, one observes that in Fig. 10.8(j) the very right portion of $\tilde{Y}_T$ almost reaches $y = 10$, but in Figs. 10.9(j) and 10.10(j) the very right portion of $\tilde{Y}_T$ only reaches $y \approx 9$ and $y \approx 8.7$. This all seems quite sensible in that one would expect poorer assessments of any of the three subcriteria to move $\tilde{Y}_T$ to the left.

10.4.1.4 *Conclusions.* These 15 cases have demonstrated that Content does indeed dominate Importance and Depth and that a higher assessment for any of the three subcriteria will move $\tilde{Y}_T$ to the right.

10.4.2 Aggregation of Presentation Subcriteria

To consider all possible combinations of the inputs to the criterion of Presentation, one would need to examine a total of $5^4 = 625$ cases, because each of its four subcriteria

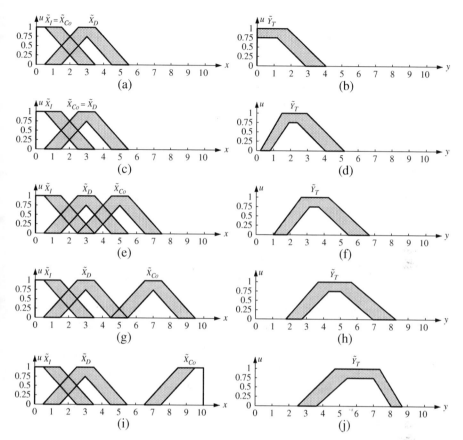

Figure 10.10. Technical Merit when Importance is Poor, Depth is Marginal, and Content varies. (a), (c), (e), (g), (i): Input FOUs when a reviewer's response to Content changes from Poor to Excellent; (b), (d), (f), (h), (j): Output $\tilde{Y}_T$ when a reviewer's response to Content changes from Poor to Excellent. The corresponding weights for the three subcriteria are shown in Fig. 10.4.

has five possible linguistic terms (Fig. 10.2) that can be chosen by a reviewer. This is even more impractical to do than it was to examine all 125 possible cases for Technical Merit so, instead, our focus is on observing the effect that subcriterion Style has on $\tilde{Y}_P$ when Clarity is fixed at Excellent and Organization and References are varied by the same amounts (recall that the weights for both Organization and References are the same; see Fig. 10.5). To do this, 15 of the 625 possible cases are studied. In all cases, $\tilde{Y}_P$ in (10.2) is computed for the four weight FOUs that are depicted in Fig. 10.5. Because $\tilde{W}_S = \tilde{W}_{Cl}$, one expects to see $\tilde{Y}_P$ move from left to right as $\tilde{X}_S$ moves from left to right and also as $\tilde{X}_O$ and $\tilde{X}_R$ simultaneously move from left to right.

10.4.2.1 Clarity is Excellent, Organization and References are Poor, and Style Varies from Poor to Excellent.

The FOUs of $\tilde{Y}_P$ for these five cases are depicted in the right-hand figures of Fig. 10.11. Each of the left-hand figures in Fig. 10.11 depicts the respective FOUs for $\tilde{X}_{Cl}$, $\tilde{X}_O$, $\tilde{X}_R$, and $\tilde{X}_S$. Note that $\tilde{X}_{Cl}$ = Excellent and $\tilde{X}_O = \tilde{X}_R$ = Poor are the ones in Fig. 10.2. Only $\tilde{X}_S$ changes in the left-hand figures, and its FOUs match the ones in Fig. 10.2 for all five words.

Observe that as the reviewer's response to Style varies from Poor to Excellent, Y_P does move from left to right toward the maximal score of 10, which supports our expectation that $\tilde{Y}_P$ moves from left to right as $\tilde{X}_S$ moves from left to right.

10.4.2.2 Clarity is Excellent, Organization and References are Adequate, and Style Varies from Poor to Excellent.

The FOUs of $\tilde{Y}_P$ for these five cases are depicted in the right-hand figures of Fig. 10.12. Each of the left-hand figures in Fig. 10.12 depicts the respective FOUs for $\tilde{X}_{Cl}$, $\tilde{X}_O$, $\tilde{X}_R$, and $\tilde{X}_S$. Note that, as in Fig. 10.11, $\tilde{X}_{Cl}$ = Excellent but now $\tilde{X}_O = \tilde{X}_R$ = Adequate and these FOUs are the ones in Fig. 10.2. Again, only $\tilde{X}_S$ changes in the left-hand figures, and its FOUs match the ones in Fig. 10.2 for all five words.

Observe that as the reviewer's response to Style varies from Poor to Excellent, $\tilde{Y}_P$ does move from left to right toward the maximal score of 10, which again supports our expectation that $\tilde{Y}_P$ moves from left to right as $\tilde{X}_{Cl}$ moves from left to right.

By comparing each line of the two sets of right-hand figures in Figs. 10.11 and 10.12, observe that each of the FOUs of $\tilde{Y}_P$ for when Organization and References are Adequate are somewhat to the right of its respective FOU for when Organization and References are Poor. This also agrees with our expectation, because improving the assessments of Organization and References should improve $\tilde{Y}_P$, that is, move $\tilde{Y}_P$ further to the right.

10.4.2.3 Clarity, Organization and References are Excellent and Style Varies from Poor to Excellent.

The FOUs of $\tilde{Y}_P$ for these five cases are depicted in the right-hand figures of Fig. 10.13. Each of the left-hand figures in Fig. 10.13 depicts the respective FOUs for $\tilde{X}_{Cl}$, $\tilde{X}_O$, $\tilde{X}_R$, and $\tilde{X}_S$. Note that, as in Figs. 10.11 and 10.12, $\tilde{X}_{Cl}$ = Excellent but now $\tilde{X}_O = \tilde{X}_R$ = Excellent, where Excellent is depicted in Fig. 10.2. Again, only $\tilde{X}_S$ changes in the left-hand figures, and its FOUs match the ones in Fig. 10.2 for all five words.

Observe that as the reviewer's response to Style varies from Poor to Excellent, $\tilde{Y}_P$ once again moves from left to right toward the maximal score of 10, which continues to support our expectation that $\tilde{Y}_P$ moves from left to right as $\tilde{X}_{Cl}$ moves from left to right.

By comparing each line of the two sets of right-hand figures in Figs. 10.13 and 10.12, observe that each of the FOUs of $\tilde{Y}_P$ for when Organization and References are Excellent are somewhat to the right of their respective FOUs for when Organization and References are Adequate. This also continues to agree with our expecta-

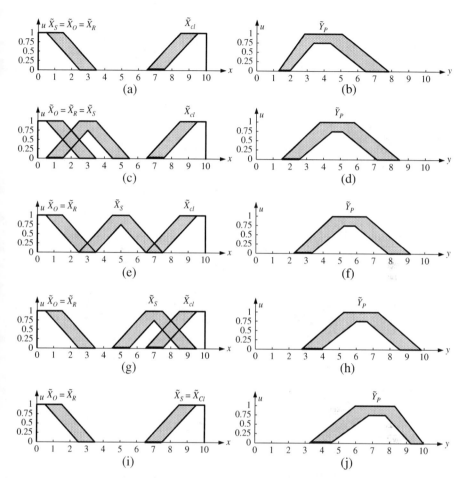

Figure 10.11. Presentation when Clarity is Excellent, Organization and References are Poor, and Style varies. (a), (c), (e), (g), (i): Input FOUs when a reviewer's response to Style changes from Poor to Excellent; (b), (d), (f), (h), (j): Output $\tilde{Y}_P$ when a reviewer's response to Style changes from Poor to Excellent. The corresponding weights for the three subcriteria are shown in Fig. 10.5.

tion, because improving the assessments of Organization and References should improve $\tilde{Y}_P$, that is, move $\tilde{Y}_P$ further to the right.

Finally, observe that the five cases in Fig. 10.12 represent an improvement of the respective cases in Fig. 10.11, and the five cases in Fig. 10.13 represent an even greater improvement of those cases. These improvements (which correspond to better reviews within the criterion of Presentation) are evident in all respective right-hand figure FOUs in Figs. 10.11–10.13 by their moving toward the right. For example, comparing Fig. (j) in these figures, one observes that in Fig. 10.11(j)

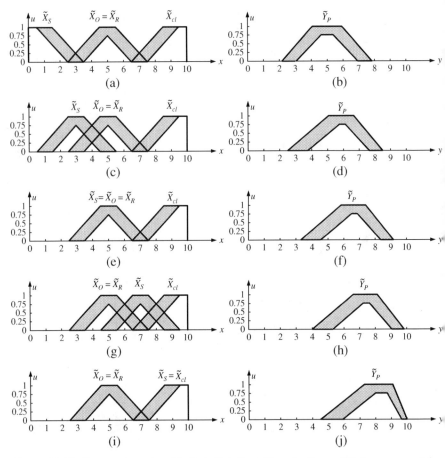

Figure 10.12. Presentation when Clarity is Excellent, Organization and References are Adequate, and Style varies. (a), (c), (e), (g), (i): Input FOUs when a reviewer's response to Style changes from Poor to Excellent; (b), (d), (f), (h), (j): Output $\tilde{Y}_P$ when a reviewer's response to Style changes from Poor to Excellent. The corresponding weights for the three subcriteria are shown in Fig. 10.5.

the left portion of $\tilde{Y}_P$ begins at $y \approx 3.3$ and the very right portion of $\tilde{Y}_P$ reaches $y = 10$, in Fig. 10.12(j) the left portion of $\tilde{Y}_P$ begins at $y \approx 4.5$ and the very right portion of $\tilde{Y}_P$ also reaches $y = 10$, and, in Fig. 10.13(j) the left portion of $\tilde{Y}_P$ begins at $y \approx 6.5$ and not only does the very right portion of $\tilde{Y}_P$ also reach $y = 10$, but $\tilde{Y}_P$ has changed its shape from that of an interior FOU to that of a right-shoulder FOU.

This all seems quite sensible in that one would expect higher assessments of any of the three subcriteria to move $\tilde{Y}_P$ to the right.

10.4.2.4 *Conclusions*. These 15 cases have demonstrated that $\tilde{Y}_P$ moves from left to right as $\tilde{X}_S$ moves from left to right and also as $\tilde{X}_O$ and $\tilde{X}_R$ simultaneously move from left to right.

10.4.3 Aggregation at the Reviewer Level

This section assumes that there are three reviewers for a paper submission, and that Technical Merit and Presentation have already had their subcategories aggregated, leading to $\tilde{Y}_{jT}$ and $\tilde{Y}_{jP}$ ($j = 1, 2, 3$). $\tilde{Y}_{jT}$ and $\tilde{Y}_{jP}$, whose shapes in this section are pre-

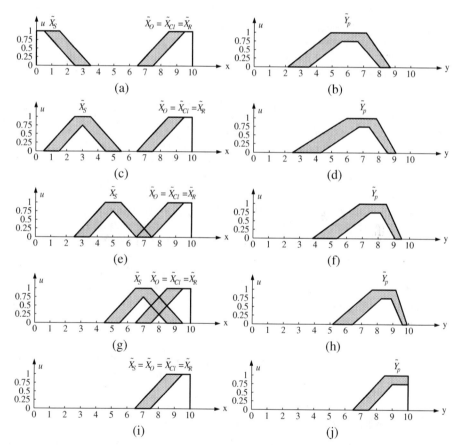

Figure 10.13. Presentation when Clarity, Organization and References are Excellent, and Style varies. (a), (c), (e), (g), (i): Input FOUs when a reviewer's response to Style changes from Poor to Excellent; (b), (d), (f), (h), (j): Output $\tilde{Y}_P$ when a reviewer's response to Style changes from Poor to Excellent. The corresponding weights for the three subcriteria are shown in Fig. 10.5.

specified by us,[3] are then aggregated using the LWA in equation (10.3), in which $\tilde{Y}_{jT}$ and $\tilde{Y}_{jP}$ are weighted using their respective weight FOUs that are depicted in Fig. 10.6, where, as previously agreed upon, heavier weight is given to Technical Merit than to Presentation. The results are $\tilde{Y}_{Rj}, j = 1, 2, 3$.

10.4.3.1   *Presentation is Good and Technical Merit Varies.* In this case, all of the reviewers agree that Presentation is Good, but they disagree about Technical Merit. Reviewer 1 rates Technical Merit as Poor, Reviewer 2 rates Technical Merit as Adequate, and Reviewer 3 rates Technical Merit as Excellent, where Good, Poor, Adequate, and Excellent are in Fig. 10.2. $\tilde{Y}_{jT}$ and $\tilde{Y}_{jP}$ are depicted in Figs. 10.14(a)–(c) for Reviewers 1–3, respectively. In those figures, $\tilde{Y}_{jP}$ is fixed at Good and only $\tilde{Y}_{jT}$ varies from one figure to the next. Figure 10.14(d) depicts $\tilde{Y}_{R1}$, $\tilde{Y}_{R2}$, and $\tilde{Y}_{R3}$. Observe that these FOUs are spread out, indicating substantial disagreement among the reviewers, and that as the rating for Technical Merit improves, $\tilde{Y}_{Rj}$ moves to the right; hence, $\tilde{Y}_{R3} > \tilde{Y}_{R2} > \tilde{Y}_{R1}$, where $>$ is used here to denote "further to the right of."

10.4.3.2   *Technical Merit is Good and Presentation Varies.* In this case, all of the reviewers agree that Technical Merit is Good, but they disagree about Presentation; hence, this case is the opposite of the one in Section 10.4.3.1. Reviewer 1 now rates Presentation as Poor, Reviewer 2 rates Presentation as Adequate, and Reviewer 3 rates Presentation as Excellent. $\tilde{Y}_{jT}$ and $\tilde{Y}_{jP}$ are depicted in Figs. 10.15(a)–(c) for Reviewers 1–3, respectively. In those figures, $\tilde{Y}_{jT}$ is fixed at Good and only $\tilde{Y}_{jP}$ varies from one figure to the next. Fig. 10.15(d) depicts $\tilde{Y}_{R1}$, $\tilde{Y}_{R2}$, and $\tilde{Y}_{R3}$.

Observe that these FOUs are much more bunched together and have considerably more overlap than the ones in Fig. 10.14(d). So, even though there is considerable disagreement among the reviewers about Presentation, this does not make as much difference in $\tilde{Y}_{Rj}$ as did the disagreement about Technical Merit in Fig. 10.14(d). While it is true that an improved rating for Presentation moves $\tilde{Y}_{Rj}$ further to the right, this effect on $\tilde{Y}_{Rj}$ is nowhere as dramatic as the effect of an improved rating for Technical Merit has on $\tilde{Y}_{Rj}$.

10.4.3.3   *Conclusions.* As expected, a higher rating for Technical Merit has a much greater effect on $\tilde{Y}_{Rj}$ than does a comparable rating for Presentation.

10.4.4   Aggregation at the AE Level

This section builds upon the results in Section 10.4.3. It assumes there are three reviewers of a submission and their reviews have been aggregated using equation (10.3). Here, the focus is on what effects different levels of reviewer expertise

---

[3]In Section 10.4.5, they will be determined by beginning with three completed generic review forms.

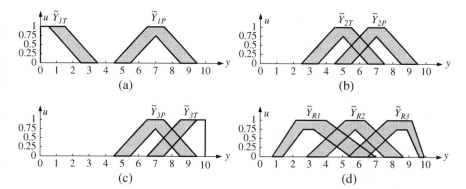

Figure 10.14. The three reviewers have the same opinion about Presentation (Good) and different opinions about Technical Merit. (a), (b), and (c): Reviewers 1, 2, and 3's aggregated FOUs on Technical Merit and Presentation, respectively. (d): Reviewers 1, 2, and 3's overall FOU. The corresponding weights for the two criteria are shown in Fig. 10.6.

have on $\tilde{Y}_{AE}$ as computed by equation (10.4). One expects that reviews from reviewers who have high expertise will have more effect on $\tilde{Y}_{AE}$ than those from reviewers who have moderate or low levels of expertise, because according to Fig. 10.3, *High > Moderate > Low,* where, again, > is used to denote "further to the right of."

10.4.4.1 Presentation is Good, Technical Merit Varies, and Reviewer Expertise Varies.
This is a continuation of Section 10.4.3.1, and starts with $\tilde{Y}_{R1}$,

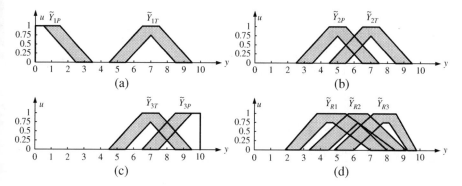

Figure 10.15. The three reviewers have the same opinion about Technical Merit (Good) and different opinions about Presentation. (a), (b), and (c): Reviewers 1, 2, and 3's aggregated FOUs on Technical Merit and Presentation, respectively. (d): Reviewers 1, 2, and 3's overall FOU. The corresponding weights for the two criteria are shown in Fig. 10.6.

$\tilde{Y}_{R2}$, and $\tilde{Y}_{R3}$ that are in Fig. 10.14(d) and that are quite spread out. When Reviewer 1 is of high expertise, Reviewer 2 is of moderate expertise, and Reviewer 3 is of low expertise, their weights are depicted in Fig. 10.16(a), and equation (10.4) leads to $\tilde{Y}_{AE}$, which is depicted in Fig. 10.16(b). On the other hand, when all three reviewers are of moderate expertise, their weights are depicted in Fig. 10.16(c), and the resulting $\tilde{Y}_{AE}$ is in Fig. 10.16(d). Finally, when Reviewers 1, 2, and 3 are of low, moderate, and high expertise, respectively, their weights are depicted in Fig. 10.16(e), and the resulting $\tilde{Y}_{AE}$ is depicted in Fig. 10.16(f).

What can be concluded from all of this? First, observe that regardless of the reviewer's expertise $\tilde{Y}_{AE}$ is very spread out, so that it is very likely that the AE will recommend that the paper be rewritten. Next, observe that a better $\tilde{Y}_{AE}$ is obtained when a reviewer's $\tilde{Y}_{Rj}$ in Fig. 10.14(d) is farther to the right (e.g., Reviewer 3) and the reviewer is of high expertise. So, the expertise of the reviewer is important, as can be seen by comparing $\tilde{Y}_{AE}$ in Figs. 10.16(b), (d), and (f).

10.4.4.2 Technical Merit is Good, Presentation Varies, and Reviewer Expertise Varies.

This is a continuation of Section 10.4.3.2, and starts with $\tilde{Y}_{R1}$, $\tilde{Y}_{R2}$, and $\tilde{Y}_{R3}$ that are in Fig. 10.15(d) and are much more bunched together and have considerably more overlap than the ones in Fig. 10.14(d). When Reviewer 1 is of

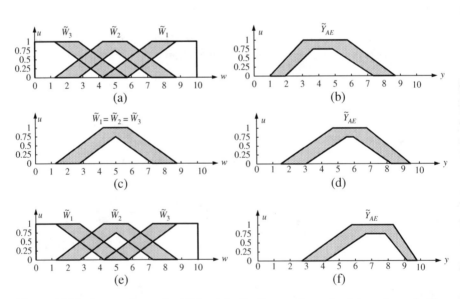

Figure 10.16. Aggregation at the AE level for the three reviewers' opinions shown in Fig. 10.14(d), when reviewer expertise varies. (a), (c), (e): weights for the three reviewers; (b), (d) and (f): the corresponding $\tilde{Y}_{AE}$.

high expertise, Reviewer 2 is of moderate expertise, and Reviewer 3 is of low expertise, their weights are depicted in Fig. 10.17(a), and equation (10.4) leads to $\tilde{Y}_{AE}$ that is depicted in Fig. 10.17(b). On the other hand, when all three reviewers are of moderate expertise, their weights are depicted in Fig. 10.17(c), and the resulting $\tilde{Y}_{AE}$ is in Fig. 10.17(d). Finally, when Reviewers 1, 2, and 3 are of low, moderate, and high expertise, respectively, their weights are depicted in Fig. 10.17(e), and the resulting $\tilde{Y}_{AE}$ is depicted in Fig. 10.17(f).

As in Fig. 10.16, one may ask: "What can be concluded from all of this?" Again, observe from Fig. 10.17 that, regardless of the reviewer's expertise, $\tilde{Y}_{AE}$ is very spread out (although not quite as much as in Fig. 10.16), so that, again, it is very likely that the AE will recommend that the paper be rewritten. Observe again that a better $\tilde{Y}_{AE}$ is obtained when a reviewer's $\tilde{Y}_{Rj}$ in Fig. 10.15(d) is farther to the right (e.g., Reviewer 3) and the reviewer is of high expertise. So, again the expertise of the reviewer is important, as can be seen by comparing $\tilde{Y}_{AE}$ in Figs. 10.17(b), (d), and (f).

Finally, when the respective right-hand figures in Figs. 10.16 and 10.17 are compared one observes that they are quite similar looking; however, the FOUs in Fig. 10.17 are shifted to the right of their comparable FOUs in Fig. 10.16. This is because Reviewer 3 provides the highest assessment for this paper, so that, as his weight increases, his review dominates the reviews from the two other reviewers.

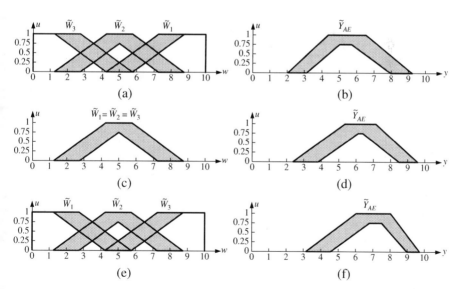

Figure 10.17. Aggregation at the AE level for the three reviewers' opinions shown in Fig. 10.15(d), when reviewer expertise varies. (a), (c), (e): weights for the three reviewers; (b), (d), and (f): the corresponding $\tilde{Y}_{AE}$.

10.4.4.3 Conclusions. In practice when an AE receives three widely different reviews the result is a recommendation that the paper be rewritten. The JPJA gives results that seem to be consistent with this.

10.4.5 Complete Reviews

This section provides three examples of the complete JPJA for different kinds of reviews so that one can gain confidence that the JPJA will be a useful assistant to an AE. In all examples, there are three reviewers.

10.4.5.1 A Submission that Would be Accepted. The reviewers' three completed generic review forms are depicted in Figs. 10.18(a)–(c). Observe that all of the linguistic assessments are in the Good or Excellent columns, suggesting that this paper probably will be accepted. Will the JPJA arrive at this recommendation?

The three reviewers' aggregated FOUs for Technical Merit and Presentation are depicted in Figs. 10.18(d)–(f). These FOUs were computed using equations (10.1) and (10.2). Observe that all of the FOUs are toward the right side of the scale 0–10, suggesting that things are looking good for this submission.

The reviewers' overall FOUs are shown in Fig. 10.18(g). These FOUs were computed using equation (10.3). The three overall FOUs look very similar because the three review forms are very similar. Observe that all of the overall FOUs are also toward the right side of the scale 0–10, suggesting that things are looking even better for this submission.

The weights for each of the reviewers are shown in Fig. 10.18(h). They are used together with the overall FOUs in Fig. 10.18(g) in equation (10.4) to obtain the aggregated FOU for the AE, $\tilde{Y}_{AE}$, depicted in Fig. 10.18(i). Observe that $\tilde{Y}_{AE}$ is also toward the right side of the scale 0–10, suggesting that things are looking very good for this submission; however, we are not going to leave things to a subjective "look" to make the final publication judgment. Instead, $\tilde{Y}_{AE}$ is sent to the decoder.

The decoder computes Vlachos and Sergiadis's subsethood measure (see Section 4.4.3) between $\tilde{Y}_{AE}$ and the three words in the decoding codebook (Fig. 10.7):

$$ss_{VS}(\tilde{Y}_{AE}, Reject) = 0$$

$$ss_{VS}(\tilde{Y}_{AE}, Rewrite) = 0.23$$

$$ss_{VS}(\tilde{Y}_{AE}, Accept) = 0.77$$

Because $ss_{VS}(\tilde{Y}_{AE}, Accept)$ is much larger than the other two subsethoods and it is greater than 0.5, the AE can recommend "Accept" with high confidence, so the JPJA has made the recommendation that agrees with our earlier stated intuition.

10.4.5.2 A Submission that Would be Rejected. The reviewer's three completed generic review forms are depicted in Figs. 10.19(a)–(c). Reviewer 1 has

	Poor	Marginal	Adequate	Good	Excellent
Technical Merit:					
Importance	( )	( )	( )	(X)	( )
Content	( )	( )	( )	( )	(X)
Depth	( )	( )	( )	( )	(X)
Presentation:					
Style	( )	( )	( )	( )	(X)
Organization	( )	( )	( )	( )	(X)
Clarity	( )	( )	( )	( )	(X)
Reference	( )	( )	( )	(X)	( )
Expertise:	Low		Moderate		High
Your Expertise	( )		( )		(X)

(a)

	Poor	Marginal	Adequate	Good	Excellent
Technical Merit:					
Importance	( )	( )	( )	( )	(X)
Content	( )	( )	( )	( )	(X)
Depth	( )	( )	( )	( )	(X)
Presentation:					
Style	( )	( )	( )	(X)	( )
Organization	( )	( )	( )	( )	(X)
Clarity	( )	( )	( )	(X)	( )
Reference	( )	( )	( )	( )	(X)
Expertise:	Low		Moderate		High
Your Expertise	( )		(X)		( )

(b)

	Poor	Marginal	Adequate	Good	Excellent
Technical Merit:					
Importance	( )	( )	( )	(X)	( )
Content	( )	( )	( )	( )	(X)
Depth	( )	( )	( )	( )	(X)
Presentation:					
Style	( )	( )	( )	(X)	( )
Organization	( )	( )	( )	( )	(X)
Clarity	( )	( )	( )	( )	(X)
Reference	( )	( )	( )	(X)	( )
Expertise:	Low		Moderate		High
Your Expertise	( )		(X)		( )

(c)

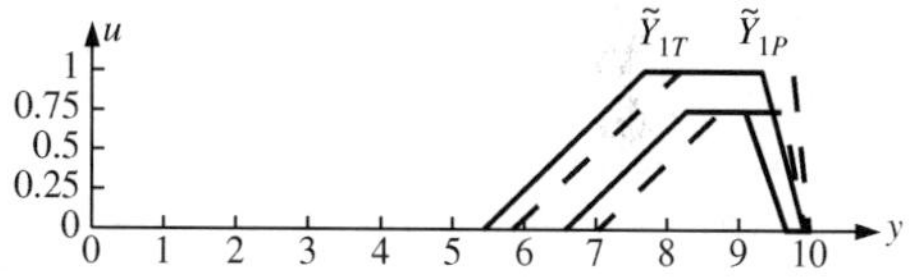

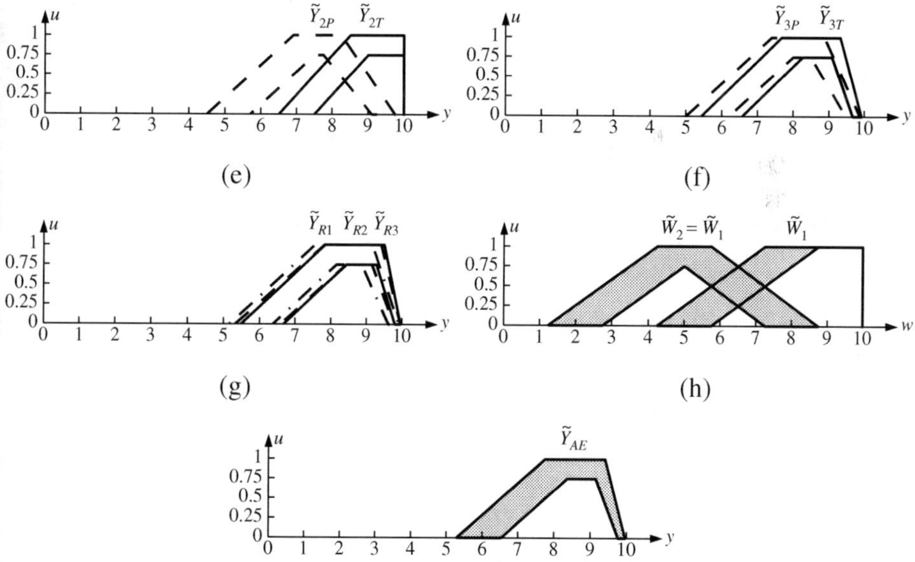

Figure 10.18. The first complete paper review example. (a), (b), (c): the completed review forms; (d), (e), (f): aggregated Technical Merit and Presentation FOUs for the three reviewers; (g): overall FOUs of the three reviewers; (h): the weights associated with the three reviewers; (i): the aggregated AE's FOU in relation to the three categories.

assessed all of the subcategories as either Adequate or Good, but his expertise is Low. Reviewers 2 and 3 have assessed all of the subcategories as Poor, Marginal, or Adequate, and their levels of expertise are Moderate and High, respectively. An AE will tend to put more credence on the reviews from Reviewers 2 and 3 than on the review from Reviewer 1, suggesting that this paper will probably be rejected. Will the JPJA also arrive at this recommendation?

The three reviewers' aggregated FOUs for Technical Merit and Presentation are depicted in Figs. 10.19(d)–(f). Observe that the FOUs for the more knowledgeable Reviewers 2 and 3 are toward the left on the scale 0–10. This suggests that things are not looking good for this submission.

The reviewers' overall FOUs are shown in Fig. 10.19(g). The overall FOUs for the more knowledgeable Reviewers 2 and 3 are very clearly shifted to the left on the scale 0–10, suggesting that things are looking even worse for this submission.

The weights for each of the reviewers are shown in Fig. 10.19(h). They are used together with the overall FOUs in Fig. 10.19(g) in equation (10.4) to obtain the aggregated FOU for the AE, $\tilde{Y}_{AE}$, depicted in Fig. 10.19(i). Observe that $\tilde{Y}_{AE}$ is also toward the left side of the scale 0–10, suggesting that things are looking very bad for this submission.

Indeed, when $\tilde{Y}_{AE}$ is sent to the decoder the following results are obtained:

$$ss_{VS}\,(\tilde{Y}_{AE},Reject\,)=0.67$$

$$ss_{VS}\,(\tilde{Y}_{AE},Rewrite\,)=0.35$$

$$ss_{VS}\,(\tilde{Y}_{AE},Accept)=0.01$$

Because $ss_{VS}(\tilde{Y}_{AE}$, Reject) is much larger than the other two subsethoods and it is larger than 0.5, the AE can recommend Reject with high confidence. Once again, the JPJA has provided a recommendation that agrees with our earlier stated intuition.

10.4.5.3 *A Submission that Would be Rewritten.* The reviewer's three completed generic review forms are depicted in Figs. 10.20(a)–(c). Reviewers 1 and 2 have assessed all of the subcategories as Adequate, Good, or Excellent and their levels of expertise are High and Moderate, respectively. Reviewer 3 has assessed all of the subcategories as Good and Excellent, but his level of expertise is Low. An AE will, therefore, tend to put more credence on the reviews from Reviewers 1 and 2 than on the review from Reviewer 3; however, it is not clear from the actual reviews whether the paper will be accepted or will have to be rewritten. How (or) will this ambiguity be seen by the JPJA?

The three reviewers' aggregated FOUs for Technical Merit and Presentation are depicted in Figs. 10.20(d)–(f). Observe that the FOUs for the more knowledgeable Reviewers 1 and 2 are more toward the center of the scale 0–10, whereas the FOU for the least knowledgeable Reviewer 3 is more toward the right of that scale. This suggests mixed reviews for this submission.

	Poor	Marginal	Adequate	Good	Excellent
Technical Merit:					
Importance	( )	( )	(X)	( )	( )
Content	( )	( )	( )	(X)	( )
Depth	( )	( )	( )	(X)	( )
Presentation:					
Style	( )	( )	( )	(X)	( )
Organization	( )	( )	(X)	( )	( )
Clarity	( )	( )	(X)	( )	( )
Reference	( )	( )	( )	(X)	( )
Expertise:	Low		Moderate		High
Your Expertise	(X)		( )		( )

(a)

	Poor	Marginal	Adequate	Good	Excellent
Technical Merit:					
Importance	(X)	( )	( )	( )	( )
Content	( )	(X)	( )	( )	( )
Depth	(X)	( )	( )	( )	( )
Presentation:					
Style	( )	(X)	( )	( )	( )
Organization	( )	( )	(X)	( )	( )
Clarity	( )	(X)	( )	( )	( )
Reference	( )	(X)	( )	( )	( )
Expertise:	Low		Moderate		High
Your Expertise	( )		(X)		( )

(b)

	Poor	Marginal	Adequate	Good	Excellent
Technical Merit:					
Importance	(X)	( )	( )	( )	( )
Content	(X)	( )	( )	( )	( )
Depth	( )	( )	(X)	( )	( )
Presentation:					
Style	( )	( )	(X)	( )	( )
Organization	( )	(X)	( )	( )	( )
Clarity	( )	( )	(X)	( )	( )
Reference	(X)	( )	( )	( )	( )
Expertise:	Low		Moderate		High
Your Expertise	( )		( )		(X)

(c)

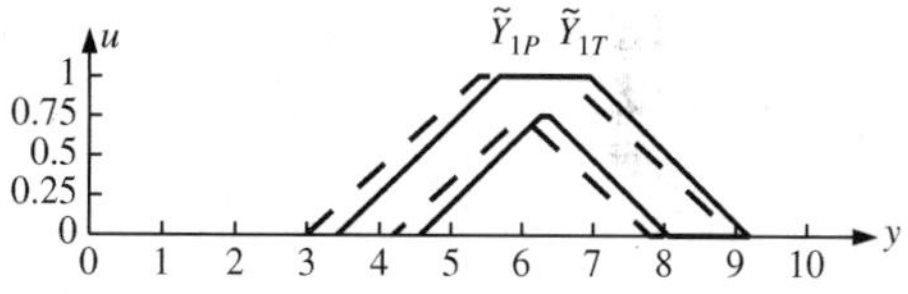

(d) 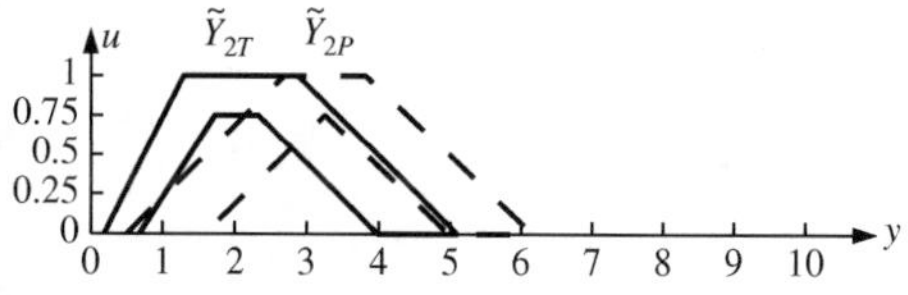   (e) 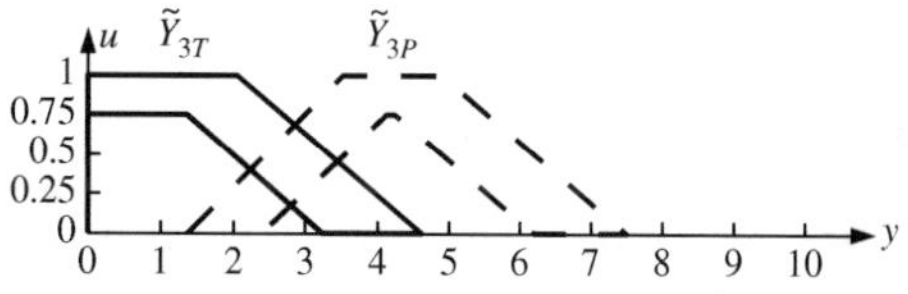   (f) 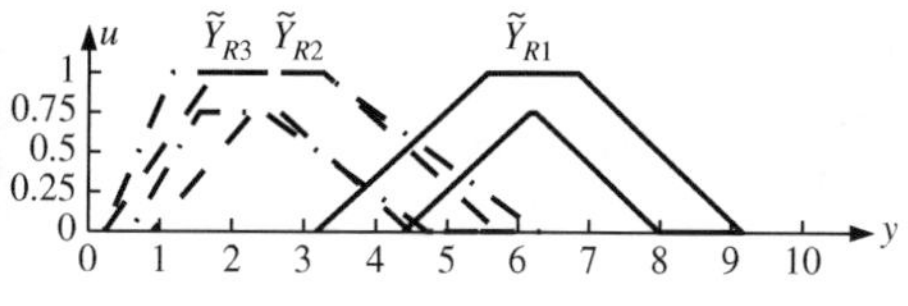   (g) 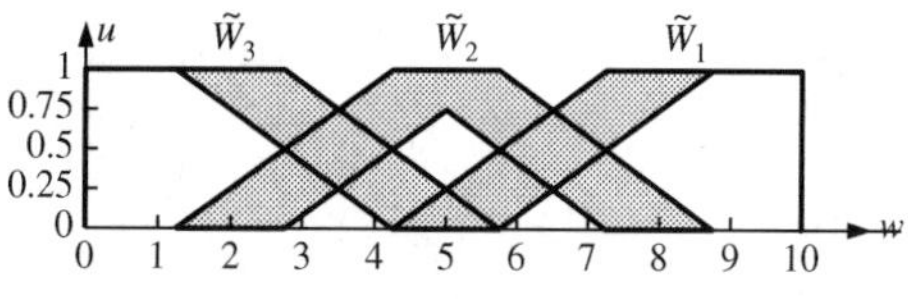   (h) 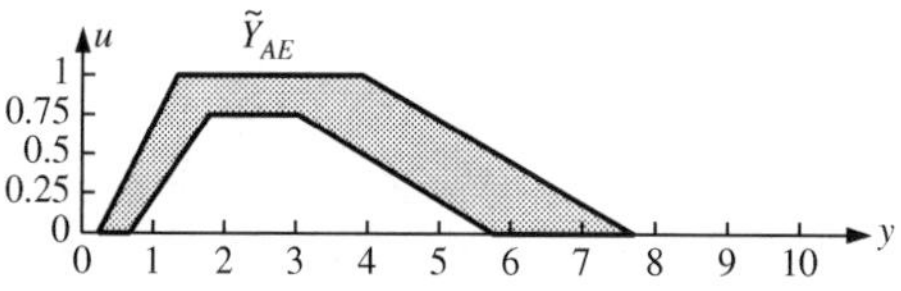   (i)

Figure 10.19. The second complete paper review example. (a), (b), (c): the completed review forms; (d), (e), (f): aggregated Technical Merit and Presentation FOUs for the three reviewers; (g): overall FOUs of the three reviewers; (h): the weights associated with the three reviewers; (i): the aggregated AE's FOU in relation to the three categories.

	Poor	Marginal	Adequate	Good	Excellent
Technical Merit:					
Importance	( )	( )	(X)	( )	( )
Content	( )	( )	( )	( )	(X)
Depth	( )	( )	( )	(X)	( )
Presentation:					
Style	( )	( )	( )	( )	(X)
Organization	( )	( )	( )	( )	(X)
Clarity	( )	( )	(X)	( )	( )
Reference	( )	( )	( )	(X)	( )
Expertise:	Low		Moderate		High
Your Expertise	( )		( )		(X)

(a)

	Poor	Marginal	Adequate	Good	Excellent
Technical Merit:					
Importance	( )	( )	(X)	( )	( )
Content	( )	( )	( )	(X)	( )
Depth	( )	( )	( )	( )	(X)
Presentation:					
Style	( )	( )	( )	(X)	( )
Organization	( )	( )	( )	(X)	( )
Clarity	( )	( )	( )	( )	(X)
Reference	( )	( )	( )	( )	(X)
Expertise:	Low		Moderate		High
Your Expertise	( )		(X)		( )

(b)

	Poor	Marginal	Adequate	Good	Excellent
Technical Merit:					
Importance	( )	( )	( )	(X)	( )
Content	( )	( )	( )	( )	(X)
Depth	( )	( )	( )	( )	(X)
Presentation:					
Style	( )	( )	( )	( )	(X)
Organization	( )	( )	( )	( )	(X)
Clarity	( )	( )	( )	( )	(X)
Reference	( )	( )	( )	(X)	( )
Expertise:	Low		Moderate		High
Your Expertise	(X)		( )		( )

(c)

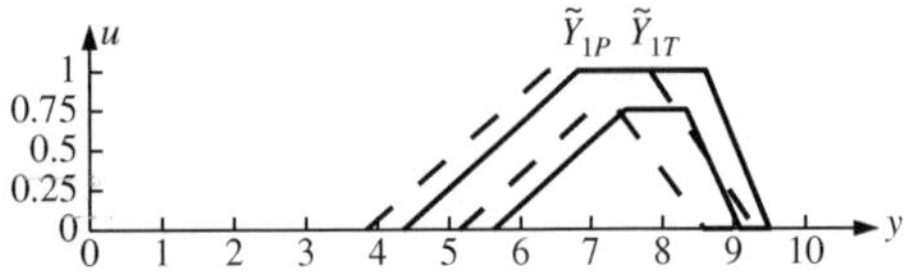

(d)

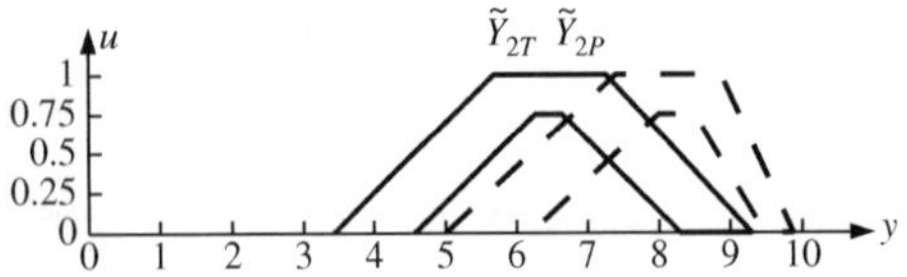

(e)

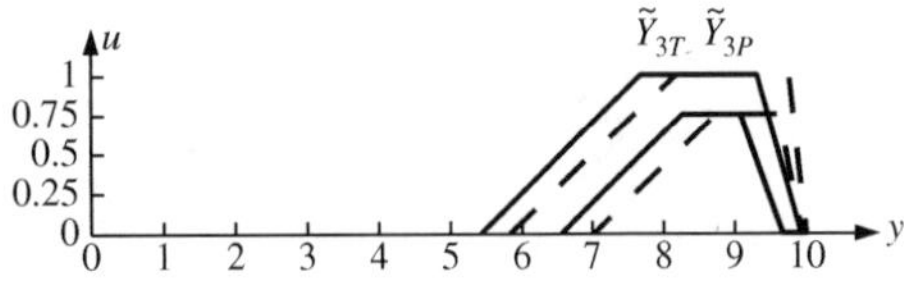

(f)

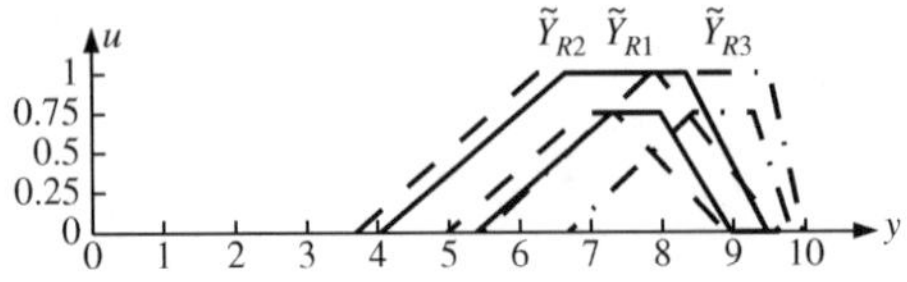

(g)

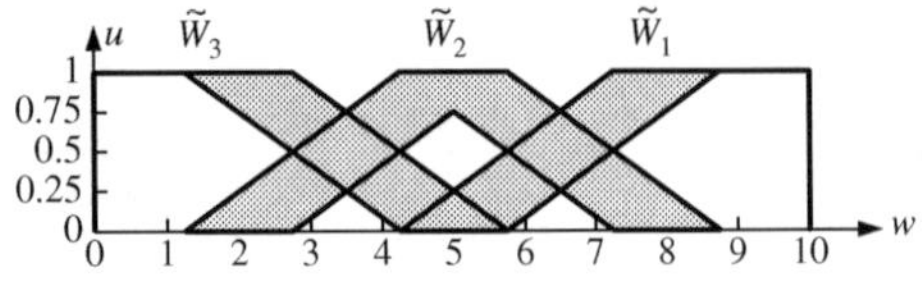

(h)

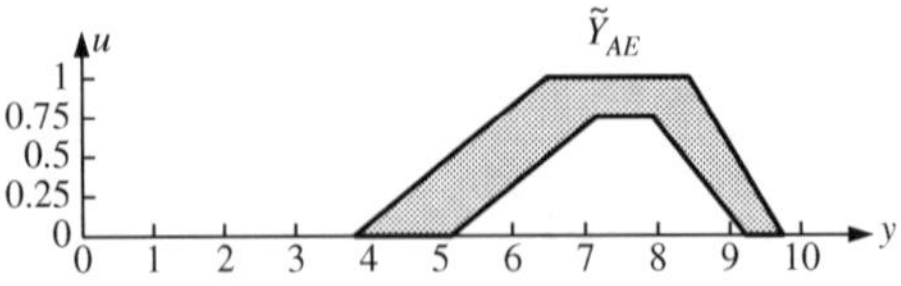

(i)

Figure 10.20. The third complete paper review example. (a), (b), (c): the completed review forms; (d), (e), (f): aggregated Technical Merit and Presentation FOUs for the three reviewers; (g): overall FOUs of the three reviewers; (h): the weights associated with the three reviewers; (i): the aggregated AE's FOU in relation to the three categories.

The reviewers' overall FOUs are shown in Fig. 10.20(g). Comparing this figure with Fig. 10.18(g), it is clear that the reviewers' overall FOUs for the accepted paper are all to the right of 5 on the scale of 0–10, whereas the reviewers' overall FOUs for the present case cover a larger range on that scale, going from around 3.7 to 9.8, some of which lies to the left of 5. This again supports the notion of mixed reviews for this submission.

The weights for each of the reviewers are shown in Fig. 10.20(h). They are used together with the overall FOUs in Fig. 10.20(g) in equation (10.4) to obtain the aggregated FOU for the AE, $\tilde{Y}_{AE}$, depicted in Fig. 10.20(i). Observe that $\tilde{Y}_{AE}$ covers a large range on the scale of 0–10, going from around 3.8 to 9.7, some of which lies to the left of 5. Compare this to $\tilde{Y}_{AE}$ in Fig. 10.18(i) that lies to the right of 5. It seems that the AE is getting mixed reviews for this submission.

Indeed, when $\tilde{Y}_{AE}$ is sent to the decoder the following results are obtained:

$$ss_{VS}(\tilde{Y}_{AE}, Reject) = 0.01$$

$$ss_{VS}(\tilde{Y}_{AE}, Rewrite) = 0.48$$

$$ss_{VS}(\tilde{Y}_{AE}, Accept) = 0.43$$

Because $ss_{VS}(\tilde{Y}_{AE}, Rewrite)$ and $ss_{VS}(\tilde{Y}_{AE}, Accept)$ are close in value and both are below 0.5, the AE must recommend either Accept or Rewrite. Past history for such close calls indicates that the AE will choose the Rewrite category because $ss_{VS}(\tilde{Y}_{AE}, Accept)$ is well below 0.5 and is too close to $ss_{VS}(\tilde{Y}_{AE}, Rewrite)$ for him to rationally choose the Accept category.

So, when a submission receives reviews from which it is unclear whether the paper will be accepted or will have to be rewritten this shows up in the JPJA as subsethoods of two categories that are very close and both are less than 0.5. A comparable situation would occur for a paper whose reviews led to close values of $ss_{VS}(\tilde{Y}_{AE}, Reject)$ and $ss_{VS}(\tilde{Y}_{AE}, Rewrite)$.

10.4.5.4 Conclusions. From these three complete examples, the JPJA is providing recommendations that agree with anticipated recommendations. This suggests that the JPJA will be a very useful assistant to an AE.

10.5 CONCLUSIONS

The examples in this chapter have demonstrated that the Per-C is a very useful tool for hierarchical and distributed decision making. In this chapter, all inputs to the JPJA have been words that were modeled as IT2 FSs; however, from the results in Chapter 9, we know that the Per-C can also easily aggregate mixed inputs of numbers, intervals, and words; hence, the Per-C has great potential in complex hierarchical and distributed decision-making problems.

REFERENCE

D. Wu and J. M. Mendel, "Aggregation using the linguistic weighted average and interval type-2 fuzzy sets," *IEEE Trans. on Fuzzy Systems,* vol. 15, no. 6, pp. 1145–1161, 2007.

CHAPTER 11

Conclusions

11.1 PERCEPTUAL COMPUTING METHODOLOGY

Perceptual computing is a methodology for assisting people to make subjective judgments. The perceptual computer (Per-C) is our instantiation of perceptual computing. Although there are lots of details needed in order to implement the Per-C's three components—encoder, decoder, and CWW engine—and they are covered in Chapters 2–6, it is when the Per-C is applied to specific applications, as is done in Chapters 7–10, that the focus on the methodology becomes clear. Stepping back from those details, the methodology of perceptual computing is:

1. Focus on an application (A).
2. Establish a vocabulary (or vocabularies) for A.
3. Collect interval end-point data from a group of subjects (representative of the subjects who will use the Per-C) for all of the words in the vocabulary.
4. Map the collected word data into word FOUs by using the *Interval Approach* (Chapter 3). The result of doing this is the codebook (or codebooks) for A, and completes the design of the encoder of the Per-C.
5. Choose an appropriate CWW engine for A. It will map IT2 FSs into one or more IT2 FS.
6. If an existing CWW engine is available for A, then use its available mathematics to compute its output(s) (Chapters 5 and 6). Otherwise, develop such mathematics for your new kind of CWW engine. Your new CWW engine should be constrained so that its output(s) resemble the FOUs in the codebook(s) for A.
7. Map the IT2 FS outputs from the CWW engine into a recommendation at the output of the decoder. If the recommendation is a word, rank, or class, then use existing mathematics to accomplish this mapping (Chapter 4). Otherwise, develop such mathematics for your new kind of decoder.

The constraint in Step 6, that the output FOU of the CWW engine should resemble the FOUs in the codebook(s) for A, is the major difference between perceptual computing and function approximation applications of FSs and systems.

Perceptual Computing. By Jerry M. Mendel and Dongrui Wu **311**

11.2 PROPOSED GUIDELINES FOR CALLING SOMETHING CWW

Guidelines are needed for when something such as the Per-C is called computing with words (CWW), or else CWW will just be a relabeling of what we are already doing. The following proposed guidelines are in the form of three tests, all of which we suggest must be passed or else the work should not be called CWW. A fourth test is optional but is strongly suggested.

1. *A word must lead to a membership function rather than a membership function leading to a word.* When one begins with an FS, one begins with the MF of that set, that is, a mathematical description of that set. It matters not what that FS is called because the same MF is associated with each and every name chosen for the set, and when the FS is programmed for a computer, the computer does not care about the name of the FS, it only implements the mathematical formula of the MF. For example, if temperature is partitioned into three overlapping intervals, and FSs are established for the three partitions, these sets could be called low, medium, and high, T_1, T_2, and T_3, or any other three names.

   On the other hand, when one begins with a word and wants to use a FS to model it, then some knowledge or information about the word has to lead to the FS. Just as there can be different kinds of models that describe a dynamical system, there can be different kinds of FS models that describe a word. When physical laws are used to model a dynamical system, then one obtains an internal representation of the system. When only data are available about a dynamical system, then one obtains an external representation of the system. Similarly, when some laws about words are used to model them, then one obtains an internal representation of the words. When data are available about words, then one obtains an external representation about the words. So, for example, when interval data are collected for words and those intervals are then mapped into FOUs, an external IT2 FS model is obtained for each word.

2. *Numbers alone may not activate the CWW engine (e.g., if–then rules).* Numbers are modeled as singleton FSs and there is nothing fuzzy about them. At least one word must activate the CWW engine and it must be modeled by a nonsingleton FS, for example, a fuzzy number. If the CWW engine is comprised of rules, then singleton fuzzification alone is not permitted, because a fuzzy singleton is not a legitimate model of a word. Rules must be activated by FSs, and so in CWW one is always in the so-called nonsingleton fuzzification situation. This is very different from a rule-based fuzzy logic system that is used for function-approximation kinds of applications, in which almost everyone uses singleton fuzzification to keep things simple.

3. *The output from CWW must be at least a word and not just a number.* CWW implies "words in and words out"; however, people also like to get data to back up the words (e.g., if your supervisor tells you your performance is un-

satisfactory, then you ask "why?" and the answer to this has to be backed up with data), so words and data are okay as outputs from CWW. Words alone are okay for CWW, but data alone are not okay as outputs from CWW, for example, for a rule-based CWW engine, if the output is only a defuzzified number, then this is not CWW (it's a fuzzy logic system or a fuzzy logic controller, etc.). If, however, that defuzzified number is somehow mapped into a word, then this is CWW, and the combined defuzzified number and its associated word are also CWW. An example of a mapping that leads to both a number and a word is ranking. For example, proposals A, B, C, and D are ranked 2 (next to the best), 4 (worst), 1 (best), and 3 (next to the worst), respectively. Of course, in CWW something other than defuzzification may be used to aggregate fired-rule output sets, for example, a fuzzy weighted average or a linguistic weighted average, leading to another FS that is mapped into the word it most closely resembles.

4. *Because words mean different things to different people, they should be modeled using at least IT2 FSs.* A consequence of using at least IT2 FSs as models for words is that all computations performed by a CWW engine will then be valid for at least IT2 FSs. Another consequence of this requirement is that researchers who have developed novel and interesting ideas for CWW in the framework of T1 FSs could reexamine those ideas using at least IT2 FSs.

   This test is "optional" so as not to exclude much research on CWW that uses T1 FSs, even though we strongly believe that this test should also be a requirement for CWW, because, as we have explained in Chapter 3, it is scientifically incorrect to model a word using a T1 FS.

The above tests are easy to apply to any article that uses CWW in its title or claims to be about CWW. If Tests 1–3 are passed, then using the phrase CWW is okay; otherwise, it is not. Failing any one or all of these tests does not diminish the work's importance; it serves to distinguish the work from works about CWW. In this way, a clear distinction will appear between fuzzy logic in CWW and fuzzy logic as not in CWW. Confusion will be reduced and this will benefit the entire fuzzy logic field.

INDEX

Printed in the United States
By Bookmasters